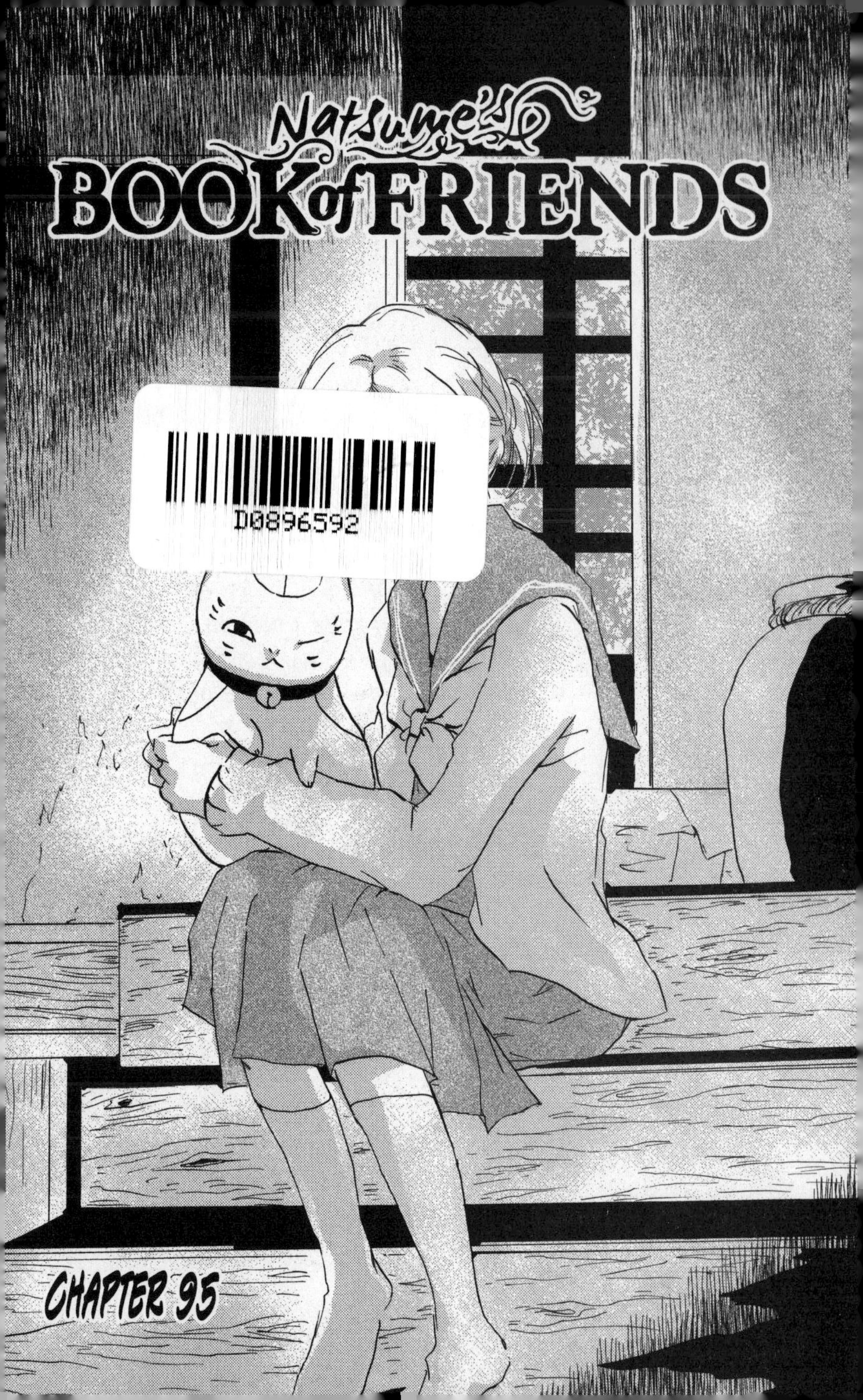
Natsume's
BOOK of FRIENDS
CHAPTER 95

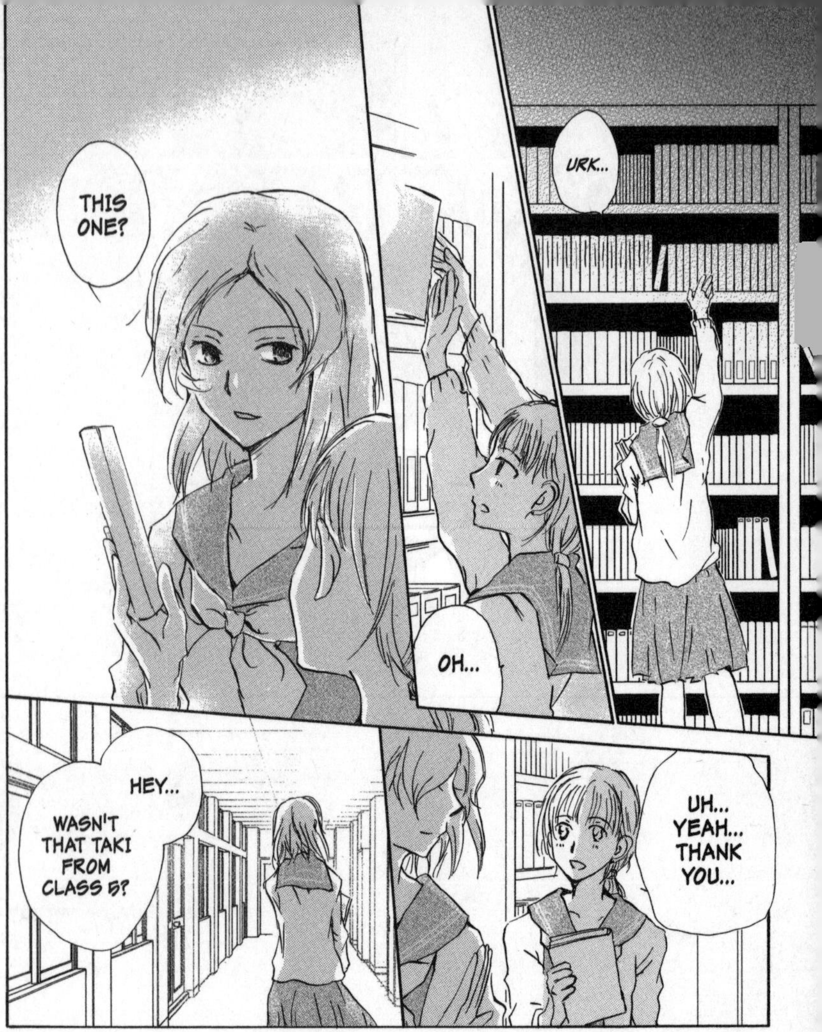
URK...
OH...
THIS ONE?
UH... YEAH... THANK YOU...
HEY... WASN'T THAT TAKI FROM CLASS 5?

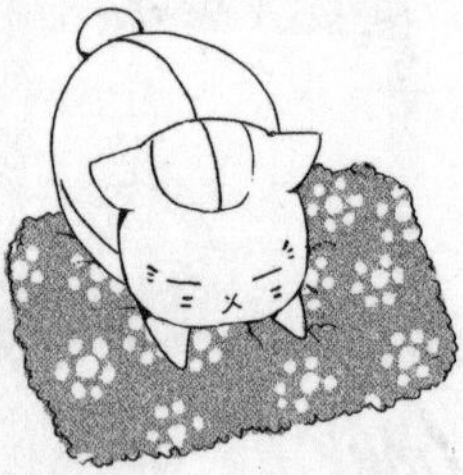

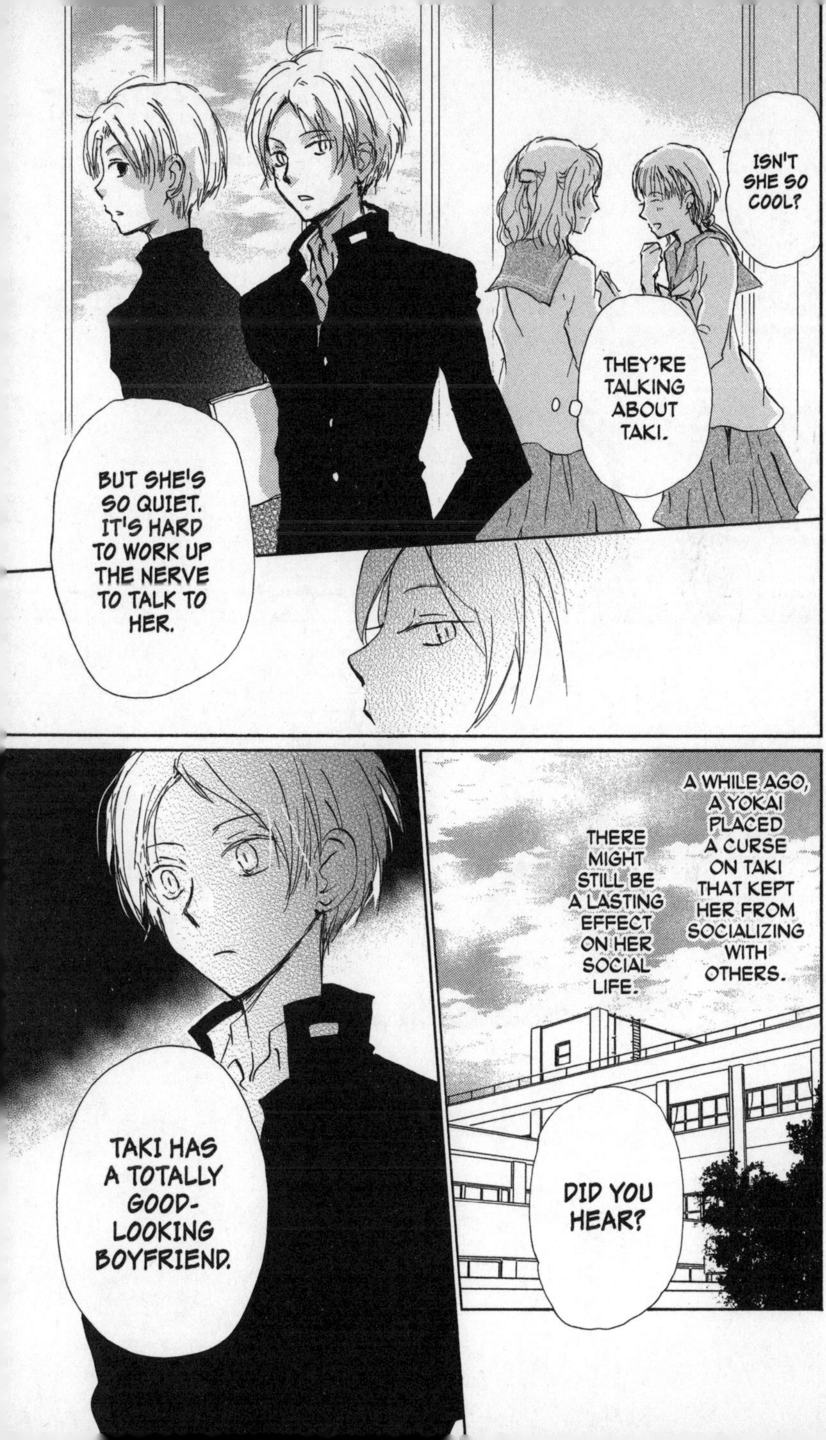
ISN'T SHE SO COOL?
THEY'RE TALKING ABOUT TAKI.
BUT SHE'S SO QUIET. IT'S HARD TO WORK UP THE NERVE TO TALK TO HER.
A WHILE AGO, A YOKAI PLACED A CURSE ON TAKI THAT KEPT HER FROM SOCIALIZING WITH OTHERS.
THERE MIGHT STILL BE A LASTING EFFECT ON HER SOCIAL LIFE.
DID YOU HEAR?
TAKI HAS A TOTALLY GOOD-LOOKING BOYFRIEND.

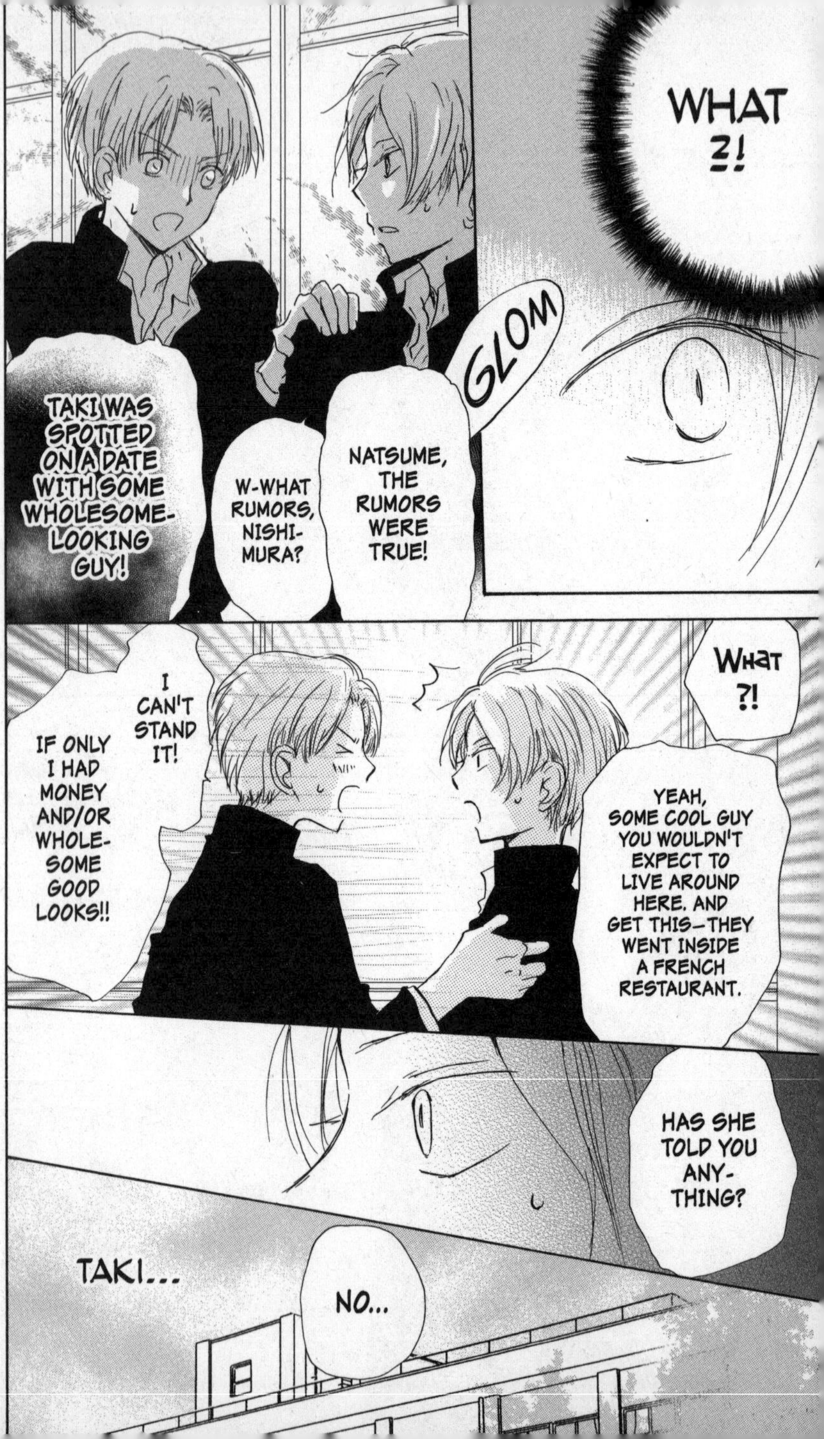
WHAT ?!
GLOM
NATSUME, THE RUMORS WERE TRUE!
W-WHAT RUMORS, NISHIMURA?
TAKI WAS SPOTTED ON A DATE WITH SOME WHOLESOME-LOOKING GUY!
WHAT ?!
YEAH, SOME COOL GUY YOU WOULDN'T EXPECT TO LIVE AROUND HERE. AND GET THIS—THEY WENT INSIDE A FRENCH RESTAURANT.
I CAN'T STAND IT!
IF ONLY I HAD MONEY AND/OR WHOLE-SOME GOOD LOOKS!!
HAS SHE TOLD YOU ANY-THING?
NO...
TAKI...

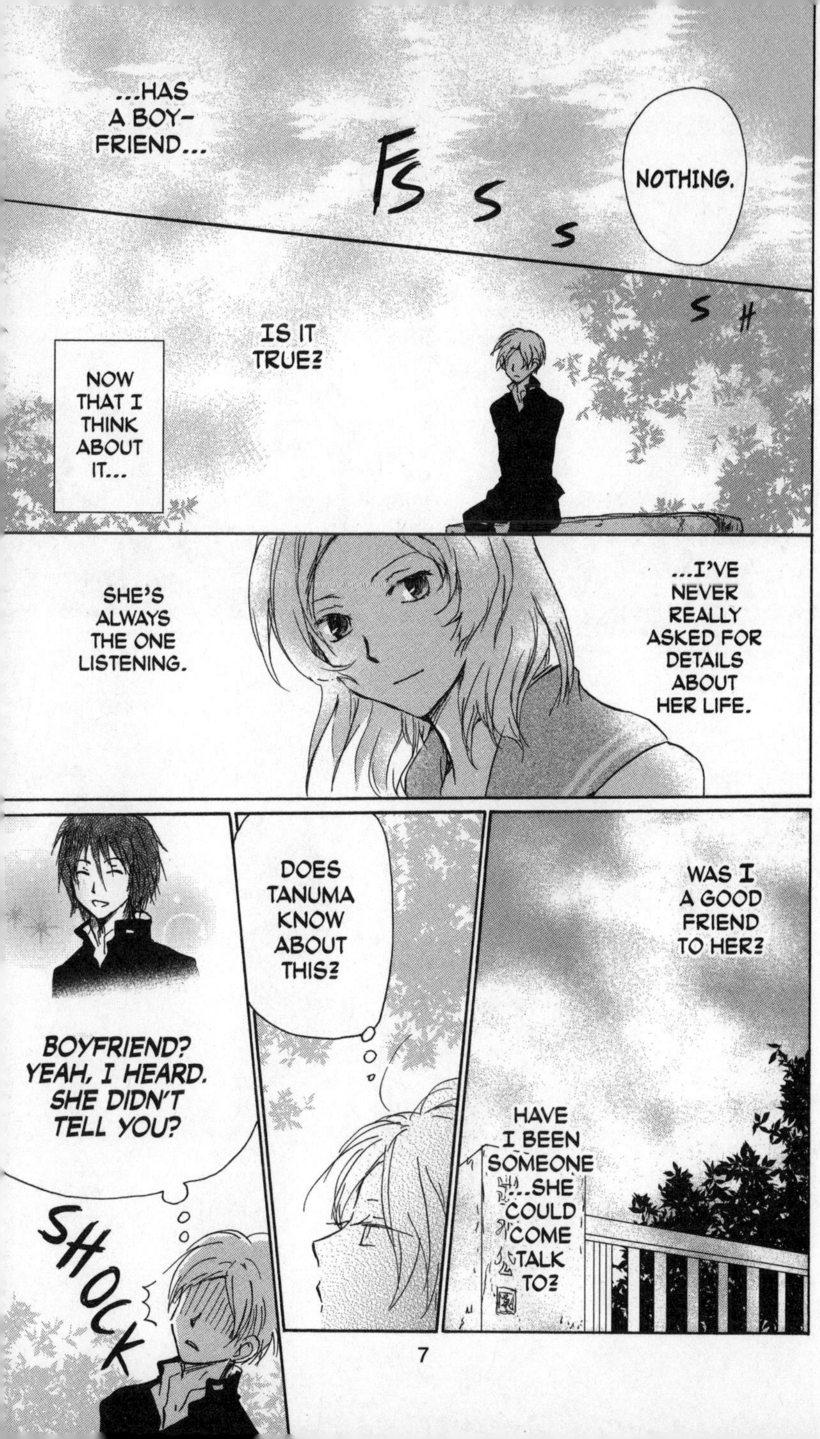
NOTHING.
FSSS
...HAS A BOY-FRIEND...
SH
IS IT TRUE?
NOW THAT I THINK ABOUT IT...
...I'VE NEVER REALLY ASKED FOR DETAILS ABOUT HER LIFE.
SHE'S ALWAYS THE ONE LISTENING.
WAS I A GOOD FRIEND TO HER?
HAVE I BEEN SOMEONE ...SHE COULD COME TALK TO?
DOES TANUMA KNOW ABOUT THIS?
BOYFRIEND? YEAH, I HEARD. SHE DIDN'T TELL YOU?
SHOCK

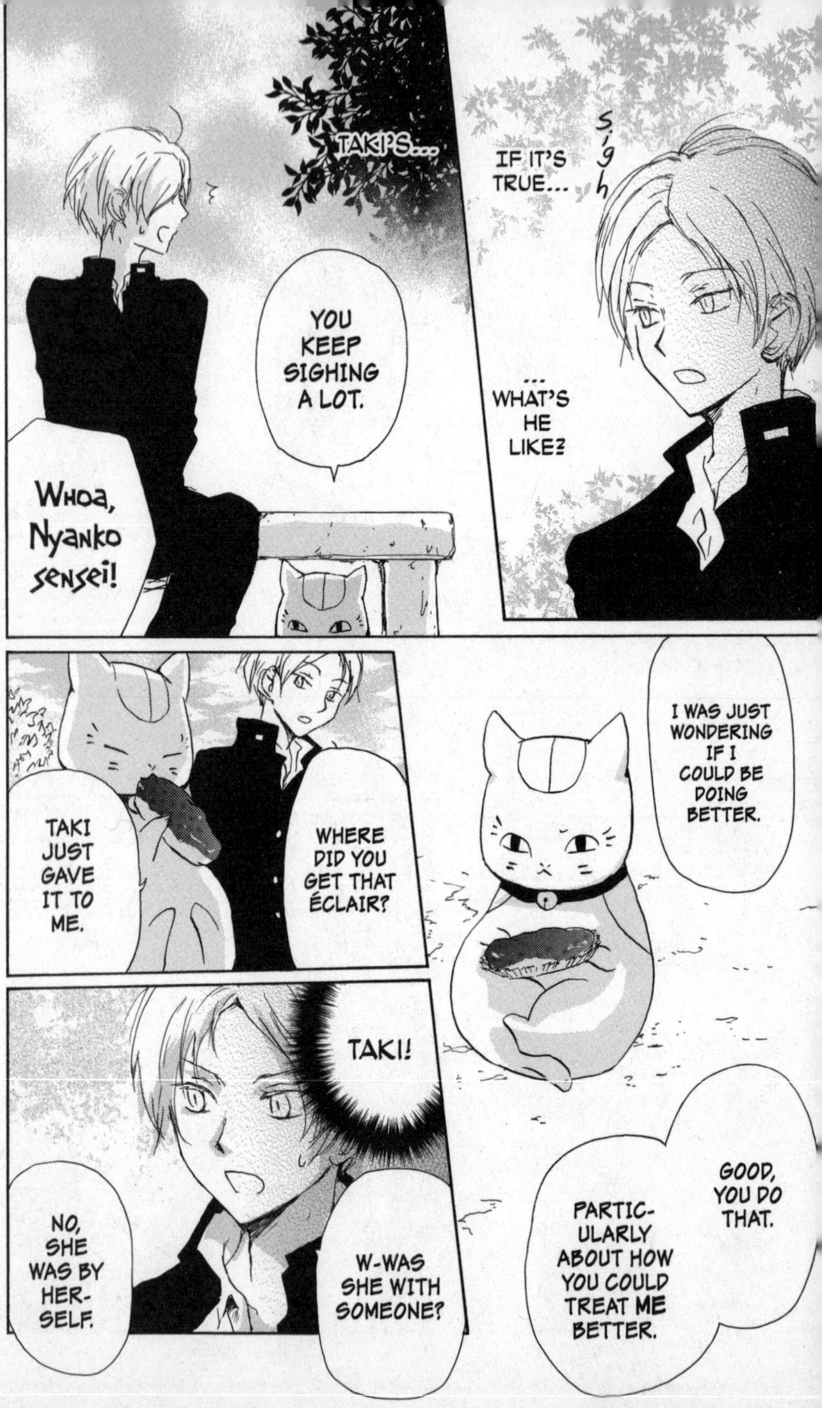
Sigh
IF IT'S TRUE...
...WHAT'S HE LIKE?
TAKI'S...
YOU KEEP SIGHING A LOT.
Whoa, Nyanko sensei!
I WAS JUST WONDERING IF I COULD BE DOING BETTER.
GOOD, YOU DO THAT.
PARTIC-ULARLY ABOUT HOW YOU COULD TREAT ME BETTER.
WHERE DID YOU GET THAT ÉCLAIR?
TAKI JUST GAVE IT TO ME.
TAKI!
W-WAS SHE WITH SOMEONE?
NO, SHE WAS BY HER-SELF.

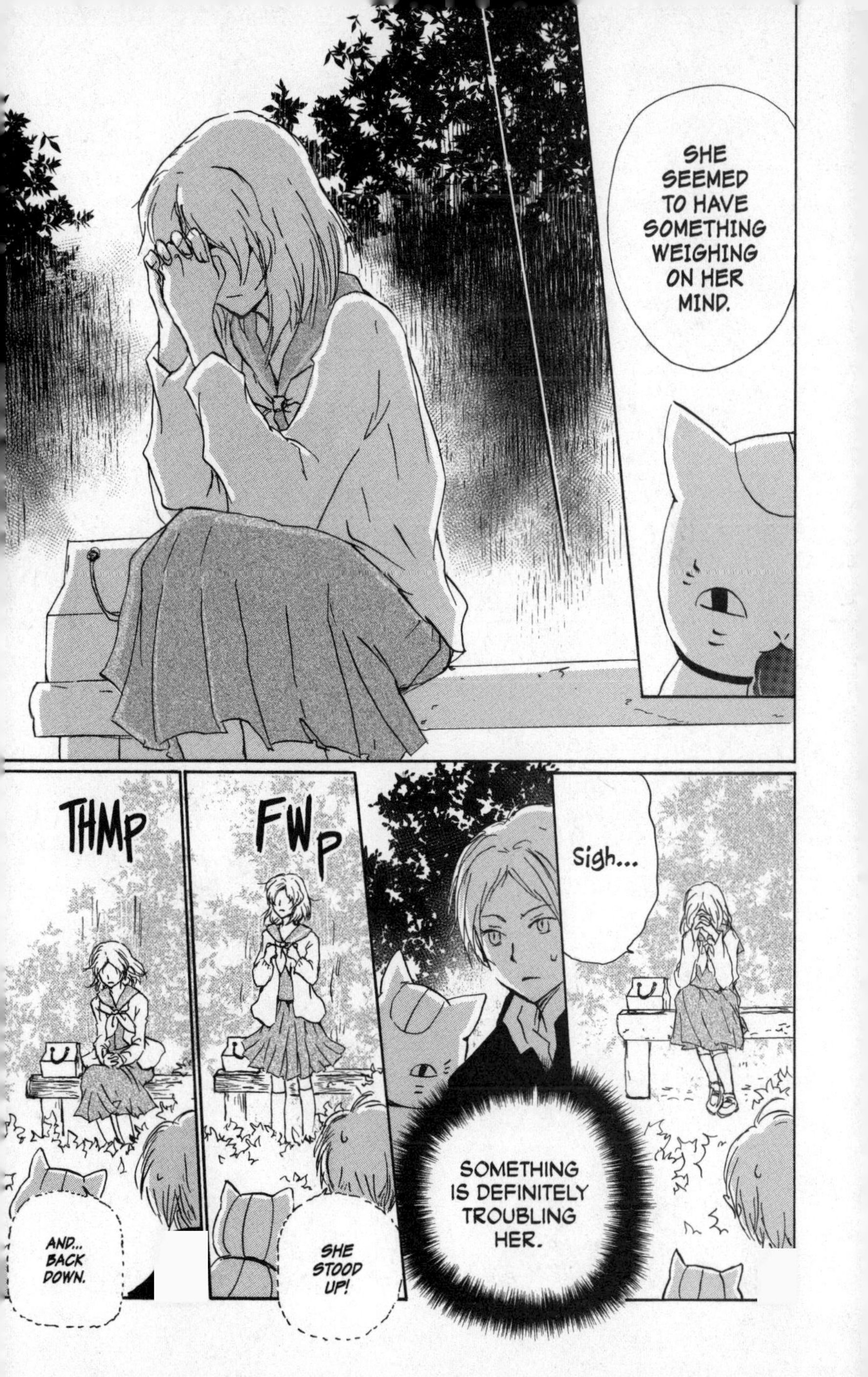
SHE SEEMED TO HAVE SOMETHING WEIGHING ON HER MIND.
Sigh...
SOMETHING IS DEFINITELY TROUBLING HER.
FWP
SHE STOOD UP!
THMP
AND... BACK DOWN.

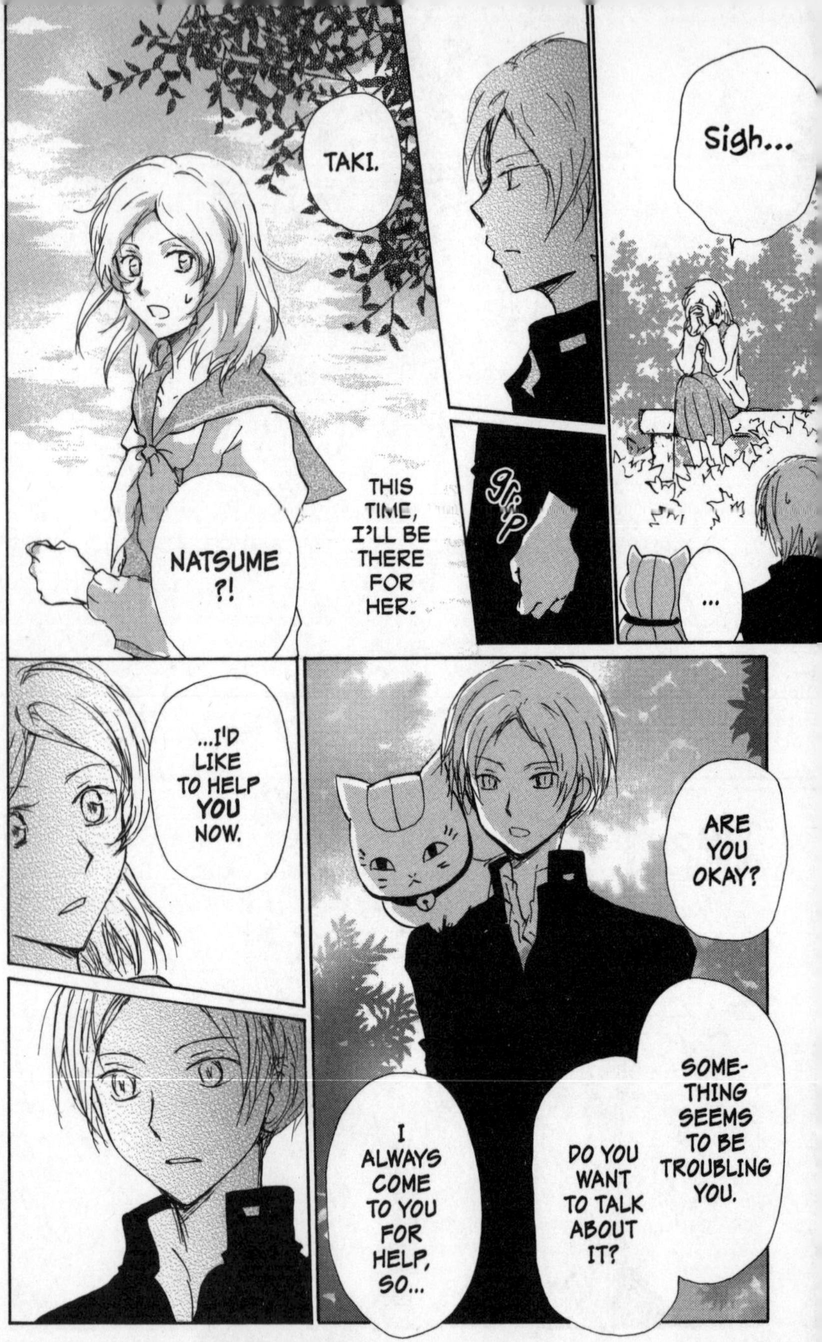

Sigh...
...
grip
TAKI.
THIS TIME, I'LL BE THERE FOR HER.
NATSUME?!
ARE YOU OKAY?
SOME-THING SEEMS TO BE TROUBLING YOU.
DO YOU WANT TO TALK ABOUT IT?
I ALWAYS COME TO YOU FOR HELP, SO...
...I'D LIKE TO HELP YOU NOW.

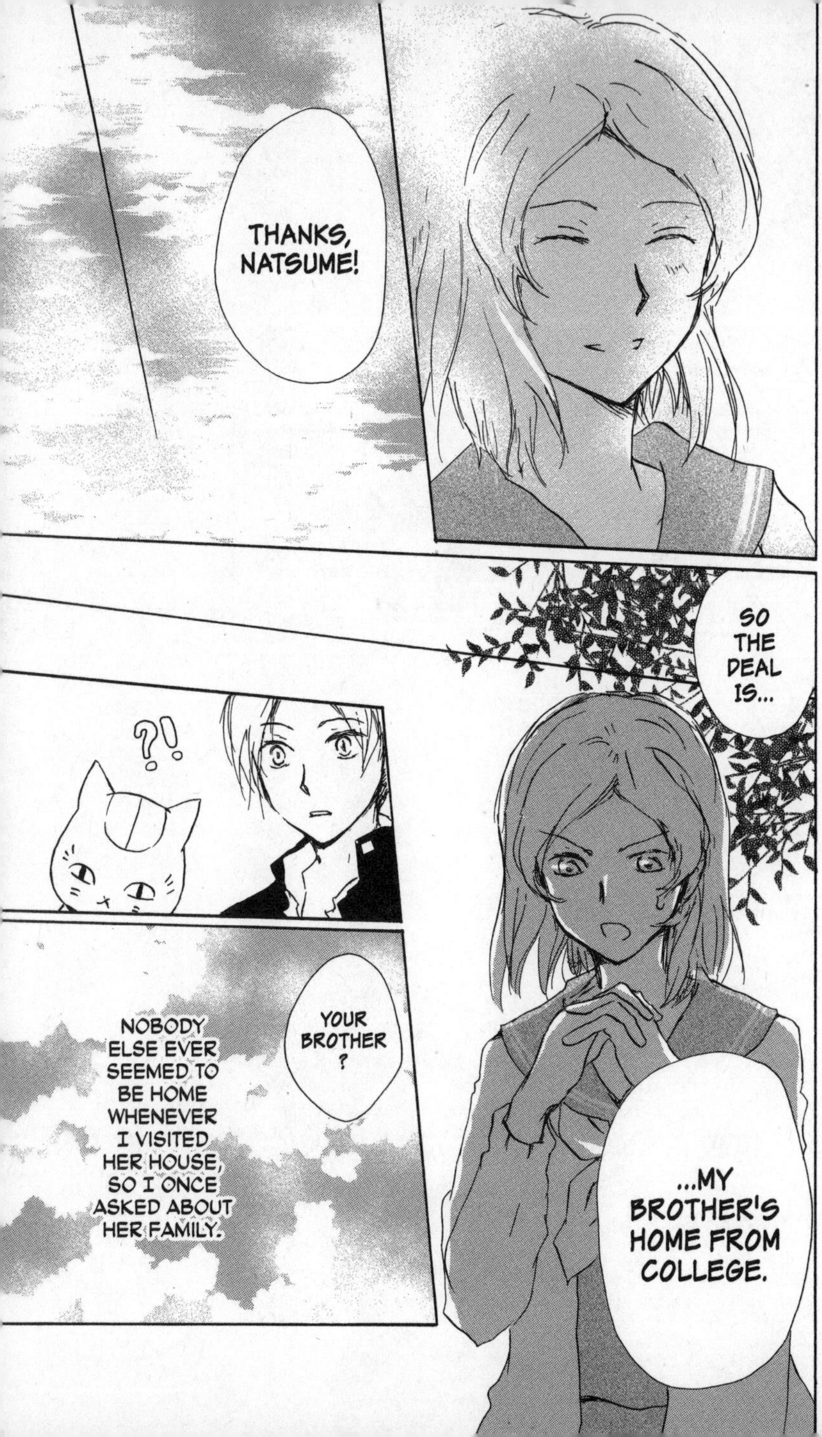
THANKS, NATSUME!
SO THE DEAL IS...
...MY BROTHER'S HOME FROM COLLEGE.
?!
YOUR BROTHER?
NOBODY ELSE EVER SEEMED TO BE HOME WHENEVER I VISITED HER HOUSE, SO I ONCE ASKED ABOUT HER FAMILY.

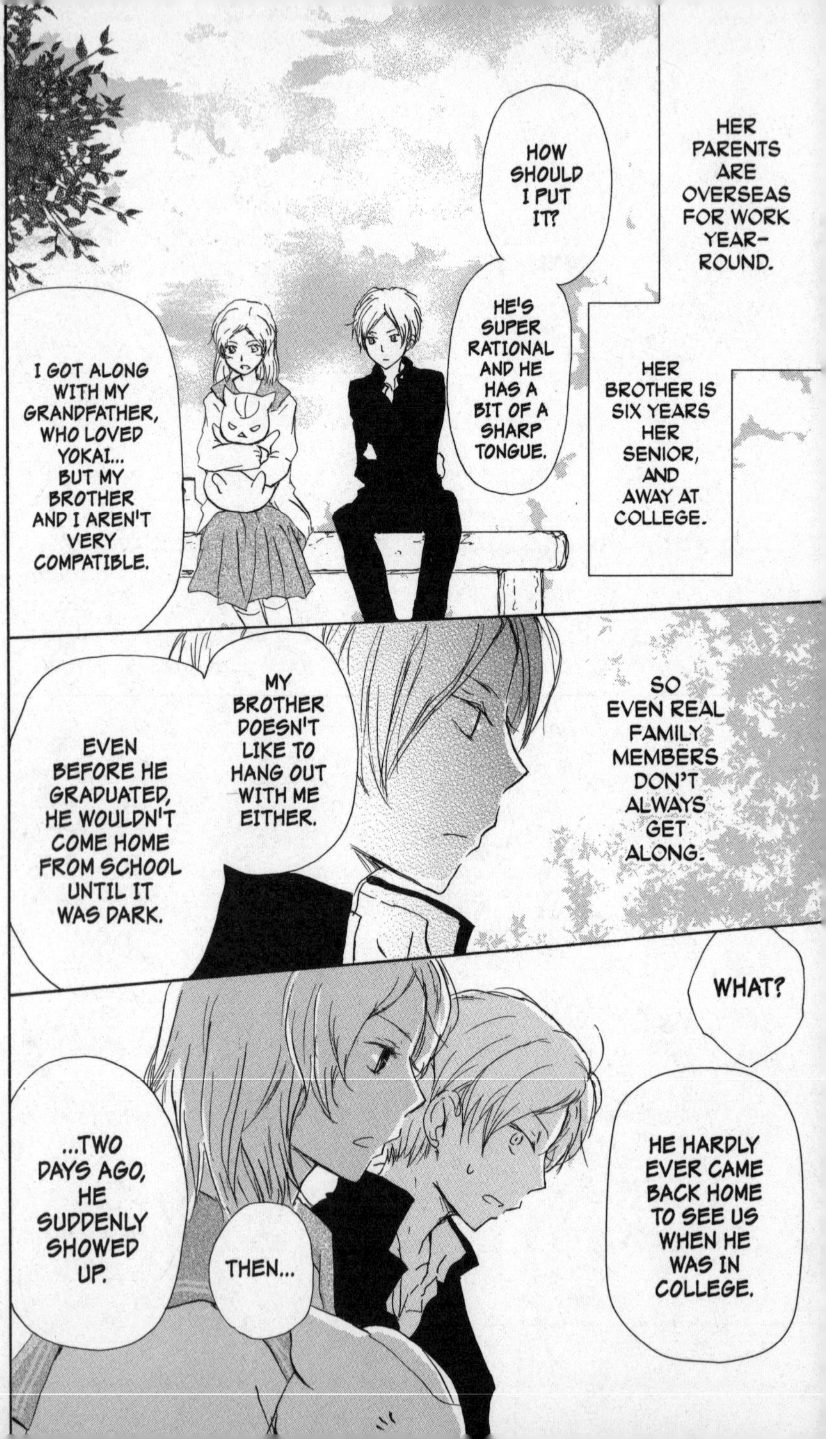
HER PARENTS ARE OVERSEAS FOR WORK YEAR-ROUND.
HOW SHOULD I PUT IT?
HER BROTHER IS SIX YEARS HER SENIOR, AND AWAY AT COLLEGE.
HE'S SUPER RATIONAL AND HE HAS A BIT OF A SHARP TONGUE.
I GOT ALONG WITH MY GRANDFATHER, WHO LOVED YOKAI... BUT MY BROTHER AND I AREN'T VERY COMPATIBLE.
SO EVEN REAL FAMILY MEMBERS DON'T ALWAYS GET ALONG.
MY BROTHER DOESN'T LIKE TO HANG OUT WITH ME EITHER.
EVEN BEFORE HE GRADUATED, HE WOULDN'T COME HOME FROM SCHOOL UNTIL IT WAS DARK.
WHAT?
HE HARDLY EVER CAME BACK HOME TO SEE US WHEN HE WAS IN COLLEGE.
THEN...
...TWO DAYS AGO, HE SUDDENLY SHOWED UP.

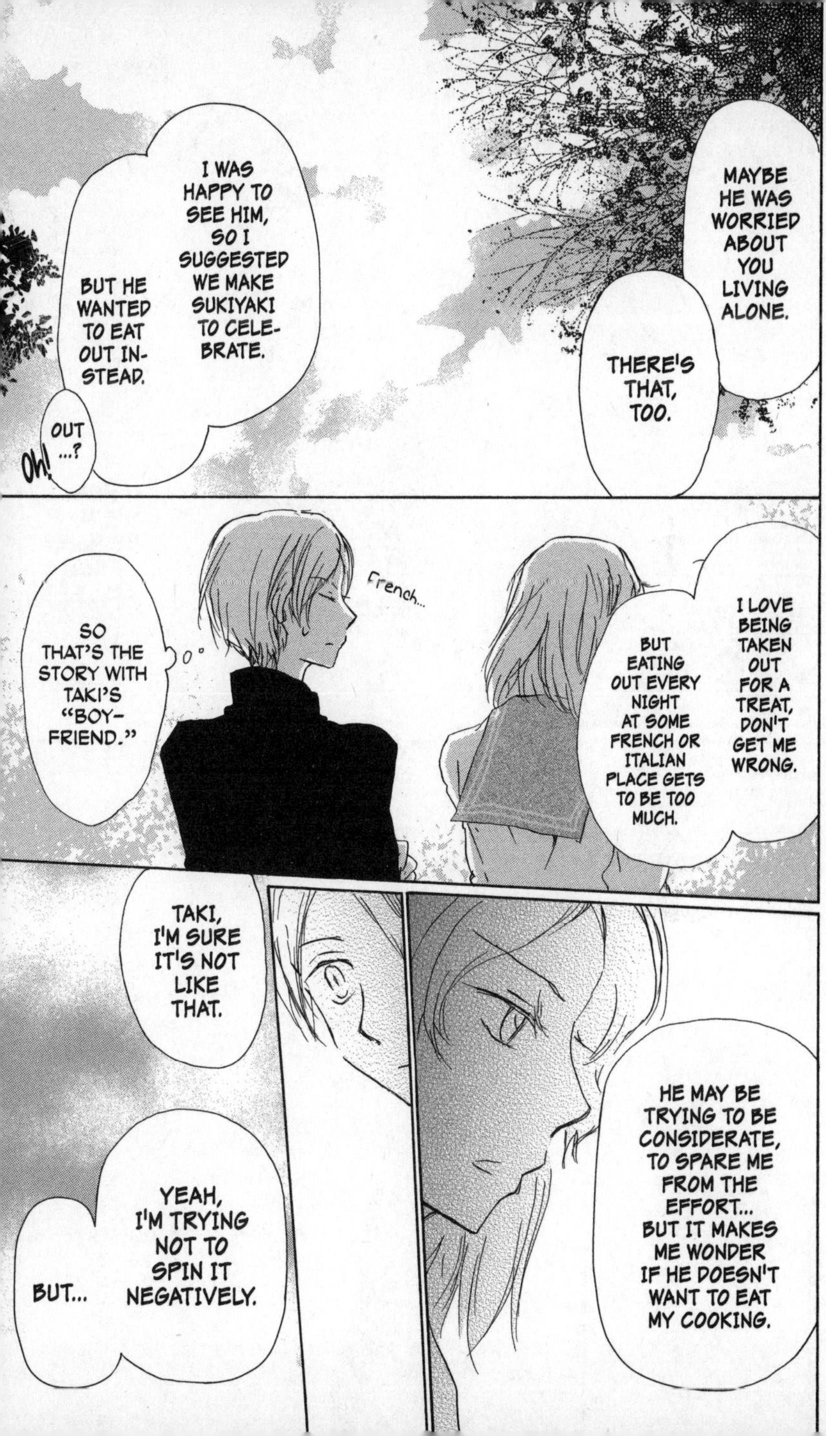
MAYBE HE WAS WORRIED ABOUT YOU LIVING ALONE.
THERE'S THAT, TOO.
I WAS HAPPY TO SEE HIM, SO I SUGGESTED WE MAKE SUKIYAKI TO CELEBRATE.
BUT HE WANTED TO EAT OUT INSTEAD.
OUT ...?
Oh!
I LOVE BEING TAKEN OUT FOR A TREAT, DON'T GET ME WRONG.
BUT EATING OUT EVERY NIGHT AT SOME FRENCH OR ITALIAN PLACE GETS TO BE TOO MUCH.
French...
SO THAT'S THE STORY WITH TAKI'S "BOY-FRIEND."
HE MAY BE TRYING TO BE CONSIDERATE, TO SPARE ME FROM THE EFFORT... BUT IT MAKES ME WONDER IF HE DOESN'T WANT TO EAT MY COOKING.
TAKI, I'M SURE IT'S NOT LIKE THAT.
YEAH, I'M TRYING NOT TO SPIN IT NEGATIVELY.
BUT...

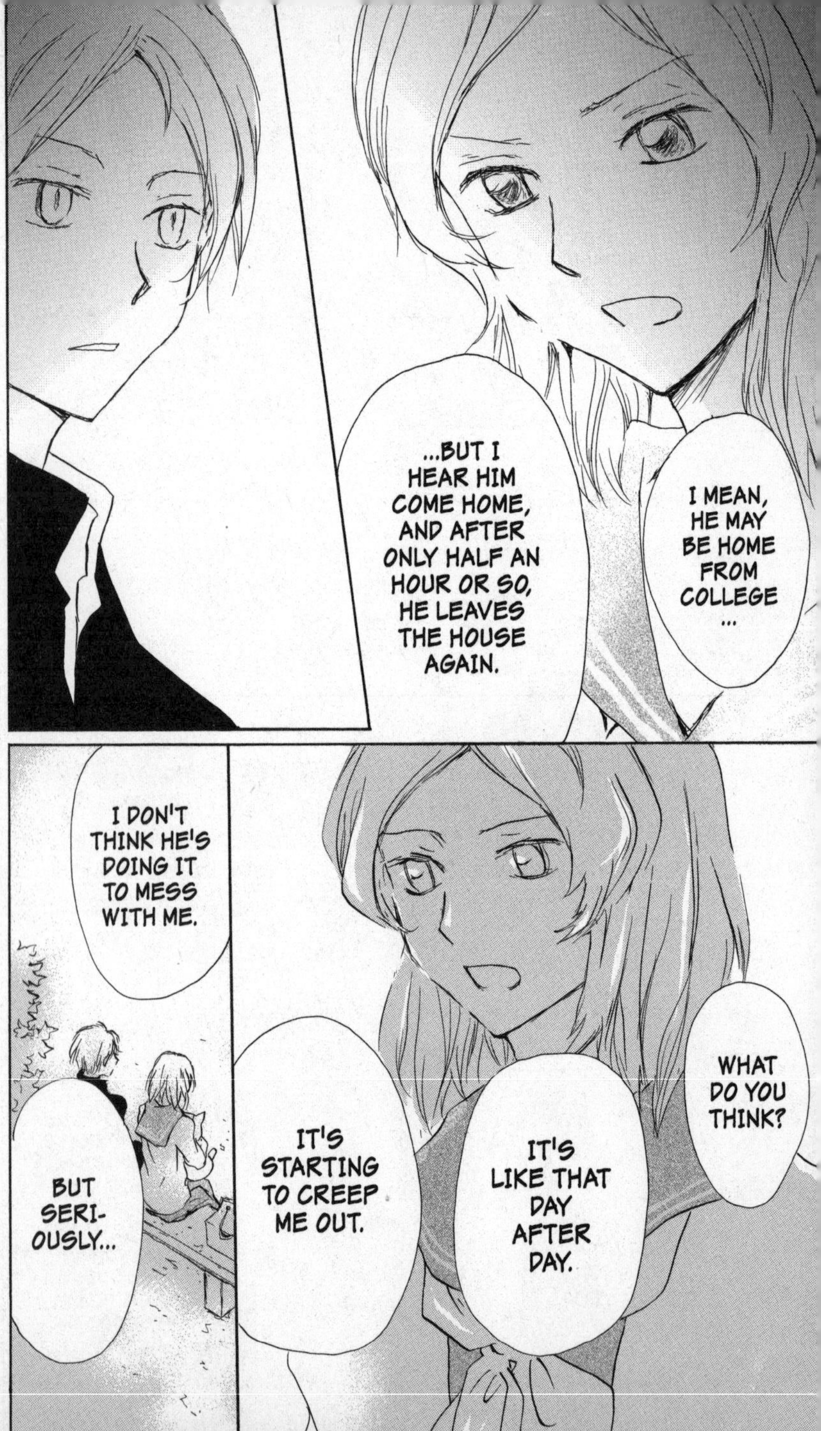
I MEAN, HE MAY BE HOME FROM COLLEGE ...
...BUT I HEAR HIM COME HOME, AND AFTER ONLY HALF AN HOUR OR SO, HE LEAVES THE HOUSE AGAIN.
WHAT DO YOU THINK?
IT'S LIKE THAT DAY AFTER DAY.
IT'S STARTING TO CREEP ME OUT.
I DON'T THINK HE'S DOING IT TO MESS WITH ME.
BUT SERI-OUSLY...

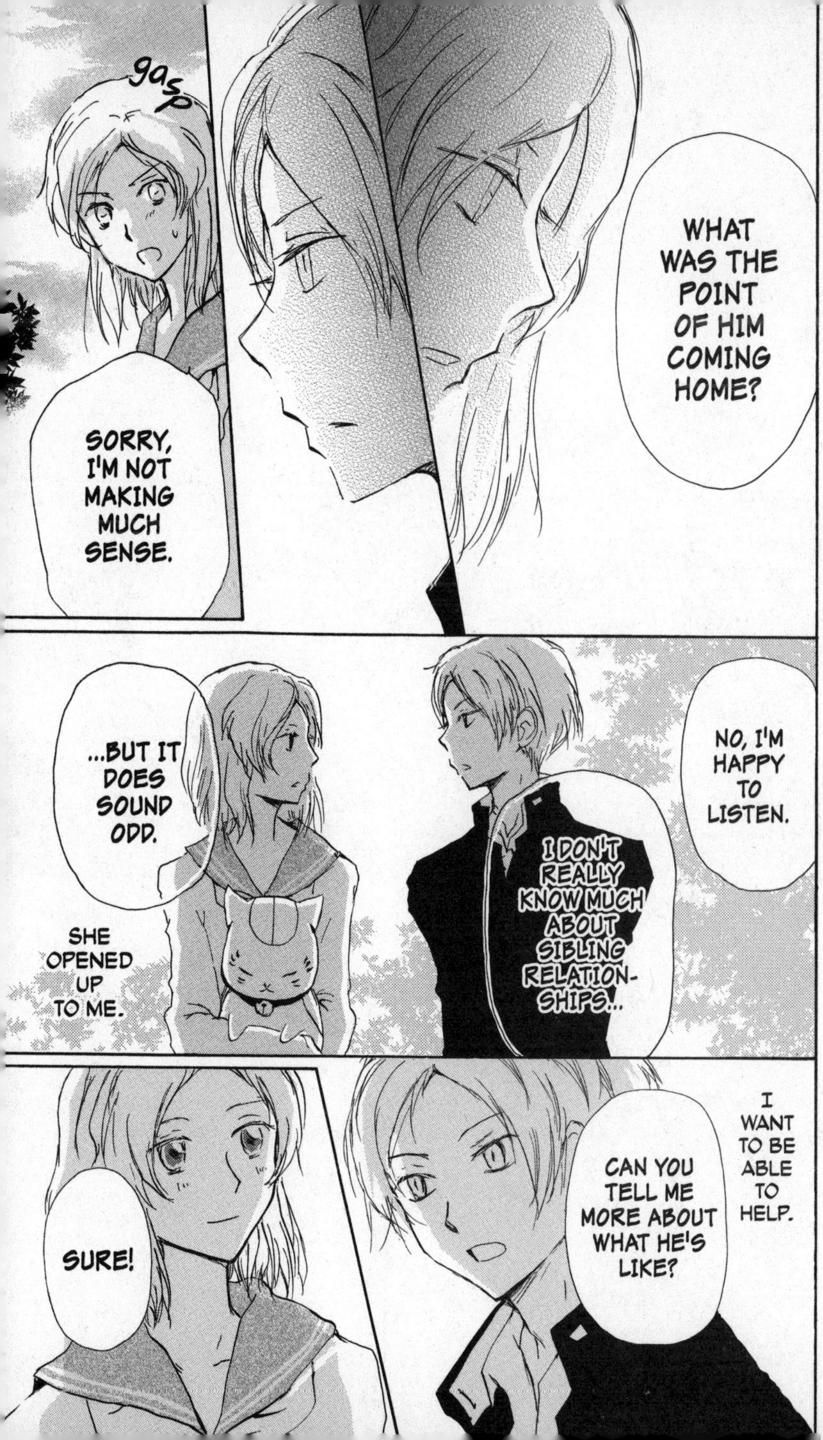
WHAT WAS THE POINT OF HIM COMING HOME?
gasp
SORRY, I'M NOT MAKING MUCH SENSE.
NO, I'M HAPPY TO LISTEN.
I DON'T REALLY KNOW MUCH ABOUT SIBLING RELATION-SHIPS...
...BUT IT DOES SOUND ODD.
SHE OPENED UP TO ME.
I WANT TO BE ABLE TO HELP.
CAN YOU TELL ME MORE ABOUT WHAT HE'S LIKE?
SURE!

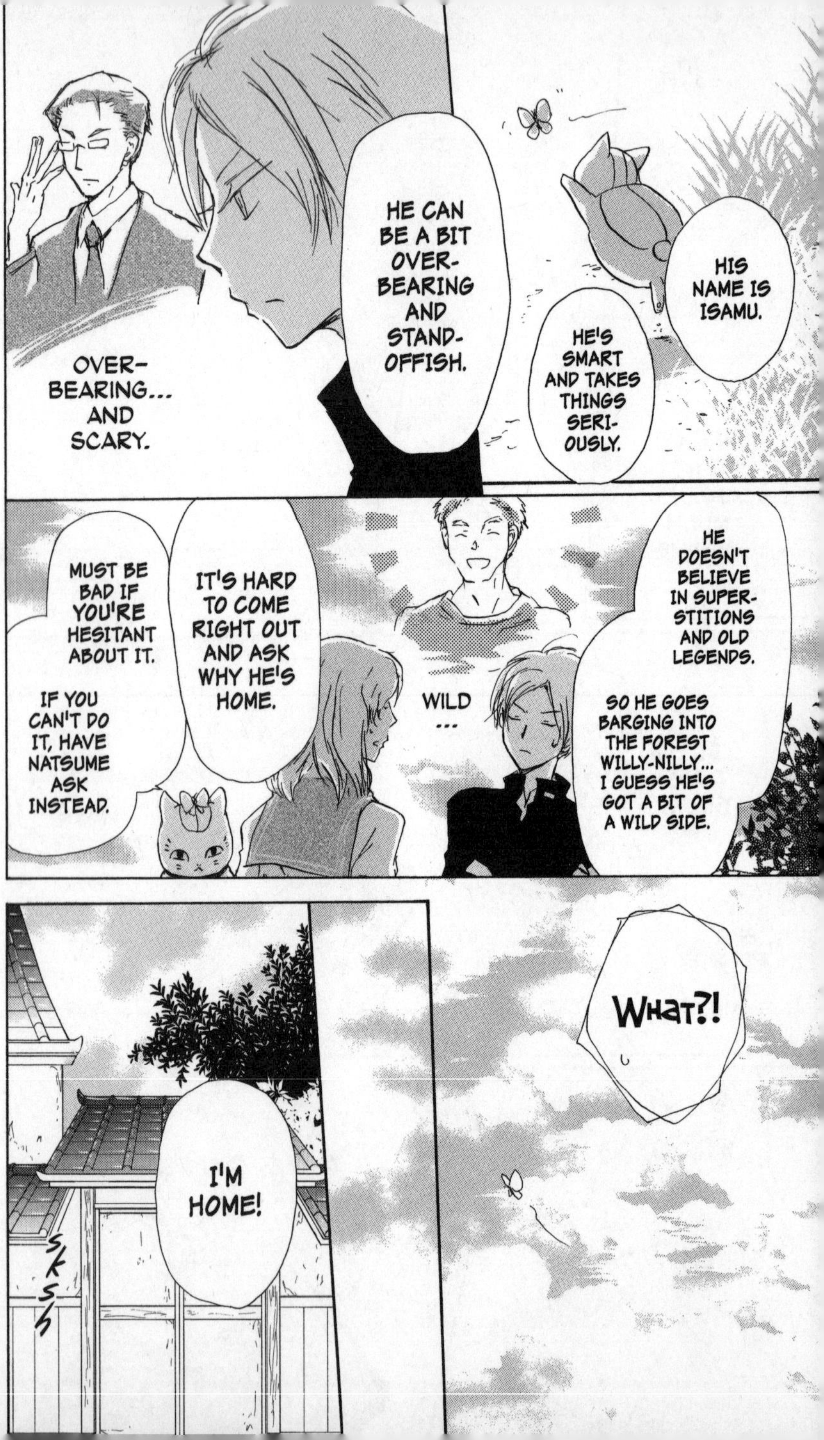
HIS NAME IS ISAMU.
HE'S SMART AND TAKES THINGS SERI-OUSLY.
HE CAN BE A BIT OVER-BEARING AND STAND-OFFISH.
OVER-BEARING... AND SCARY.
HE DOESN'T BELIEVE IN SUPER-STITIONS AND OLD LEGENDS.
SO HE GOES BARGING INTO THE FOREST WILLY-NILLY... I GUESS HE'S GOT A BIT OF A WILD SIDE.
WILD ...
IT'S HARD TO COME RIGHT OUT AND ASK WHY HE'S HOME.
MUST BE BAD IF YOU'RE HESITANT ABOUT IT.
IF YOU CAN'T DO IT, HAVE NATSUME ASK INSTEAD.
WHAT?!
I'M HOME!
SKSH

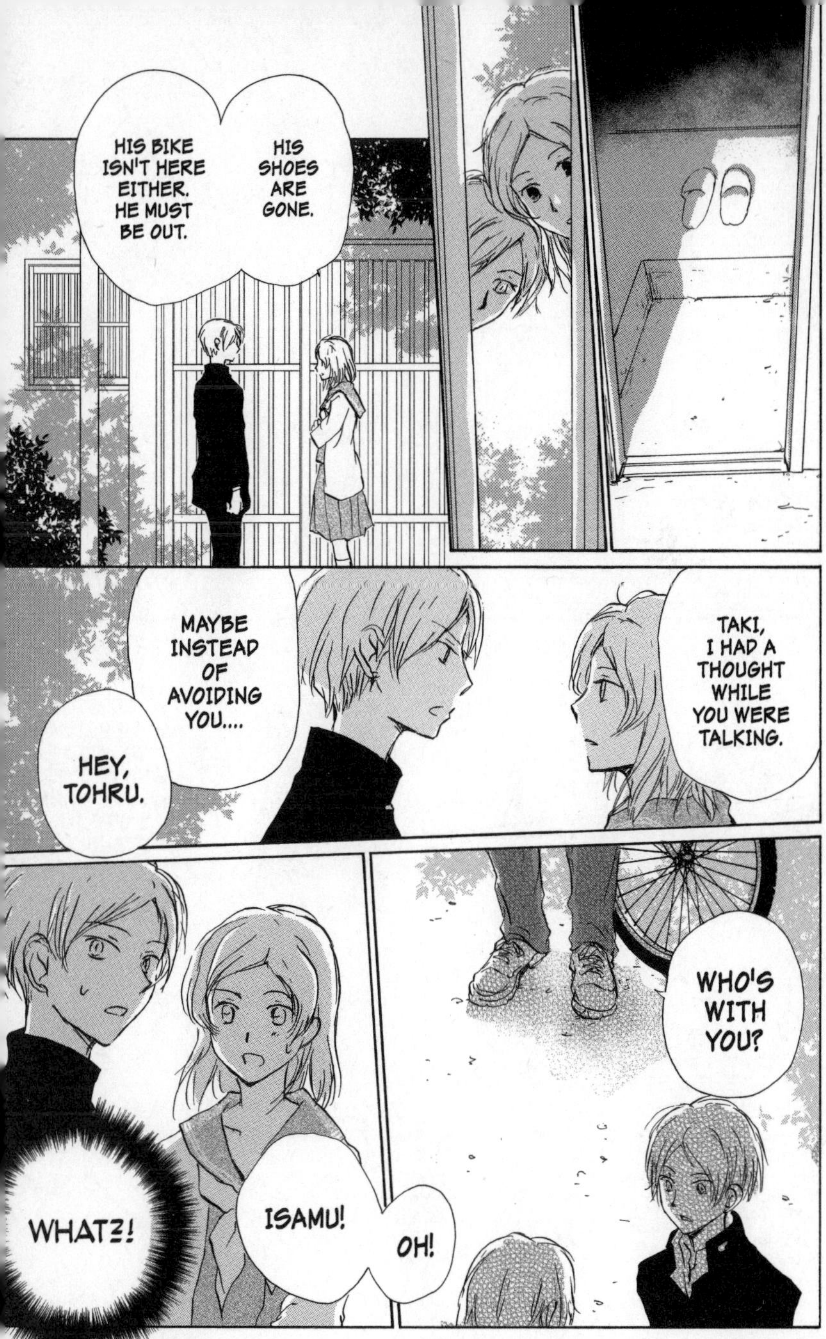
HIS SHOES ARE GONE.
HIS BIKE ISN'T HERE EITHER. HE MUST BE OUT.
TAKI, I HAD A THOUGHT WHILE YOU WERE TALKING.
MAYBE INSTEAD OF AVOIDING YOU....
HEY, TOHRU.
WHO'S WITH YOU?
OH!
ISAMU!
WHAT?!

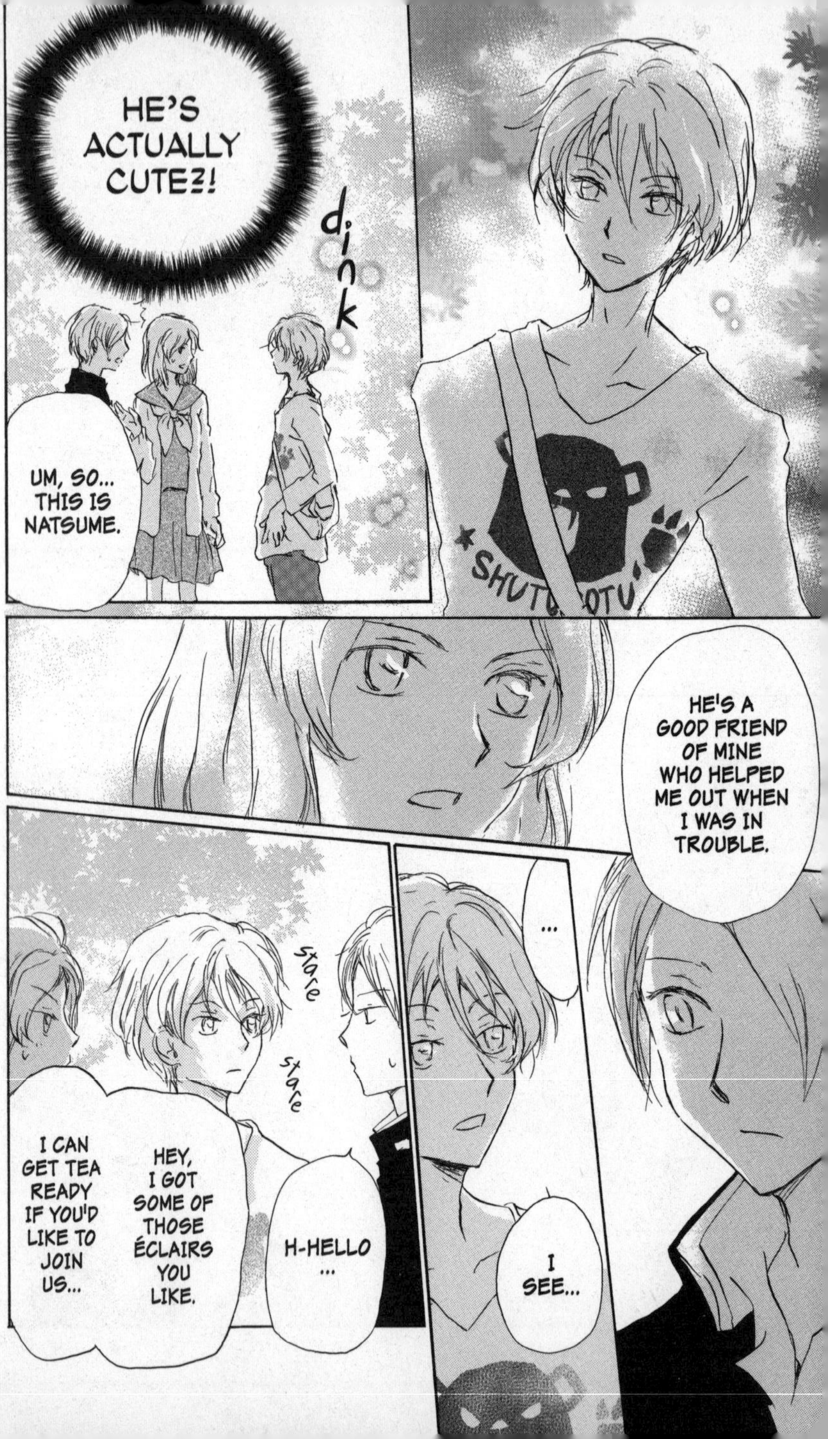
HE'S ACTUALLY CUTE?!
dink
UM, SO... THIS IS NATSUME.
HE'S A GOOD FRIEND OF MINE WHO HELPED ME OUT WHEN I WAS IN TROUBLE.
...
I SEE...
stare
stare
H-HELLO...
HEY, I GOT SOME OF THOSE ÉCLAIRS YOU LIKE.
I CAN GET TEA READY IF YOU'D LIKE TO JOIN US...

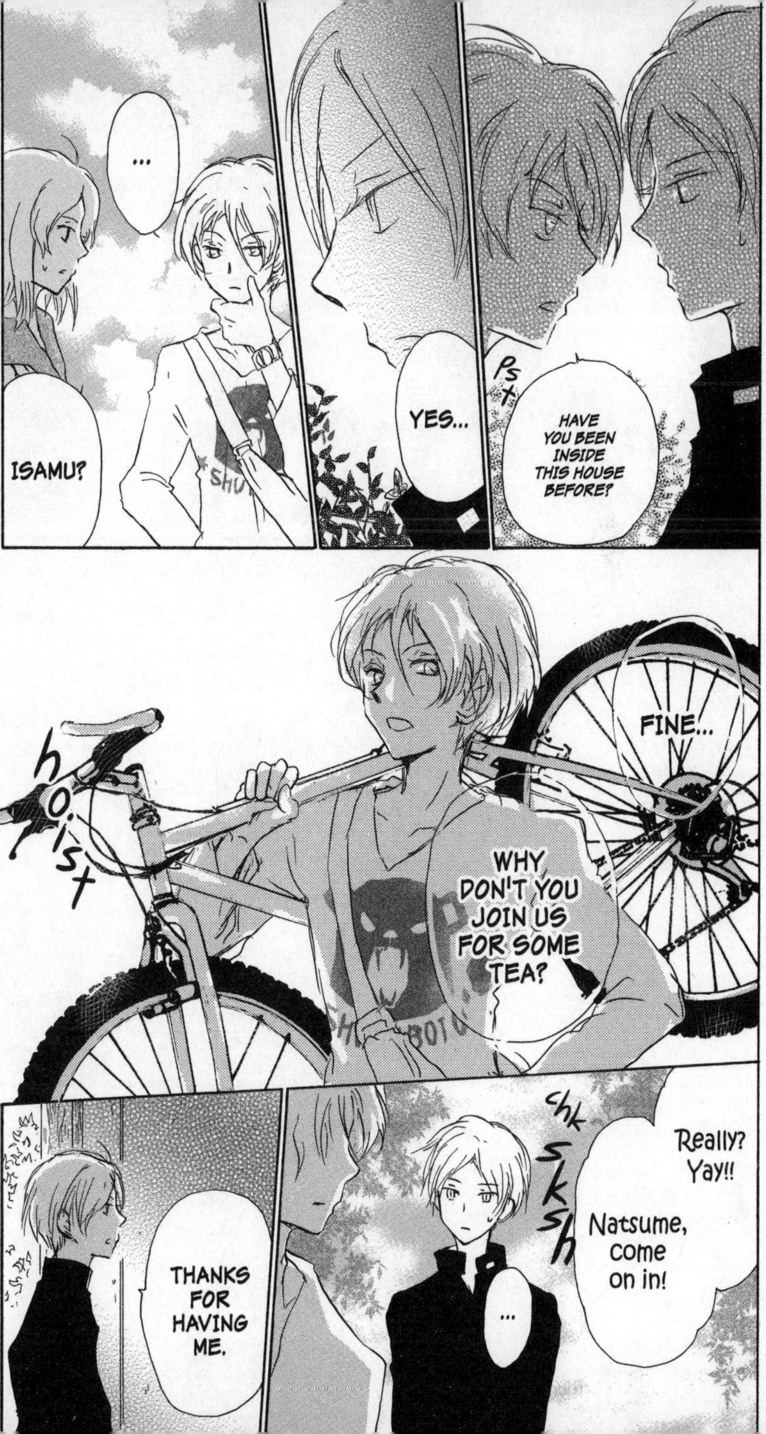
Pst
HAVE YOU BEEN INSIDE THIS HOUSE BEFORE?
YES...
...
ISAMU?
FINE...
hoist
WHY DON'T YOU JOIN US FOR SOME TEA?
chk
sksh
Really? Yay!!
Natsume, come on in!
...
THANKS FOR HAVING ME.

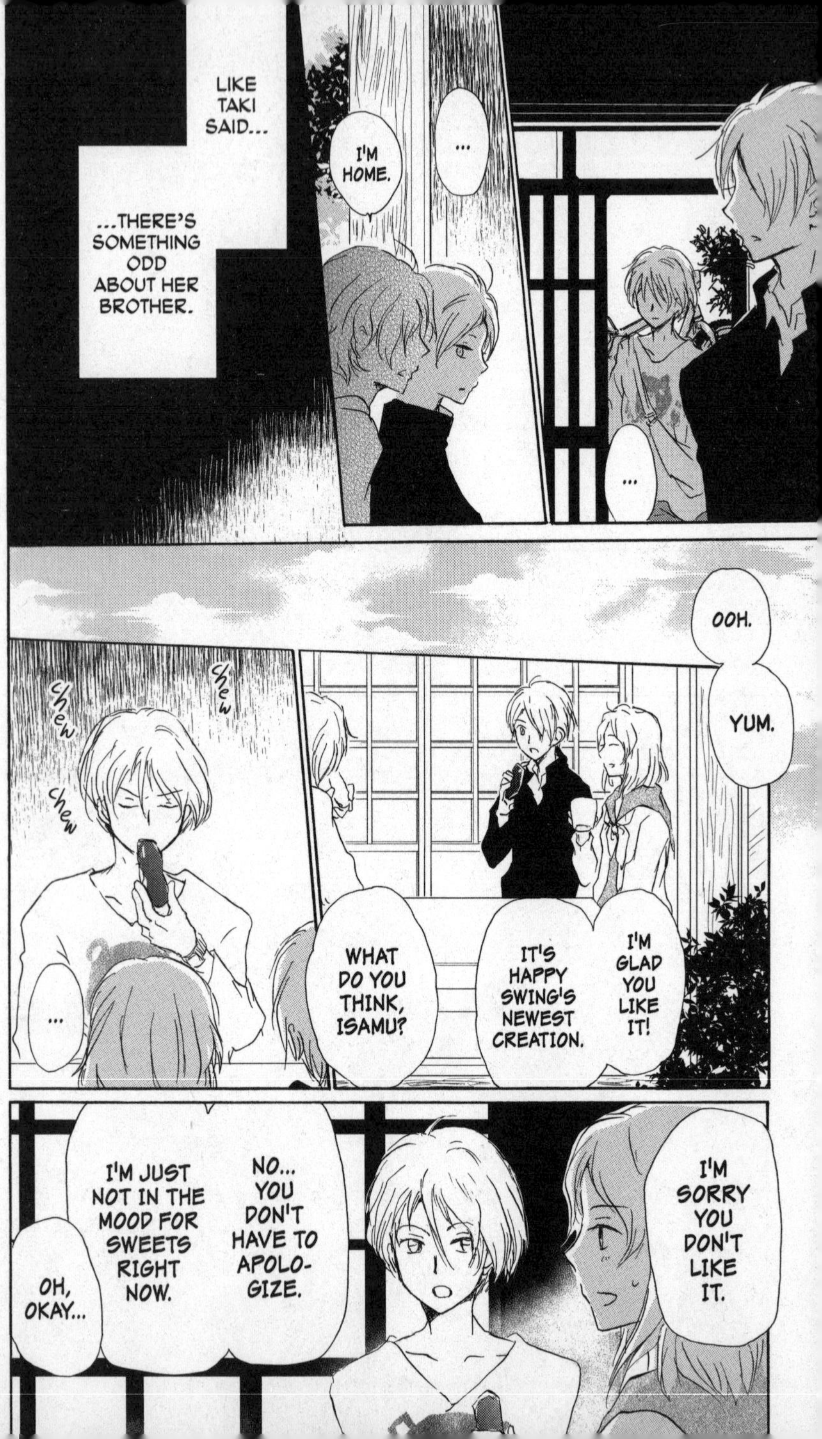
...
...
I'M HOME.
LIKE TAKI SAID...
...THERE'S SOMETHING ODD ABOUT HER BROTHER.
OOH.
YUM.
I'M GLAD YOU LIKE IT!
IT'S HAPPY SWING'S NEWEST CREATION.
WHAT DO YOU THINK, ISAMU?
chew
chew
chew
...
I'M SORRY YOU DON'T LIKE IT.
NO... YOU DON'T HAVE TO APOLOGIZE.
I'M JUST NOT IN THE MOOD FOR SWEETS RIGHT NOW.
OH, OKAY...

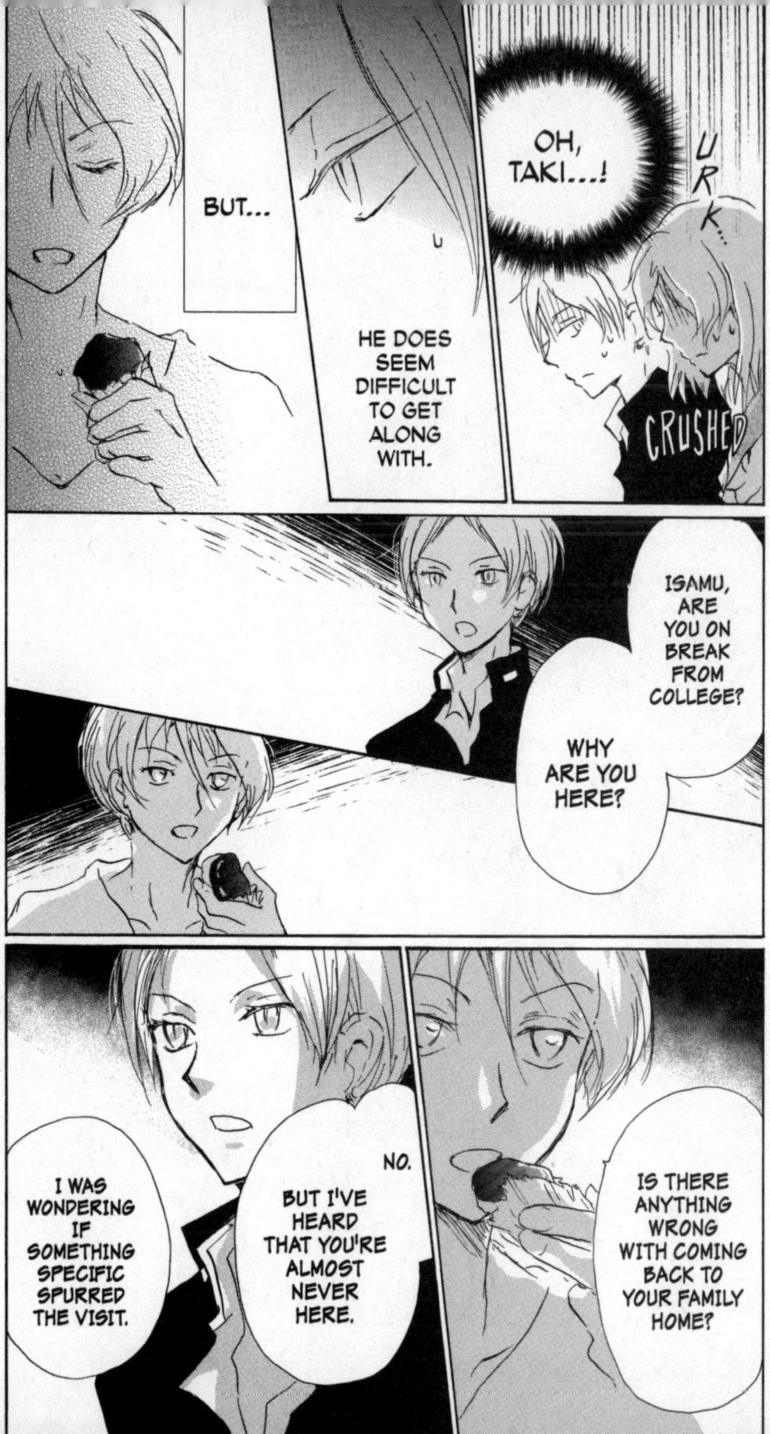
OH, TAKI...!
URK...
CRUSHED
HE DOES SEEM DIFFICULT TO GET ALONG WITH.
BUT...
ISAMU, ARE YOU ON BREAK FROM COLLEGE?
WHY ARE YOU HERE?
IS THERE ANYTHING WRONG WITH COMING BACK TO YOUR FAMILY HOME?
NO.
BUT I'VE HEARD THAT YOU'RE ALMOST NEVER HERE.
I WAS WONDERING IF SOMETHING SPECIFIC SPURRED THE VISIT.

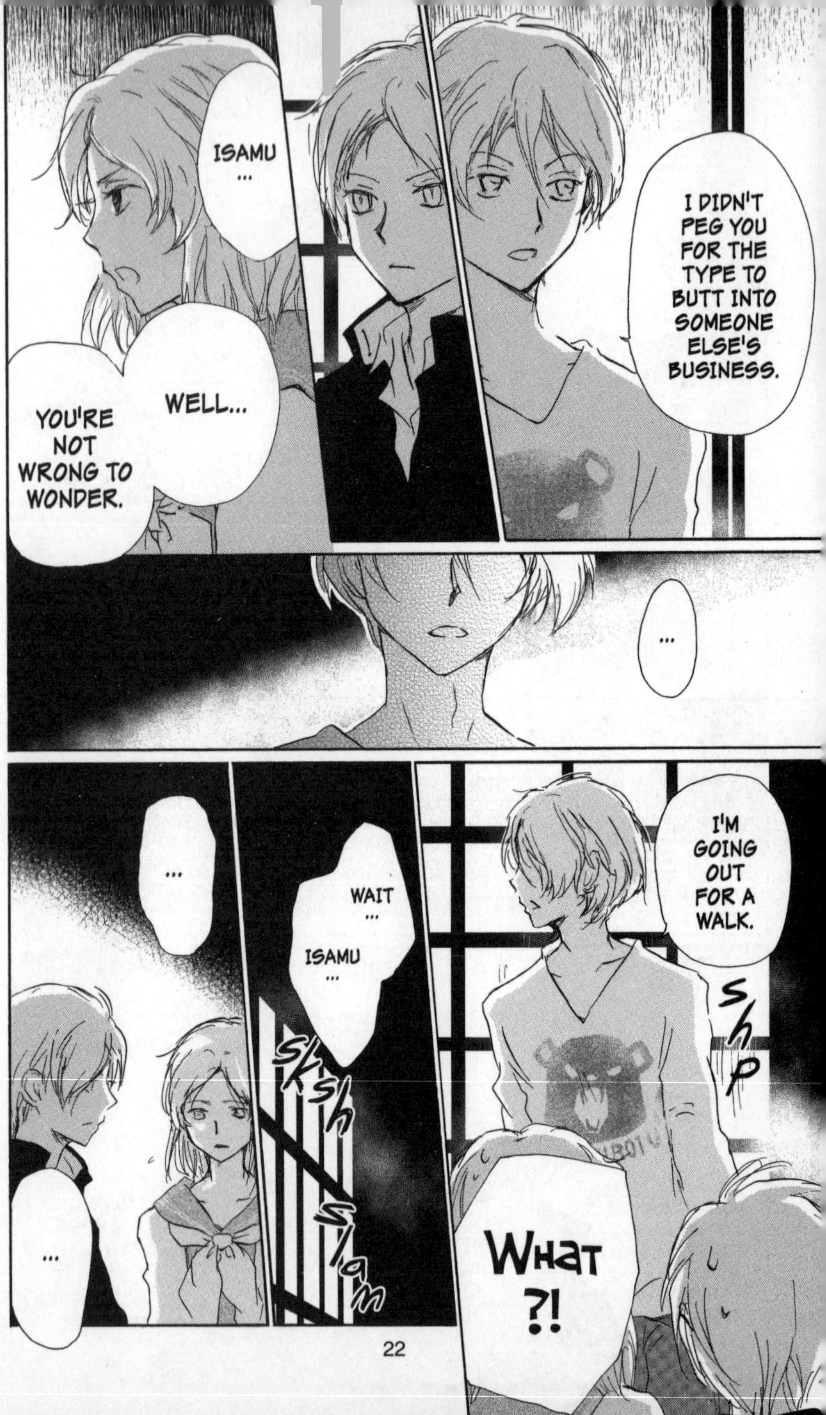
I DIDN'T PEG YOU FOR THE TYPE TO BUTT INTO SOMEONE ELSE'S BUSINESS.
ISAMU ...
WELL...
YOU'RE NOT WRONG TO WONDER.
...
I'M GOING OUT FOR A WALK.
SHP
WAIT ... ISAMU ...
SKSH SLAM
...
WHAT ?!
...

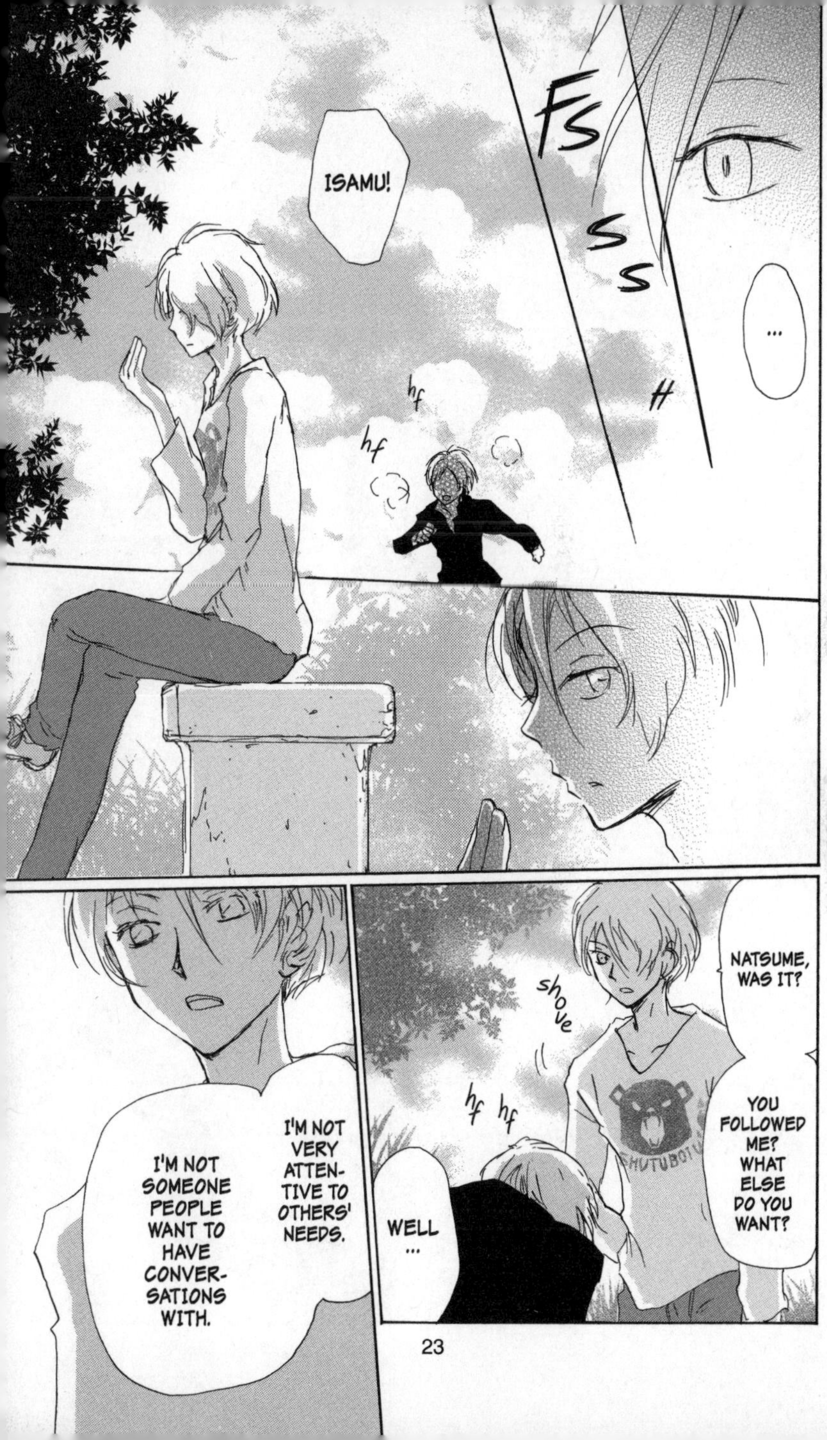
FSSSH
...
ISAMU!
hf
hf
NATSUME, WAS IT?
YOU FOLLOWED ME? WHAT ELSE DO YOU WANT?
shove
hf hf
WELL ...
I'M NOT VERY ATTEN-TIVE TO OTHERS' NEEDS.
I'M NOT SOMEONE PEOPLE WANT TO HAVE CONVER-SATIONS WITH.

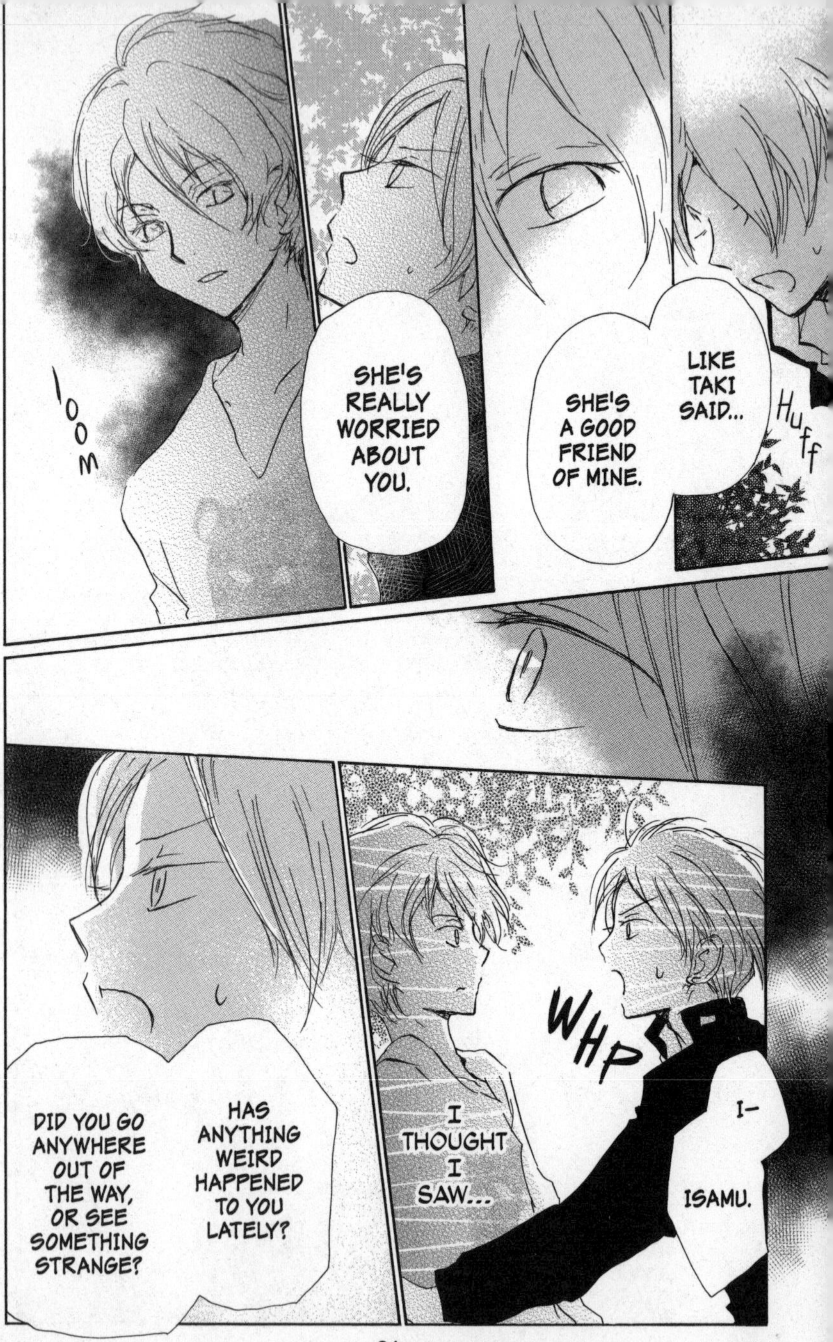
Huff
LIKE TAKI SAID...
SHE'S A GOOD FRIEND OF MINE.
SHE'S REALLY WORRIED ABOUT YOU.
loom
WHP
I—
ISAMU.
I THOUGHT I SAW...
HAS ANYTHING WEIRD HAPPENED TO YOU LATELY?
DID YOU GO ANYWHERE OUT OF THE WAY, OR SEE SOMETHING STRANGE?

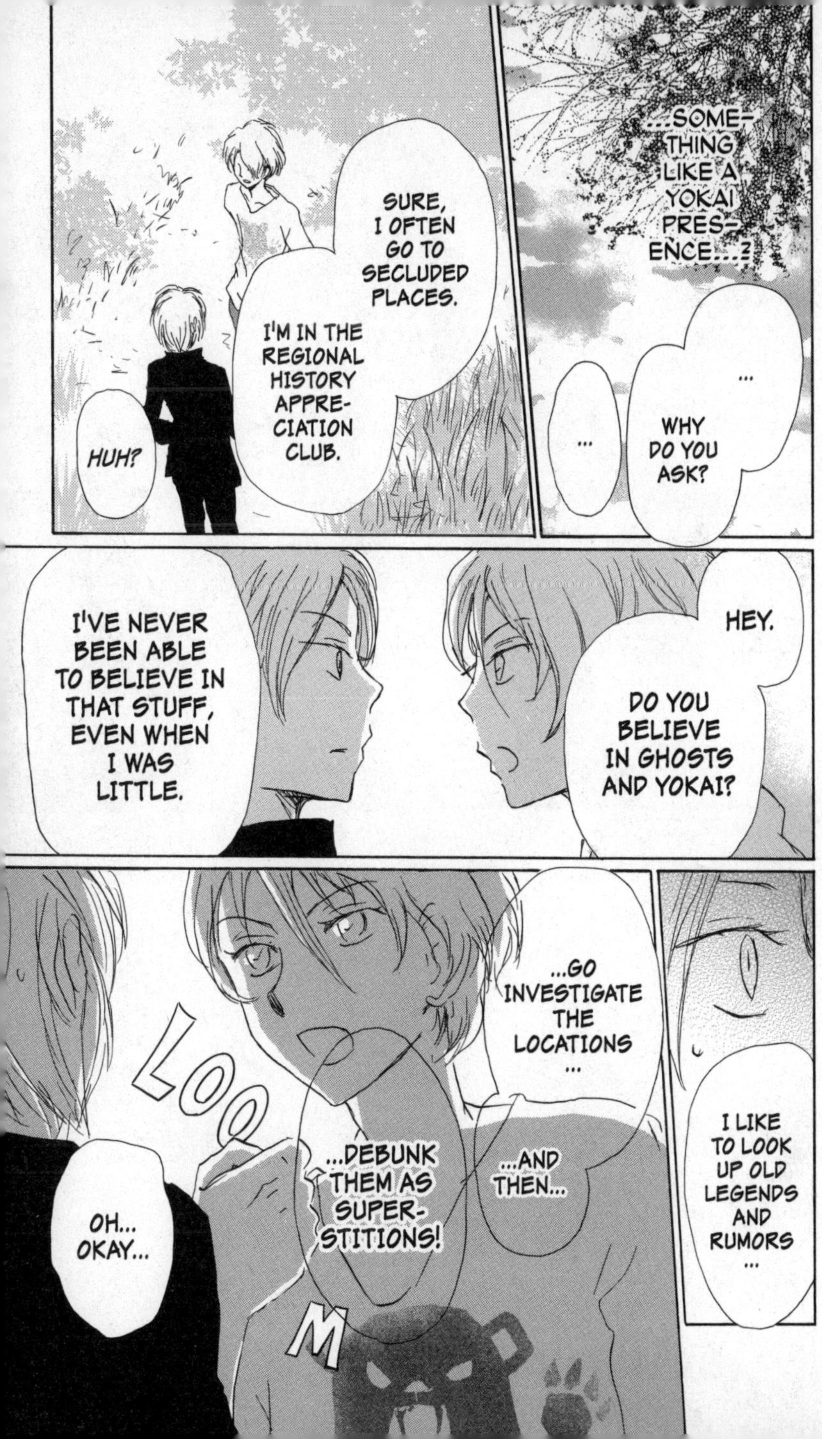
...SOMETHING LIKE A YOKAI PRESENCE...?
...
WHY DO YOU ASK?
...
SURE, I OFTEN GO TO SECLUDED PLACES.
I'M IN THE REGIONAL HISTORY APPRECIATION CLUB.
HUH?
HEY.
DO YOU BELIEVE IN GHOSTS AND YOKAI?
I'VE NEVER BEEN ABLE TO BELIEVE IN THAT STUFF, EVEN WHEN I WAS LITTLE.
I LIKE TO LOOK UP OLD LEGENDS AND RUMORS ...
...GO INVESTIGATE THE LOCATIONS ...
...AND THEN...
...DEBUNK THEM AS SUPERSTITIONS!
LOOOM
OH... OKAY...

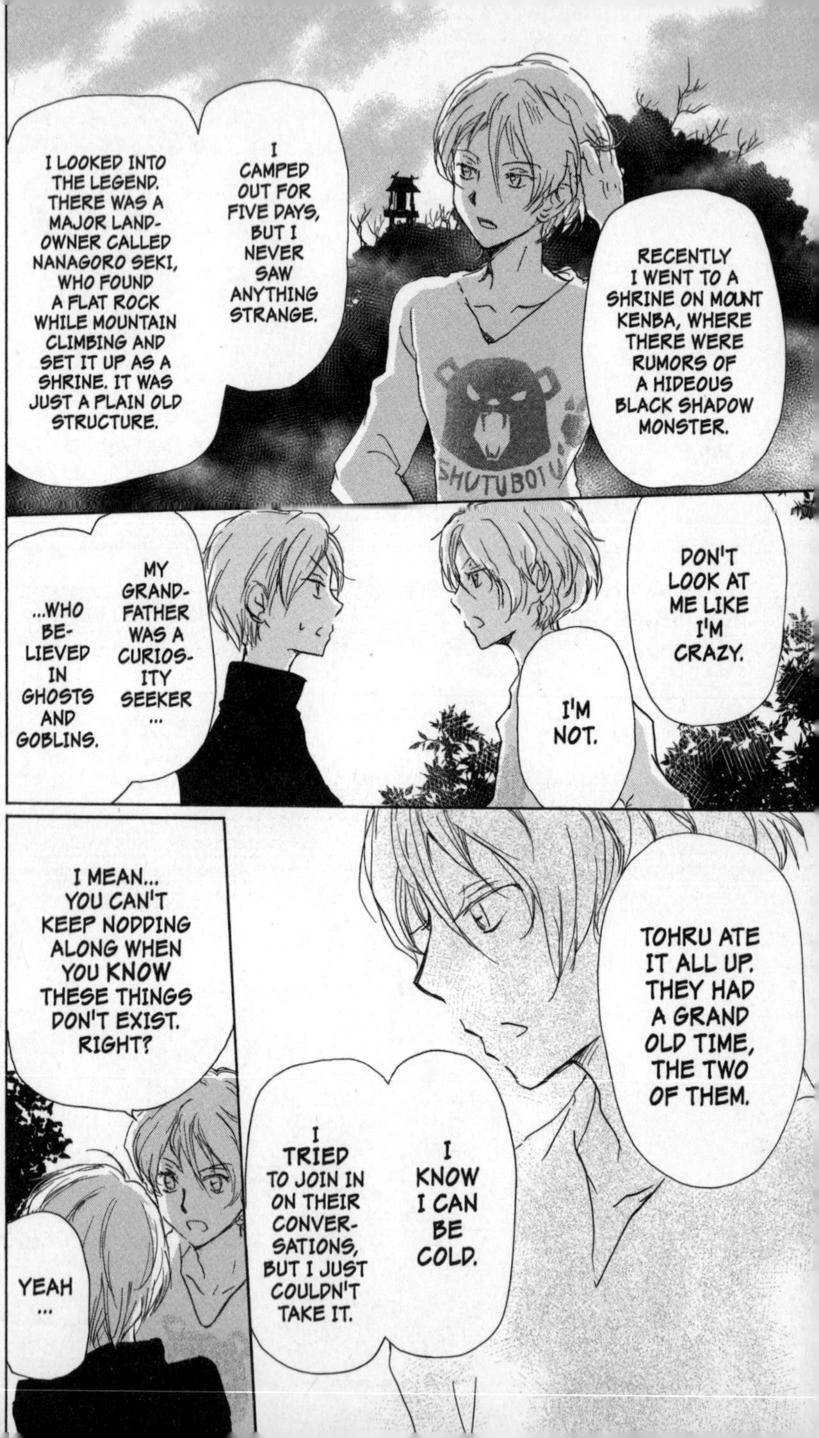
RECENTLY I WENT TO A SHRINE ON MOUNT KENBA, WHERE THERE WERE RUMORS OF A HIDEOUS BLACK SHADOW MONSTER.
I CAMPED OUT FOR FIVE DAYS, BUT I NEVER SAW ANYTHING STRANGE.
I LOOKED INTO THE LEGEND. THERE WAS A MAJOR LAND-OWNER CALLED NANAGORO SEKI, WHO FOUND A FLAT ROCK WHILE MOUNTAIN CLIMBING AND SET IT UP AS A SHRINE. IT WAS JUST A PLAIN OLD STRUCTURE.
SHUTUBOI
DON'T LOOK AT ME LIKE I'M CRAZY.
I'M NOT.
MY GRAND-FATHER WAS A CURIOS-ITY SEEKER...
...WHO BE-LIEVED IN GHOSTS AND GOBLINS.
TOHRU ATE IT ALL UP. THEY HAD A GRAND OLD TIME, THE TWO OF THEM.
I KNOW I CAN BE COLD.
I TRIED TO JOIN IN ON THEIR CONVER-SATIONS, BUT I JUST COULDN'T TAKE IT.
I MEAN... YOU CAN'T KEEP NODDING ALONG WHEN YOU KNOW THESE THINGS DON'T EXIST. RIGHT?
YEAH...

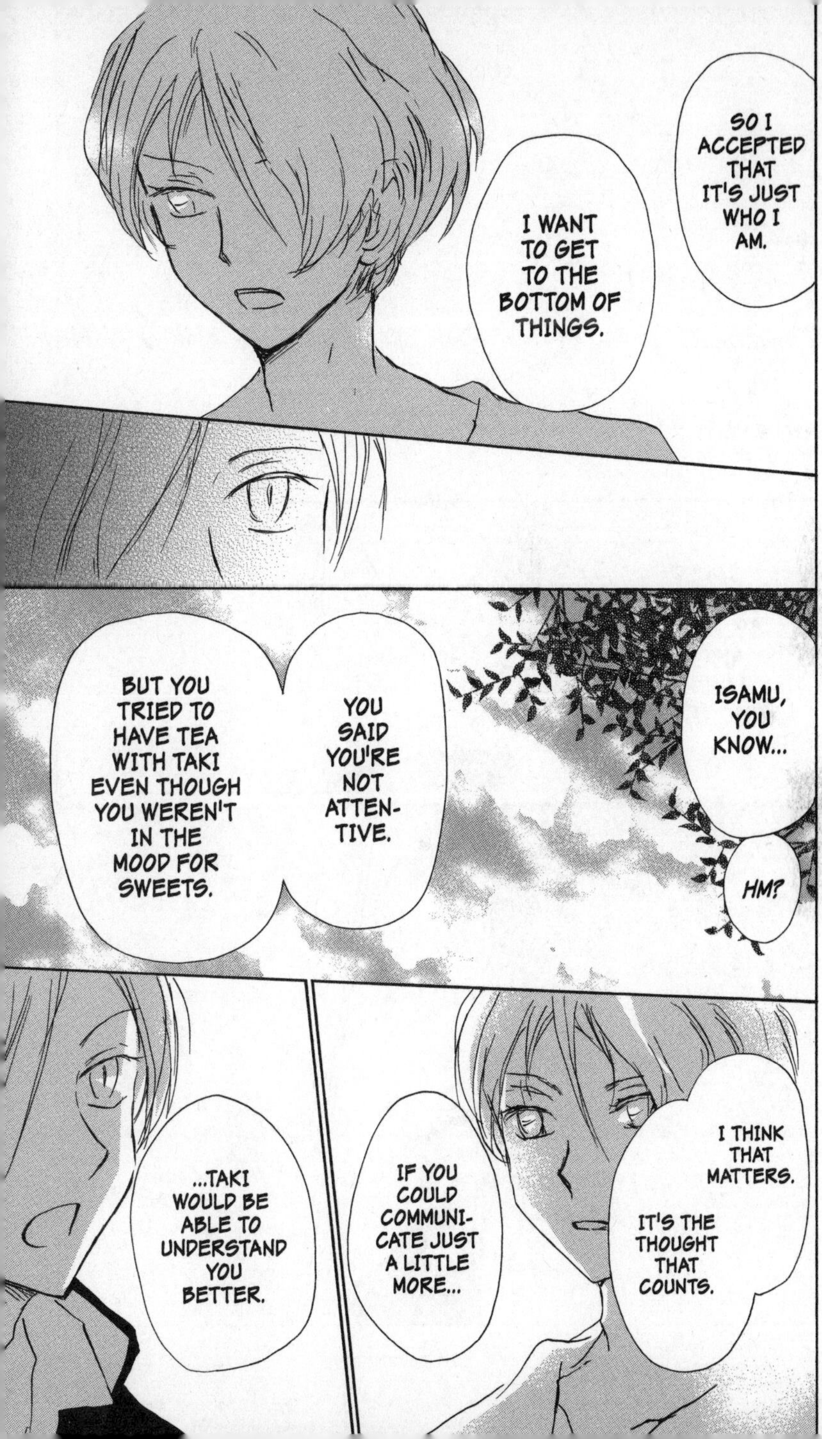
SO I ACCEPTED THAT IT'S JUST WHO I AM.
I WANT TO GET TO THE BOTTOM OF THINGS.
ISAMU, YOU KNOW...
HM?
YOU SAID YOU'RE NOT ATTEN-TIVE.
BUT YOU TRIED TO HAVE TEA WITH TAKI EVEN THOUGH YOU WEREN'T IN THE MOOD FOR SWEETS.
I THINK THAT MATTERS.
IT'S THE THOUGHT THAT COUNTS.
IF YOU COULD COMMUNI-CATE JUST A LITTLE MORE...
...TAKI WOULD BE ABLE TO UNDERSTAND YOU BETTER.

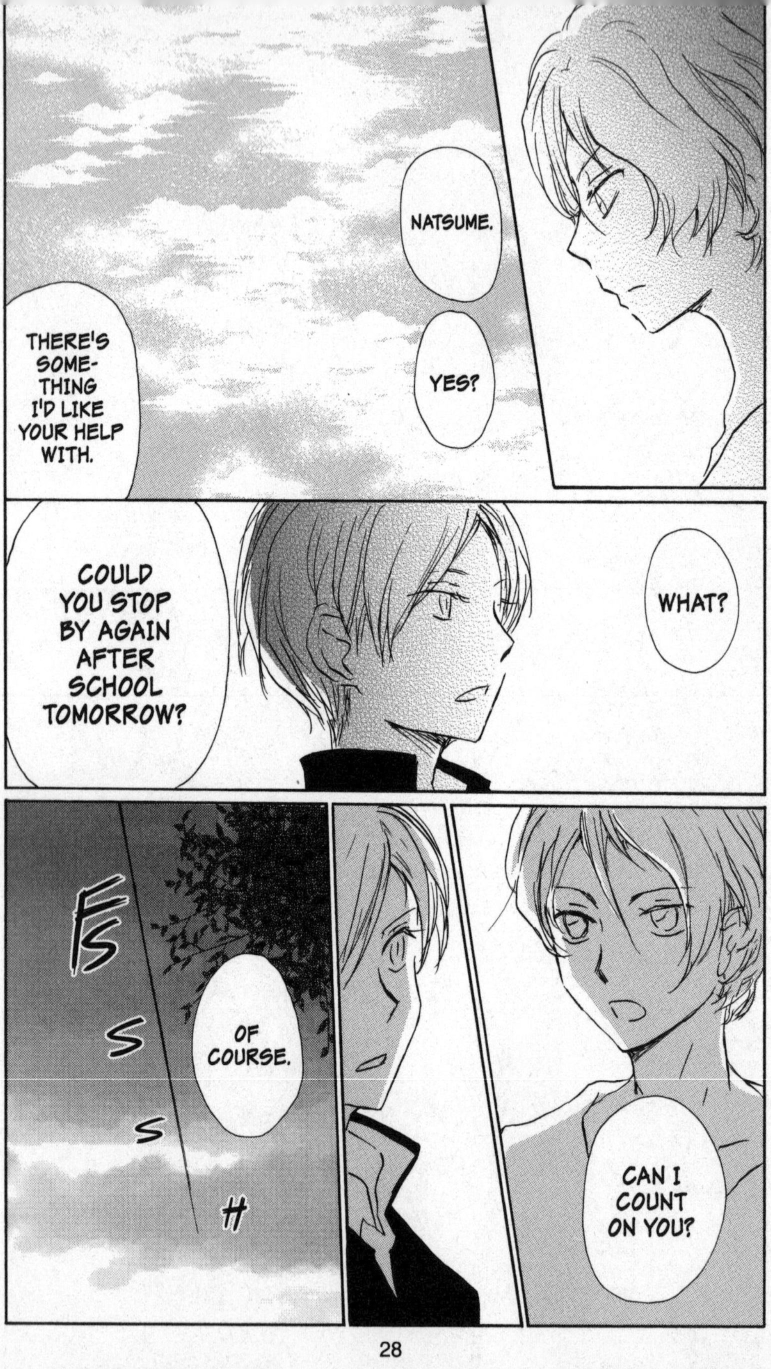
NATSUME.
YES?
THERE'S SOME-THING I'D LIKE YOUR HELP WITH.
WHAT?
COULD YOU STOP BY AGAIN AFTER SCHOOL TOMORROW?
CAN I COUNT ON YOU?
OF COURSE.
FSSSH

01

Hello, Midorikawa here. *Natsume's Book of Friends* has reached its 24th volume. I'm so touched that I've been able to keep the series going on for so long. I also have to buckle down on the responsibilities of running such a long series!

✻ LaLa Manga School Fukuoka

I was once again invited to participate in a manga seminar. Asato Shima, creator of *Kimi wa Haru ni Me wo Samasu* (You'll Wake Up in the Spring), was a fellow lecturer, and I was deeply impressed by her beautiful demo and her enthusiasm toward her creations. At the same time, I was moved by her being caught between her anxieties and her desire to help the participants. It's such a great responsibility to create something for someone to consume. I would like to take this opportunity to thank Ms. Shima, the participants and all the editors.

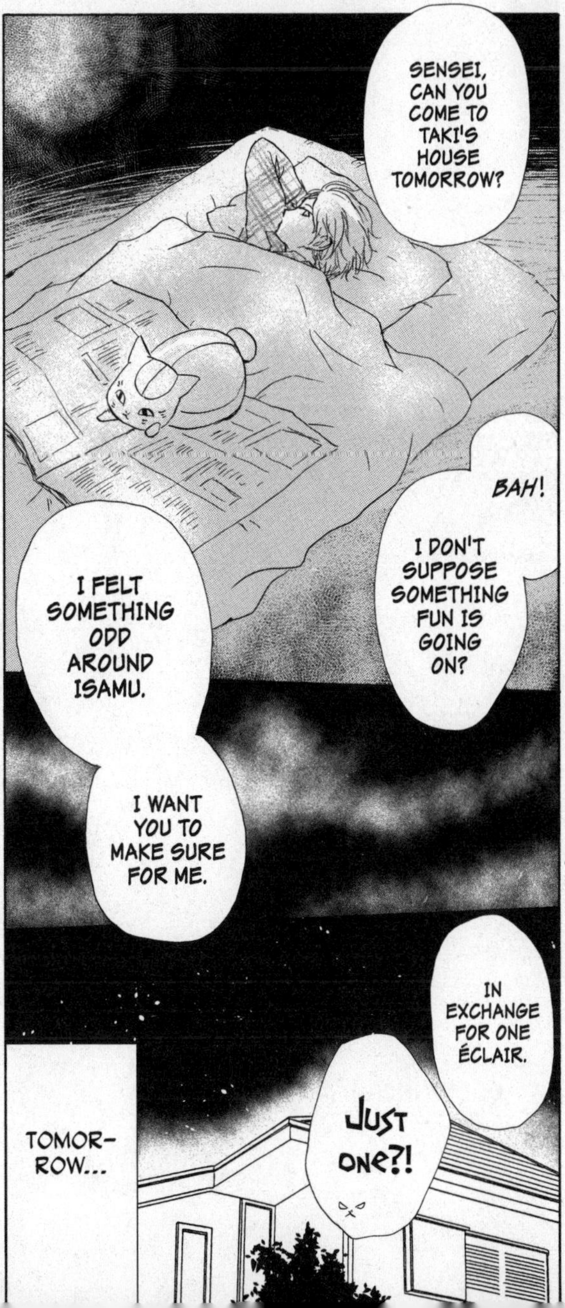
SENSEI, CAN YOU COME TO TAKI'S HOUSE TOMORROW?
BAH!
I DON'T SUPPOSE SOMETHING FUN IS GOING ON?
I FELT SOMETHING ODD AROUND ISAMU.
I WANT YOU TO MAKE SURE FOR ME.
IN EXCHANGE FOR ONE ÉCLAIR.
JUST ONE?!
TOMOR-ROW...

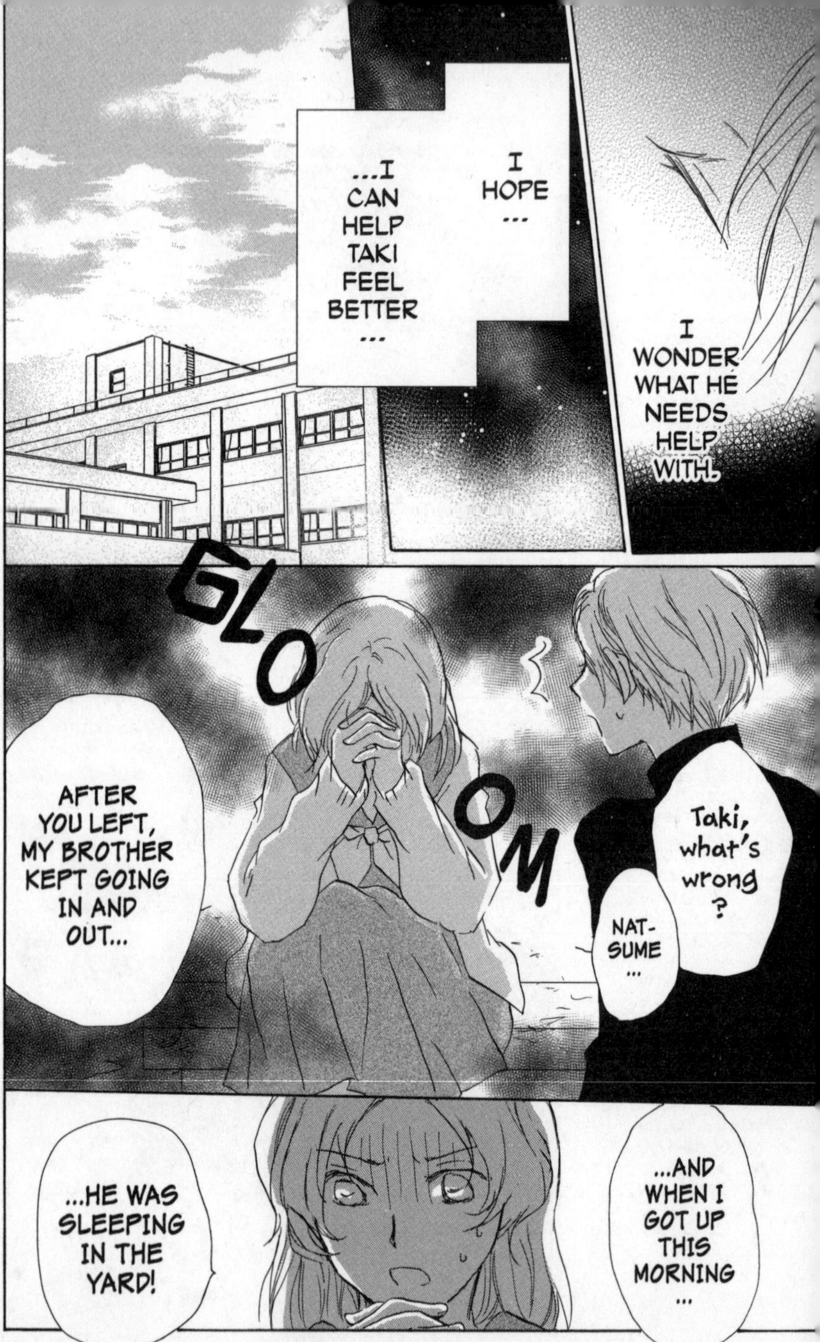
I WONDER WHAT HE NEEDS HELP WITH.
I HOPE...
...I CAN HELP TAKI FEEL BETTER...
Taki, what's wrong?
NATSUME...
GLOOM
AFTER YOU LEFT, MY BROTHER KEPT GOING IN AND OUT...
...AND WHEN I GOT UP THIS MORNING...
...HE WAS SLEEPING IN THE YARD!

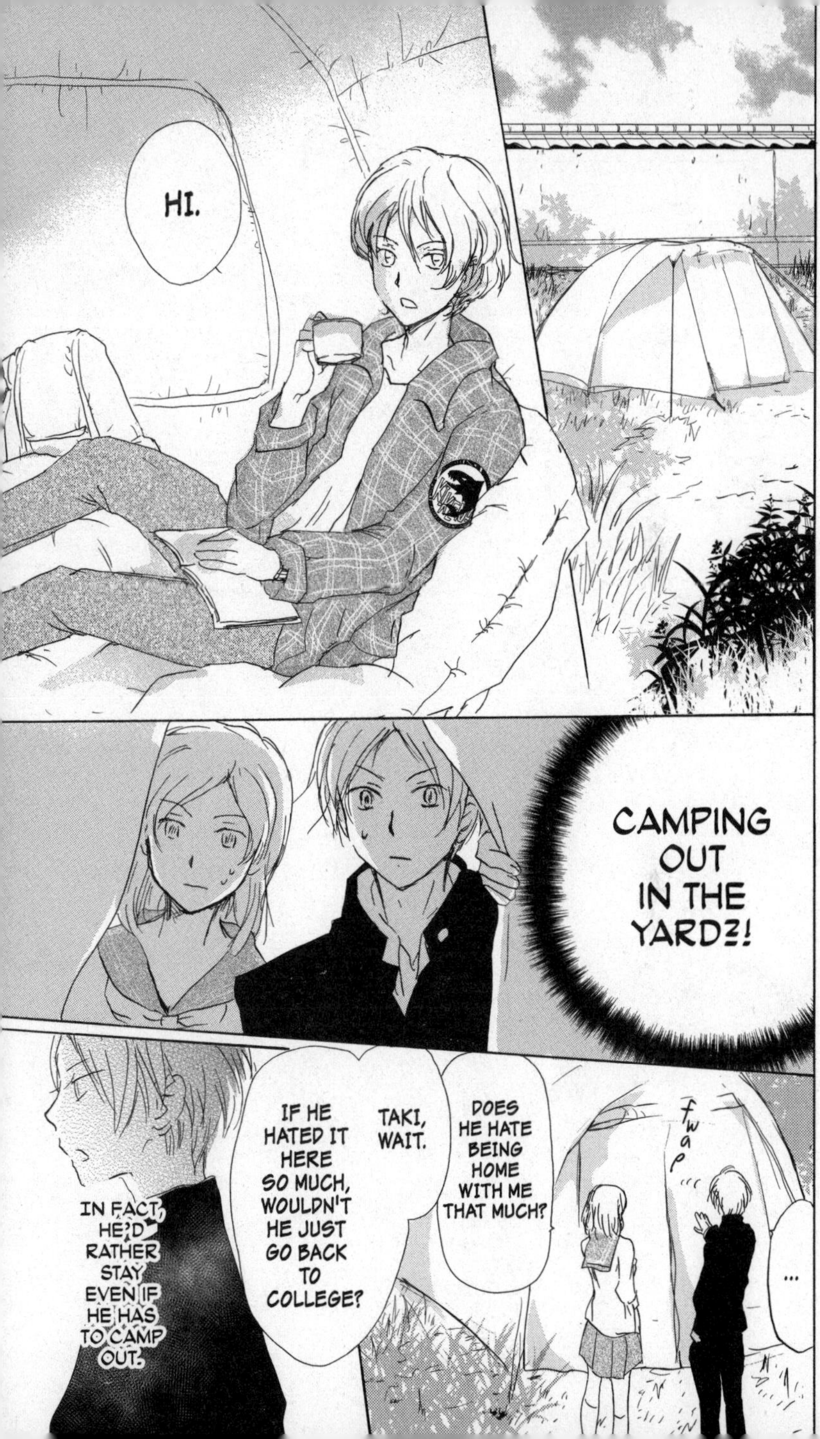
HI.
CAMPING OUT IN THE YARD?!
fwap
...
DOES HE HATE BEING HOME WITH ME THAT MUCH?
TAKI, WAIT.
IF HE HATED IT HERE SO MUCH, WOULDN'T HE JUST GO BACK TO COLLEGE?
IN FACT, HE'D RATHER STAY EVEN IF HE HAS TO CAMP OUT.

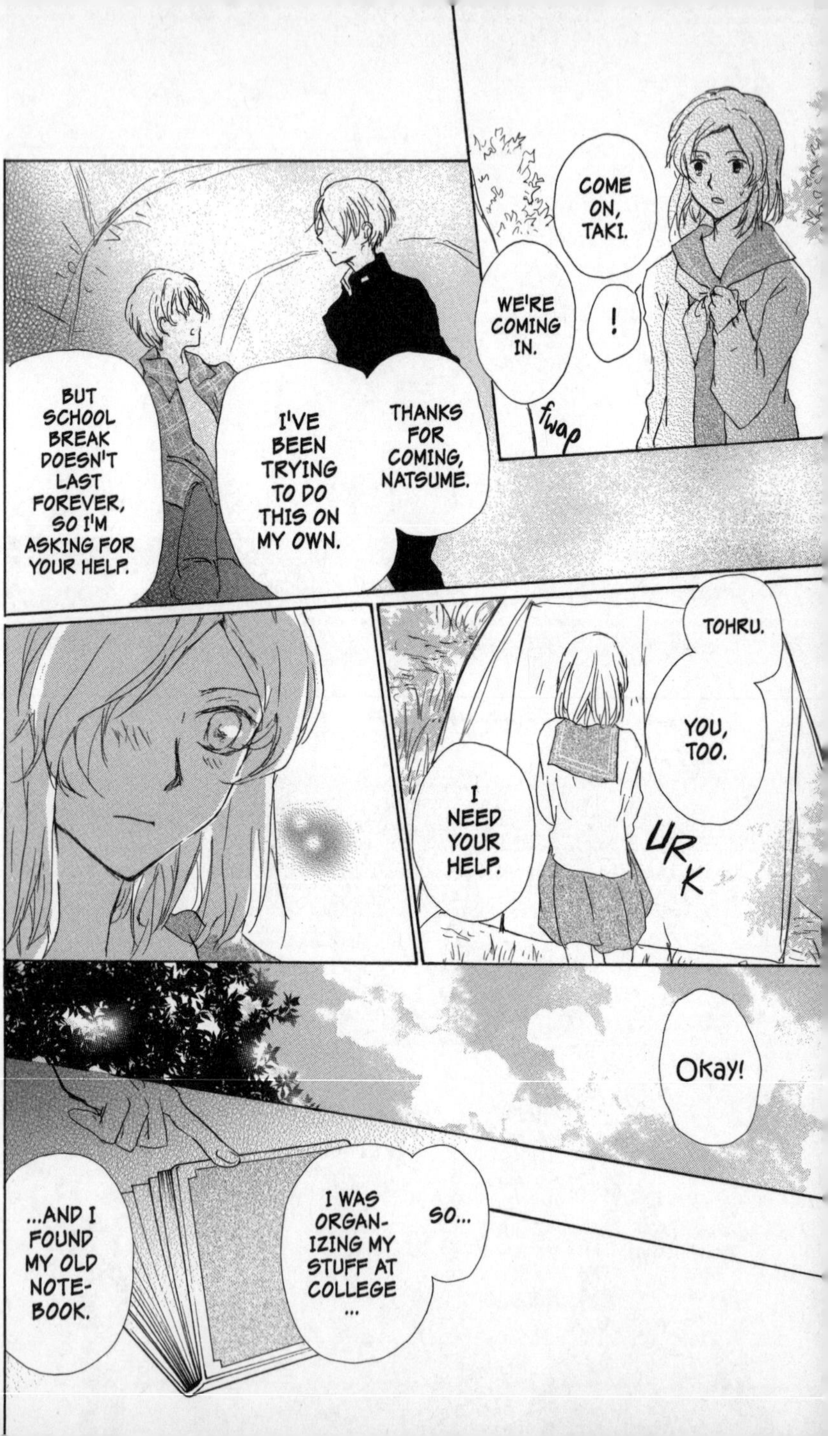
COME ON, TAKI.
!
WE'RE COMING IN.
fwap
THANKS FOR COMING, NATSUME.
I'VE BEEN TRYING TO DO THIS ON MY OWN.
BUT SCHOOL BREAK DOESN'T LAST FOREVER, SO I'M ASKING FOR YOUR HELP.
TOHRU.
YOU, TOO.
I NEED YOUR HELP.
URK
Okay!
SO...
I WAS ORGAN-IZING MY STUFF AT COLLEGE ...
...AND I FOUND MY OLD NOTE-BOOK.

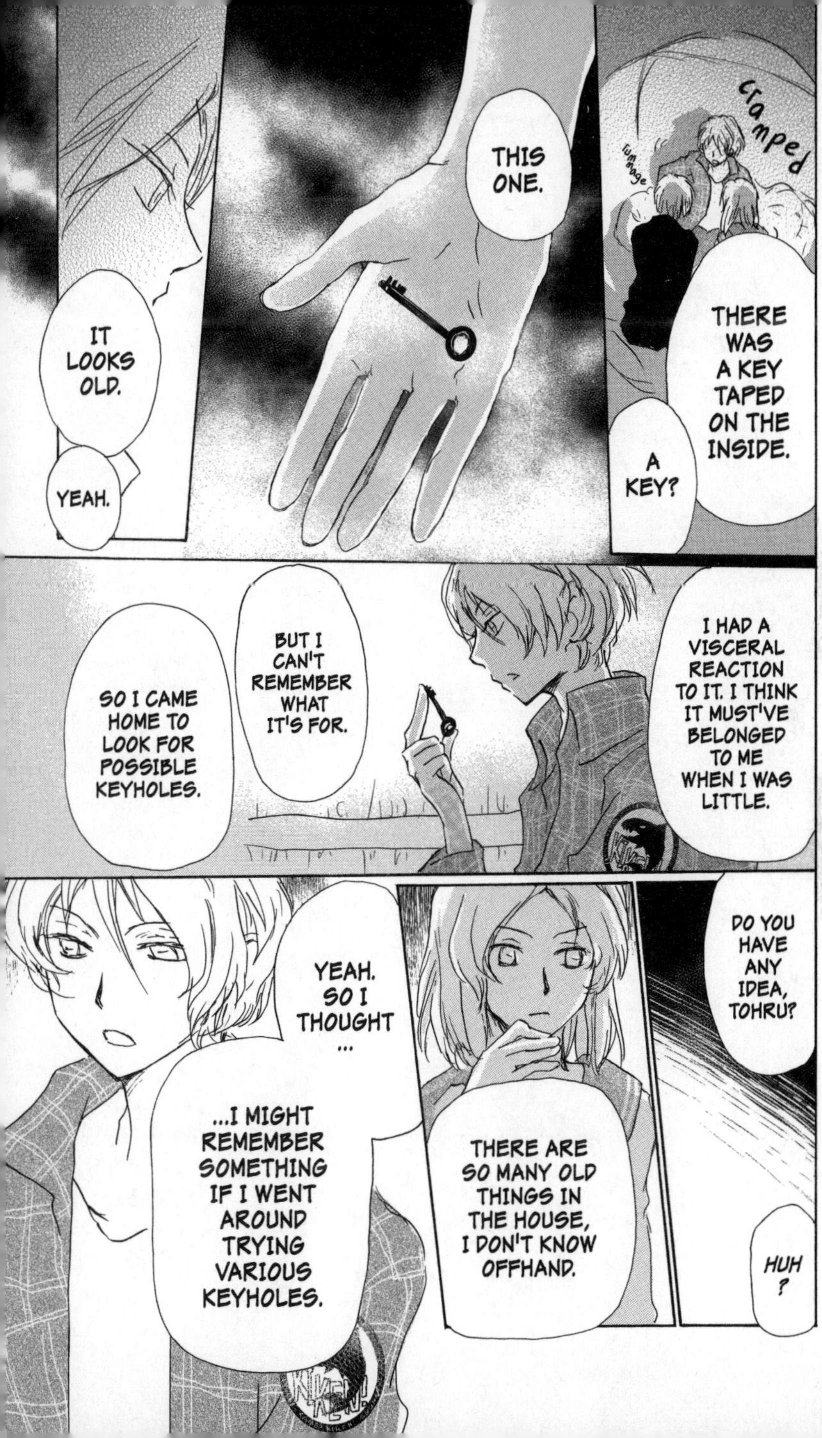
cramped
rummage
THERE WAS A KEY TAPED ON THE INSIDE.
A KEY?
THIS ONE.
IT LOOKS OLD.
YEAH.
I HAD A VISCERAL REACTION TO IT. I THINK IT MUST'VE BELONGED TO ME WHEN I WAS LITTLE.
BUT I CAN'T REMEMBER WHAT IT'S FOR.
SO I CAME HOME TO LOOK FOR POSSIBLE KEYHOLES.
DO YOU HAVE ANY IDEA, TOHRU?
HUH?
THERE ARE SO MANY OLD THINGS IN THE HOUSE, I DON'T KNOW OFFHAND.
YEAH. SO I THOUGHT ...
...I MIGHT REMEMBER SOMETHING IF I WENT AROUND TRYING VARIOUS KEYHOLES.

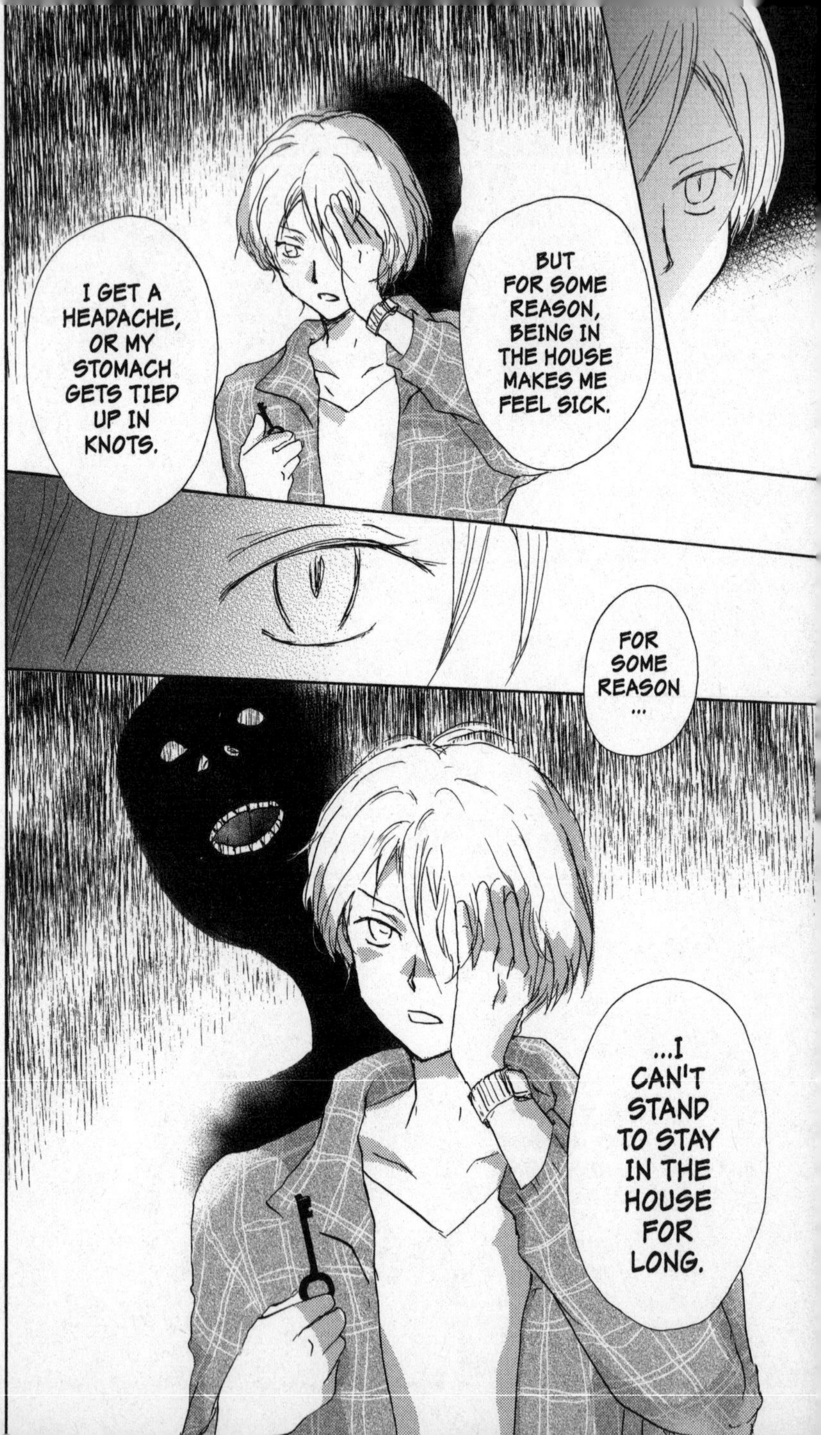
BUT FOR SOME REASON, BEING IN THE HOUSE MAKES ME FEEL SICK.
I GET A HEADACHE, OR MY STOMACH GETS TIED UP IN KNOTS.
FOR SOME REASON ...
...I CAN'T STAND TO STAY IN THE HOUSE FOR LONG.

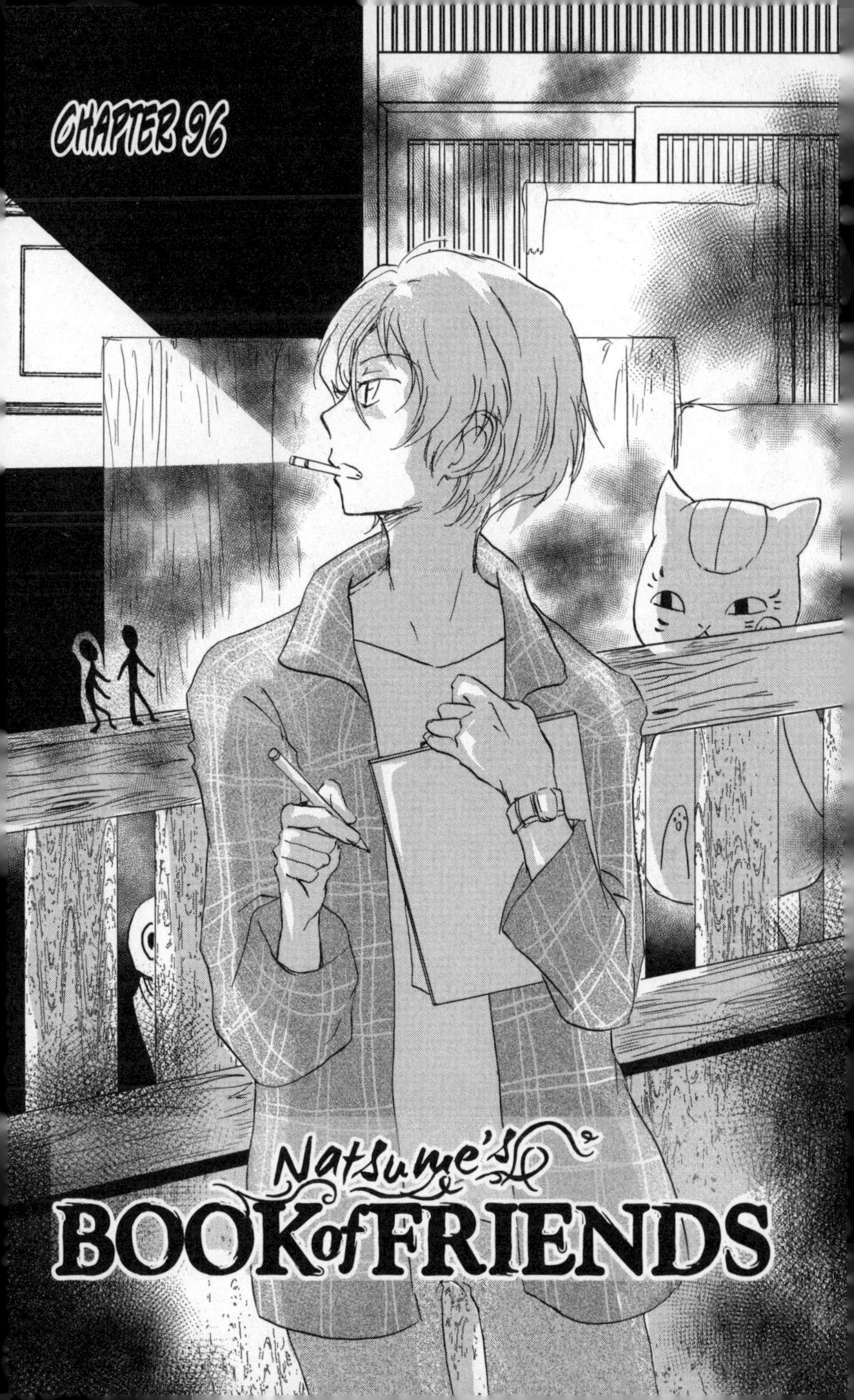
CHAPTER 96
Natsume's
BOOK of FRIENDS

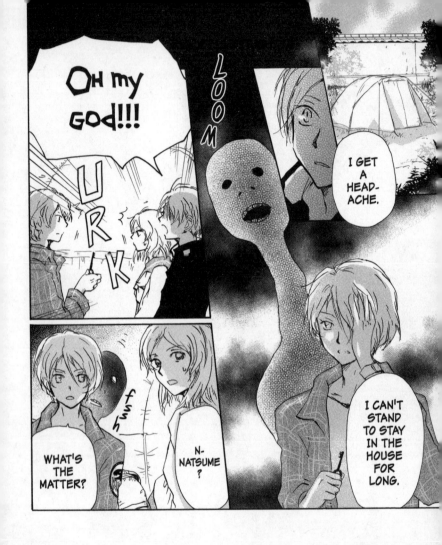

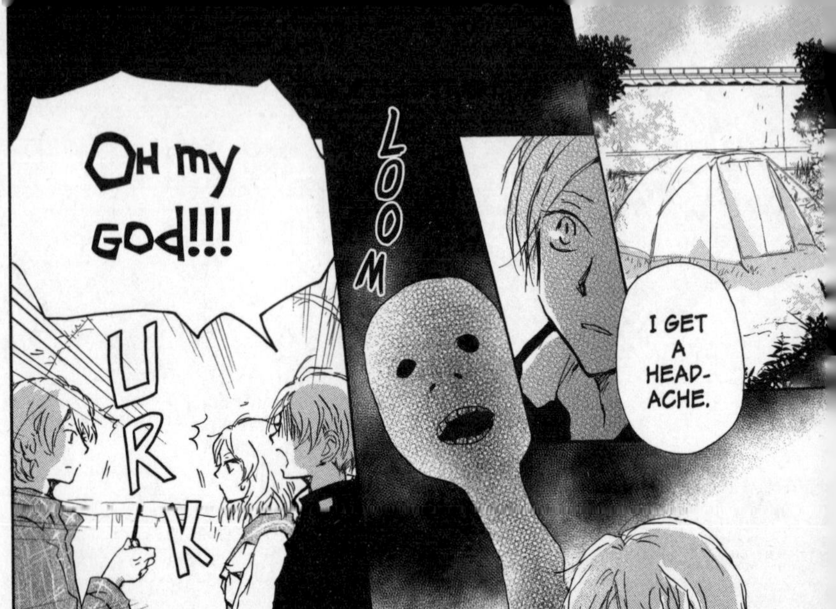
I GET A HEAD-ACHE.
LOOM
I CAN'T STAND TO STAY IN THE HOUSE FOR LONG.
OH my GOD!!!
URK
N-NATSUME?
fsuh
WHAT'S THE MATTER?

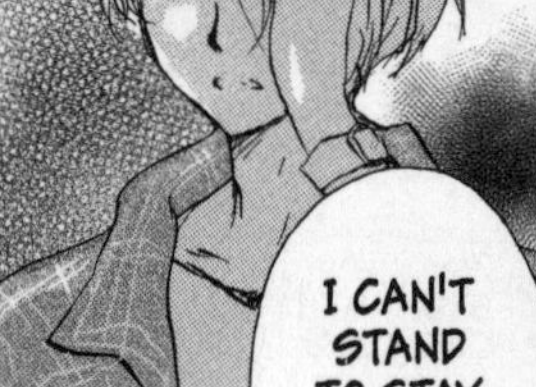

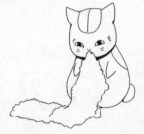

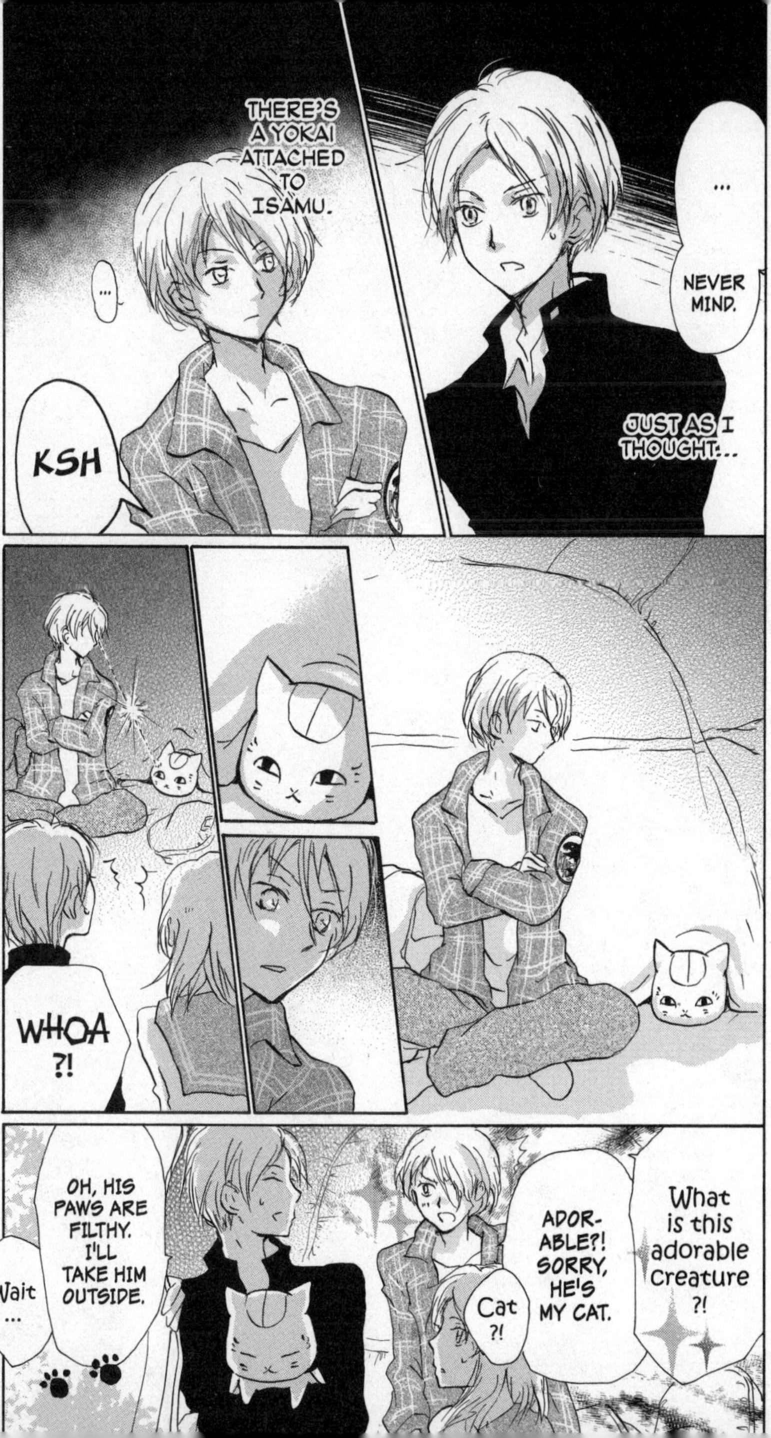
...
NEVER MIND.
JUST AS I THOUGHT...
THERE'S A YOKAI ATTACHED TO ISAMU.
...
KSH
WHOA ?!
What is this adorable creature ?!
ADOR-ABLE?! SORRY, HE'S MY CAT.
Cat ?!
OH, HIS PAWS ARE FILTHY. I'LL TAKE HIM OUTSIDE.
Wait ...

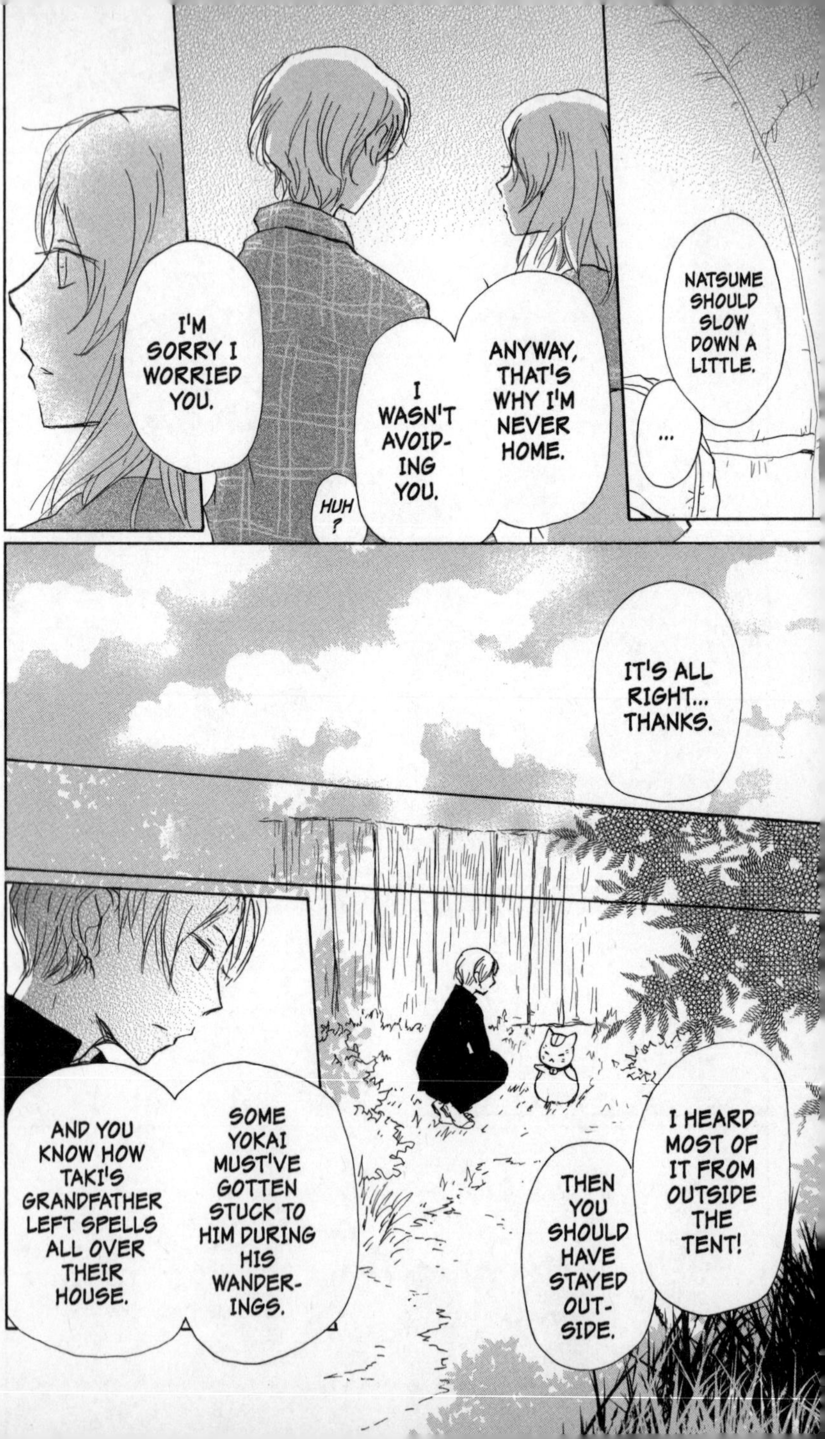
NATSUME SHOULD SLOW DOWN A LITTLE.
...
ANYWAY, THAT'S WHY I'M NEVER HOME.
I WASN'T AVOIDING YOU.
HUH?
I'M SORRY I WORRIED YOU.
IT'S ALL RIGHT... THANKS.
I HEARD MOST OF IT FROM OUTSIDE THE TENT!
THEN YOU SHOULD HAVE STAYED OUTSIDE.
SOME YOKAI MUST'VE GOTTEN STUCK TO HIM DURING HIS WANDERINGS.
AND YOU KNOW HOW TAKI'S GRANDFATHER LEFT SPELLS ALL OVER THEIR HOUSE.

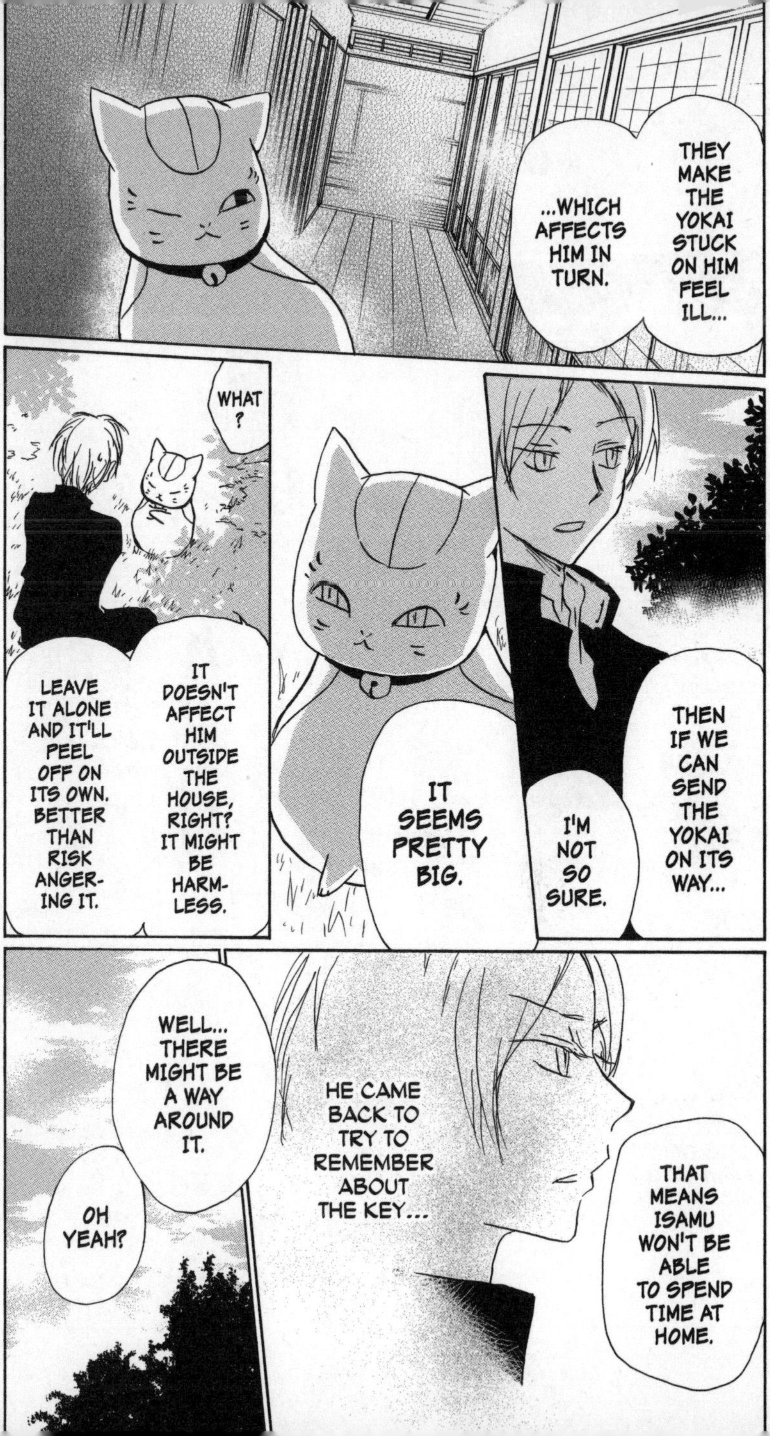
THEY MAKE THE YOKAI STUCK ON HIM FEEL ILL...
...WHICH AFFECTS HIM IN TURN.
THEN IF WE CAN SEND THE YOKAI ON ITS WAY...
I'M NOT SO SURE.
IT SEEMS PRETTY BIG.
WHAT?
IT DOESN'T AFFECT HIM OUTSIDE THE HOUSE, RIGHT? IT MIGHT BE HARMLESS.
LEAVE IT ALONE AND IT'LL PEEL OFF ON ITS OWN. BETTER THAN RISK ANGERING IT.
THAT MEANS ISAMU WON'T BE ABLE TO SPEND TIME AT HOME.
HE CAME BACK TO TRY TO REMEMBER ABOUT THE KEY...
WELL... THERE MIGHT BE A WAY AROUND IT.
OH YEAH?

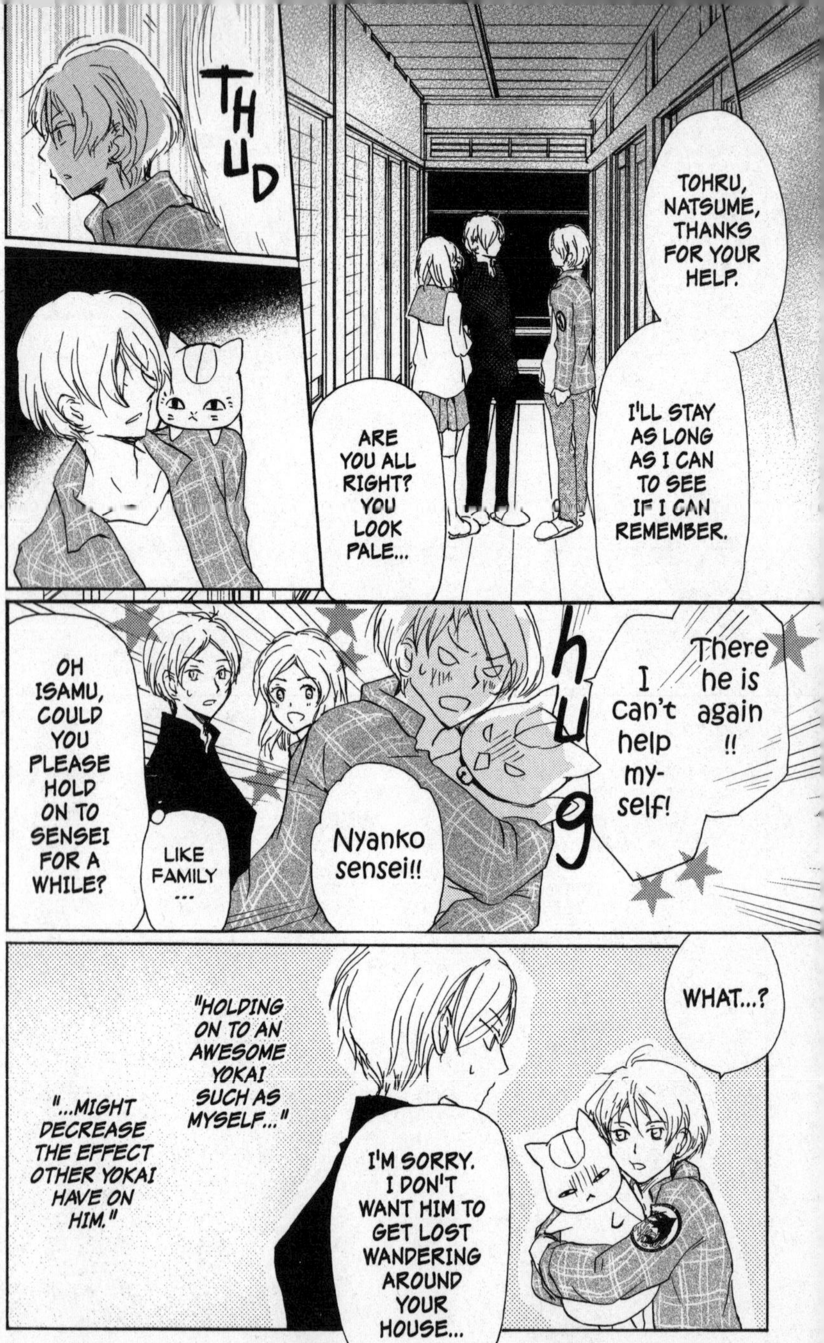
TOHRU, NATSUME, THANKS FOR YOUR HELP.
I'LL STAY AS LONG AS I CAN TO SEE IF I CAN REMEMBER.
ARE YOU ALL RIGHT? YOU LOOK PALE...
THUD
There he is again!!
I can't help myself!
hug
Nyanko sensei!!
LIKE FAMILY...
OH ISAMU, COULD YOU PLEASE HOLD ON TO SENSEI FOR A WHILE?
WHAT...?
"HOLDING ON TO AN AWESOME YOKAI SUCH AS MYSELF..."
"...MIGHT DECREASE THE EFFECT OTHER YOKAI HAVE ON HIM."
I'M SORRY. I DON'T WANT HIM TO GET LOST WANDERING AROUND YOUR HOUSE...

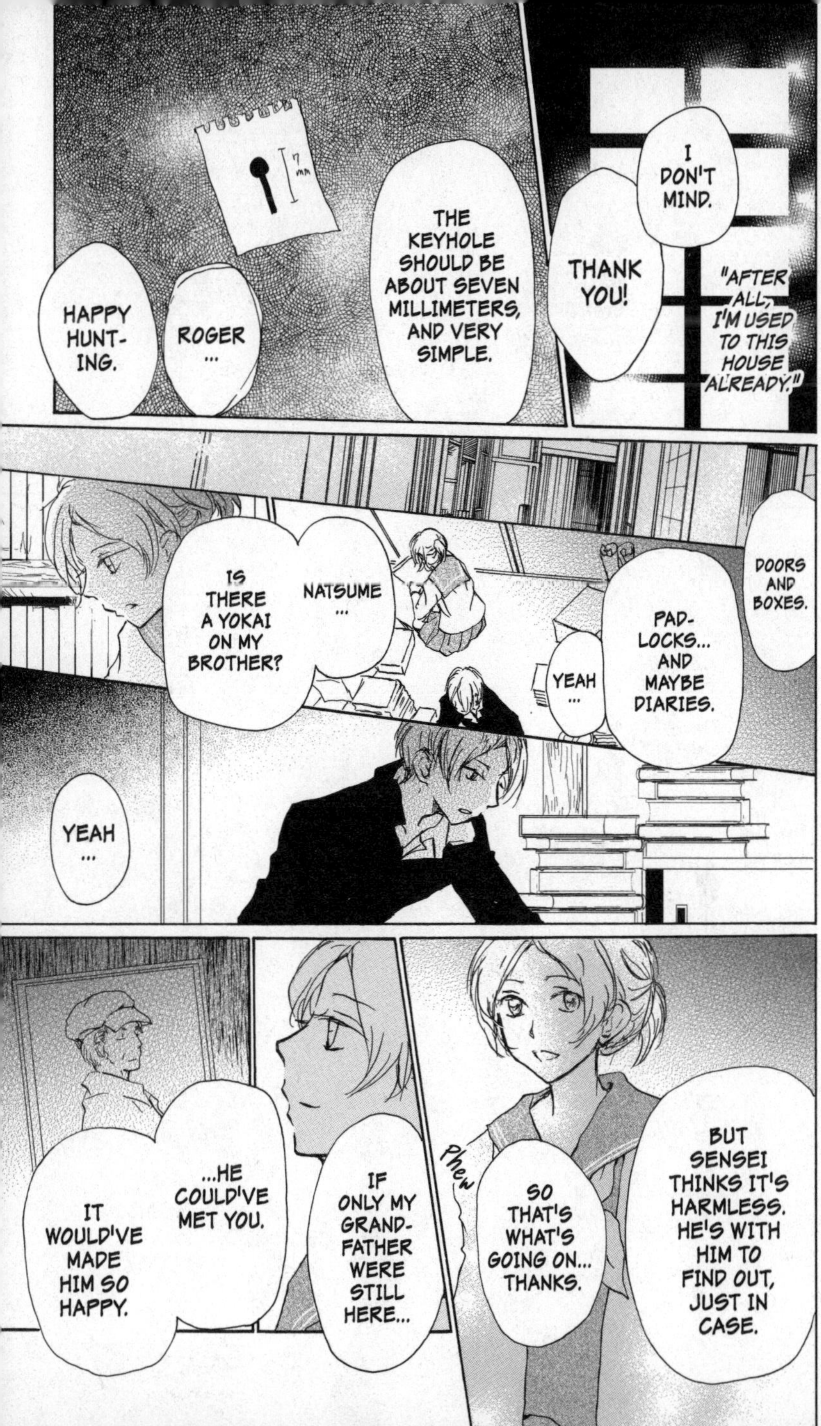

I DON'T MIND.
"AFTER ALL, I'M USED TO THIS HOUSE ALREADY."
THANK YOU!
7 mm
THE KEYHOLE SHOULD BE ABOUT SEVEN MILLIMETERS, AND VERY SIMPLE.
ROGER...
HAPPY HUNT-ING.
DOORS AND BOXES.
PAD-LOCKS... AND MAYBE DIARIES.
YEAH...
NATSUME...
IS THERE A YOKAI ON MY BROTHER?
YEAH...
BUT SENSEI THINKS IT'S HARMLESS. HE'S WITH HIM TO FIND OUT, JUST IN CASE.
SO THAT'S WHAT'S GOING ON... THANKS.
Phew
IF ONLY MY GRAND-FATHER WERE STILL HERE...
...HE COULD'VE MET YOU.
IT WOULD'VE MADE HIM SO HAPPY.

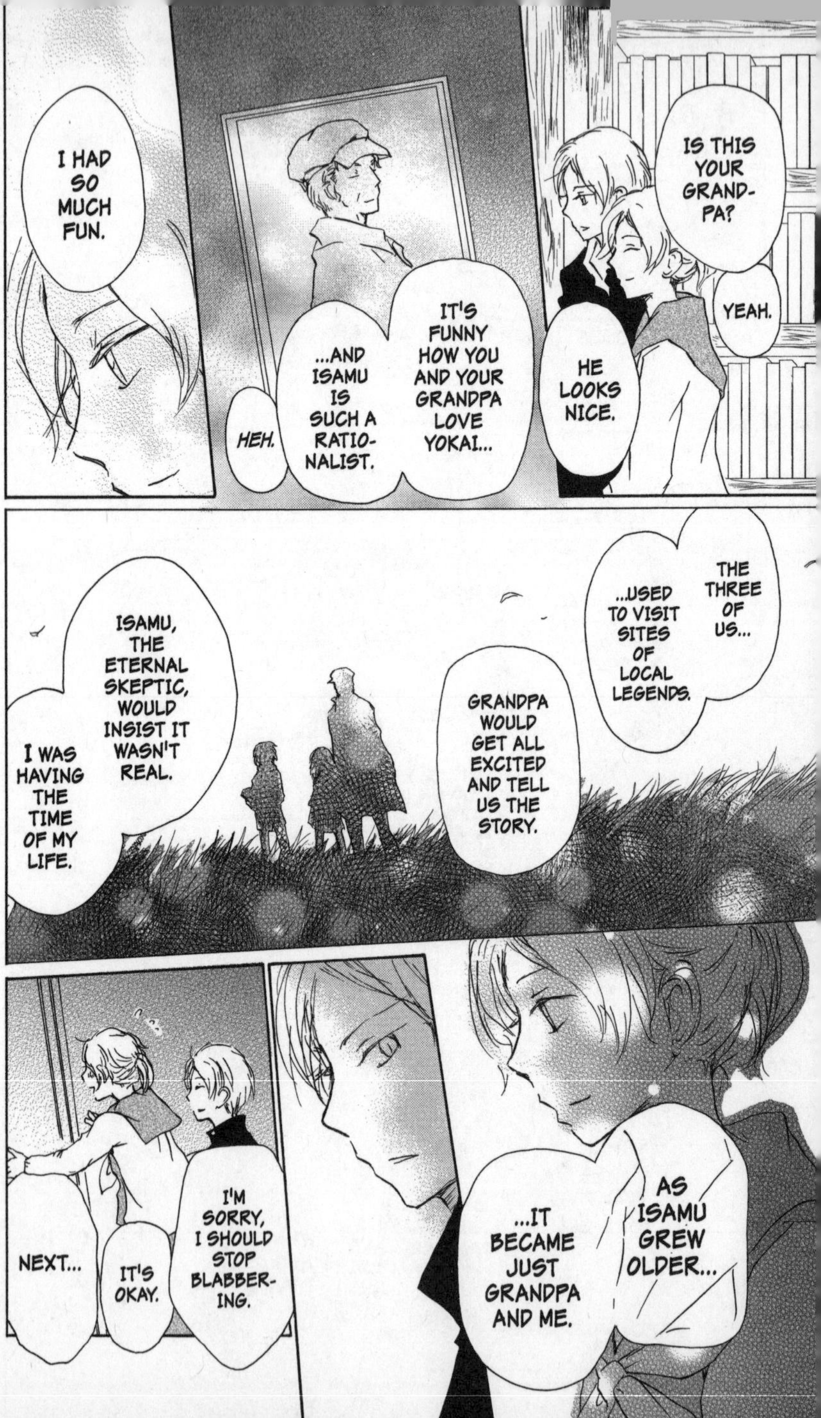
IS THIS YOUR GRANDPA?
YEAH.
HE LOOKS NICE.
IT'S FUNNY HOW YOU AND YOUR GRANDPA LOVE YOKAI...
...AND ISAMU IS SUCH A RATIONALIST.
HEH.
I HAD SO MUCH FUN.
THE THREE OF US...
...USED TO VISIT SITES OF LOCAL LEGENDS.
GRANDPA WOULD GET ALL EXCITED AND TELL US THE STORY.
ISAMU, THE ETERNAL SKEPTIC, WOULD INSIST IT WASN'T REAL.
I WAS HAVING THE TIME OF MY LIFE.
AS ISAMU GREW OLDER...
...IT BECAME JUST GRANDPA AND ME.
I'M SORRY, I SHOULD STOP BLABBERING.
IT'S OKAY.
NEXT...

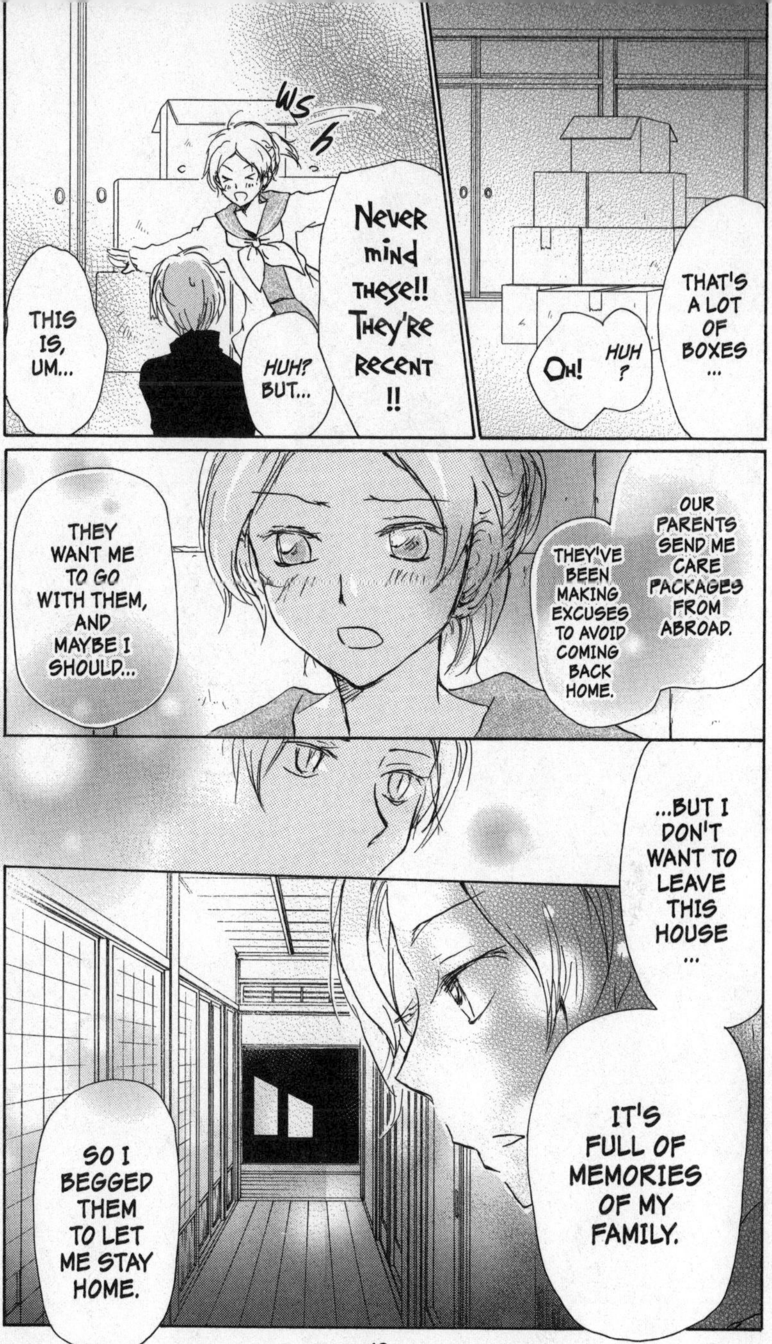
THAT'S A LOT OF BOXES...
HUH?
OH!
WSH
Never mind these!! They're recent!!
HUH? BUT...
THIS IS, UM...
OUR PARENTS SEND ME CARE PACKAGES FROM ABROAD.
THEY'VE BEEN MAKING EXCUSES TO AVOID COMING BACK HOME.
THEY WANT ME TO GO WITH THEM, AND MAYBE I SHOULD...
...BUT I DON'T WANT TO LEAVE THIS HOUSE...
IT'S FULL OF MEMORIES OF MY FAMILY.
SO I BEGGED THEM TO LET ME STAY HOME.

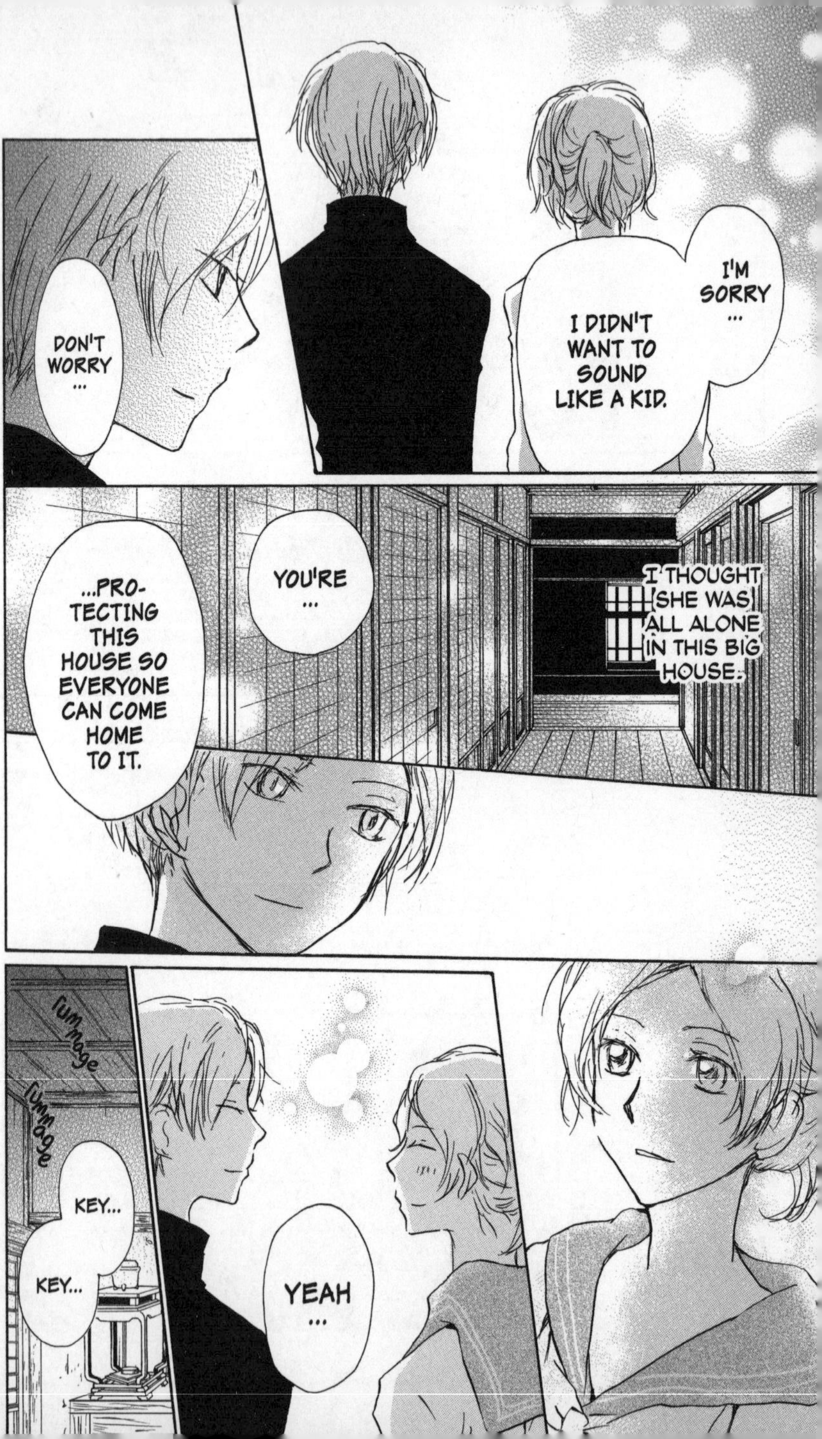
I'M SORRY ...
I DIDN'T WANT TO SOUND LIKE A KID.
DON'T WORRY ...
I THOUGHT SHE WAS ALL ALONE IN THIS BIG HOUSE.
YOU'RE ...
...PRO-TECTING THIS HOUSE SO EVERYONE CAN COME HOME TO IT.
YEAH ...
rummage
rummage
KEY...
KEY...

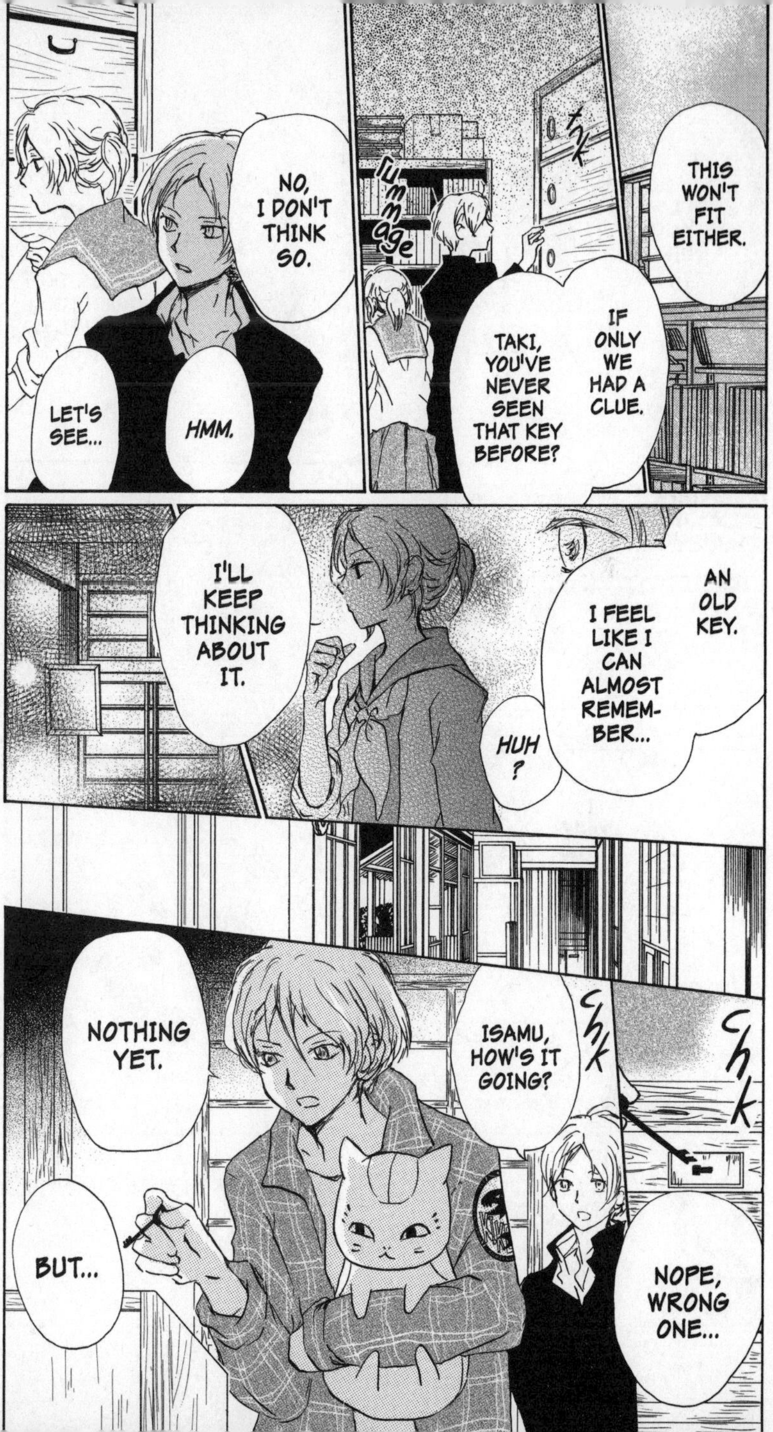
THIS WON'T FIT EITHER.
rummage
IF ONLY WE HAD A CLUE.
TAKI, YOU'VE NEVER SEEN THAT KEY BEFORE?
NO, I DON'T THINK SO.
HMM.
LET'S SEE...
AN OLD KEY.
I FEEL LIKE I CAN ALMOST REMEMBER...
HUH?
I'LL KEEP THINKING ABOUT IT.
chk
chk
ISAMU, HOW'S IT GOING?
NOPE, WRONG ONE...
NOTHING YET.
BUT...

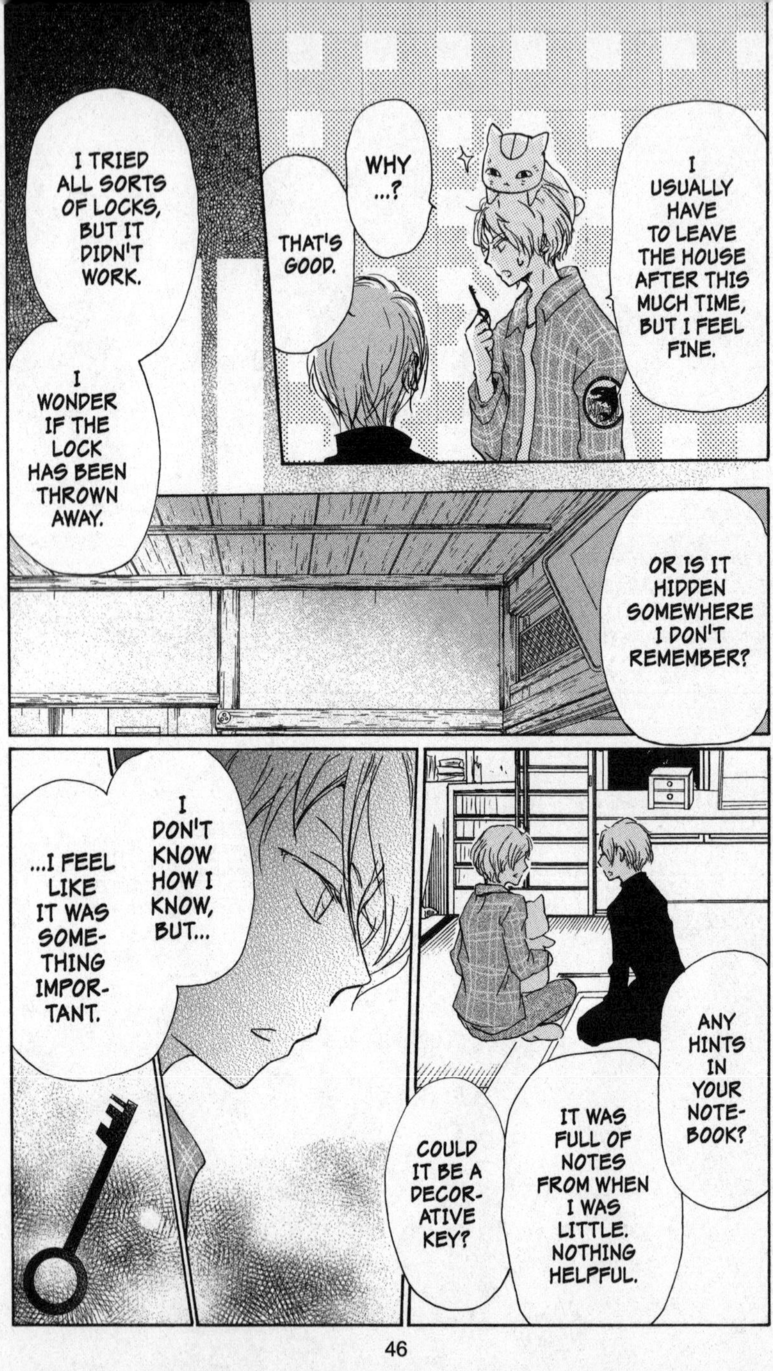
I USUALLY HAVE TO LEAVE THE HOUSE AFTER THIS MUCH TIME, BUT I FEEL FINE.
WHY ...?
THAT'S GOOD.
I TRIED ALL SORTS OF LOCKS, BUT IT DIDN'T WORK.
I WONDER IF THE LOCK HAS BEEN THROWN AWAY.
OR IS IT HIDDEN SOMEWHERE I DON'T REMEMBER?
ANY HINTS IN YOUR NOTE-BOOK?
IT WAS FULL OF NOTES FROM WHEN I WAS LITTLE. NOTHING HELPFUL.
COULD IT BE A DECOR-ATIVE KEY?
I DON'T KNOW HOW I KNOW, BUT...
...I FEEL LIKE IT WAS SOME-THING IMPOR-TANT.

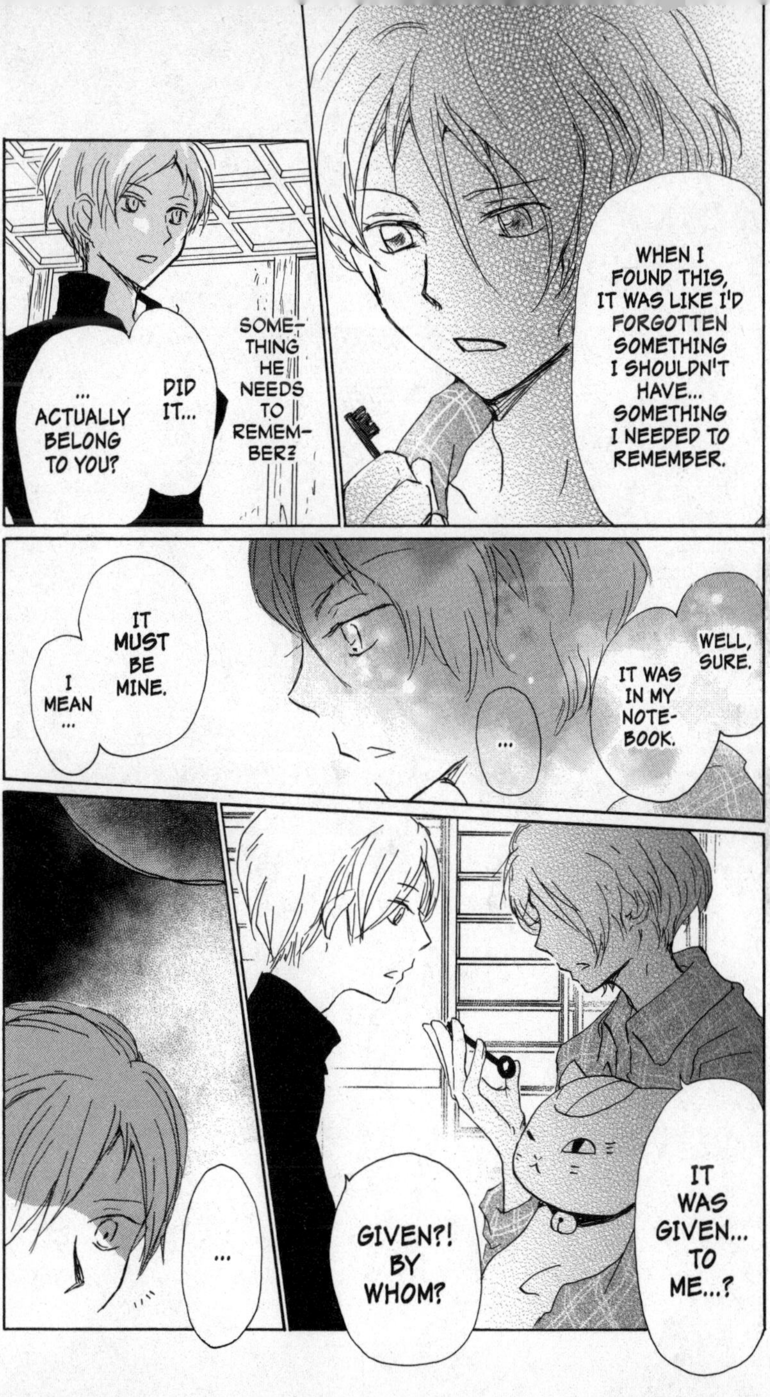
WHEN I FOUND THIS, IT WAS LIKE I'D FORGOTTEN SOMETHING I SHOULDN'T HAVE... SOMETHING I NEEDED TO REMEMBER.
SOMETHING HE NEEDS TO REMEMBER?
DID IT...
...ACTUALLY BELONG TO YOU?
WELL, SURE.
IT WAS IN MY NOTEBOOK.
...
IT MUST BE MINE.
I MEAN...
IT WAS GIVEN... TO ME...?
GIVEN?! BY WHOM?
...

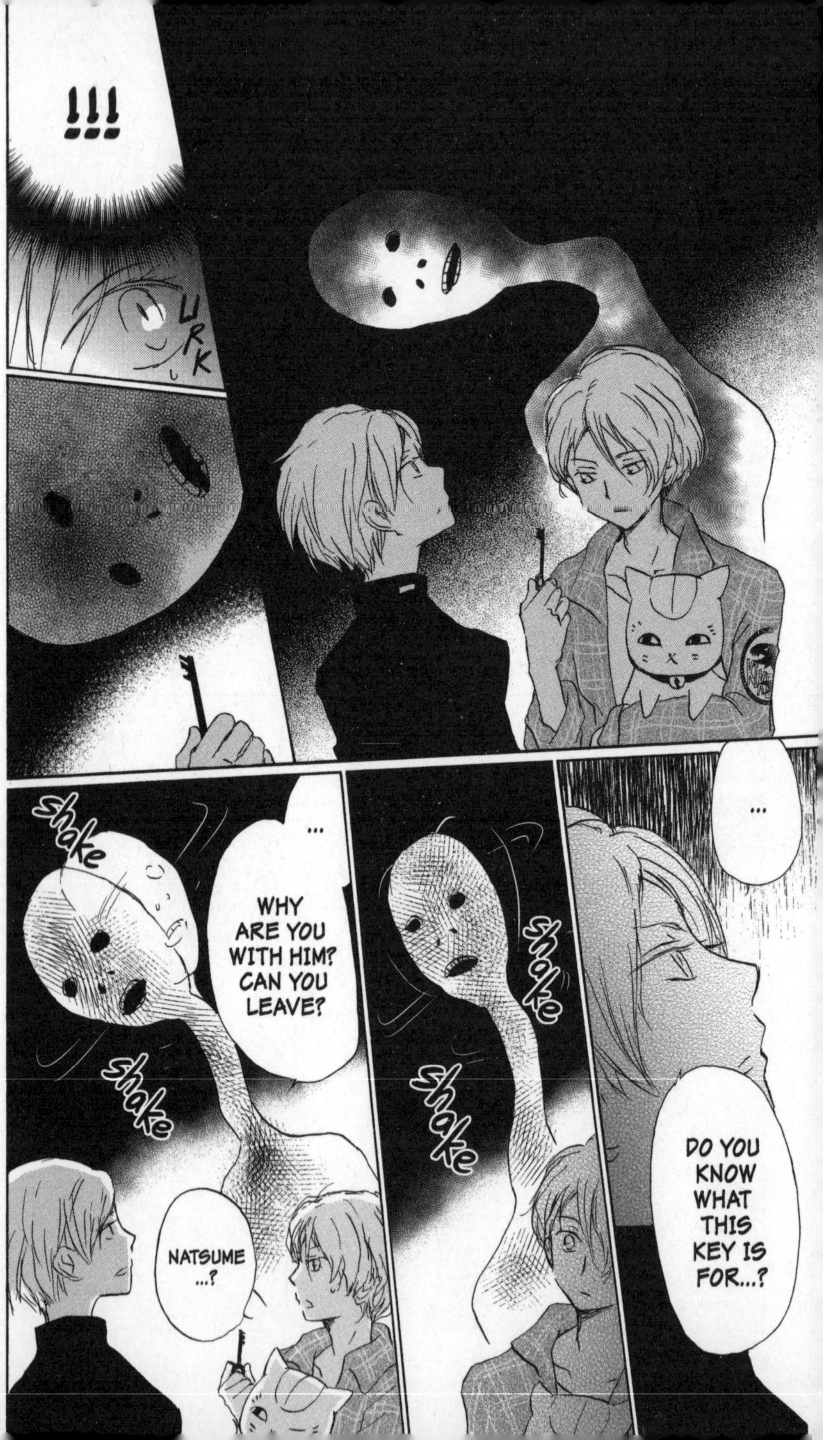
!!!
URK
...
DO YOU KNOW WHAT THIS KEY IS FOR...?
shake
shake
...
WHY ARE YOU WITH HIM? CAN YOU LEAVE?
shake
shake
NATSUME ...?

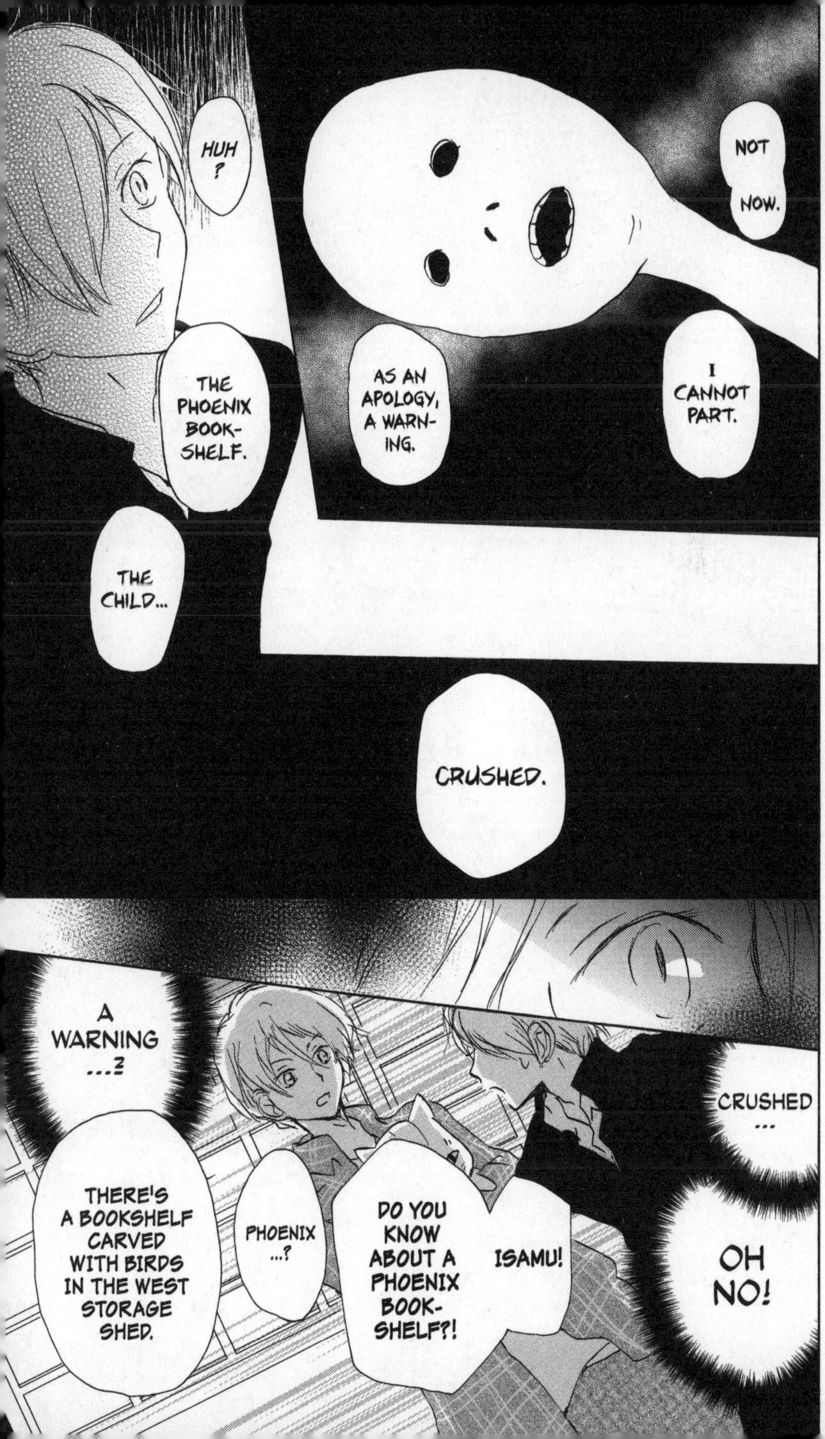
NOT NOW.
I CANNOT PART.
AS AN APOLOGY, A WARNING.
HUH?
THE PHOENIX BOOKSHELF.
THE CHILD...
CRUSHED.
CRUSHED...
A WARNING...?
OH NO!
ISAMU!
DO YOU KNOW ABOUT A PHOENIX BOOKSHELF?!
PHOENIX...?
THERE'S A BOOKSHELF CARVED WITH BIRDS IN THE WEST STORAGE SHED.

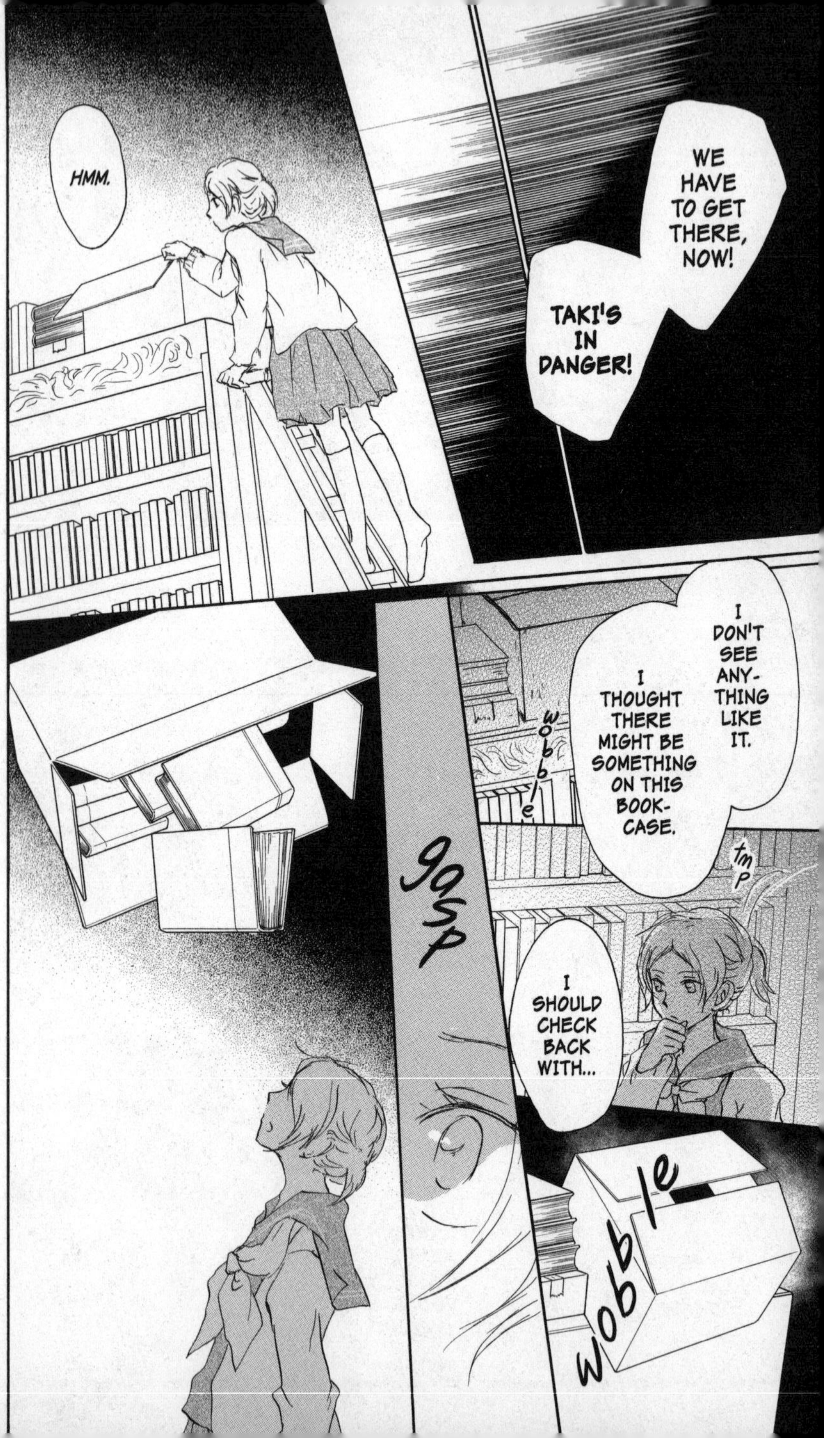

WE HAVE TO GET THERE, NOW!
TAKI'S IN DANGER!
HMM.
I DON'T SEE ANYTHING LIKE IT.
I THOUGHT THERE MIGHT BE SOMETHING ON THIS BOOK-CASE.
wobble
tmp
I SHOULD CHECK BACK WITH...
wobble
gasp

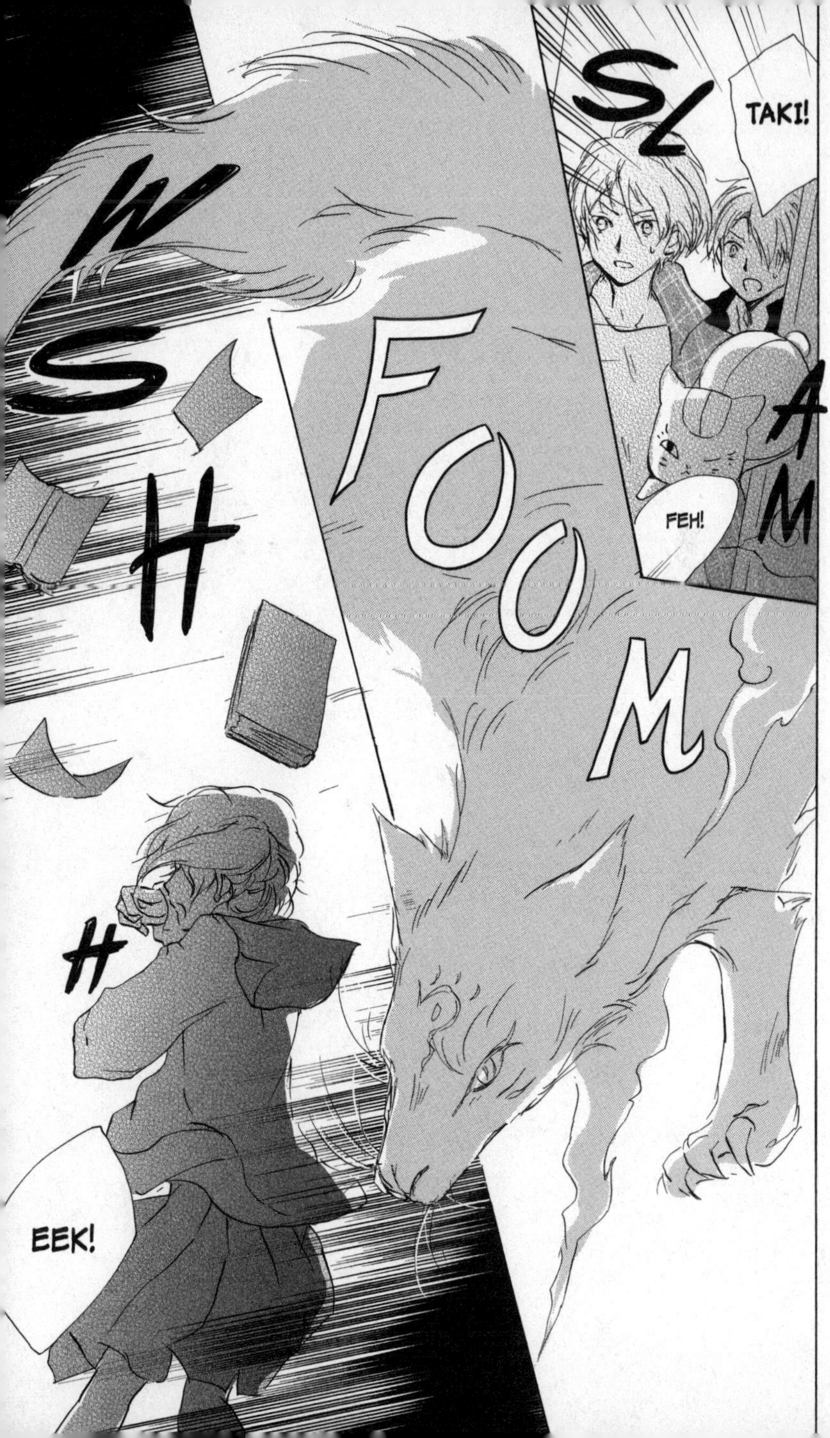
TAKI!
SLAM
FEH!
FOOM
WSHH
EEK!

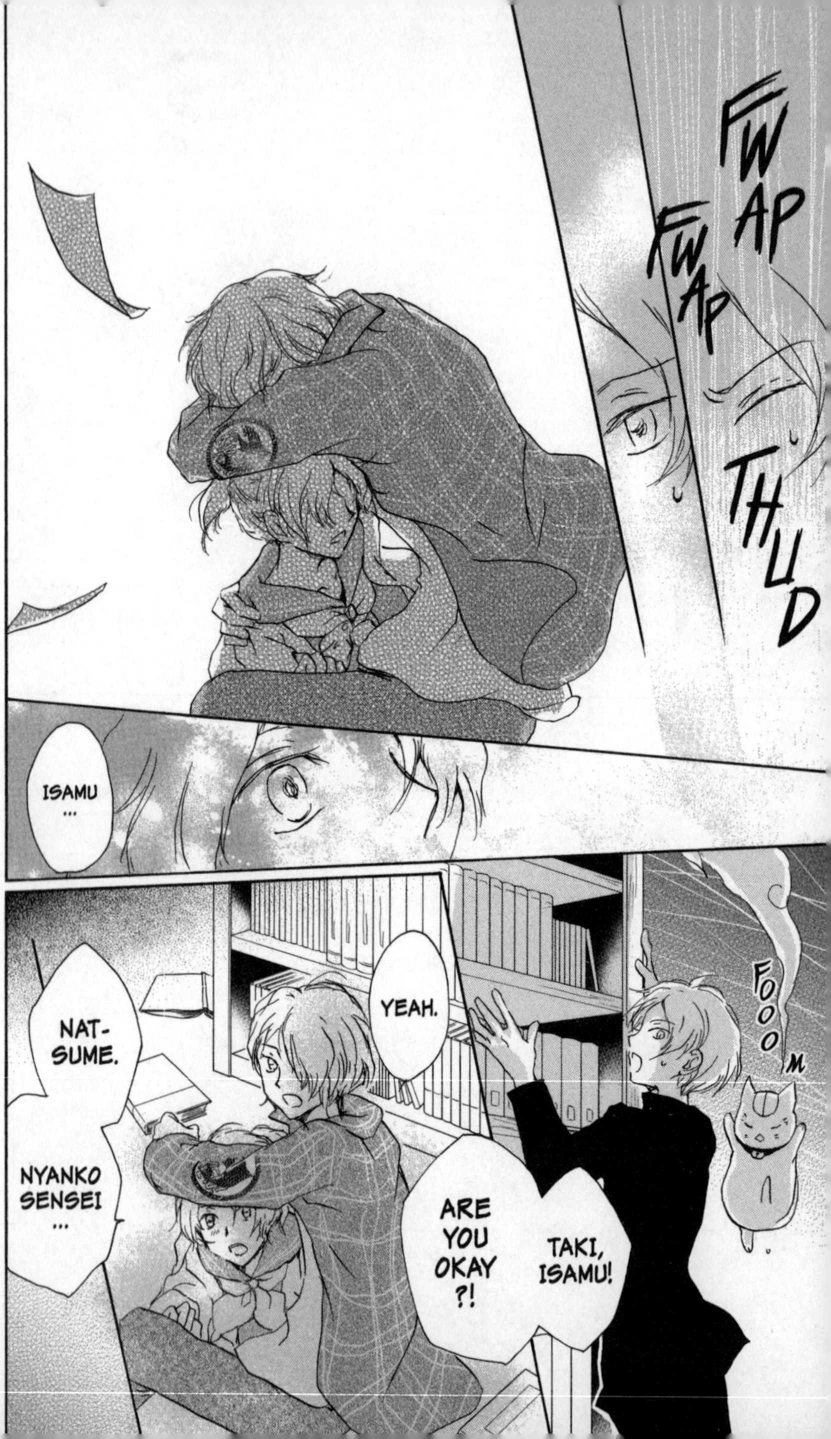
FWAP
FWAP
THUD
ISAMU ...
FOOOM
TAKI, ISAMU!
ARE YOU OKAY ?!
YEAH.
NAT-SUME.
NYANKO SENSEI ...

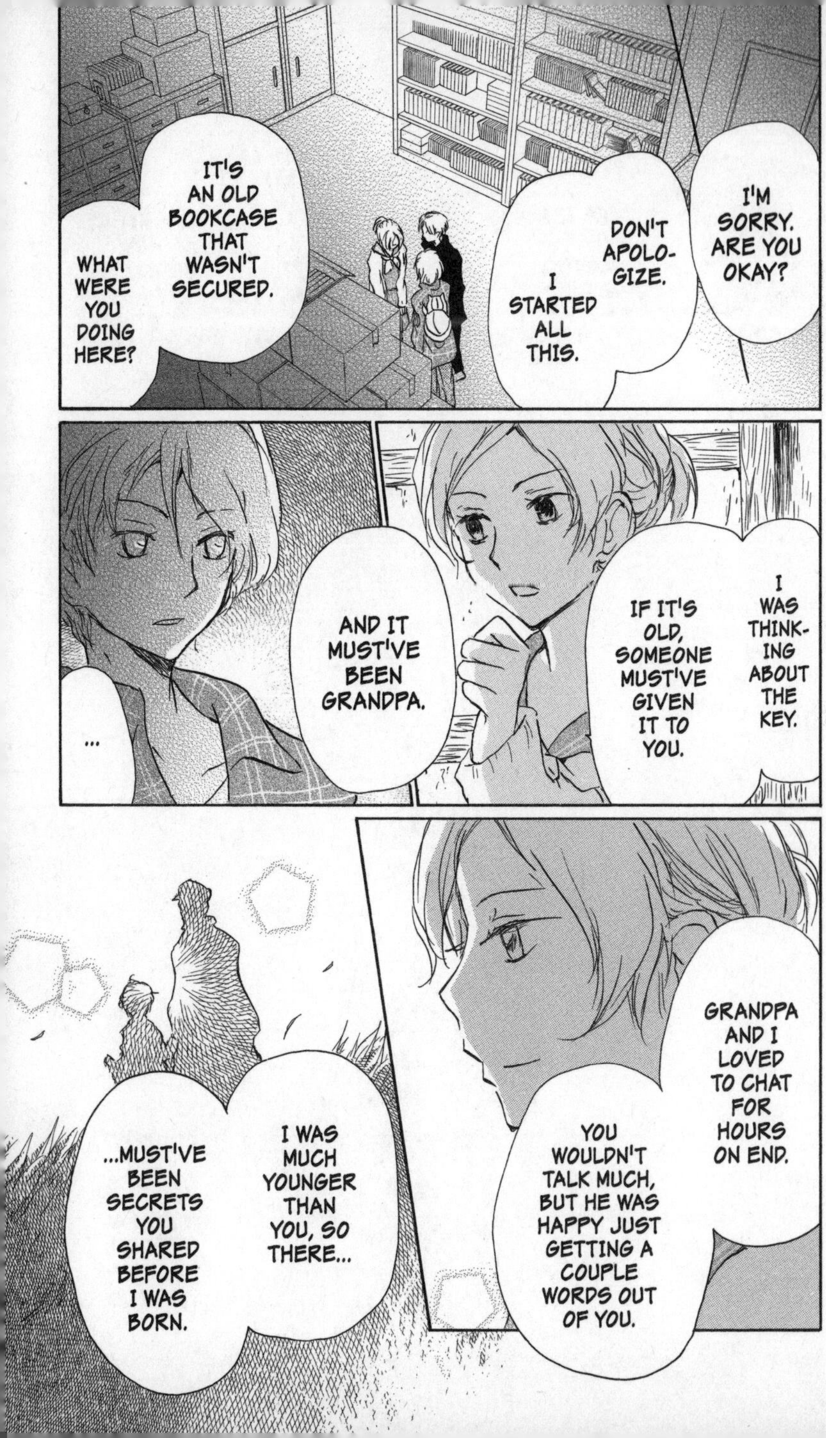
I'M SORRY. ARE YOU OKAY?
DON'T APOLOGIZE.
I STARTED ALL THIS.
IT'S AN OLD BOOKCASE THAT WASN'T SECURED.
WHAT WERE YOU DOING HERE?
I WAS THINKING ABOUT THE KEY.
IF IT'S OLD, SOMEONE MUST'VE GIVEN IT TO YOU.
AND IT MUST'VE BEEN GRANDPA.
...
GRANDPA AND I LOVED TO CHAT FOR HOURS ON END.
YOU WOULDN'T TALK MUCH, BUT HE WAS HAPPY JUST GETTING A COUPLE WORDS OUT OF YOU.
I WAS MUCH YOUNGER THAN YOU, SO THERE...
...MUST'VE BEEN SECRETS YOU SHARED BEFORE I WAS BORN.

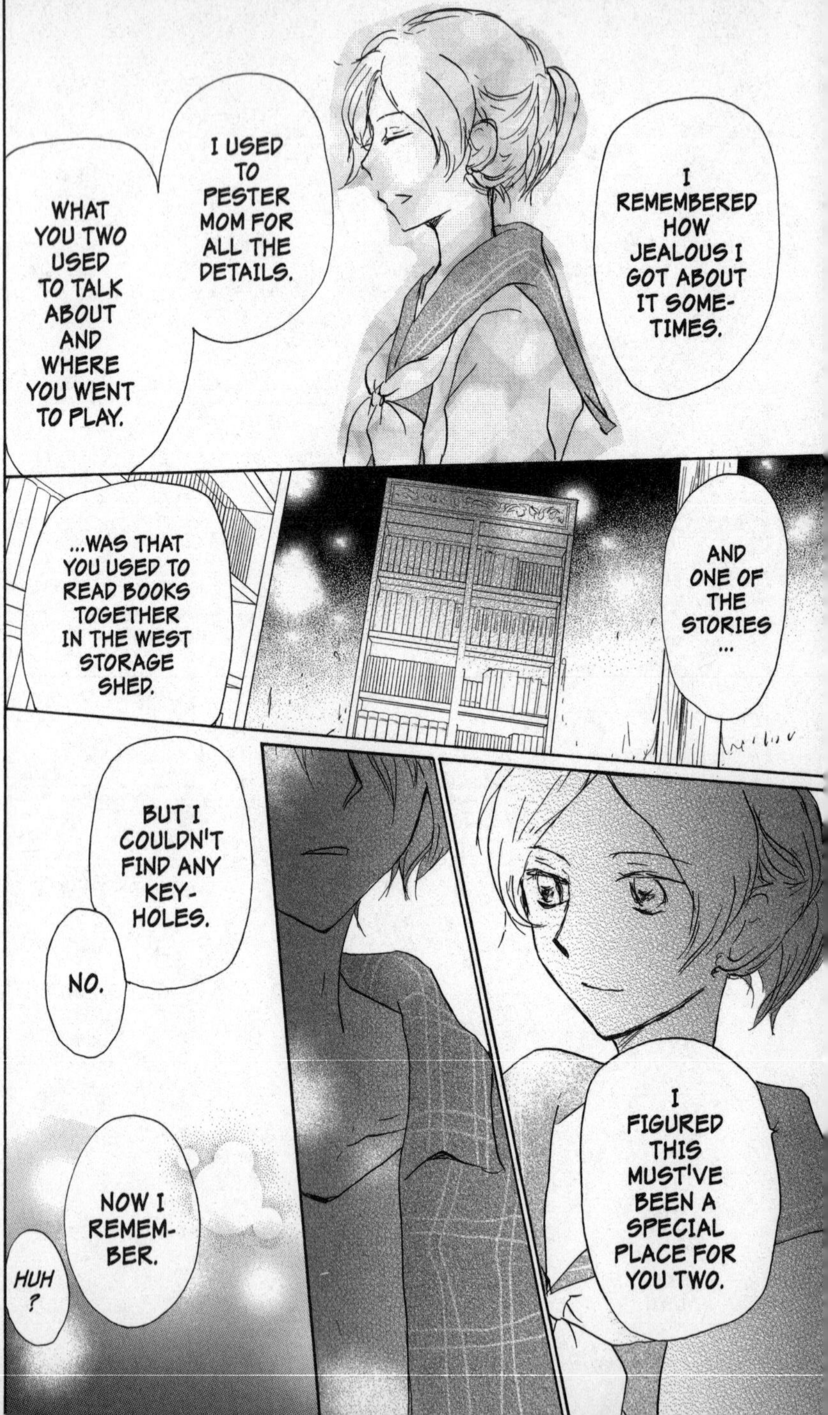

I REMEMBERED HOW JEALOUS I GOT ABOUT IT SOME-TIMES.
I USED TO PESTER MOM FOR ALL THE DETAILS.
WHAT YOU TWO USED TO TALK ABOUT AND WHERE YOU WENT TO PLAY.
AND ONE OF THE STORIES ...
...WAS THAT YOU USED TO READ BOOKS TOGETHER IN THE WEST STORAGE SHED.
I FIGURED THIS MUST'VE BEEN A SPECIAL PLACE FOR YOU TWO.
BUT I COULDN'T FIND ANY KEY-HOLES.
NO.
NOW I REMEM-BER.
HUH?

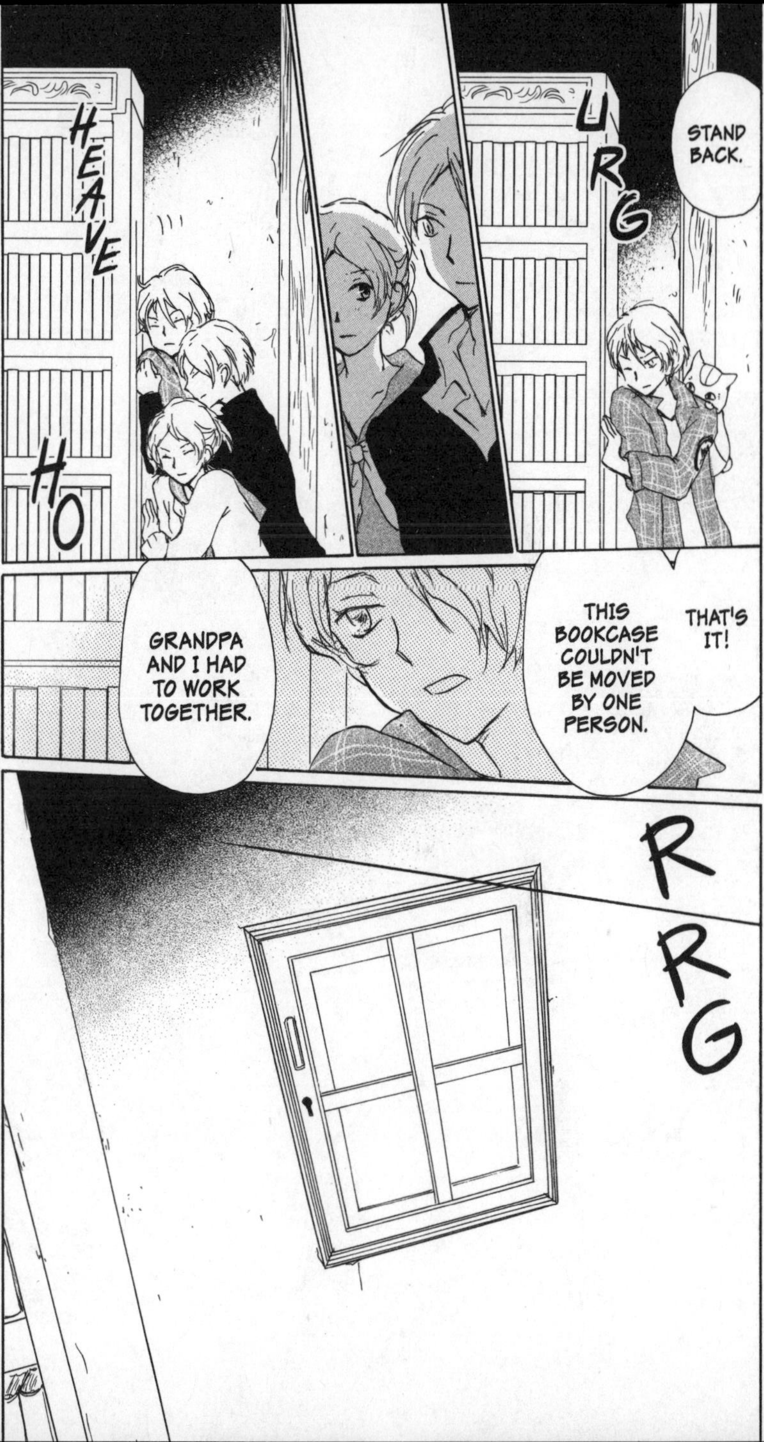
STAND BACK.
URG
HEAVE HO
THAT'S IT!
THIS BOOKCASE COULDN'T BE MOVED BY ONE PERSON.
GRANDPA AND I HAD TO WORK TOGETHER.
RRG

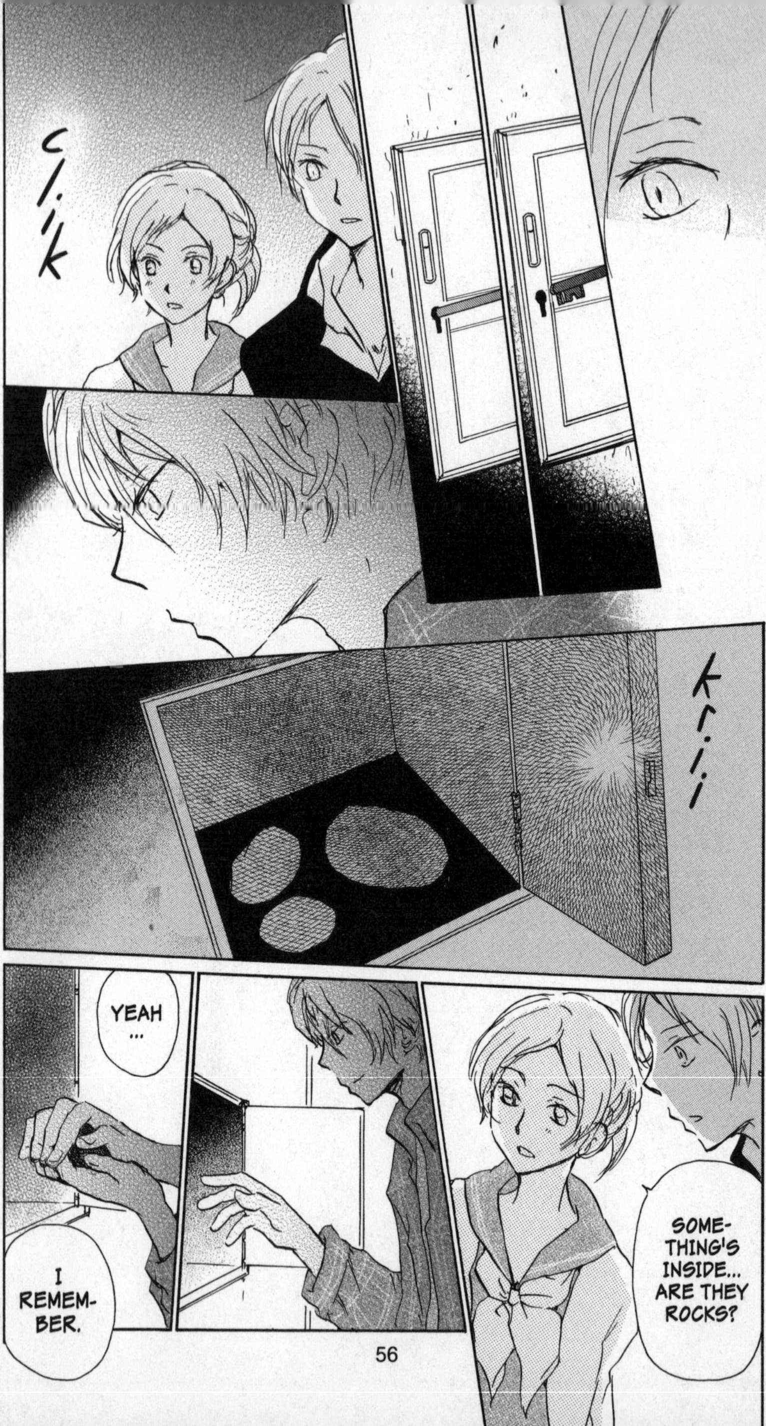
clik
krii
SOME-THING'S INSIDE... ARE THEY ROCKS?
YEAH ...
I REMEM-BER.

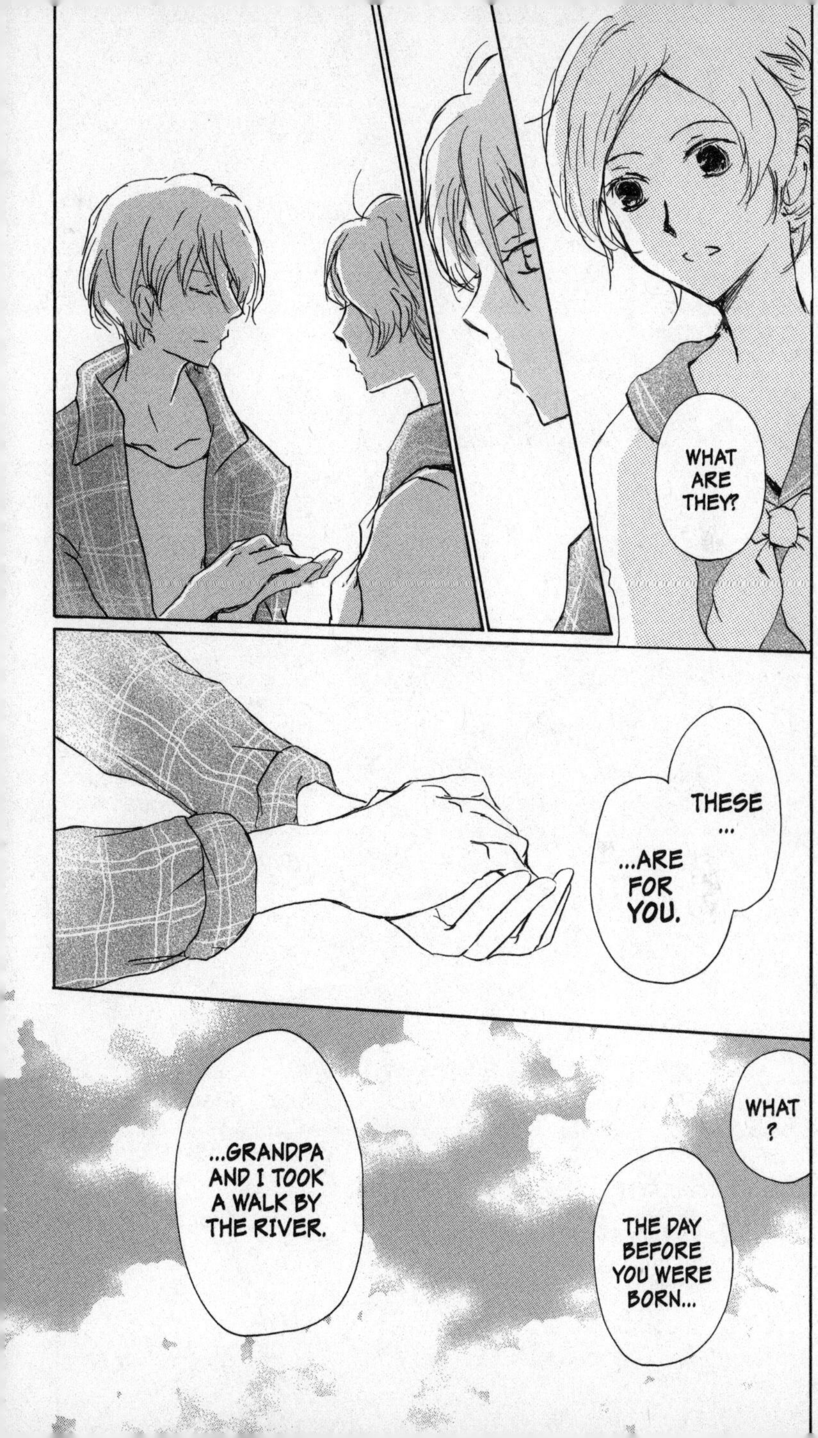
WHAT ARE THEY?
THESE ...
...ARE FOR YOU.
WHAT ?
THE DAY BEFORE YOU WERE BORN...
...GRANDPA AND I TOOK A WALK BY THE RIVER.

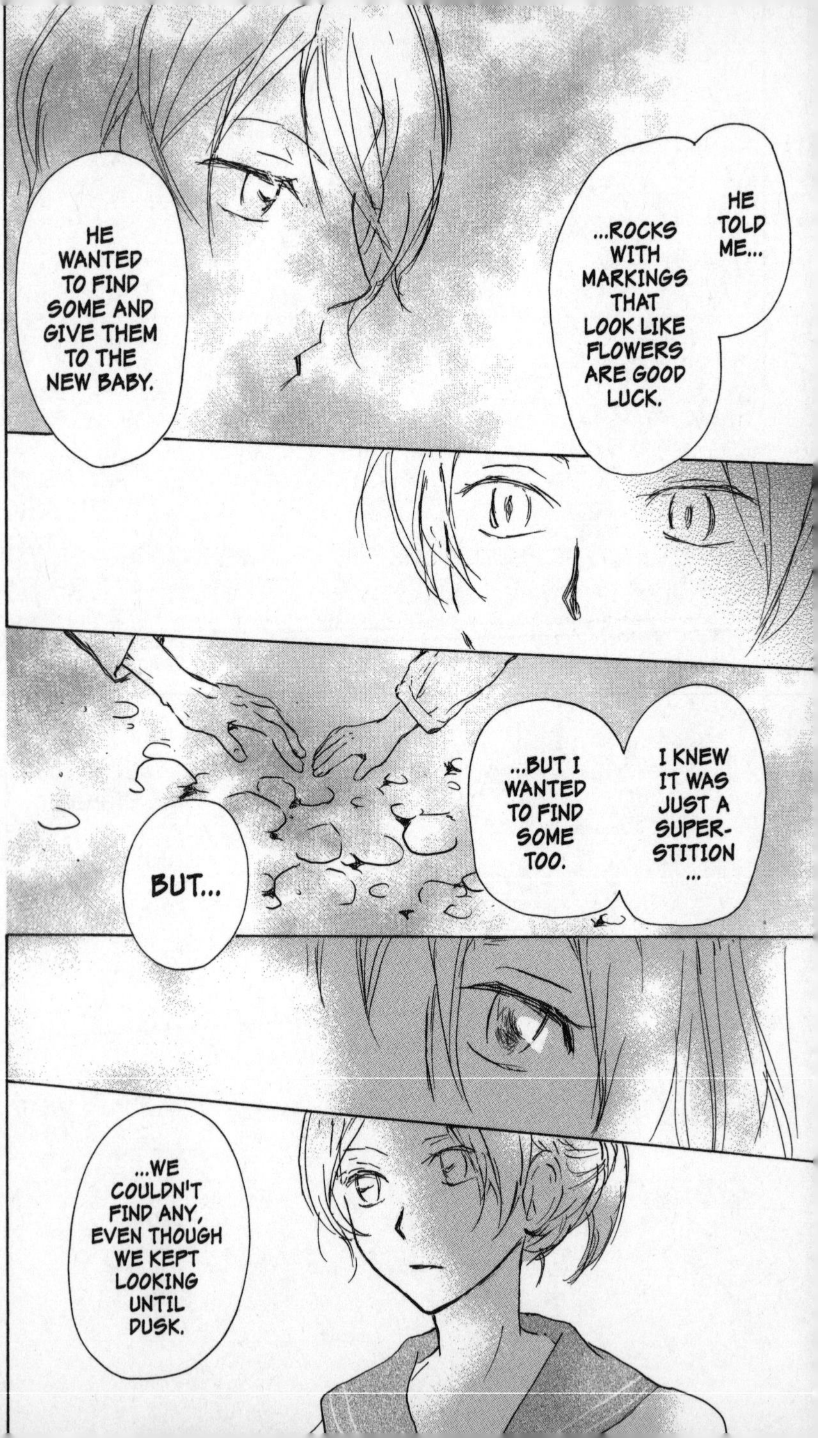
HE TOLD ME...
...ROCKS WITH MARKINGS THAT LOOK LIKE FLOWERS ARE GOOD LUCK.
HE WANTED TO FIND SOME AND GIVE THEM TO THE NEW BABY.
I KNEW IT WAS JUST A SUPER-STITION...
...BUT I WANTED TO FIND SOME TOO.
BUT...
...WE COULDN'T FIND ANY, EVEN THOUGH WE KEPT LOOKING UNTIL DUSK.

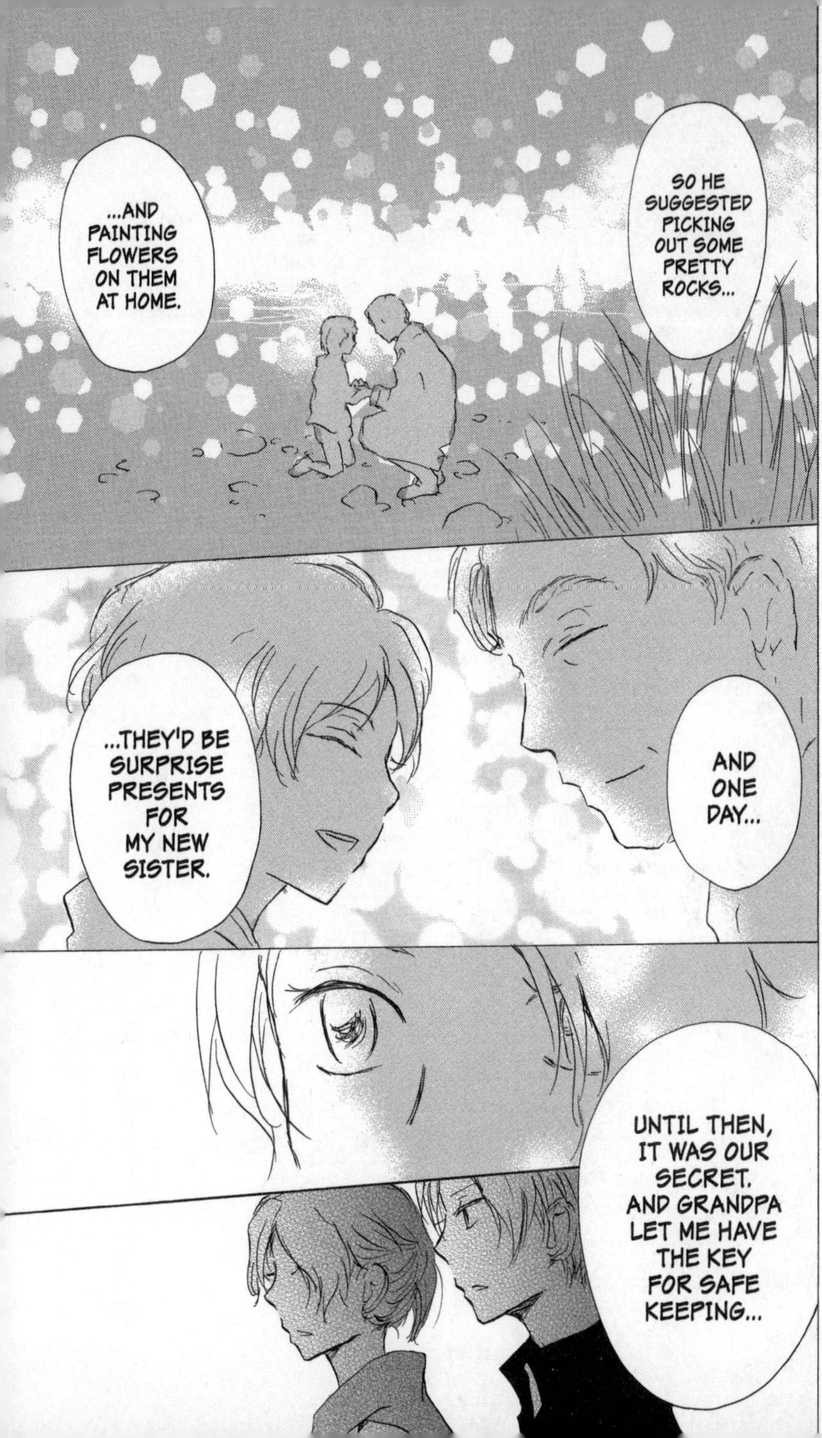
SO HE SUGGESTED PICKING OUT SOME PRETTY ROCKS...
...AND PAINTING FLOWERS ON THEM AT HOME.
AND ONE DAY...
...THEY'D BE SURPRISE PRESENTS FOR MY NEW SISTER.
UNTIL THEN, IT WAS OUR SECRET. AND GRANDPA LET ME HAVE THE KEY FOR SAFE KEEPING...

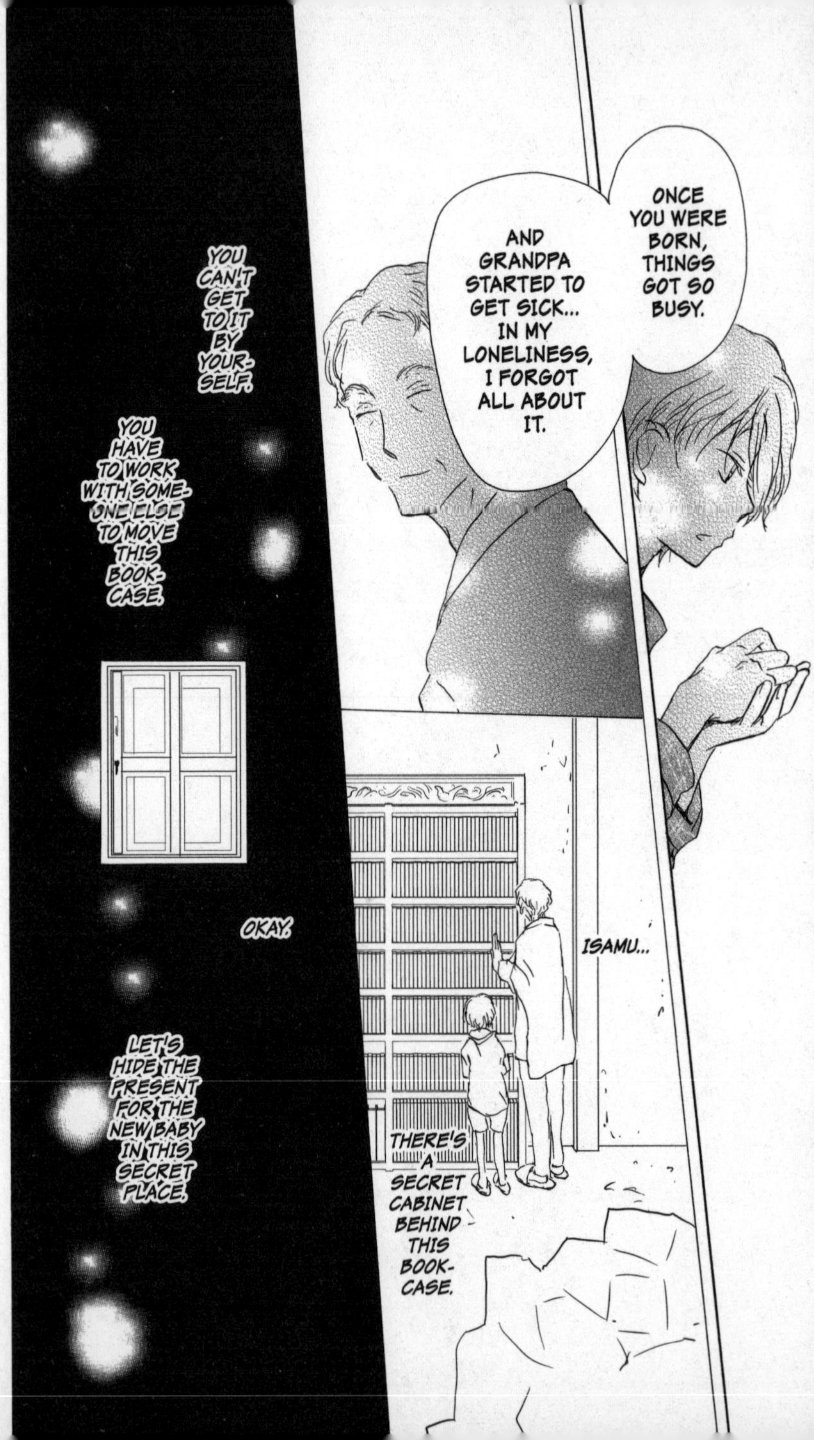
ONCE YOU WERE BORN, THINGS GOT SO BUSY.
AND GRANDPA STARTED TO GET SICK... IN MY LONELINESS, I FORGOT ALL ABOUT IT.
ISAMU...
THERE'S A SECRET CABINET BEHIND THIS BOOKCASE.
YOU CAN'T GET TO IT BY YOURSELF.
YOU HAVE TO WORK WITH SOMEONE ELSE TO MOVE THIS BOOKCASE.
OKAY.
LET'S HIDE THE PRESENT FOR THE NEW BABY IN THIS SECRET PLACE.

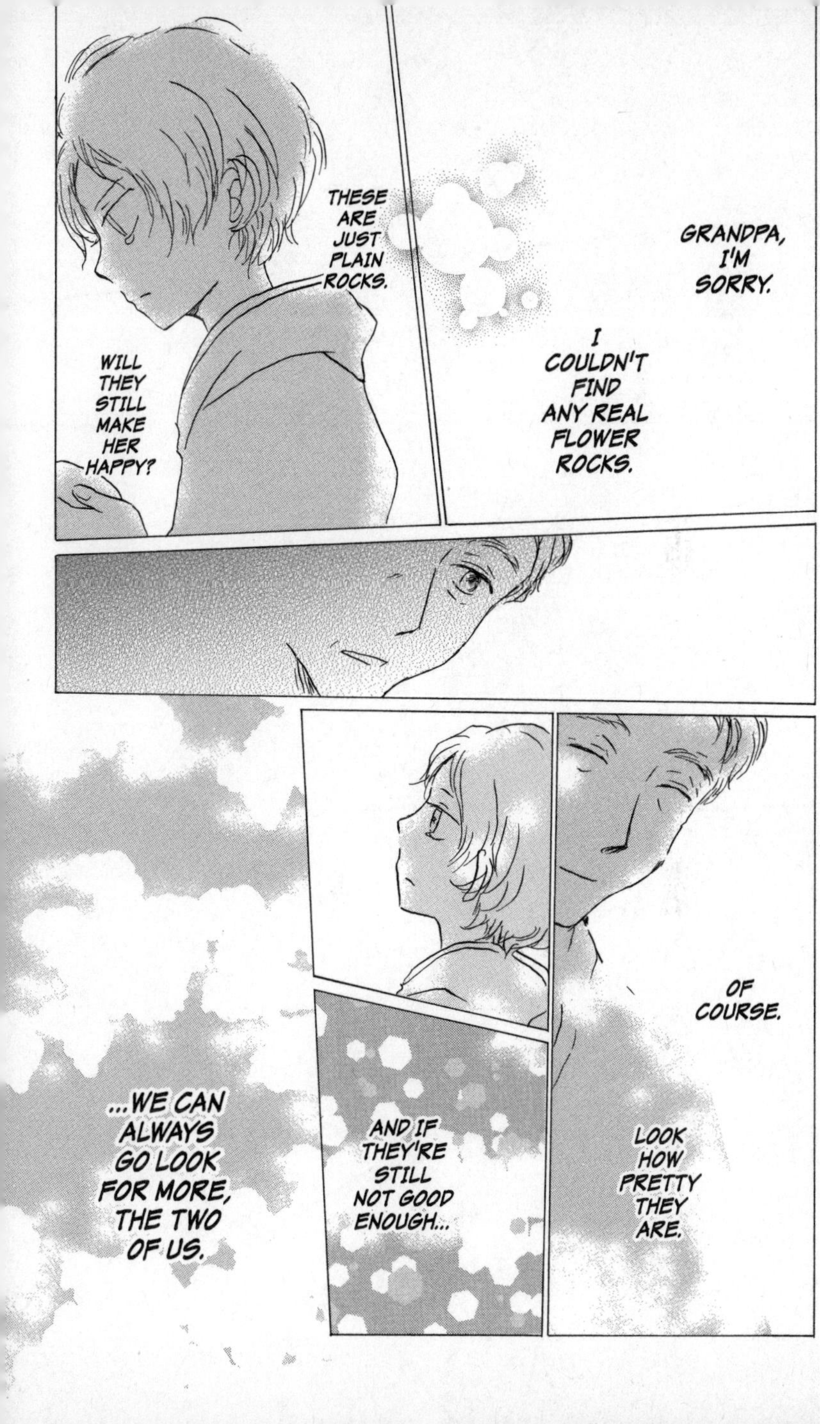
GRANDPA, I'M SORRY.
I COULDN'T FIND ANY REAL FLOWER ROCKS.
THESE ARE JUST PLAIN ROCKS.
WILL THEY STILL MAKE HER HAPPY?
OF COURSE.
LOOK HOW PRETTY THEY ARE.
AND IF THEY'RE STILL NOT GOOD ENOUGH...
...WE CAN ALWAYS GO LOOK FOR MORE, THE TWO OF US.

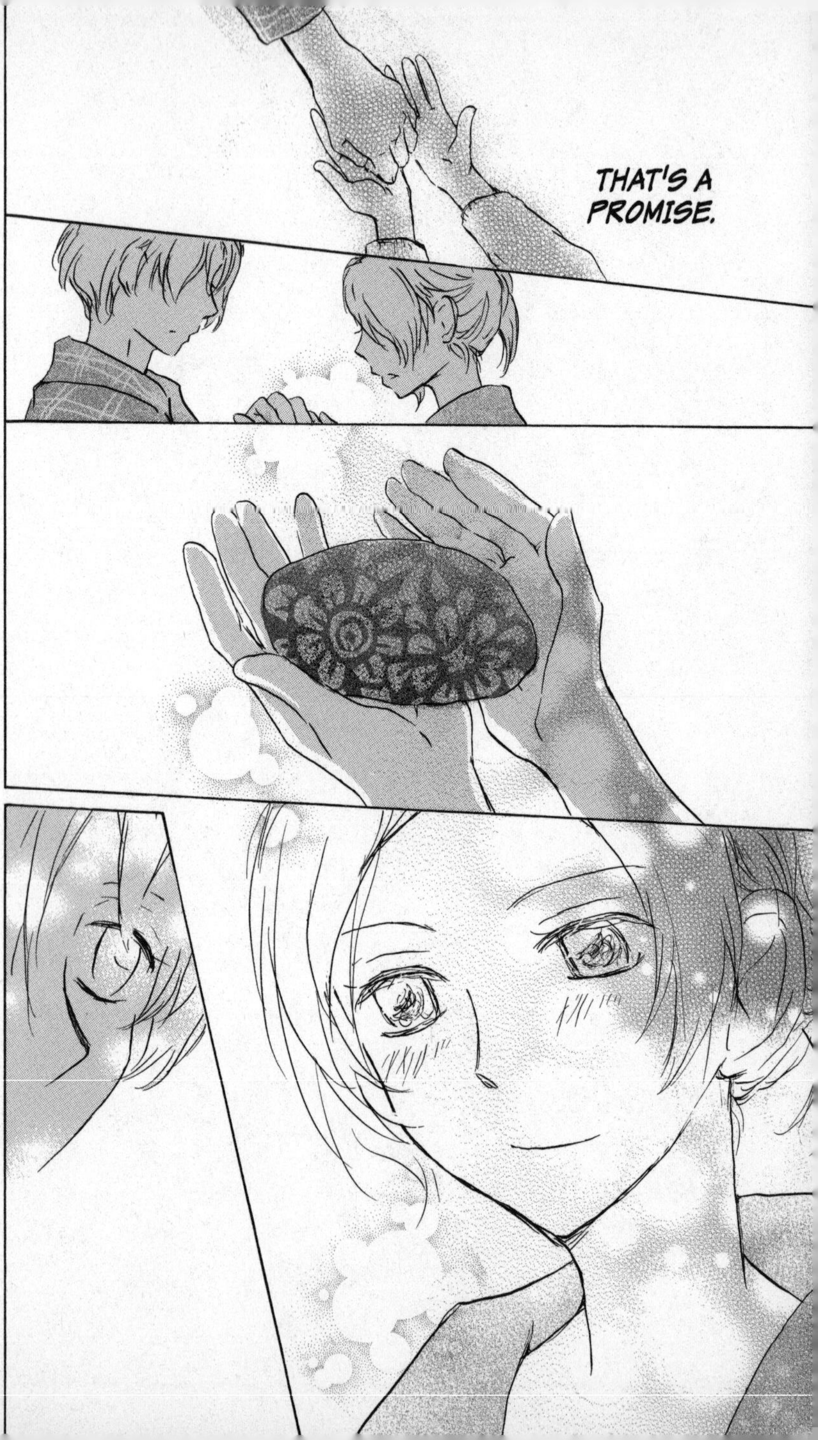
THAT'S A PROMISE.

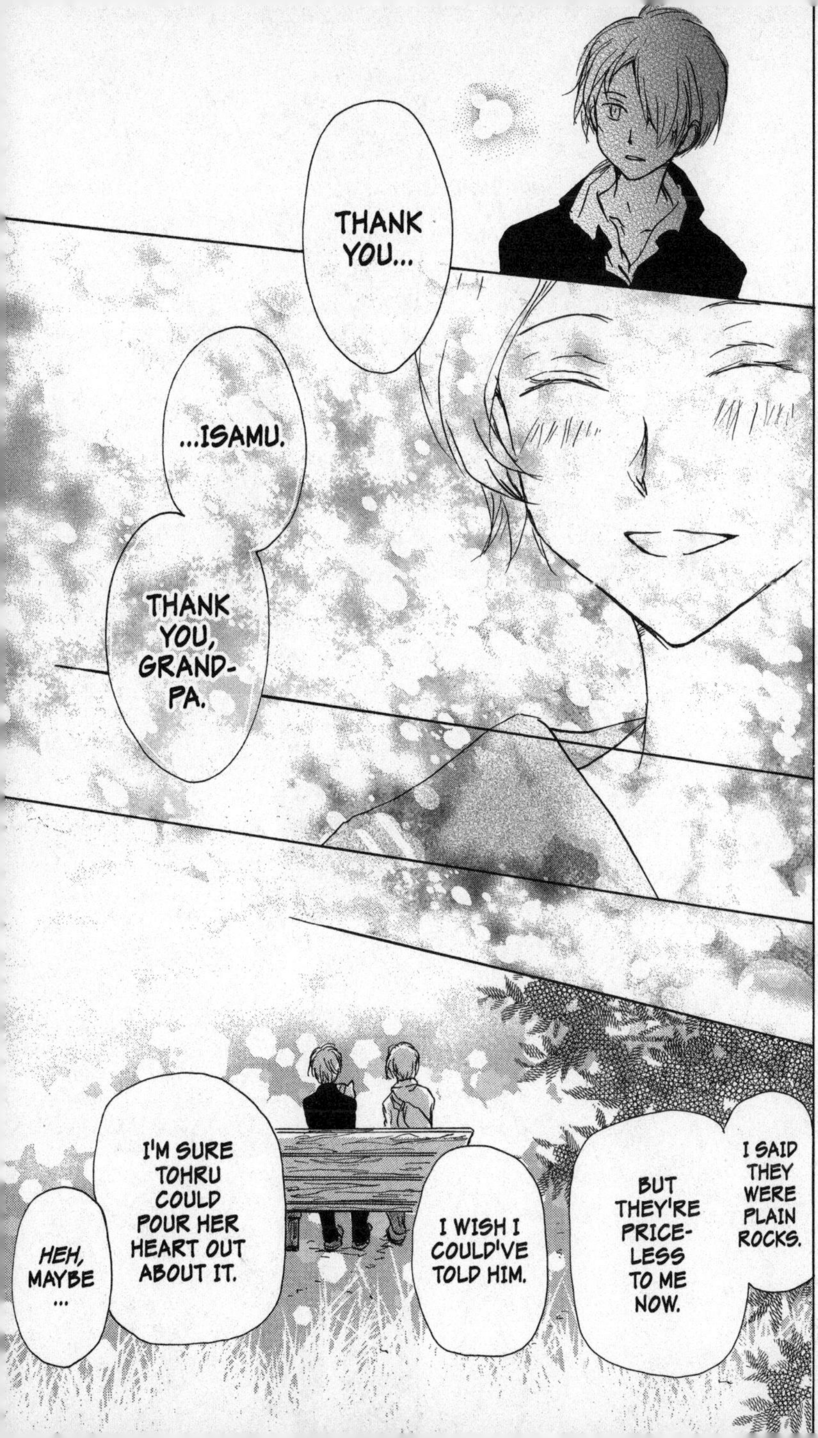
THANK YOU...
...ISAMU.
THANK YOU, GRAND-PA.
I SAID THEY WERE PLAIN ROCKS.
BUT THEY'RE PRICE-LESS TO ME NOW.
I WISH I COULD'VE TOLD HIM.
I'M SURE TOHRU COULD POUR HER HEART OUT ABOUT IT.
HEH, MAYBE ...

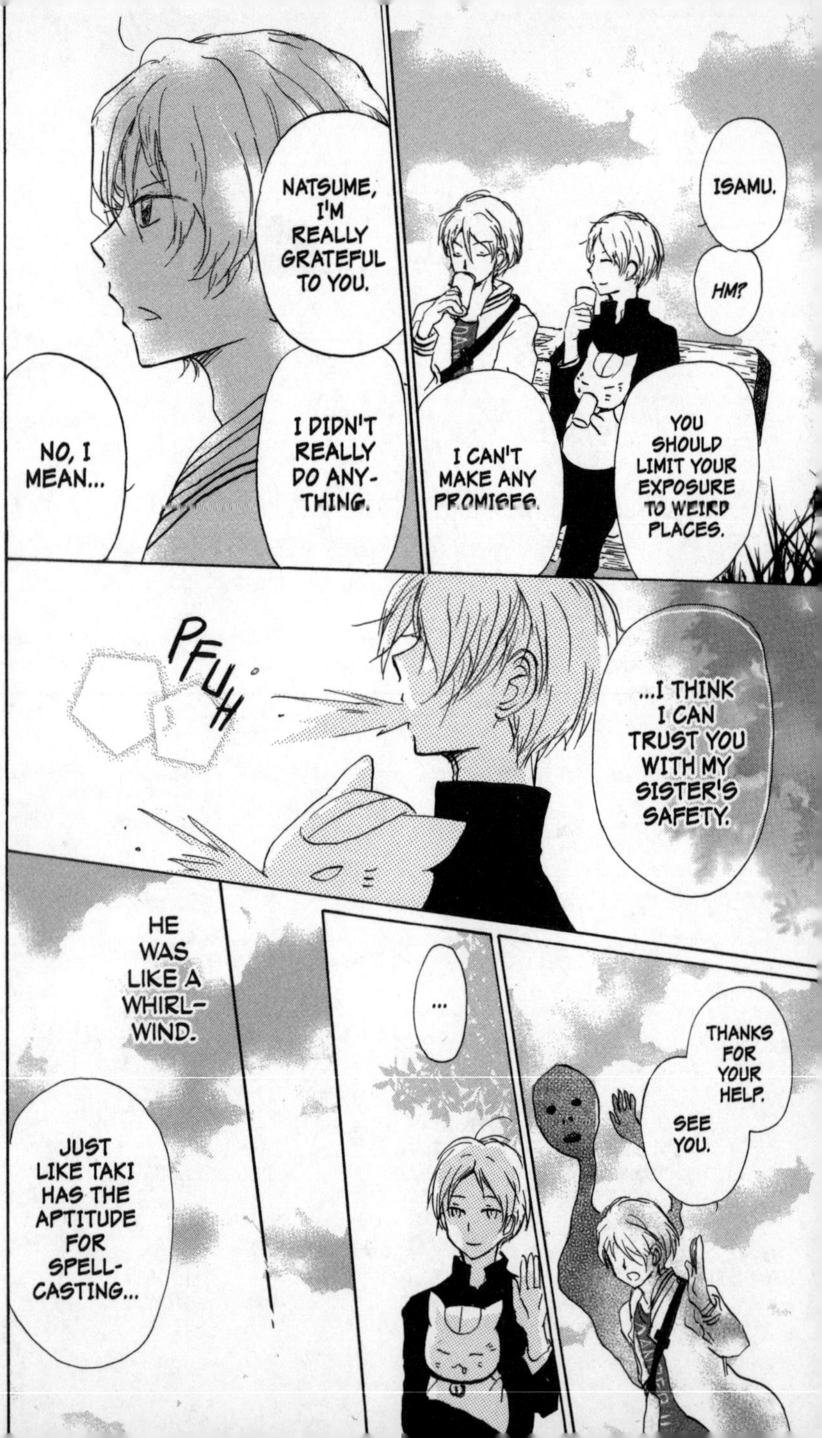

ISAMU.
HM?
YOU SHOULD LIMIT YOUR EXPOSURE TO WEIRD PLACES.
I CAN'T MAKE ANY PROMISES.
NATSUME, I'M REALLY GRATEFUL TO YOU.
I DIDN'T REALLY DO ANY-THING.
NO, I MEAN...
...I THINK I CAN TRUST YOU WITH MY SISTER'S SAFETY.
PFUH
THANKS FOR YOUR HELP.
SEE YOU.
...
HE WAS LIKE A WHIRL-WIND.
JUST LIKE TAKI HAS THE APTITUDE FOR SPELL-CASTING...

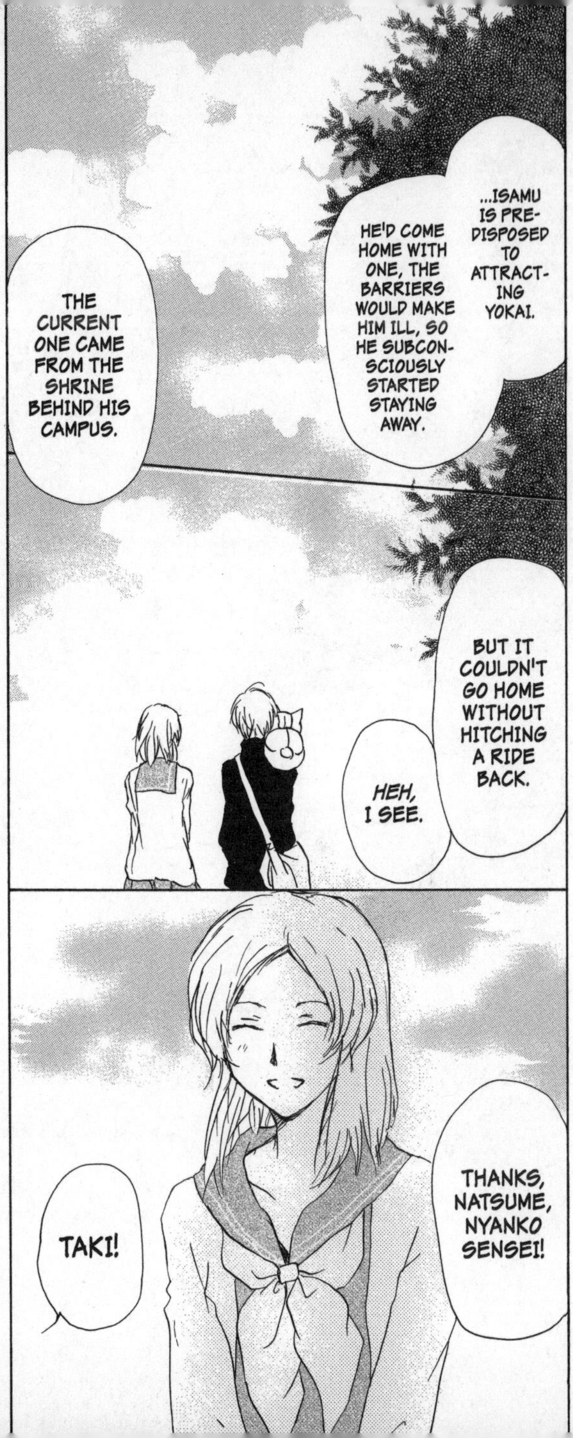
...ISAMU IS PRE-DISPOSED TO ATTRACT-ING YOKAI.
HE'D COME HOME WITH ONE, THE BARRIERS WOULD MAKE HIM ILL, SO HE SUBCON-SCIOUSLY STARTED STAYING AWAY.
THE CURRENT ONE CAME FROM THE SHRINE BEHIND HIS CAMPUS.
BUT IT COULDN'T GO HOME WITHOUT HITCHING A RIDE BACK.
HEH, I SEE.
THANKS, NATSUME, NYANKO SENSEI!
TAKI!

02

✻Taki's Brother

This story was on my mind forever, but I never had the opportunity to work it in until now. I was finally able to bring it to fruition. Taki briefly mentioned her brother previously, but I tweaked the details a bit.

I had this rigid image of the siblings raised around their grandfather in this old house, and I couldn't quite get motivated to work on the story. I recon-sidered it from a different angle, and I was finally able to bring Taki forward into the story. I always get nervous when I'm working on the family members of characters who are important to me.

It reminded me of the first time I drew Uncle Shigeru.

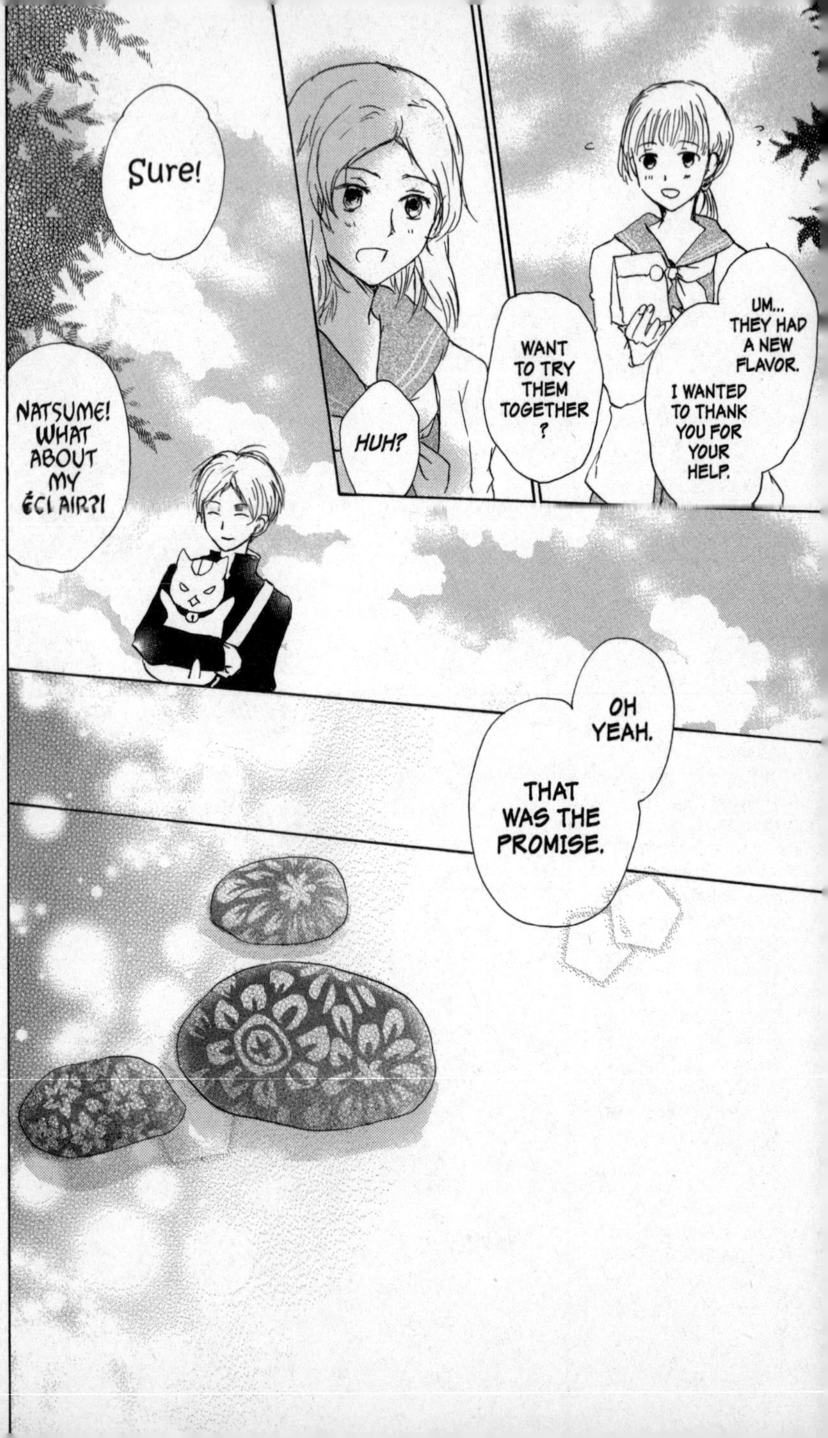
UM... THEY HAD A NEW FLAVOR.
I WANTED TO THANK YOU FOR YOUR HELP.
WANT TO TRY THEM TOGETHER?
HUH?
Sure!
NATSUME! WHAT ABOUT MY ÉCLAIR?!
OH YEAH.
THAT WAS THE PROMISE.

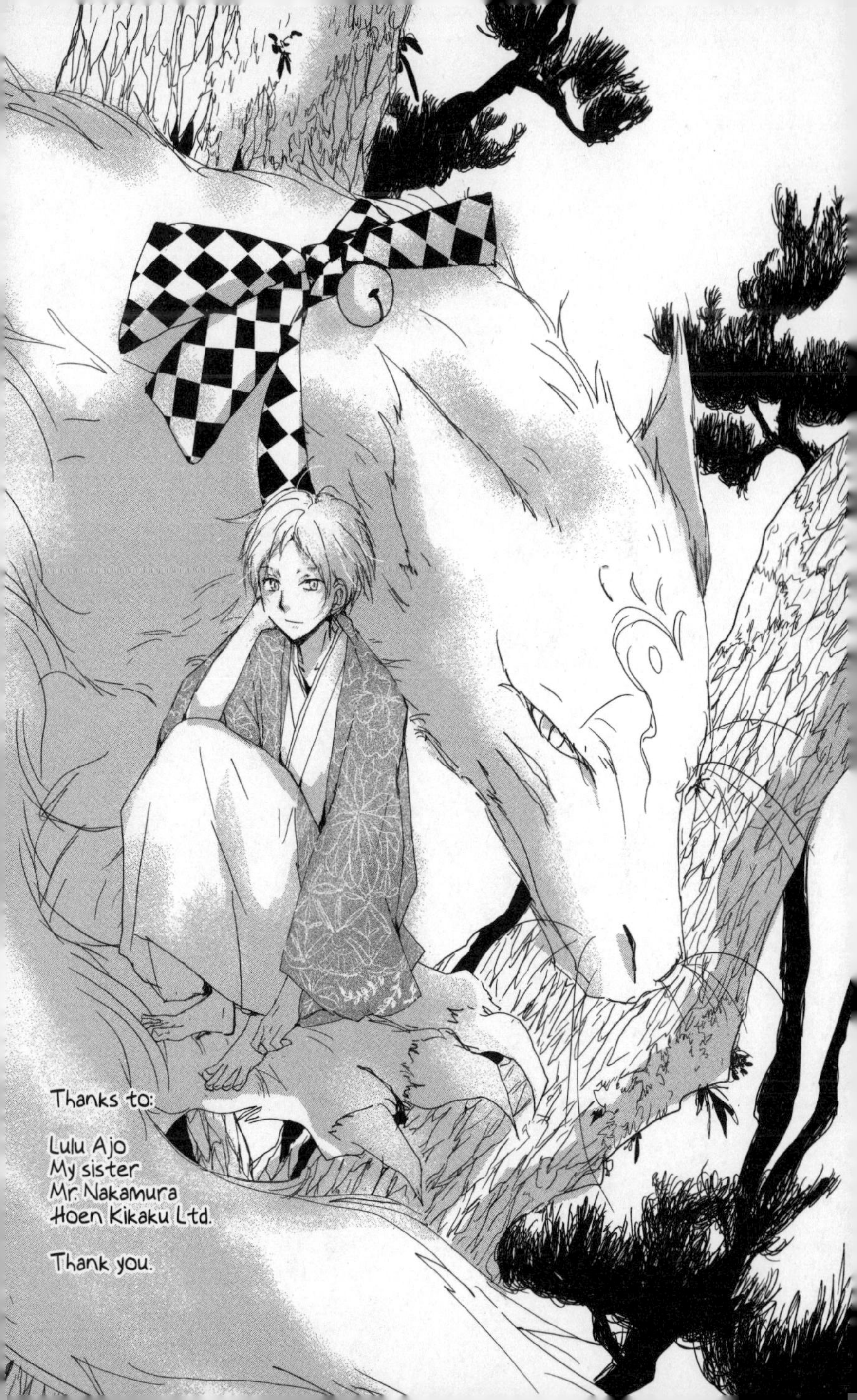
Thanks to:

Lulu Ajo
My sister
Mr. Nakamura
Hoen Kikaku Ltd.

Thank you.

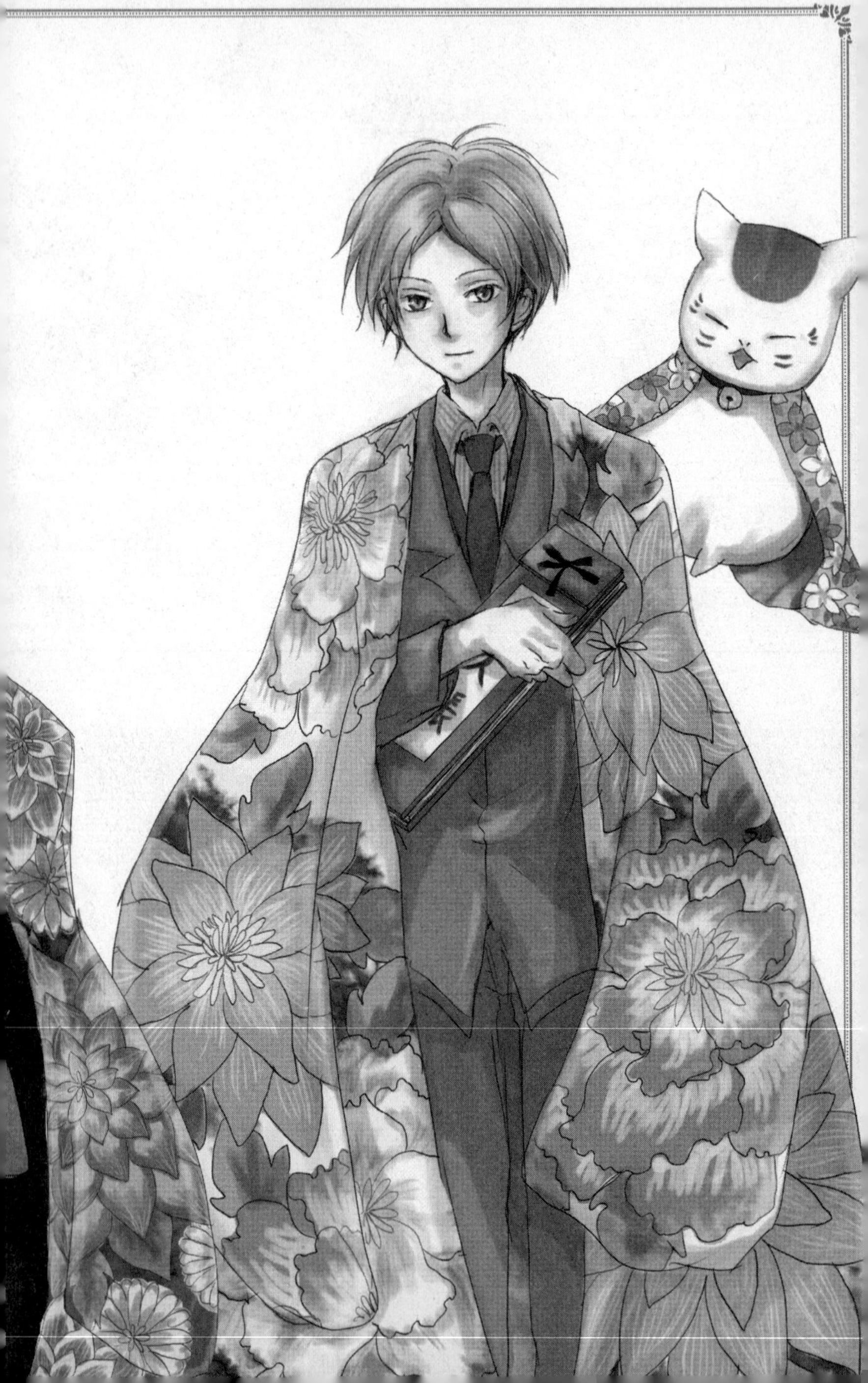

Natsume's BOOK of FRIENDS

CHAPTER 97

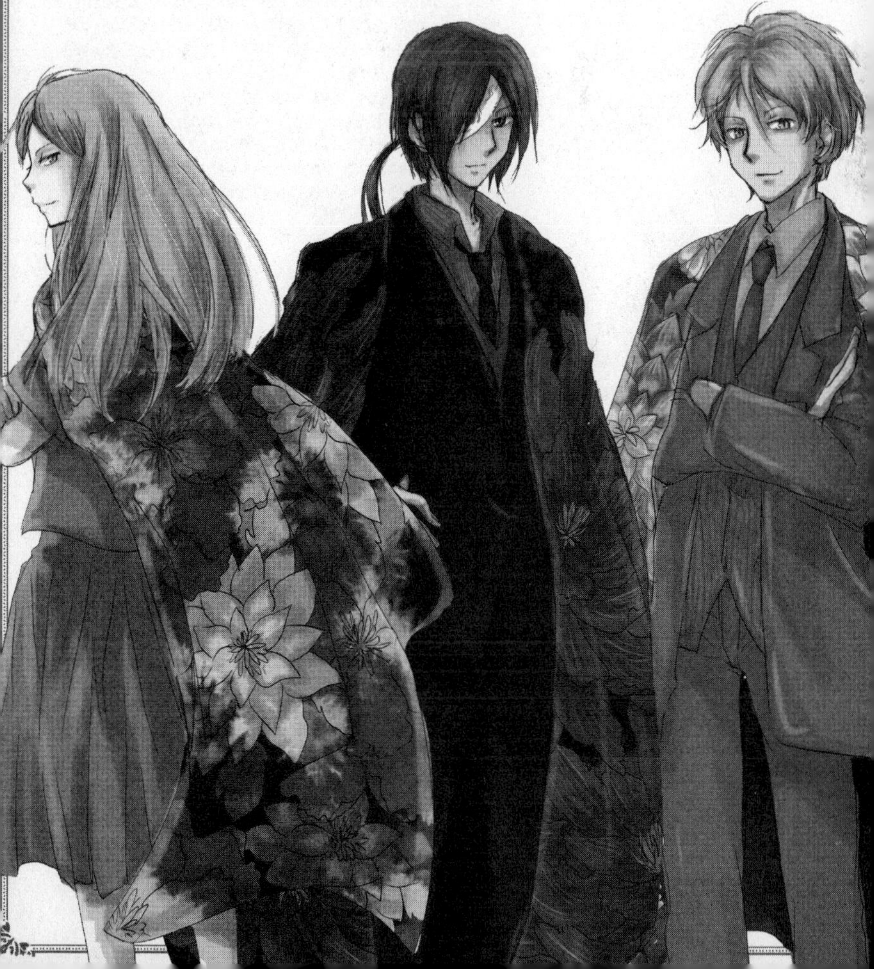

❋ Character contest

The magazine *LaLa* ran a popularity contest for the *Natsume's Book of Friends* characters.

Since the story is about Natsume and Nyanko Sensei meeting many different people going about their lives, the cast of regular characters doesn't increase very much over time. My editor and I suspected that the characters people were thinking about would depend on which story arc they'd read most recently. Nevertheless, we were very excited to check out the results.

I drew the top five characters in the spread on the previous page, which ran as the opening color illustration for the magazine first. Thanks to everyone for voting! I will continue to draw each character with passion.

Kotaro Akeboshi
illiant Detective

Betrothed
to Murder

近日公開

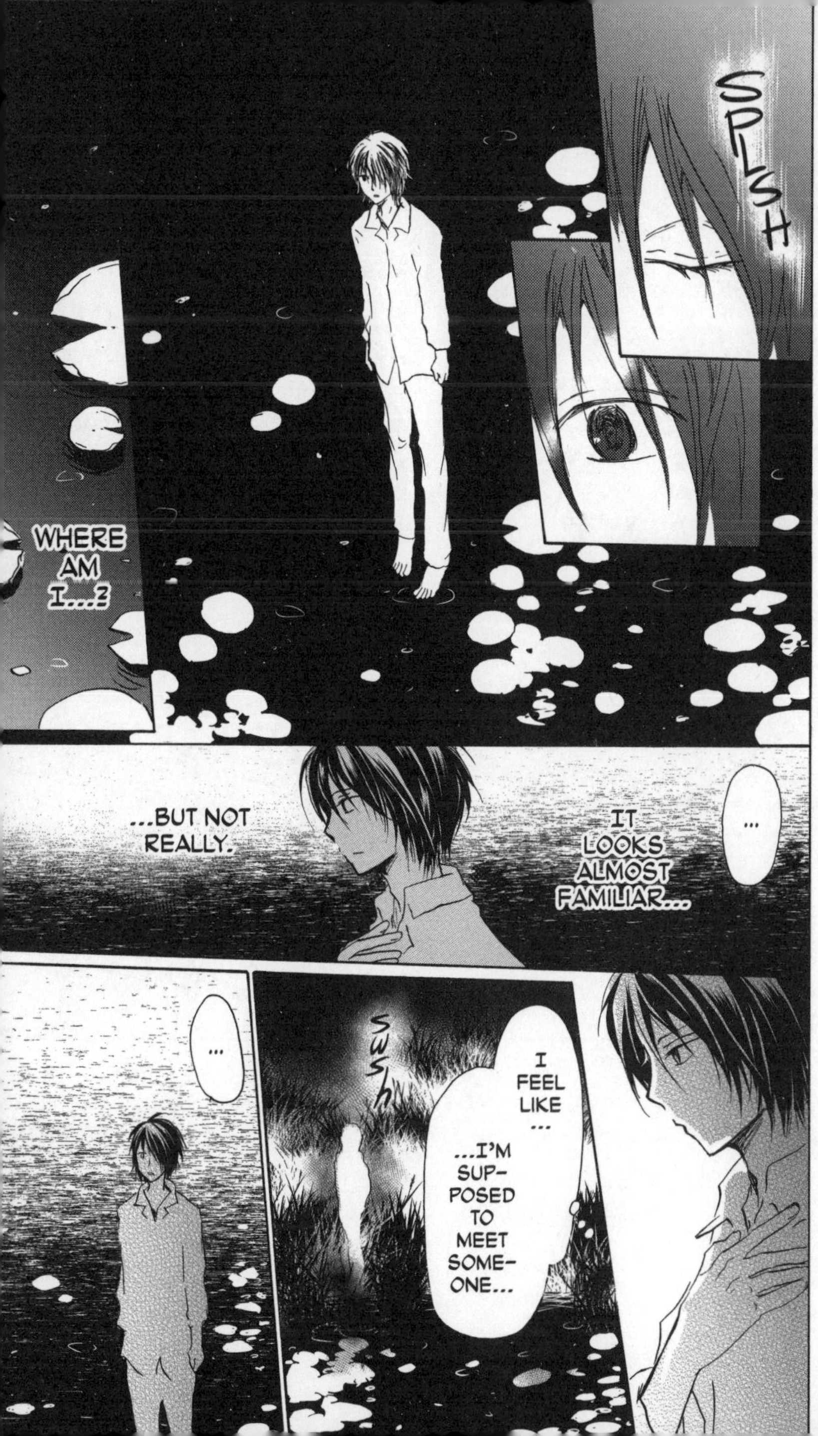
SPLSH
WHERE AM I...?
...
IT LOOKS ALMOST FAMILIAR...
...BUT NOT REALLY.
I FEEL LIKE ...
...I'M SUP-POSED TO MEET SOME-ONE...
SWSH
...

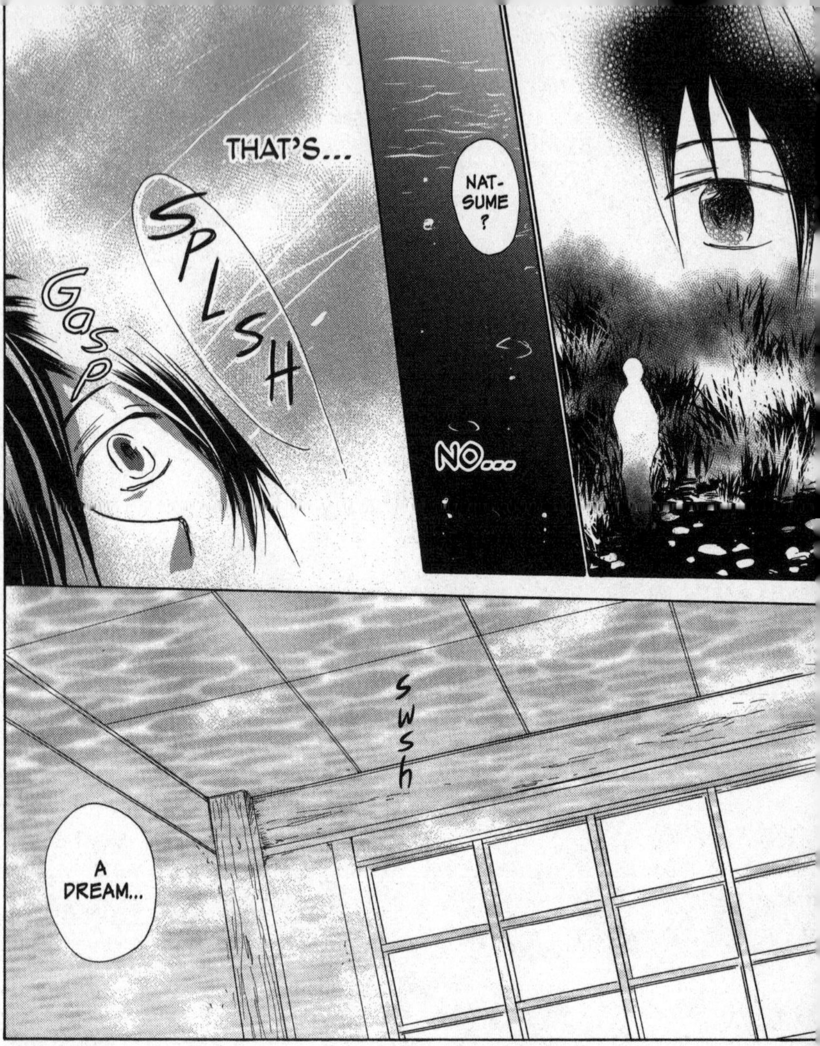
NAT-SUME?
NO...
THAT'S...
SPLSH
Gasp
SWSH
A DREAM...

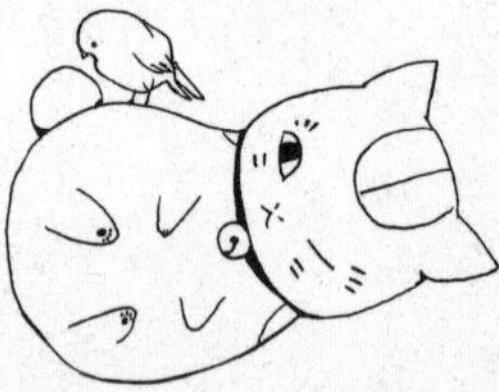

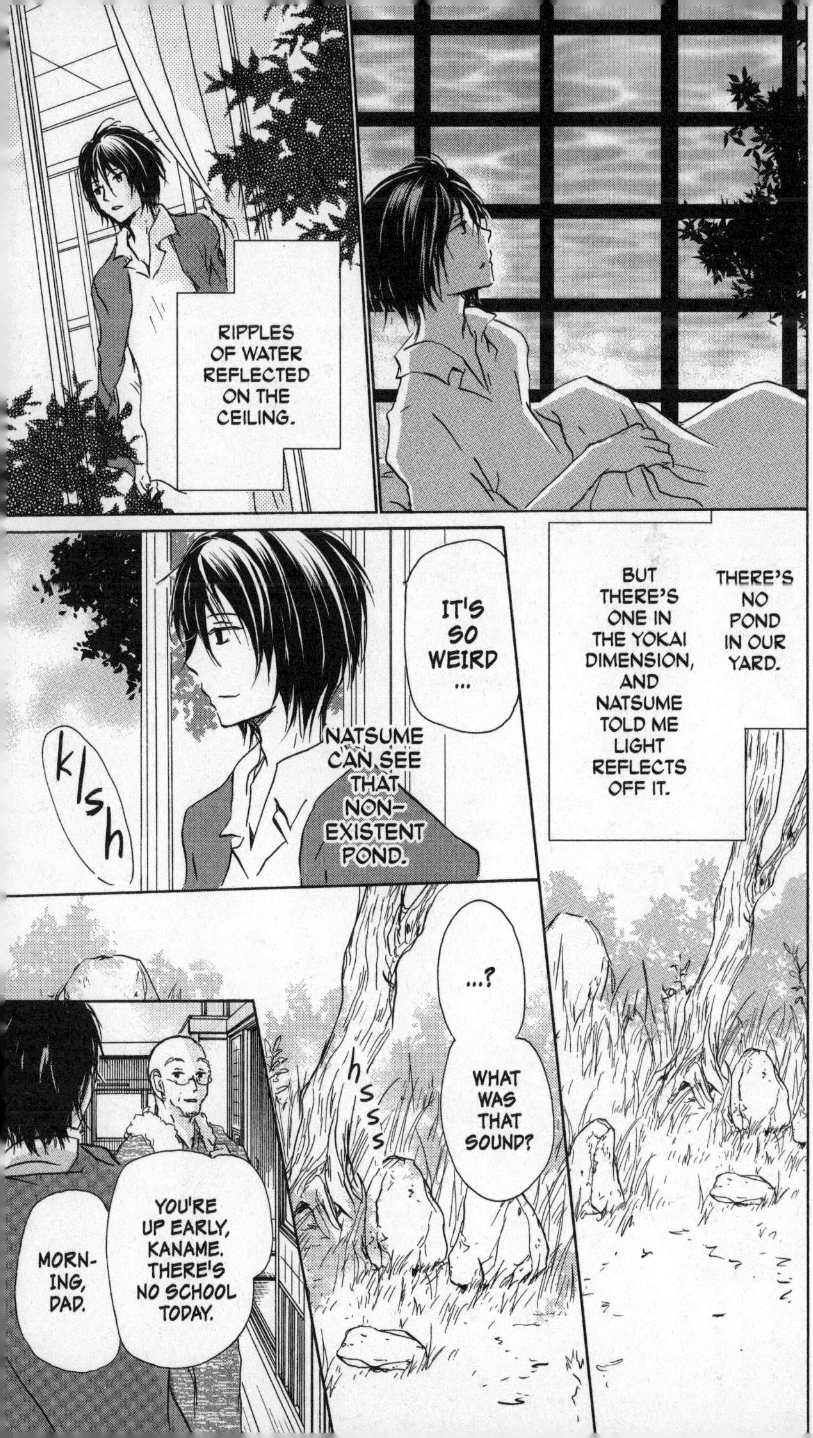
RIPPLES OF WATER REFLECTED ON THE CEILING.
THERE'S NO POND IN OUR YARD.
BUT THERE'S ONE IN THE YOKAI DIMENSION, AND NATSUME TOLD ME LIGHT REFLECTS OFF IT.
IT'S SO WEIRD...
NATSUME CAN SEE THAT NON-EXISTENT POND.
klsh
...?
WHAT WAS THAT SOUND?
hsss
YOU'RE UP EARLY, KANAME. THERE'S NO SCHOOL TODAY.
MORNING, DAD.

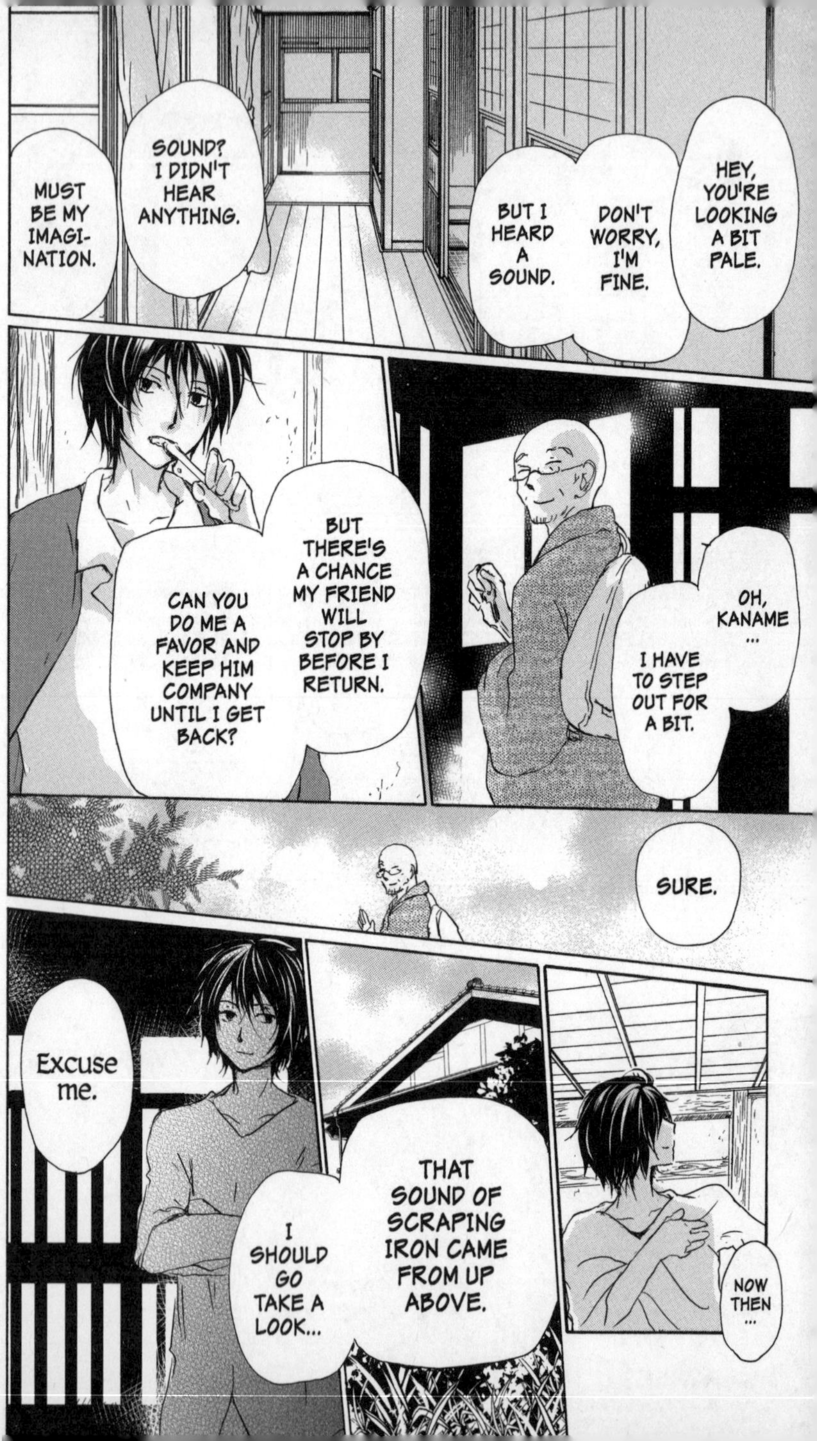
HEY, YOU'RE LOOKING A BIT PALE.
DON'T WORRY, I'M FINE.
BUT I HEARD A SOUND.
SOUND? I DIDN'T HEAR ANYTHING.
MUST BE MY IMAGI-NATION.
OH, KANAME ...
I HAVE TO STEP OUT FOR A BIT.
BUT THERE'S A CHANCE MY FRIEND WILL STOP BY BEFORE I RETURN.
CAN YOU DO ME A FAVOR AND KEEP HIM COMPANY UNTIL I GET BACK?
SURE.
NOW THEN ...
THAT SOUND OF SCRAPING IRON CAME FROM UP ABOVE.
I SHOULD GO TAKE A LOOK...
Excuse me.

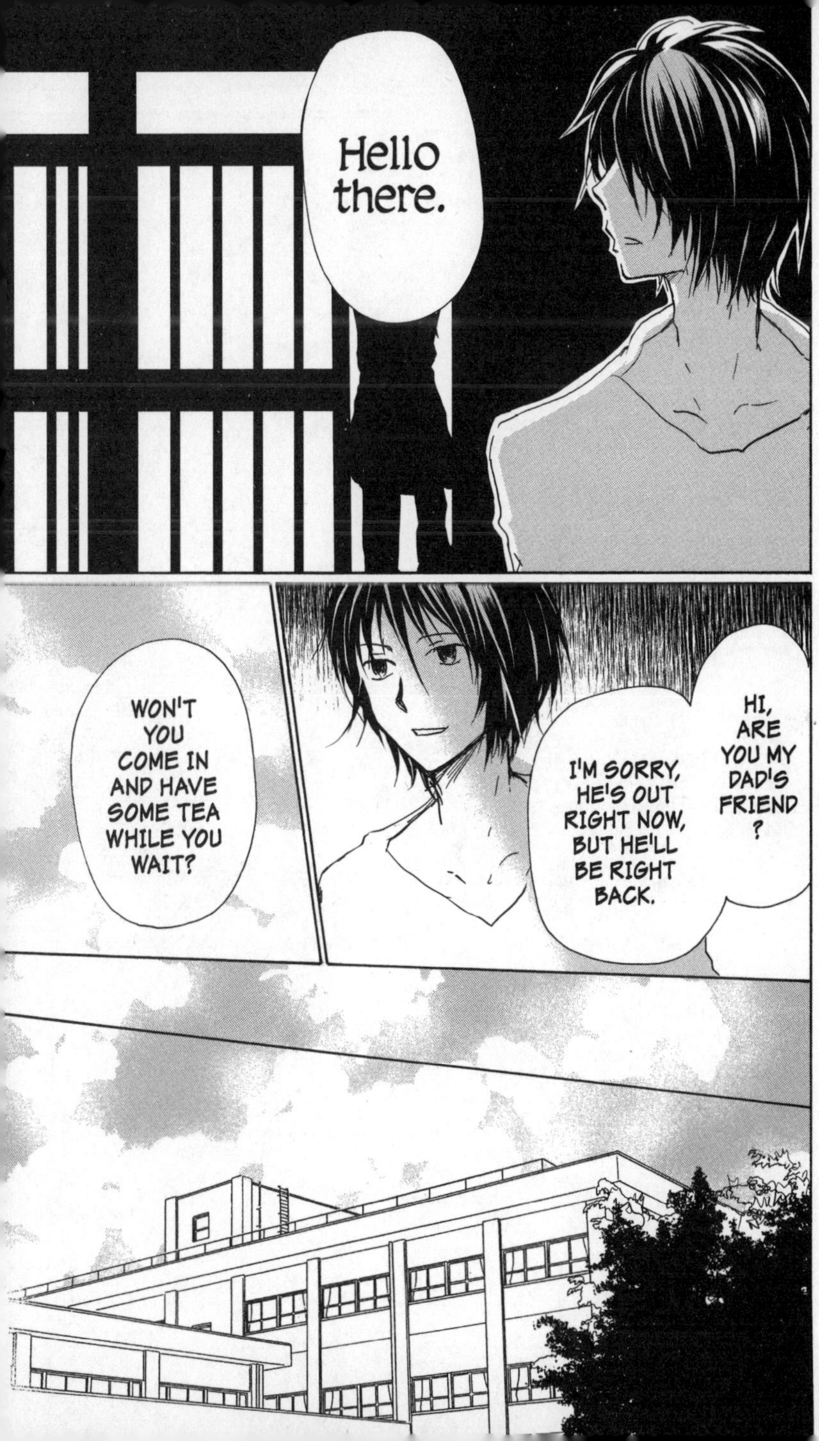
Hello there.
HI, ARE YOU MY DAD'S FRIEND?
I'M SORRY, HE'S OUT RIGHT NOW, BUT HE'LL BE RIGHT BACK.
WON'T YOU COME IN AND HAVE SOME TEA WHILE YOU WAIT?

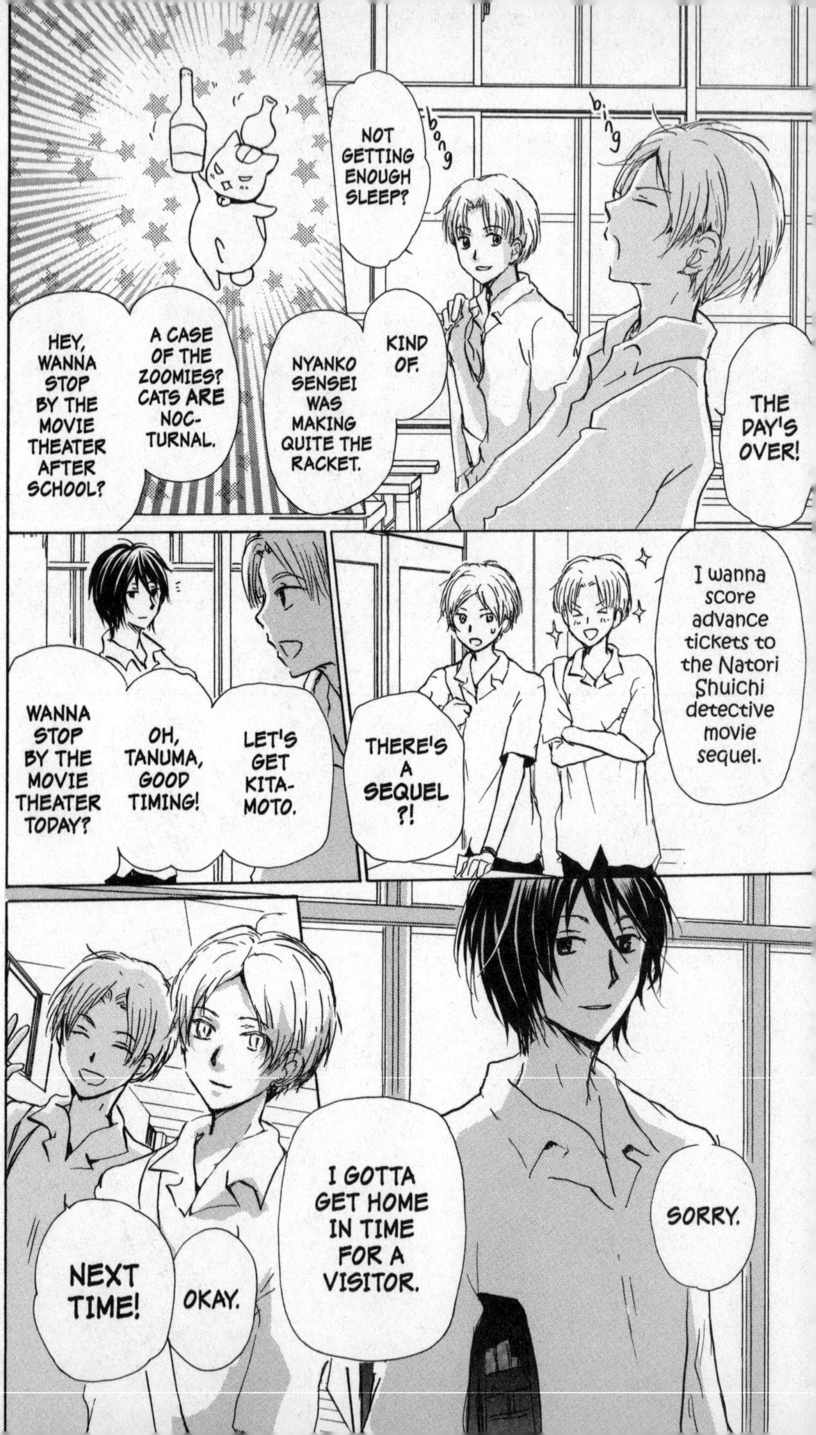
THE DAY'S OVER!
bing bong
NOT GETTING ENOUGH SLEEP?
KIND OF.
NYANKO SENSEI WAS MAKING QUITE THE RACKET.
A CASE OF THE ZOOMIES? CATS ARE NOC-TURNAL.
HEY, WANNA STOP BY THE MOVIE THEATER AFTER SCHOOL?
I wanna score advance tickets to the Natori Shuichi detective movie sequel.
THERE'S A SEQUEL?!
LET'S GET KITA-MOTO.
OH, TANUMA, GOOD TIMING!
WANNA STOP BY THE MOVIE THEATER TODAY?
SORRY.
I GOTTA GET HOME IN TIME FOR A VISITOR.
OKAY.
NEXT TIME!

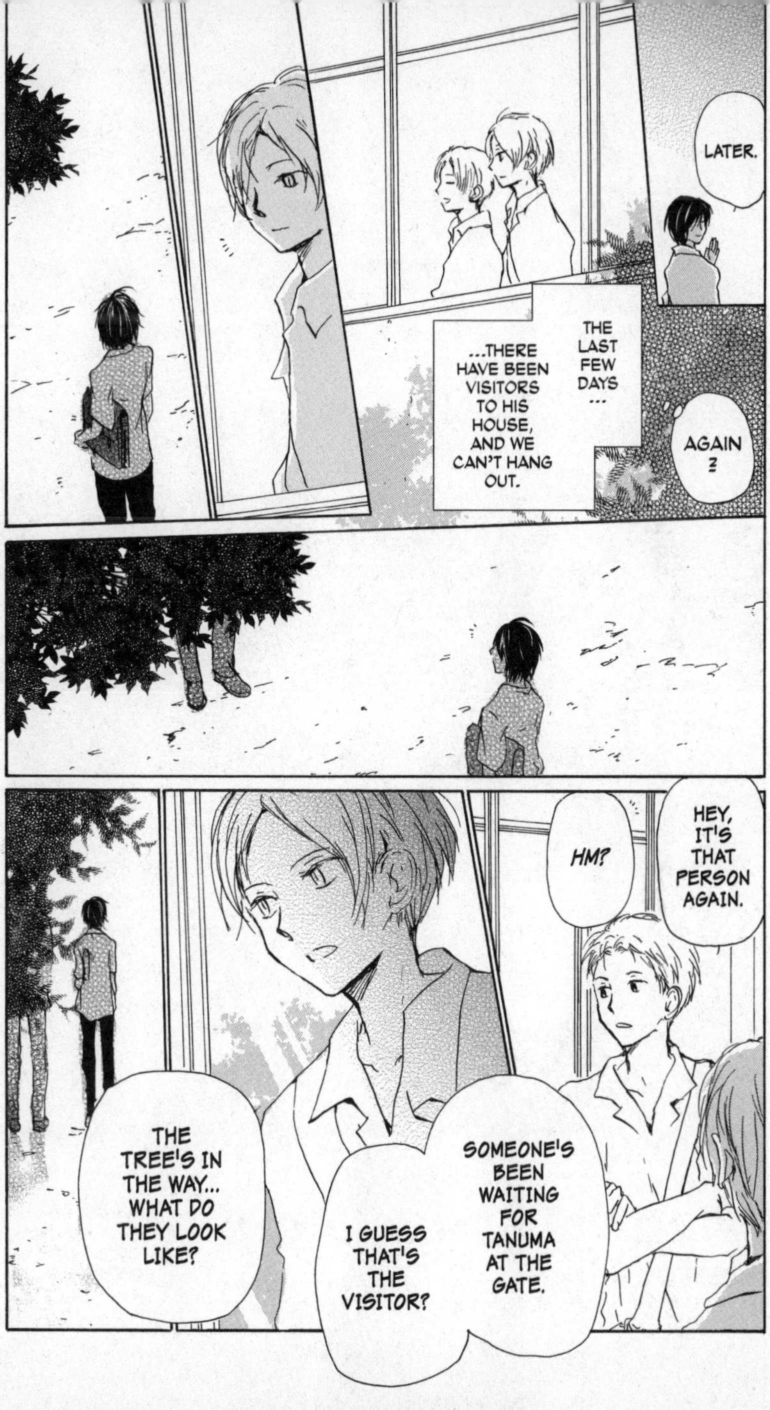
LATER.
AGAIN?
THE LAST FEW DAYS...
...THERE HAVE BEEN VISITORS TO HIS HOUSE, AND WE CAN'T HANG OUT.
HEY, IT'S THAT PERSON AGAIN.
HM?
SOMEONE'S BEEN WAITING FOR TANUMA AT THE GATE.
I GUESS THAT'S THE VISITOR?
THE TREE'S IN THE WAY... WHAT DO THEY LOOK LIKE?

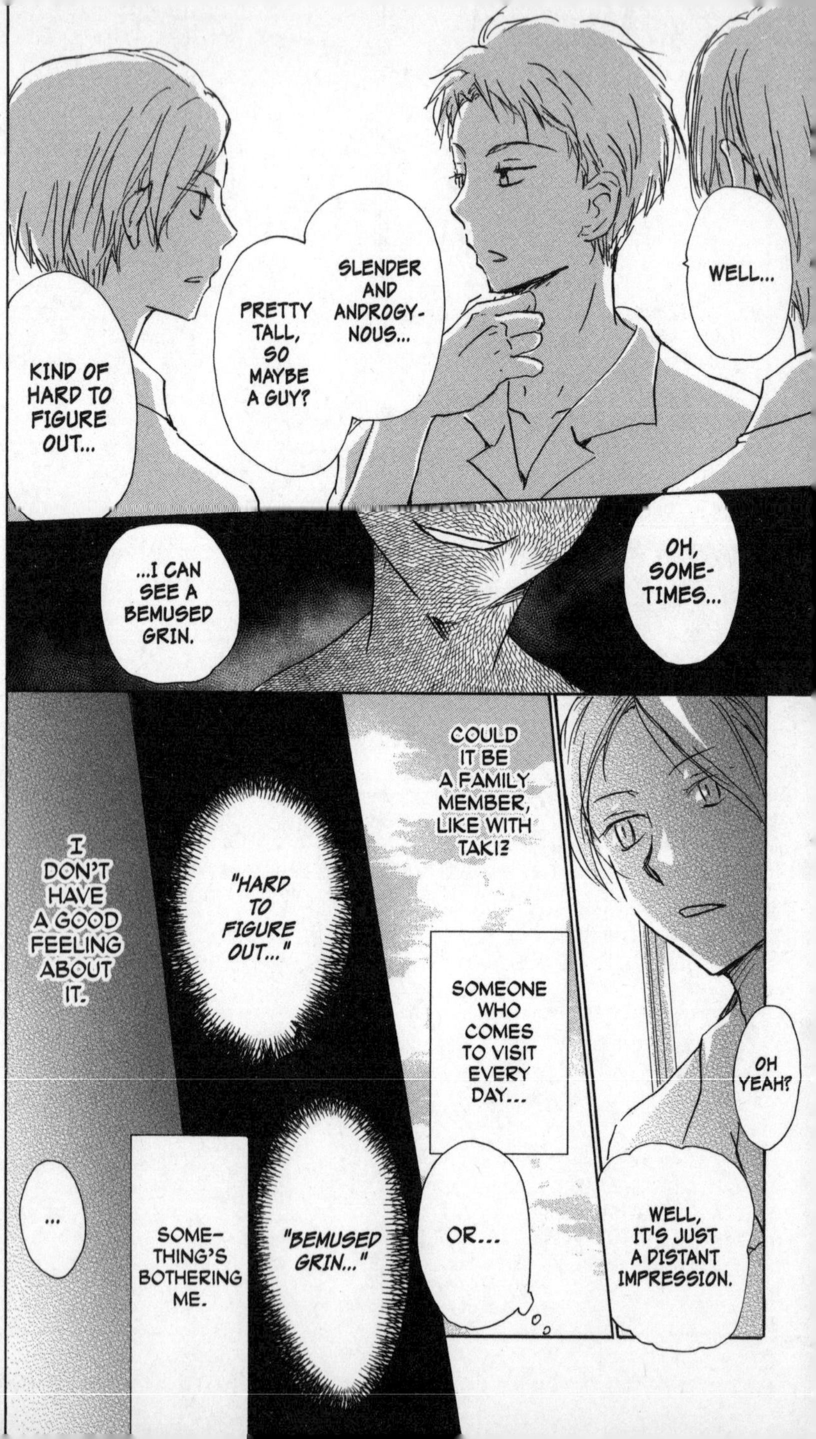
WELL...
SLENDER AND ANDROGYNOUS...
PRETTY TALL, SO MAYBE A GUY?
KIND OF HARD TO FIGURE OUT...
OH, SOMETIMES...
...I CAN SEE A BEMUSED GRIN.
COULD IT BE A FAMILY MEMBER, LIKE WITH TAKI?
OH YEAH?
SOMEONE WHO COMES TO VISIT EVERY DAY...
WELL, IT'S JUST A DISTANT IMPRESSION.
OR...
"HARD TO FIGURE OUT..."
"BEMUSED GRIN..."
SOMETHING'S BOTHERING ME.
I DON'T HAVE A GOOD FEELING ABOUT IT.
...

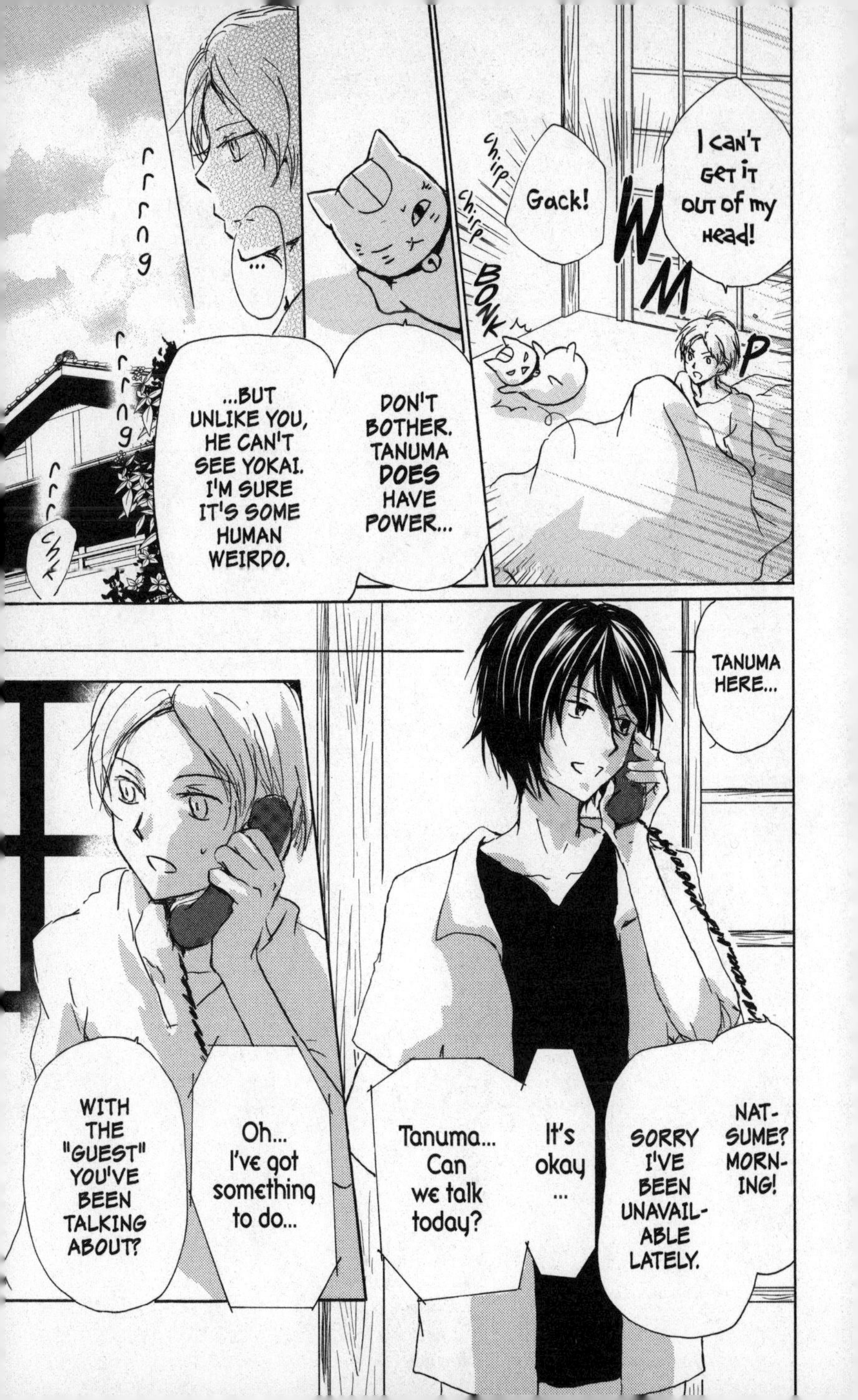
I can't get it out of my head!
WMP
Gack!
chirp
chirp
BONK
DON'T BOTHER. TANUMA DOES HAVE POWER...
...BUT UNLIKE YOU, HE CAN'T SEE YOKAI. I'M SURE IT'S SOME HUMAN WEIRDO.
rrrng
...
rrrng
rrr
TANUMA HERE...
NAT-SUME? MORN-ING!
SORRY I'VE BEEN UNAVAIL-ABLE LATELY.
It's okay...
Tanuma... Can we talk today?
Oh... I've got something to do...
WITH THE "GUEST" YOU'VE BEEN TALKING ABOUT?

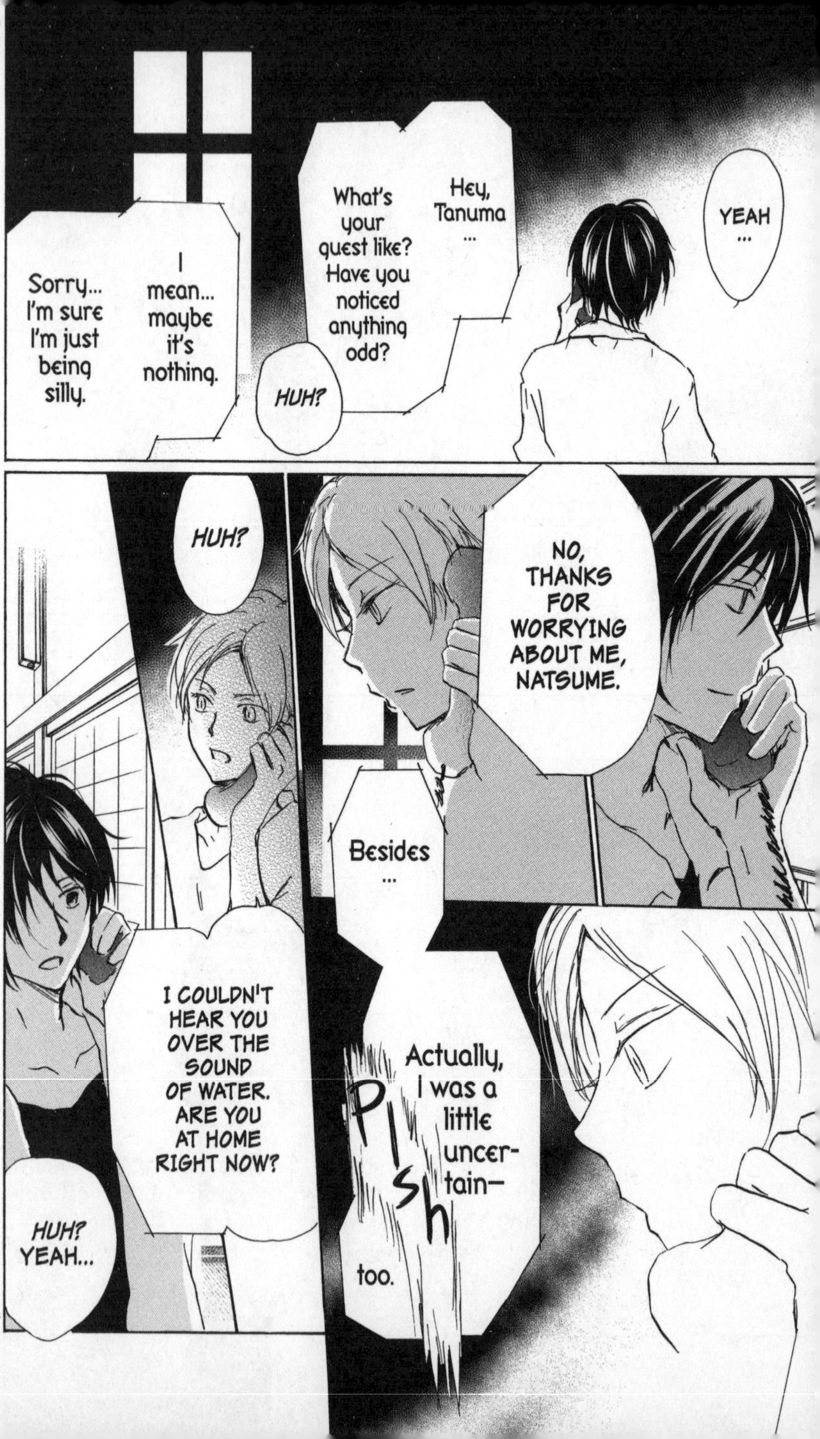
YEAH ...
Hey, Tanuma ...
What's your quest like? Have you noticed anything odd?
HUH?
I mean... maybe it's nothing.
Sorry... I'm sure I'm just being silly.
NO, THANKS FOR WORRYING ABOUT ME, NATSUME.
Besides ...
Actually, I was a little uncer-tain—
PLISH
too.
HUH?
I COULDN'T HEAR YOU OVER THE SOUND OF WATER. ARE YOU AT HOME RIGHT NOW?
HUH? YEAH...

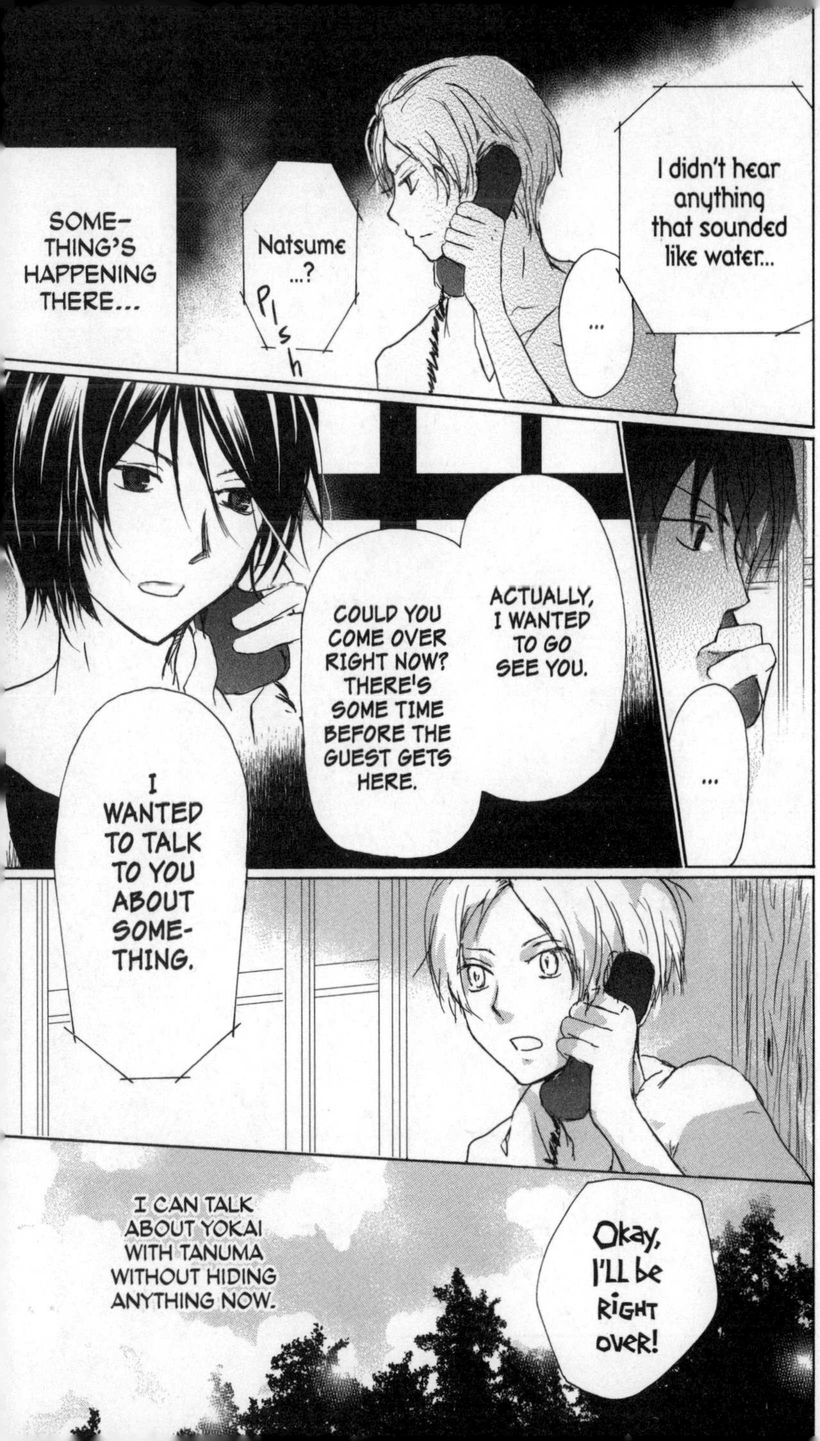
I didn't hear anything that sounded like water...
...
Natsume ...?
Plish
SOME-THING'S HAPPENING THERE...
...
ACTUALLY, I WANTED TO GO SEE YOU.
COULD YOU COME OVER RIGHT NOW? THERE'S SOME TIME BEFORE THE GUEST GETS HERE.
I WANTED TO TALK TO YOU ABOUT SOME-THING.
Okay, I'll be right over!
I CAN TALK ABOUT YOKAI WITH TANUMA WITHOUT HIDING ANYTHING NOW.

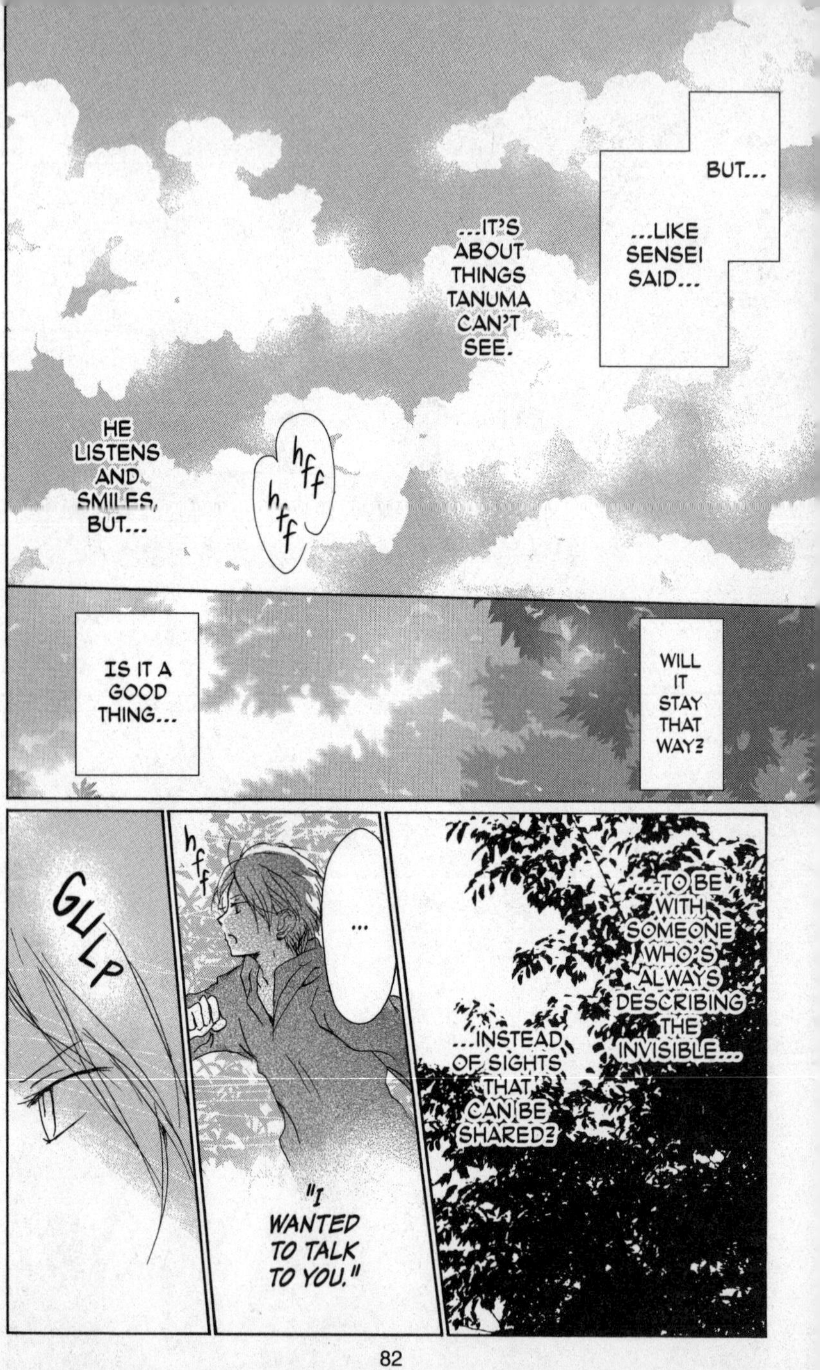
BUT...
...LIKE SENSEI SAID...
...IT'S ABOUT THINGS TANUMA CAN'T SEE.
hff hff
HE LISTENS AND SMILES, BUT...
WILL IT STAY THAT WAY?
IS IT A GOOD THING...
...TO BE WITH SOMEONE WHO'S ALWAYS DESCRIBING THE INVISIBLE...
...INSTEAD OF SIGHTS THAT CAN BE SHARED?
hff
...
"I WANTED TO TALK TO YOU."
GULP

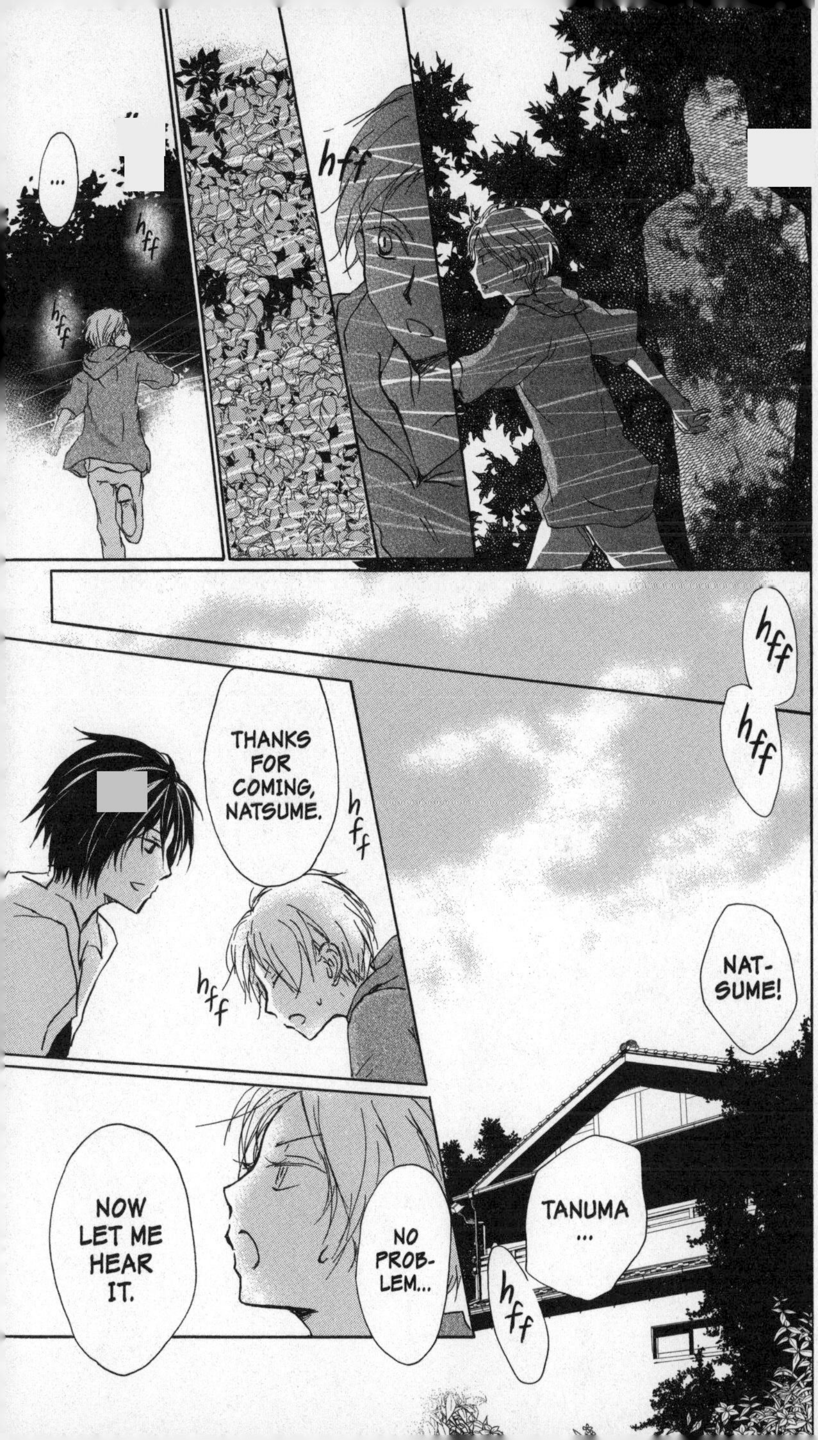
hff
...
hff
hff
hff
hff
NAT-SUME!
TANUMA ...
hff
THANKS FOR COMING, NATSUME.
hff
hff
NO PROB-LEM...
NOW LET ME HEAR IT.

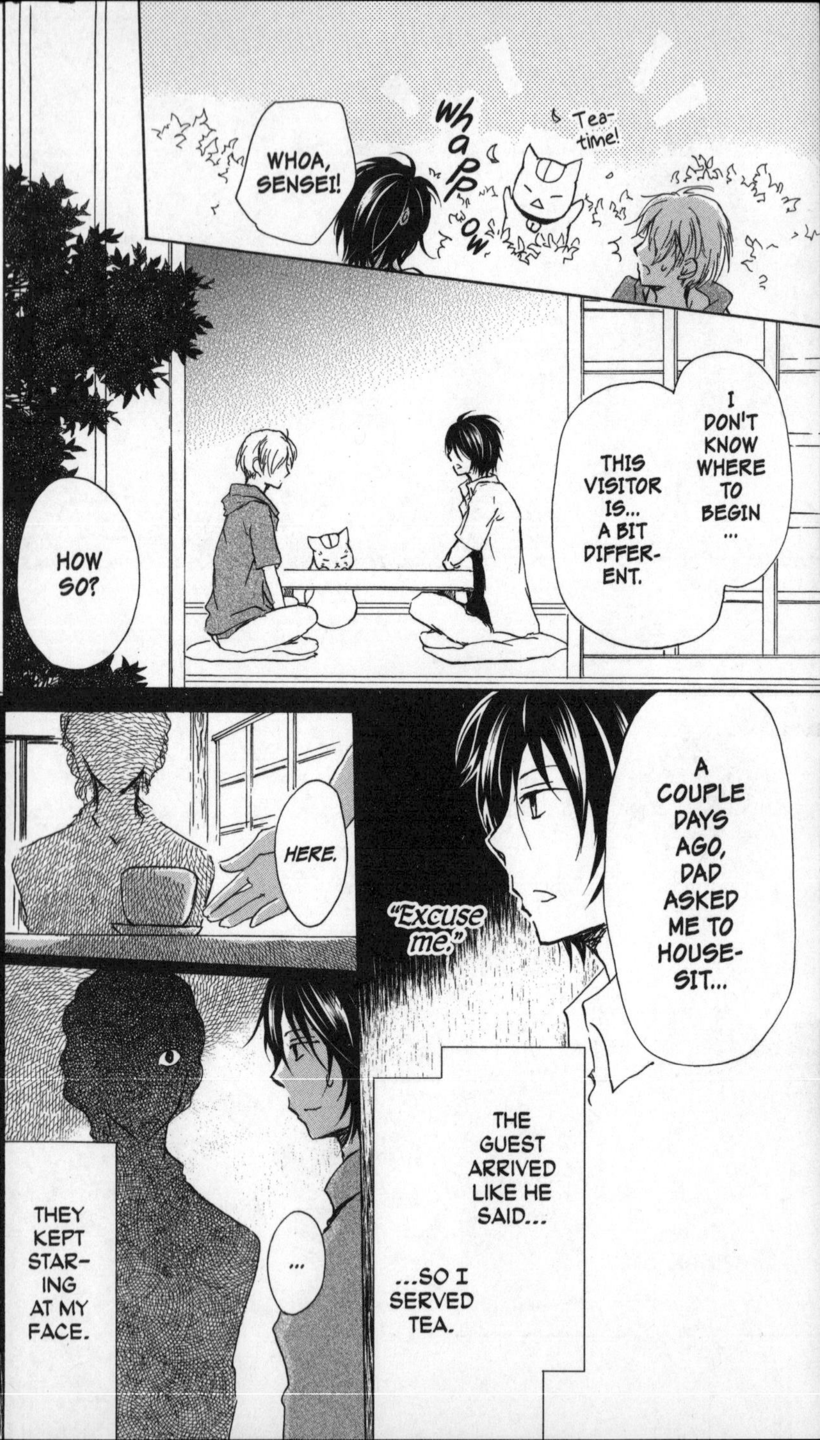
Tea-time!
WHAP POW
WHOA, SENSEI!
I DON'T KNOW WHERE TO BEGIN...
THIS VISITOR IS... A BIT DIFFERENT.
HOW SO?
A COUPLE DAYS AGO, DAD ASKED ME TO HOUSE-SIT...
"Excuse me."
HERE.
THE GUEST ARRIVED LIKE HE SAID...
...SO I SERVED TEA.
...
THEY KEPT STARING AT MY FACE.

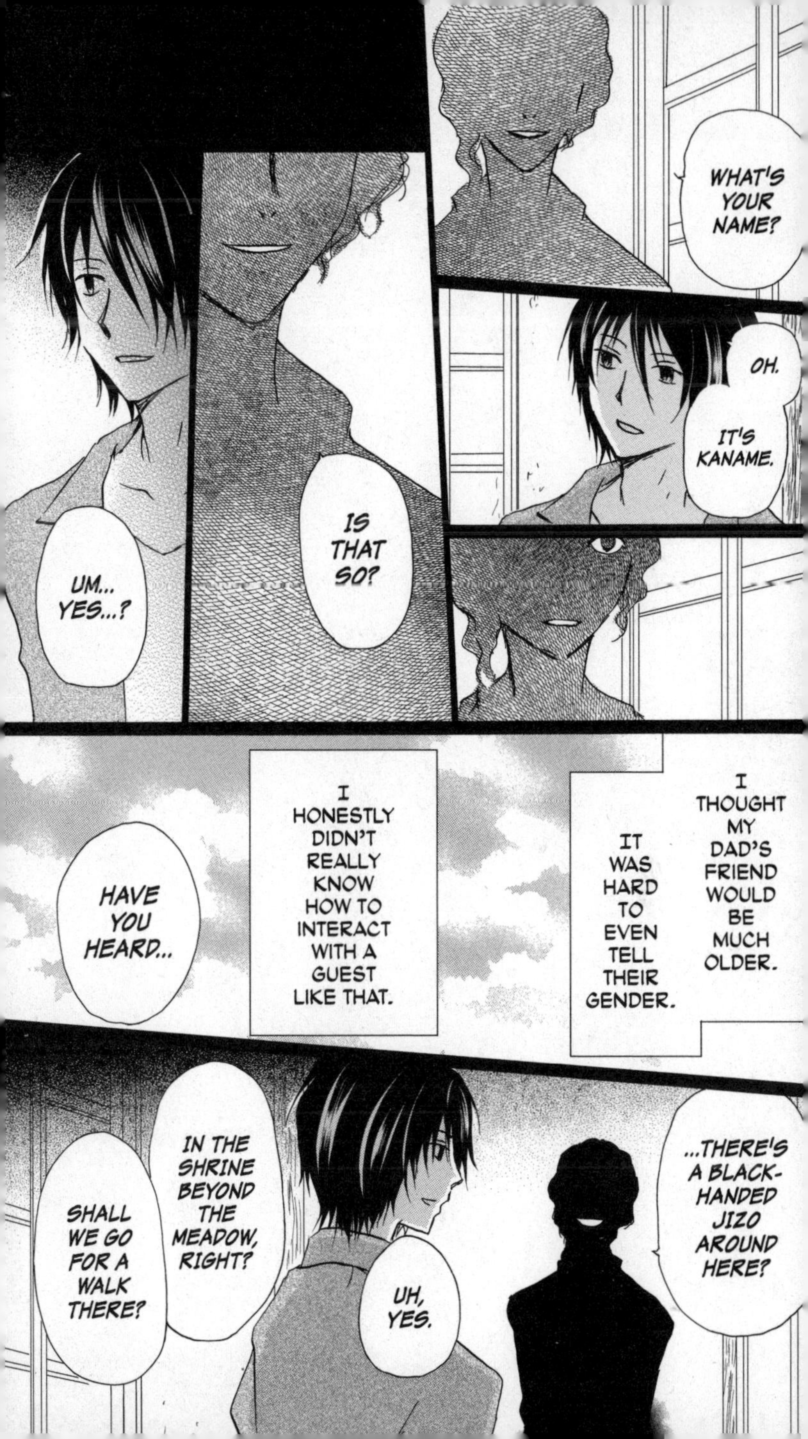
WHAT'S YOUR NAME?
OH.
IT'S KANAME.
IS THAT SO?
UM... YES...?
I THOUGHT MY DAD'S FRIEND WOULD BE MUCH OLDER.
IT WAS HARD TO EVEN TELL THEIR GENDER.
I HONESTLY DIDN'T REALLY KNOW HOW TO INTERACT WITH A GUEST LIKE THAT.
HAVE YOU HEARD...
...THERE'S A BLACK-HANDED JIZO AROUND HERE?
UH, YES.
IN THE SHRINE BEYOND THE MEADOW, RIGHT?
SHALL WE GO FOR A WALK THERE?

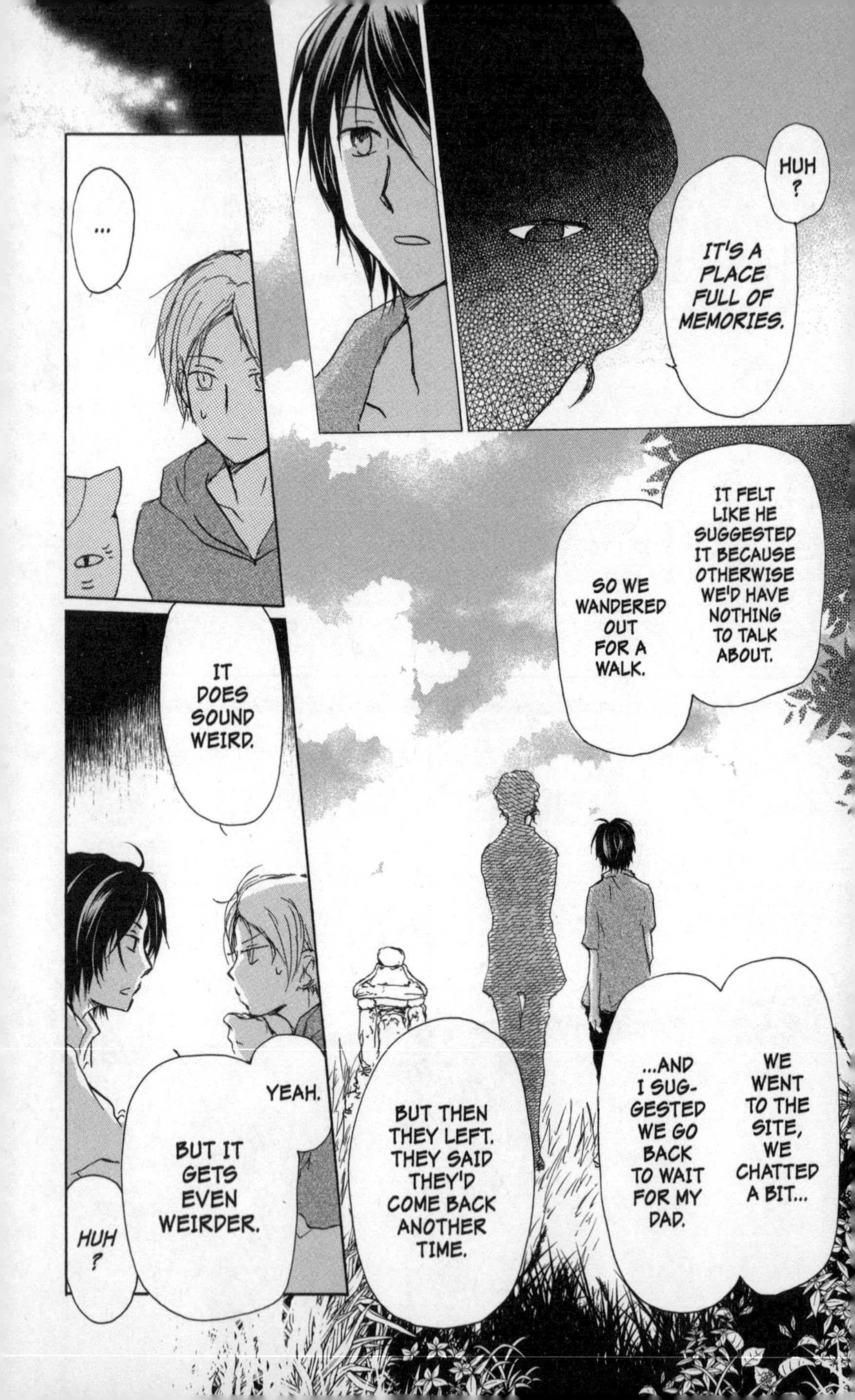
HUH?
IT'S A PLACE FULL OF MEMORIES.
...
IT FELT LIKE HE SUGGESTED IT BECAUSE OTHERWISE WE'D HAVE NOTHING TO TALK ABOUT.
SO WE WANDERED OUT FOR A WALK.
WE WENT TO THE SITE, WE CHATTED A BIT...
...AND I SUG-GESTED WE GO BACK TO WAIT FOR MY DAD.
BUT THEN THEY LEFT. THEY SAID THEY'D COME BACK ANOTHER TIME.
IT DOES SOUND WEIRD.
YEAH.
BUT IT GETS EVEN WEIRDER.
HUH?

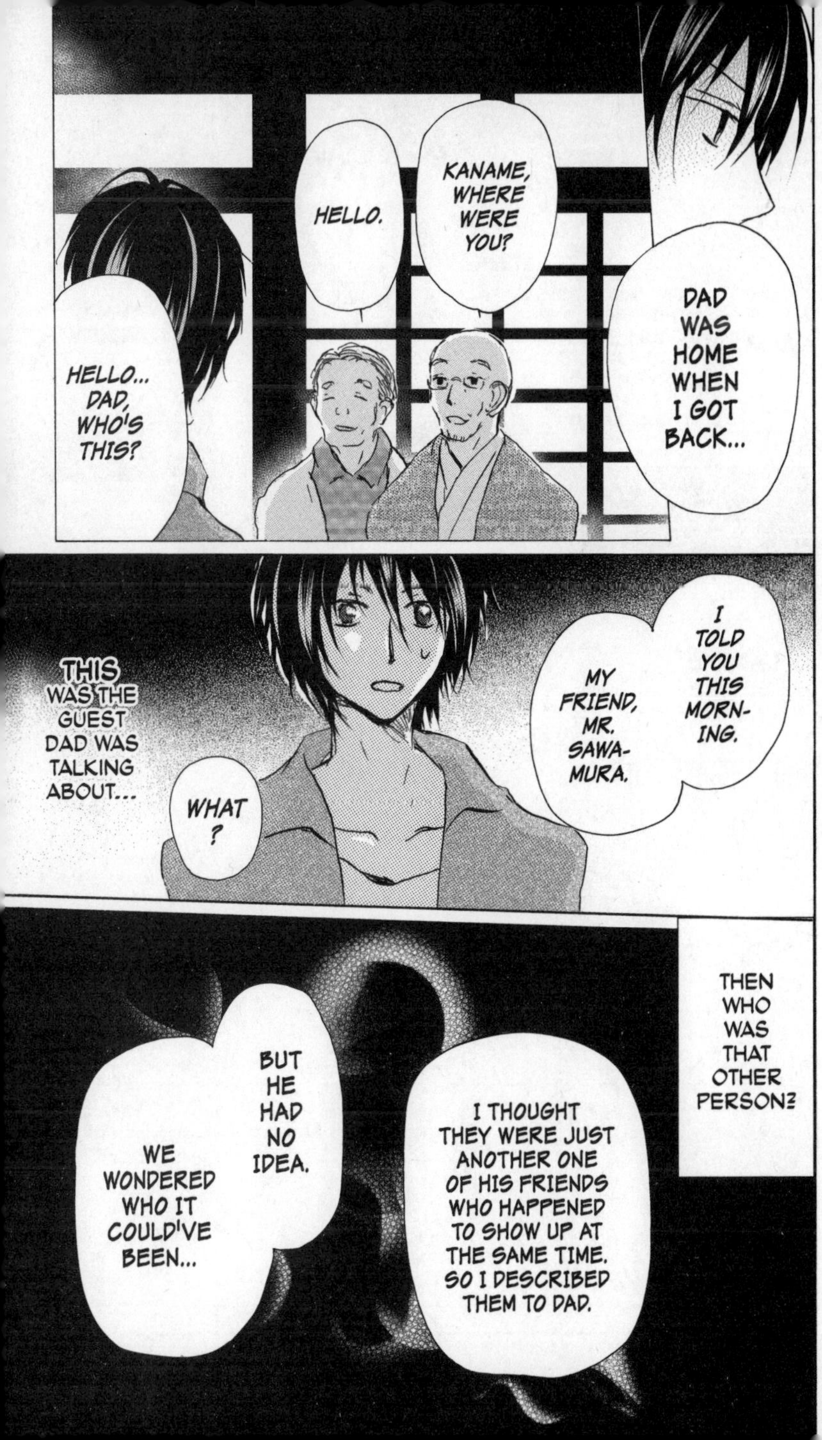
DAD WAS HOME WHEN I GOT BACK...
KANAME, WHERE WERE YOU?
HELLO.
HELLO... DAD, WHO'S THIS?
I TOLD YOU THIS MORNING.
MY FRIEND, MR. SAWAMURA.
WHAT?
THIS WAS THE GUEST DAD WAS TALKING ABOUT...
THEN WHO WAS THAT OTHER PERSON?
I THOUGHT THEY WERE JUST ANOTHER ONE OF HIS FRIENDS WHO HAPPENED TO SHOW UP AT THE SAME TIME. SO I DESCRIBED THEM TO DAD.
BUT HE HAD NO IDEA.
WE WONDERED WHO IT COULD'VE BEEN...

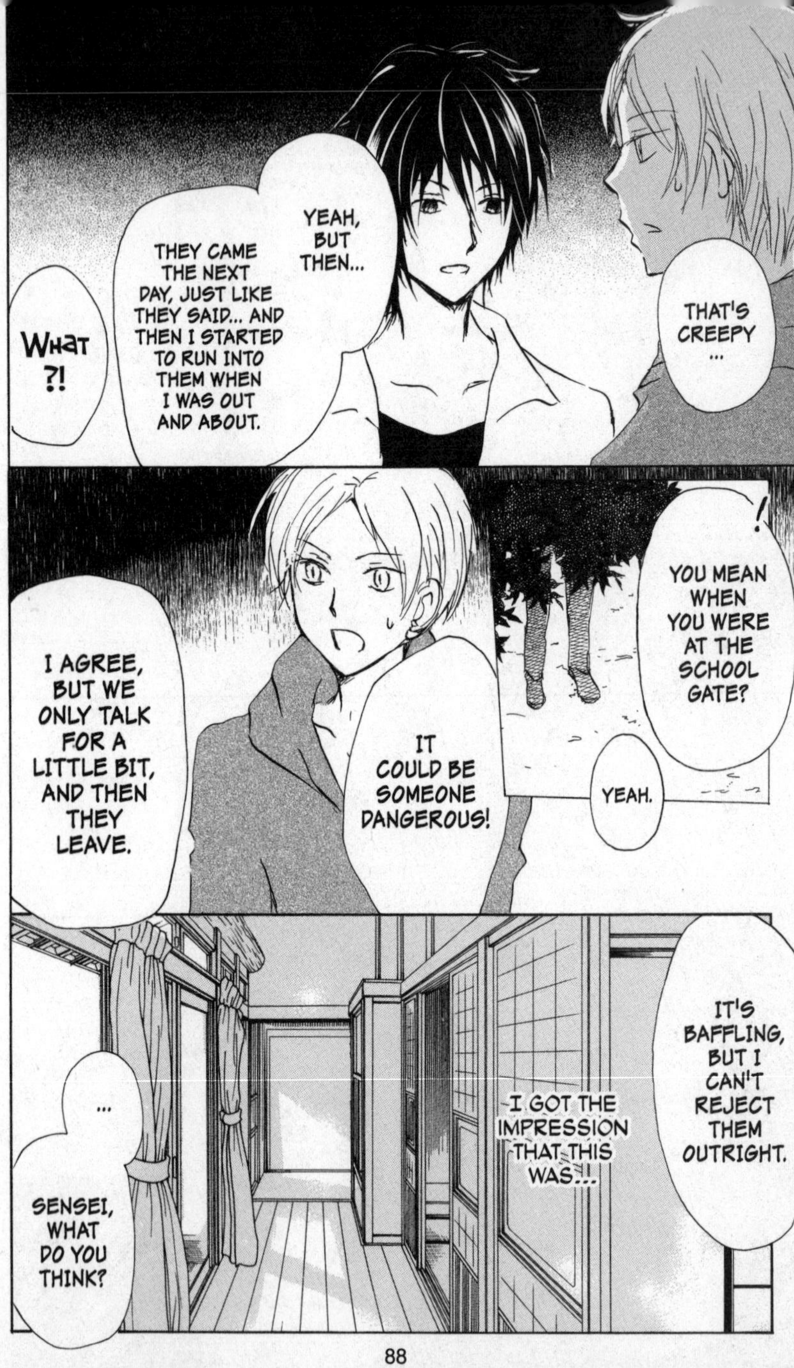
THAT'S CREEPY ...
YEAH, BUT THEN...
THEY CAME THE NEXT DAY, JUST LIKE THEY SAID... AND THEN I STARTED TO RUN INTO THEM WHEN I WAS OUT AND ABOUT.
WHAT ?!
!
YOU MEAN WHEN YOU WERE AT THE SCHOOL GATE?
YEAH.
IT COULD BE SOMEONE DANGEROUS!
I AGREE, BUT WE ONLY TALK FOR A LITTLE BIT, AND THEN THEY LEAVE.
IT'S BAFFLING, BUT I CAN'T REJECT THEM OUTRIGHT.
I GOT THE IMPRESSION THAT THIS WAS...
...
SENSEI, WHAT DO YOU THINK?

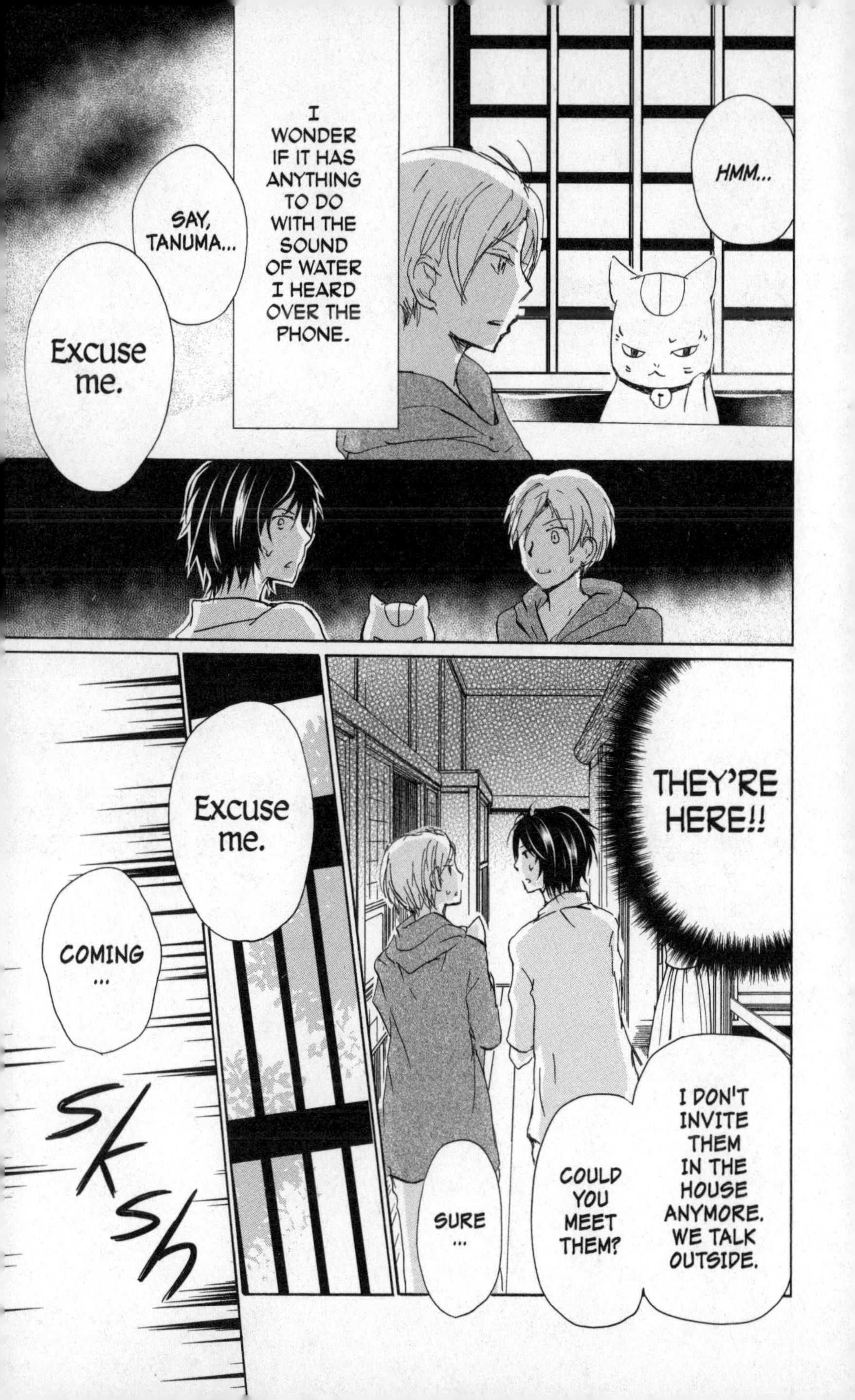
HMM...
I WONDER IF IT HAS ANYTHING TO DO WITH THE SOUND OF WATER I HEARD OVER THE PHONE.
SAY, TANUMA...
Excuse me.
THEY'RE HERE!!
I DON'T INVITE THEM IN THE HOUSE ANYMORE. WE TALK OUTSIDE.
COULD YOU MEET THEM?
SURE...
Excuse me.
COMING...
SKSH

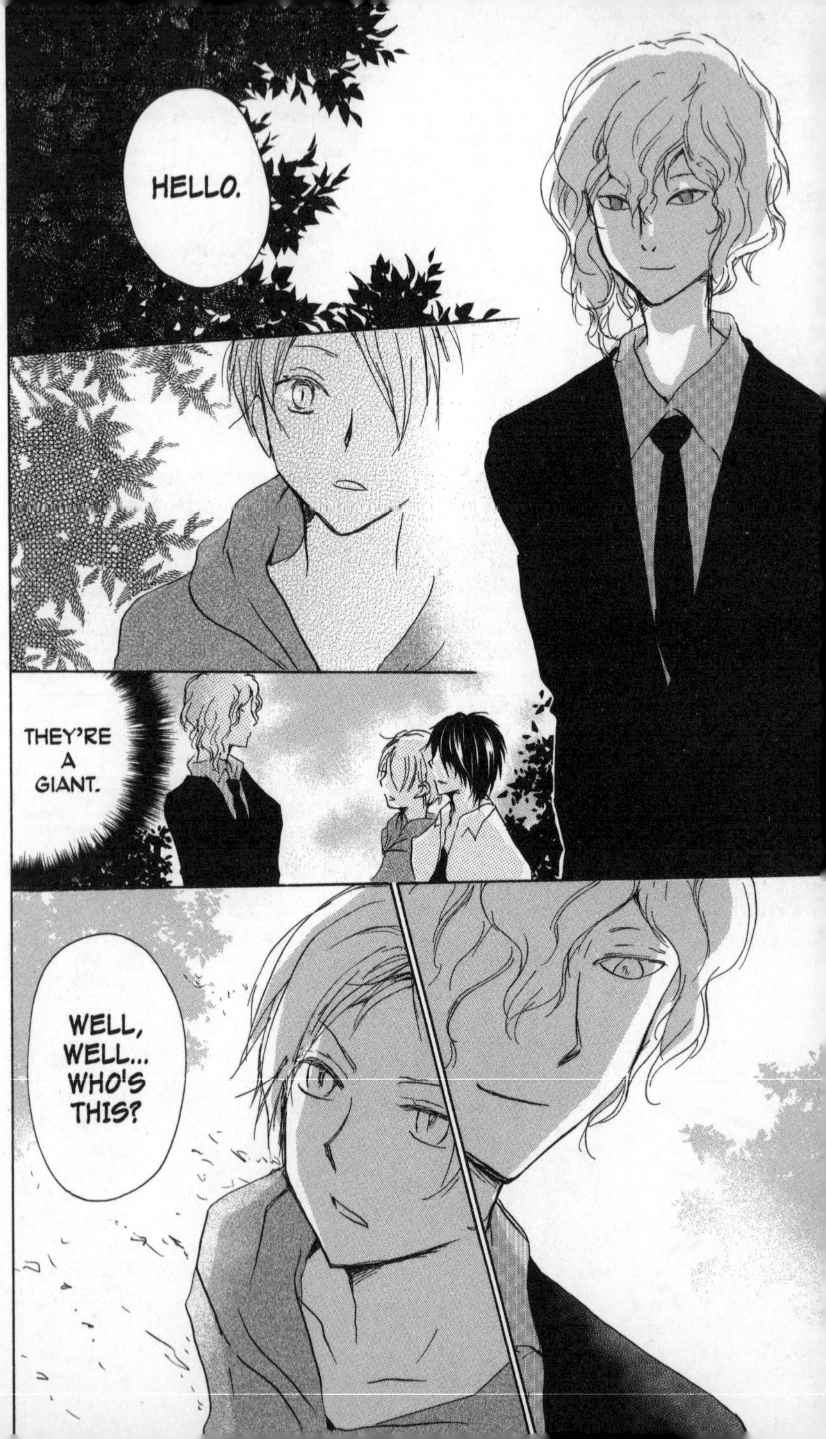
HELLO.
THEY'RE A GIANT.
WELL, WELL... WHO'S THIS?

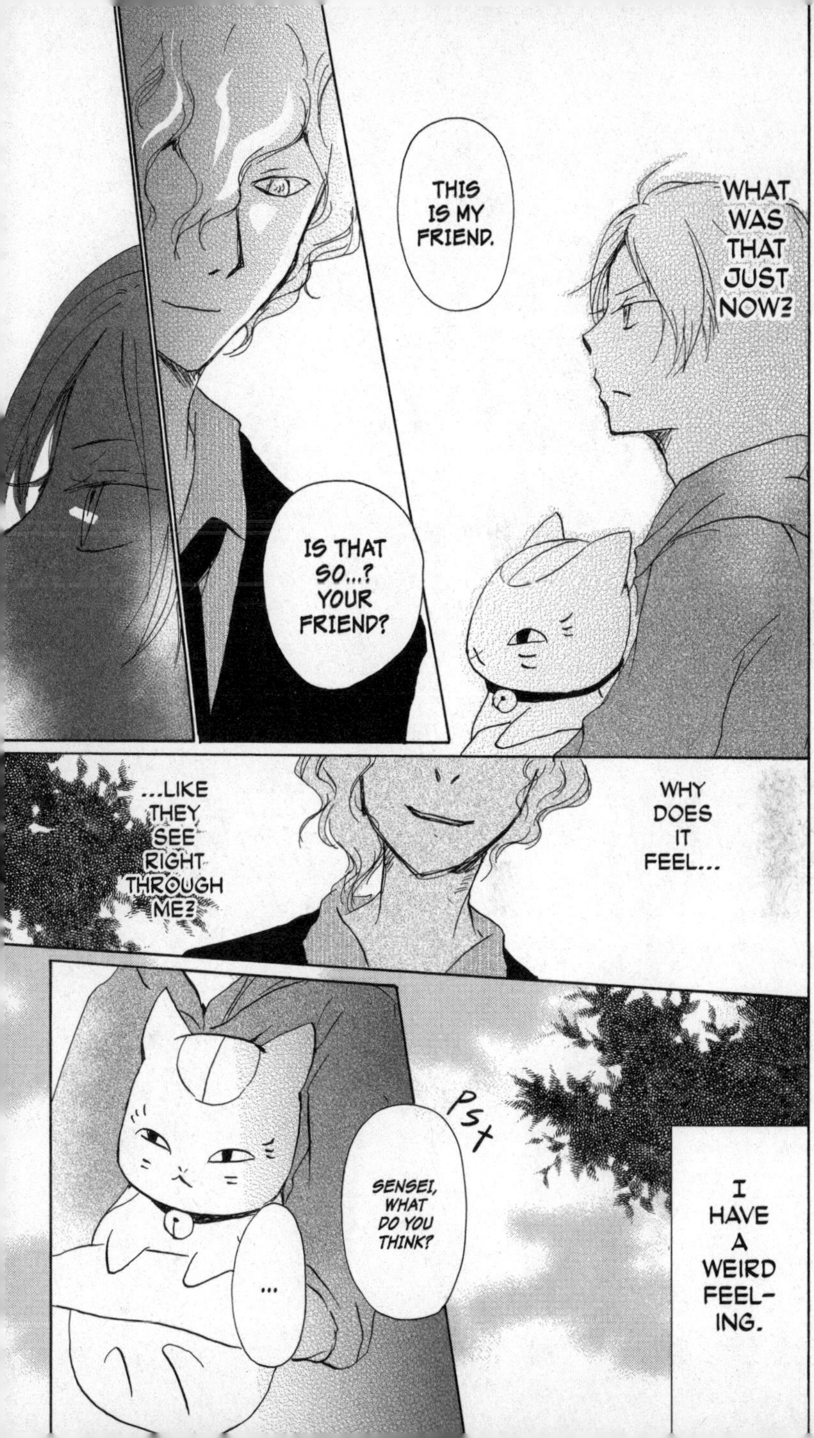
WHAT WAS THAT JUST NOW?
THIS IS MY FRIEND.
IS THAT SO...? YOUR FRIEND?
WHY DOES IT FEEL...
...LIKE THEY SEE RIGHT THROUGH ME?
I HAVE A WEIRD FEEL-ING.
Pst
SENSEI, WHAT DO YOU THINK?
...

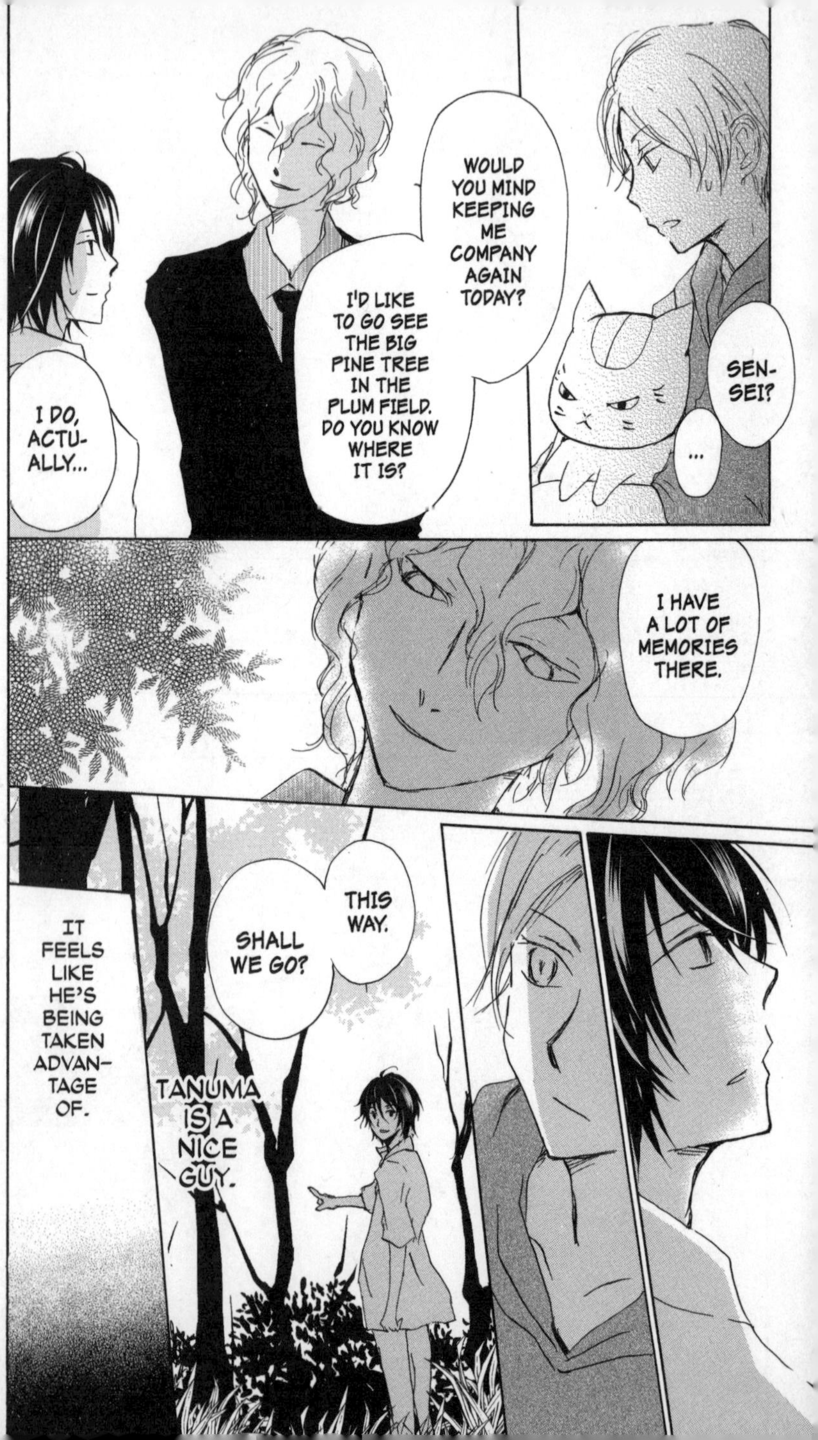

SEN-SEI?
...
WOULD YOU MIND KEEPING ME COMPANY AGAIN TODAY?
I'D LIKE TO GO SEE THE BIG PINE TREE IN THE PLUM FIELD. DO YOU KNOW WHERE IT IS?
I DO, ACTU-ALLY...
I HAVE A LOT OF MEMORIES THERE.
THIS WAY.
SHALL WE GO?
TANUMA IS A NICE GUY.
IT FEELS LIKE HE'S BEING TAKEN ADVAN-TAGE OF.

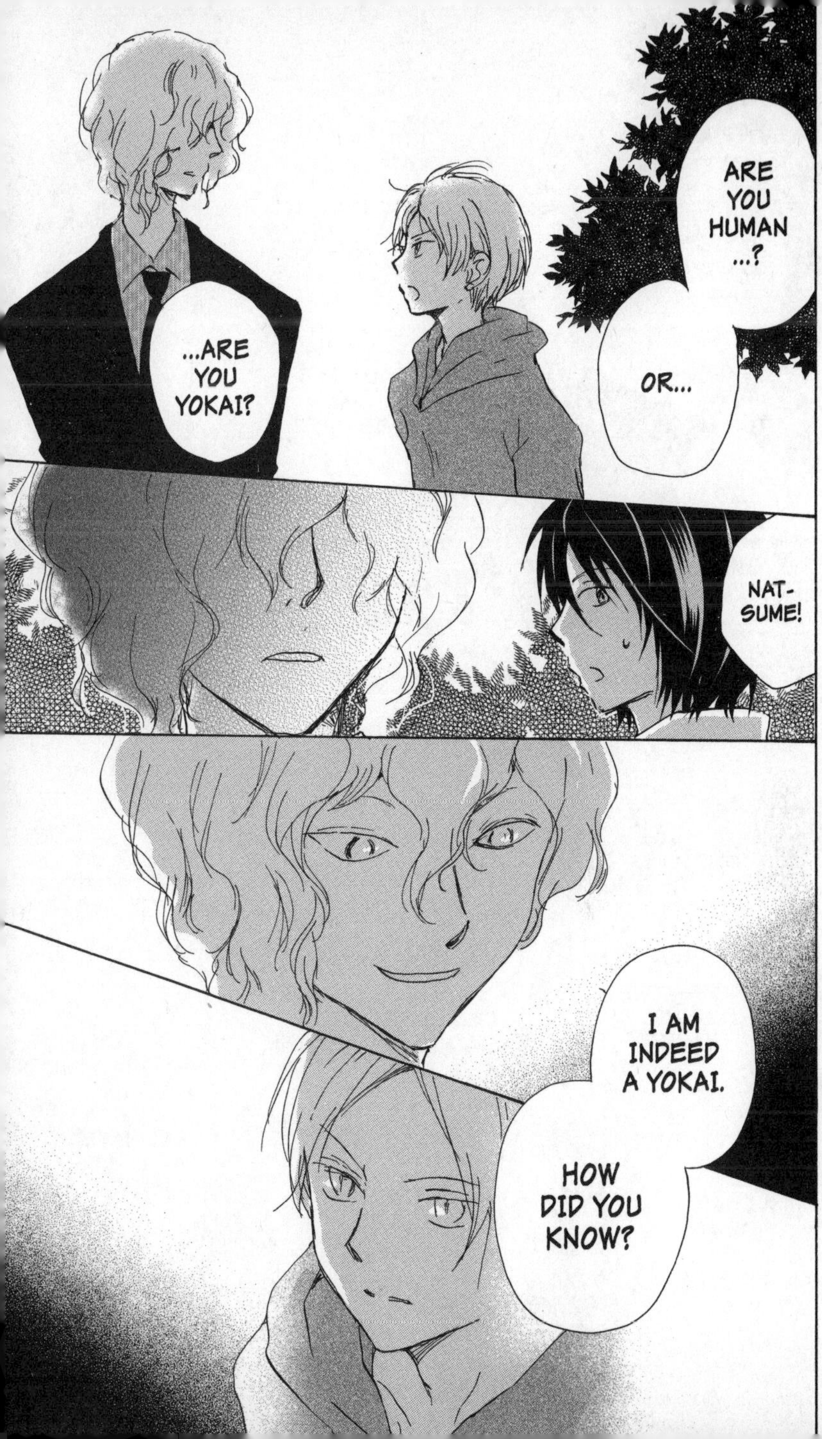
ARE YOU HUMAN ...?
OR...
...ARE YOU YOKAI?
NAT-SUME!
I AM INDEED A YOKAI.
HOW DID YOU KNOW?

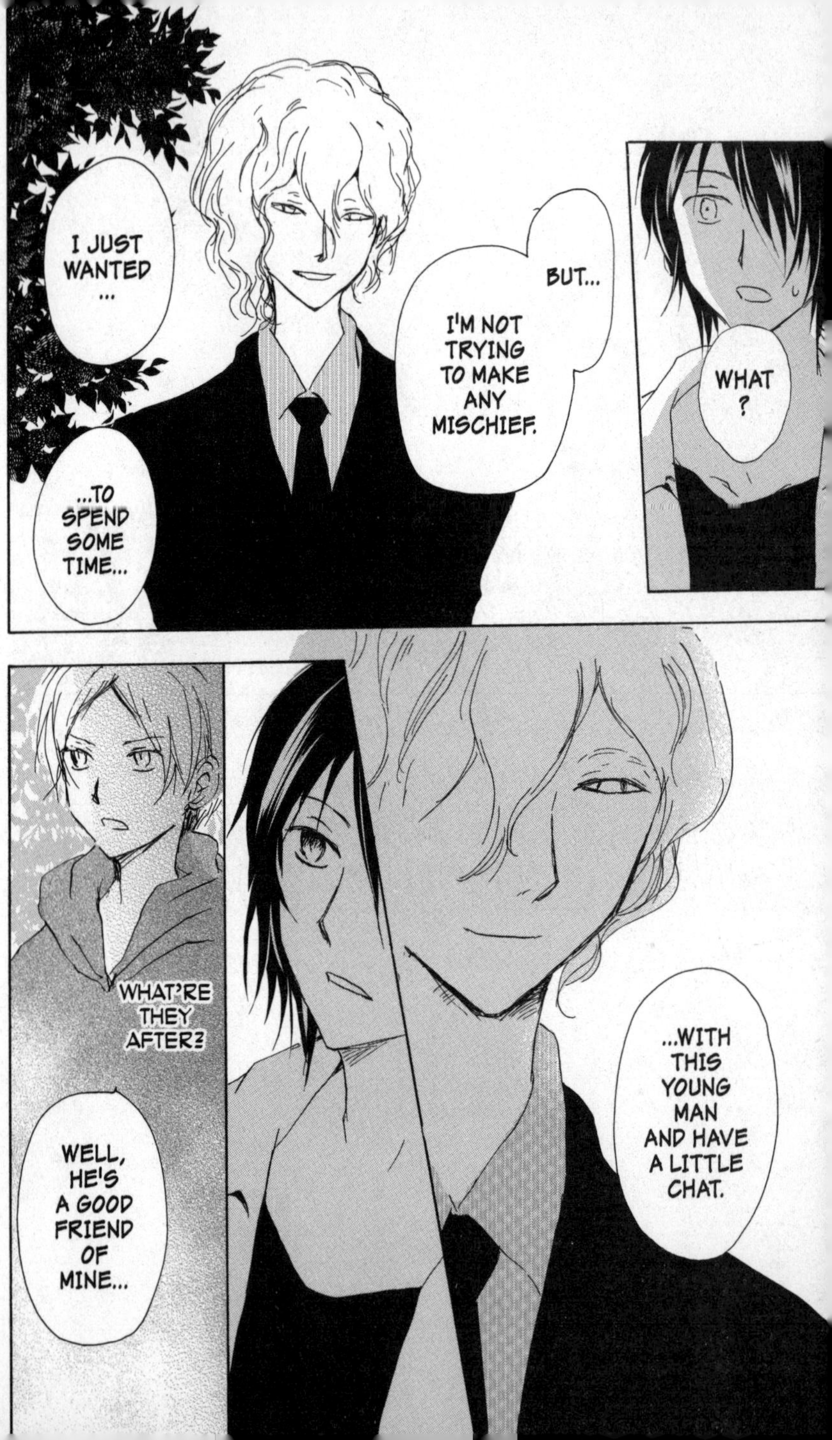
WHAT?
BUT... I'M NOT TRYING TO MAKE ANY MISCHIEF.
I JUST WANTED ...
...TO SPEND SOME TIME...
...WITH THIS YOUNG MAN AND HAVE A LITTLE CHAT.
WHAT'RE THEY AFTER?
WELL, HE'S A GOOD FRIEND OF MINE...

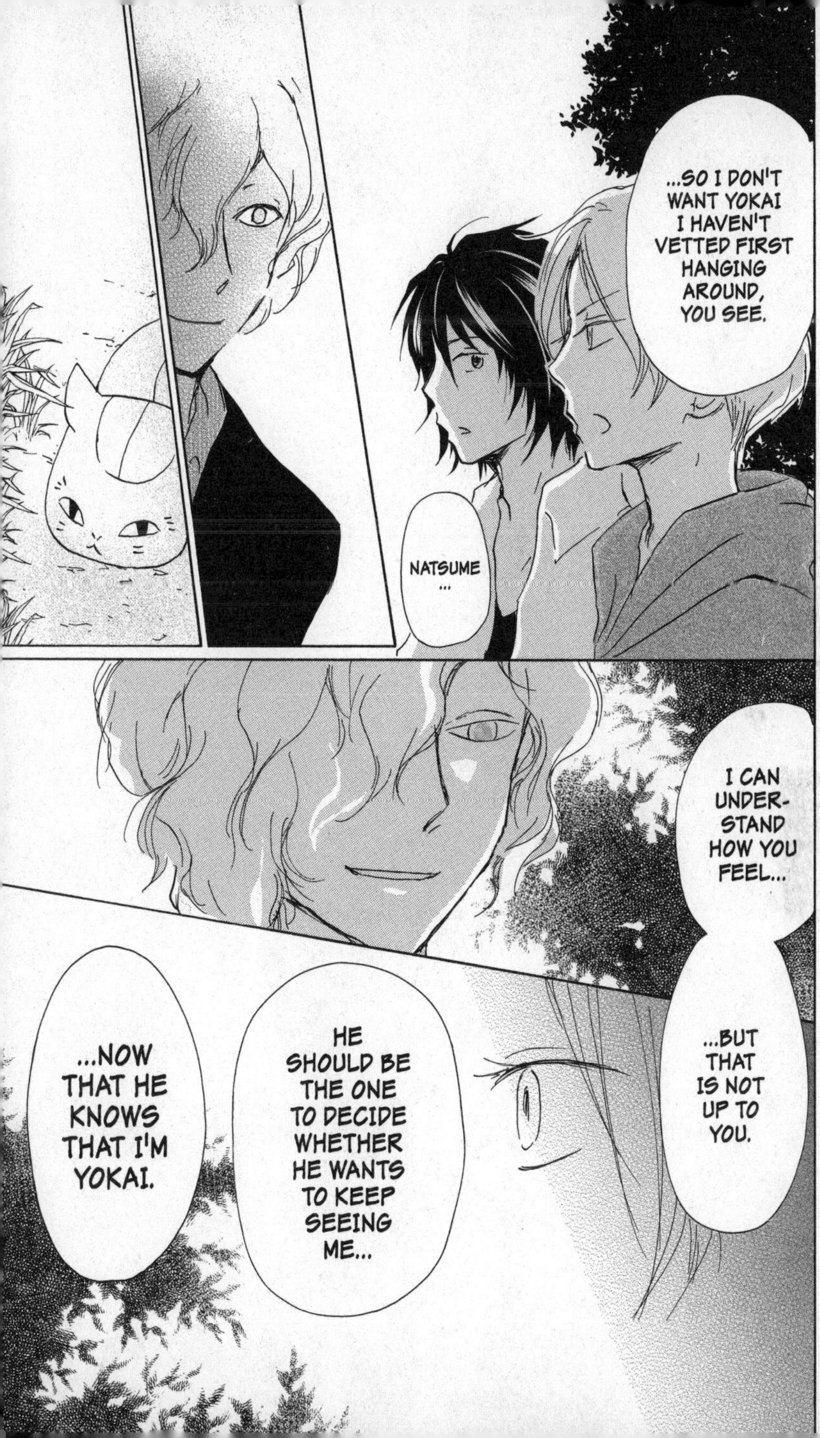
...SO I DON'T WANT YOKAI I HAVEN'T VETTED FIRST HANGING AROUND, YOU SEE.
NATSUME...
I CAN UNDER-STAND HOW YOU FEEL...
...BUT THAT IS NOT UP TO YOU.
HE SHOULD BE THE ONE TO DECIDE WHETHER HE WANTS TO KEEP SEEING ME...
...NOW THAT HE KNOWS THAT I'M YOKAI.

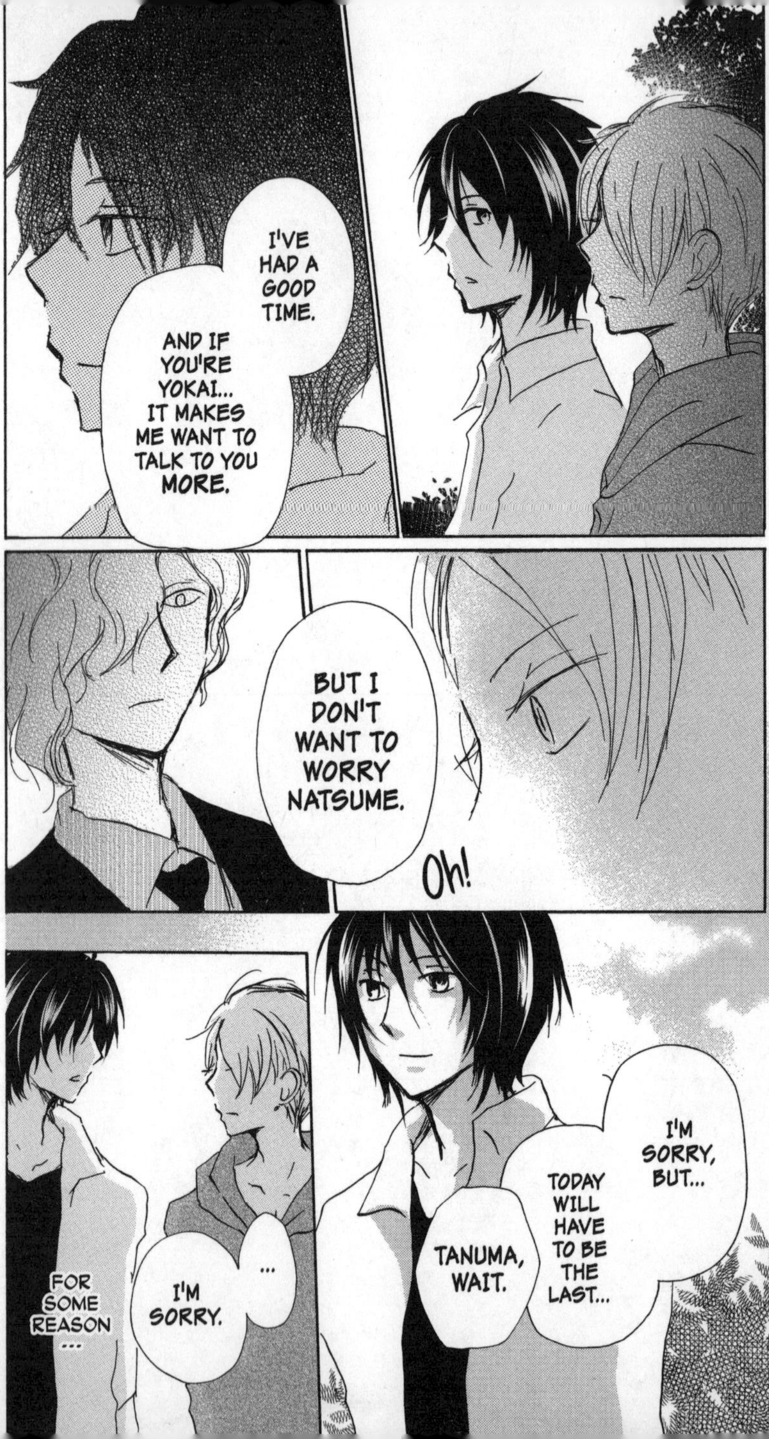
I'VE HAD A GOOD TIME.
AND IF YOU'RE YOKAI... IT MAKES ME WANT TO TALK TO YOU MORE.
BUT I DON'T WANT TO WORRY NATSUME.
Oh!
I'M SORRY, BUT...
TODAY WILL HAVE TO BE THE LAST...
TANUMA, WAIT.
...
I'M SORRY.
FOR SOME REASON ...

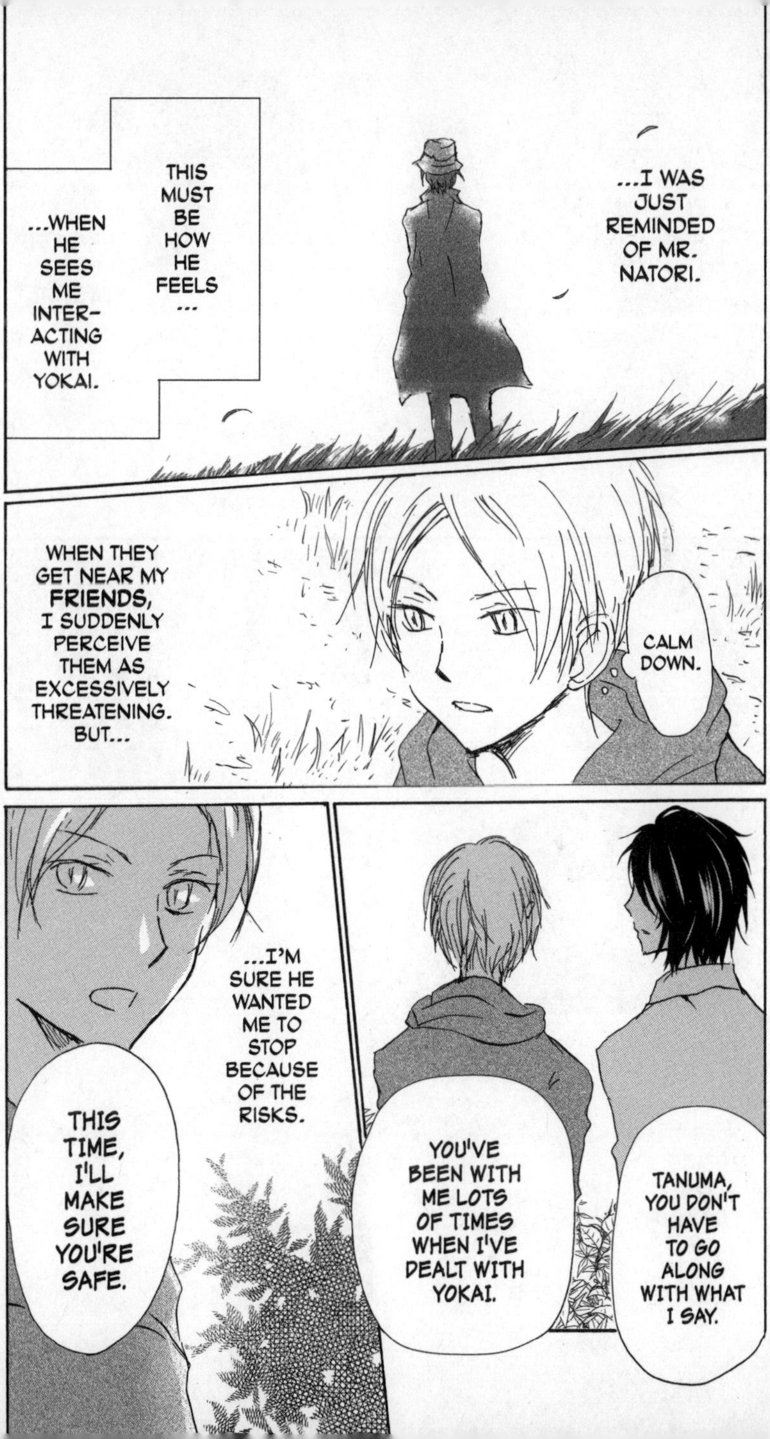
...I WAS JUST REMINDED OF MR. NATORI.
THIS MUST BE HOW HE FEELS...
...WHEN HE SEES ME INTERACTING WITH YOKAI.
CALM DOWN.
WHEN THEY GET NEAR MY **FRIENDS**, I SUDDENLY PERCEIVE THEM AS EXCESSIVELY THREATENING. BUT...
TANUMA, YOU DON'T HAVE TO GO ALONG WITH WHAT I SAY.
YOU'VE BEEN WITH ME LOTS OF TIMES WHEN I'VE DEALT WITH YOKAI.
...I'M SURE HE WANTED ME TO STOP BECAUSE OF THE RISKS.
THIS TIME, I'LL MAKE SURE YOU'RE SAFE.

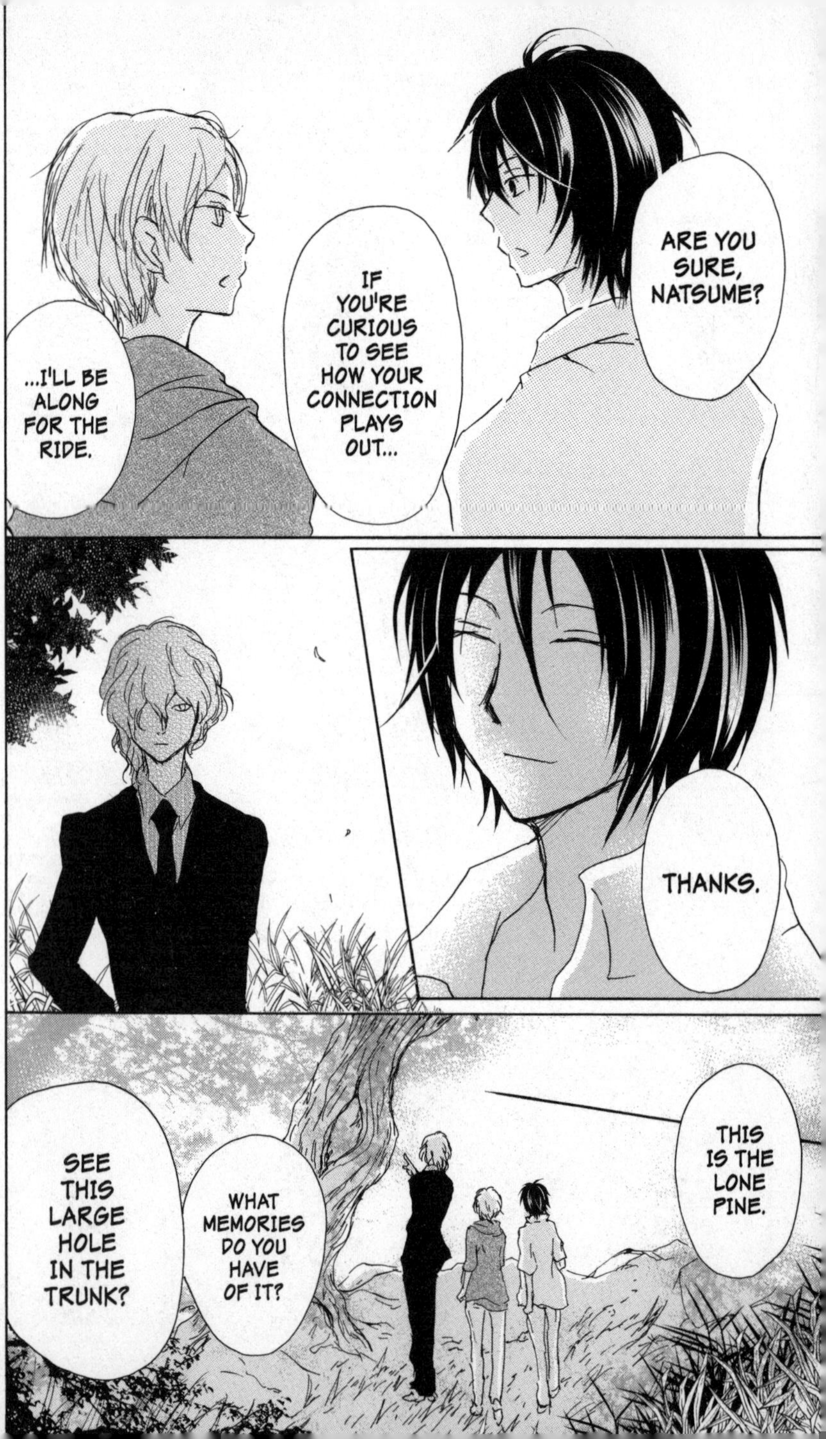
ARE YOU SURE, NATSUME?
IF YOU'RE CURIOUS TO SEE HOW YOUR CONNECTION PLAYS OUT...
...I'LL BE ALONG FOR THE RIDE.
THANKS.
THIS IS THE LONE PINE.
WHAT MEMORIES DO YOU HAVE OF IT?
SEE THIS LARGE HOLE IN THE TRUNK?

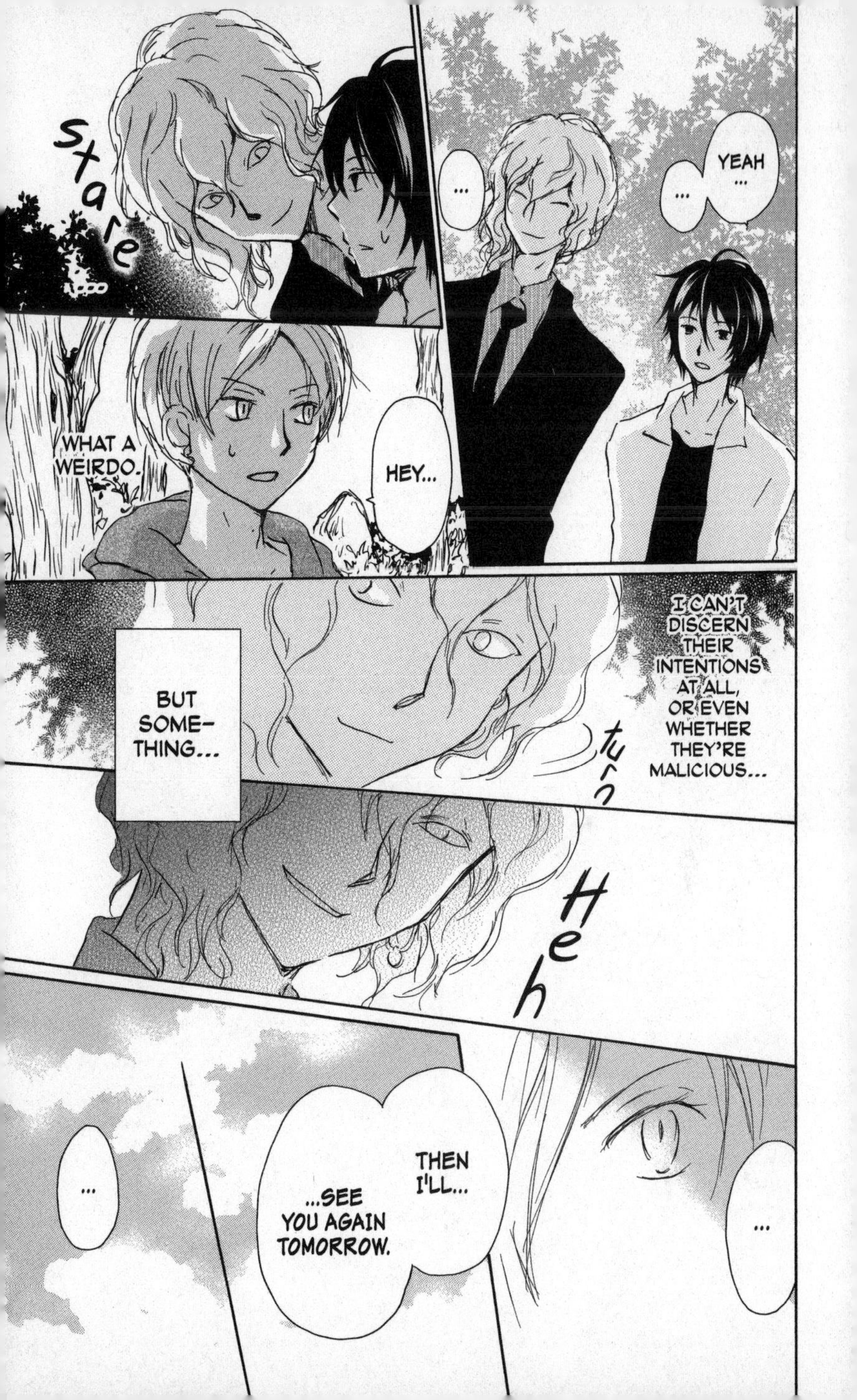
YEAH ...
...
...
stare...
HEY...
WHAT A WEIRDO.
I CAN'T DISCERN THEIR INTENTIONS AT ALL, OR EVEN WHETHER THEY'RE MALICIOUS...
turn
BUT SOME-THING...
Heh
...
THEN I'LL...
...SEE YOU AGAIN TOMORROW.
...

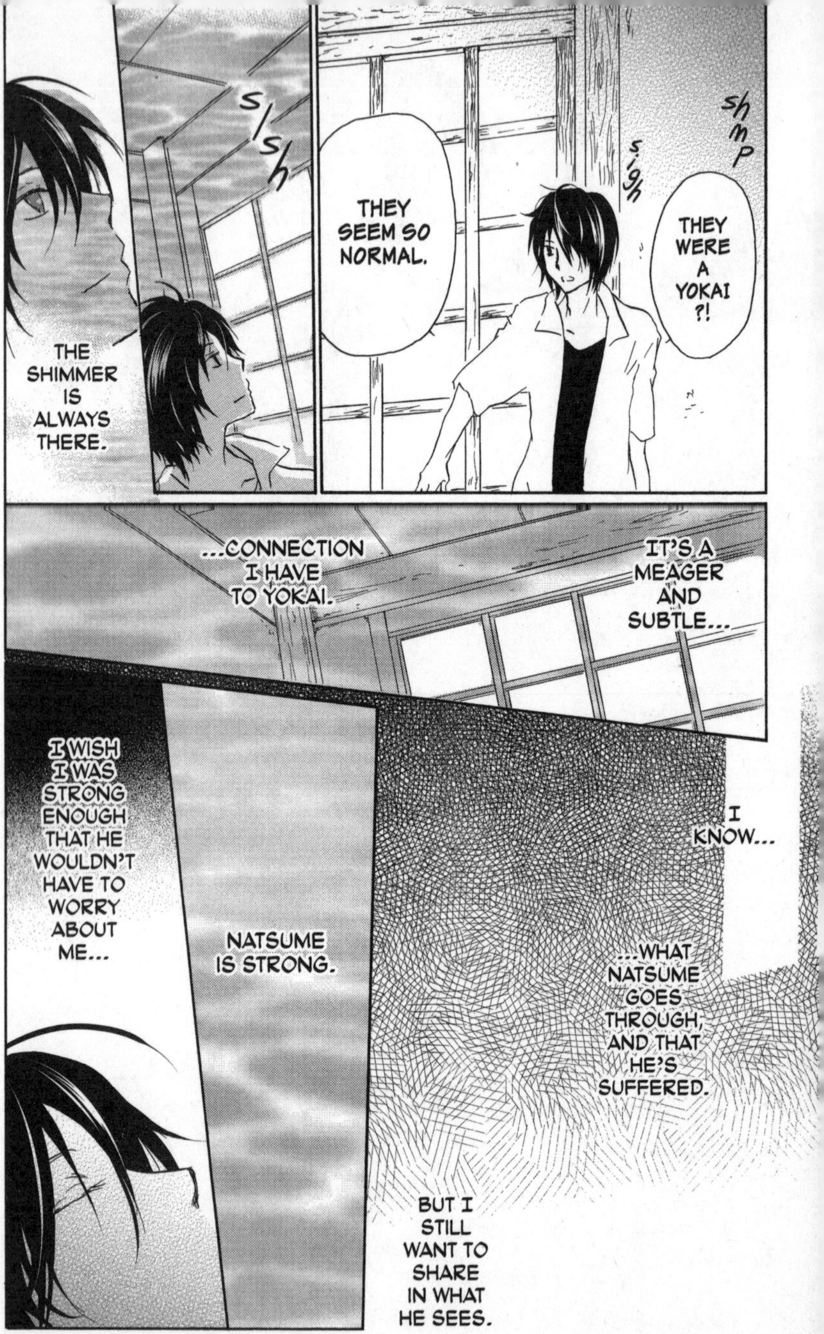
shmp
sigh
THEY WERE A YOKAI ?!
THEY SEEM SO NORMAL.
sish
THE SHIMMER IS ALWAYS THERE.
IT'S A MEAGER AND SUBTLE...
...CONNECTION I HAVE TO YOKAI.
I KNOW...
...WHAT NATSUME GOES THROUGH, AND THAT HE'S SUFFERED.
NATSUME IS STRONG.
I WISH I WAS STRONG ENOUGH THAT HE WOULDN'T HAVE TO WORRY ABOUT ME...
BUT I STILL WANT TO SHARE IN WHAT HE SEES.

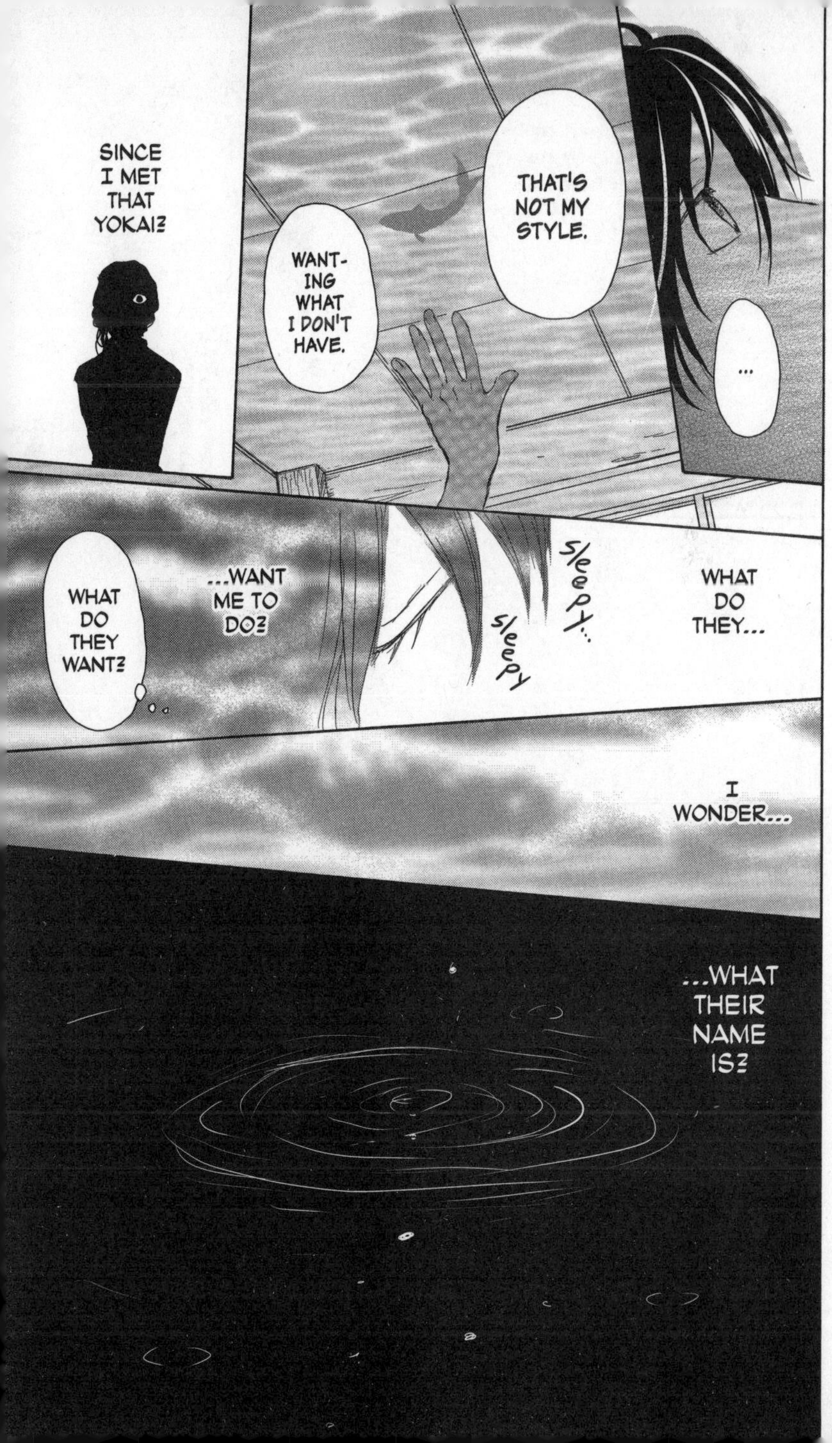

...
THAT'S NOT MY STYLE.
WANT-ING WHAT I DON'T HAVE.
SINCE I MET THAT YOKAI?
WHAT DO THEY...
sleepy... sleepy
...WANT ME TO DO?
WHAT DO THEY WANT?
I WONDER...
...WHAT THEIR NAME IS?

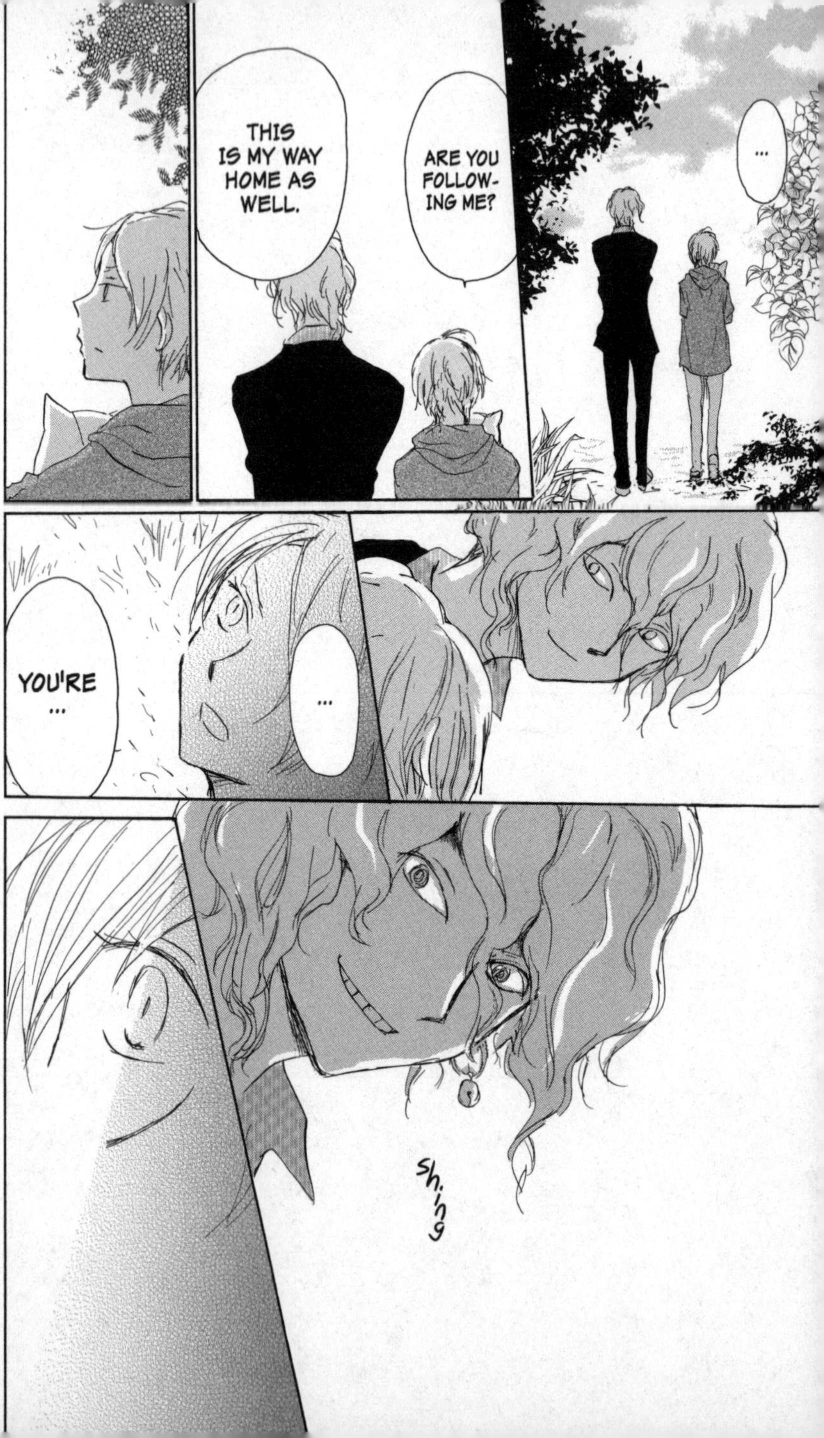
...
ARE YOU FOLLOW-ING ME?
THIS IS MY WAY HOME AS WELL.
...
YOU'RE ...
shing

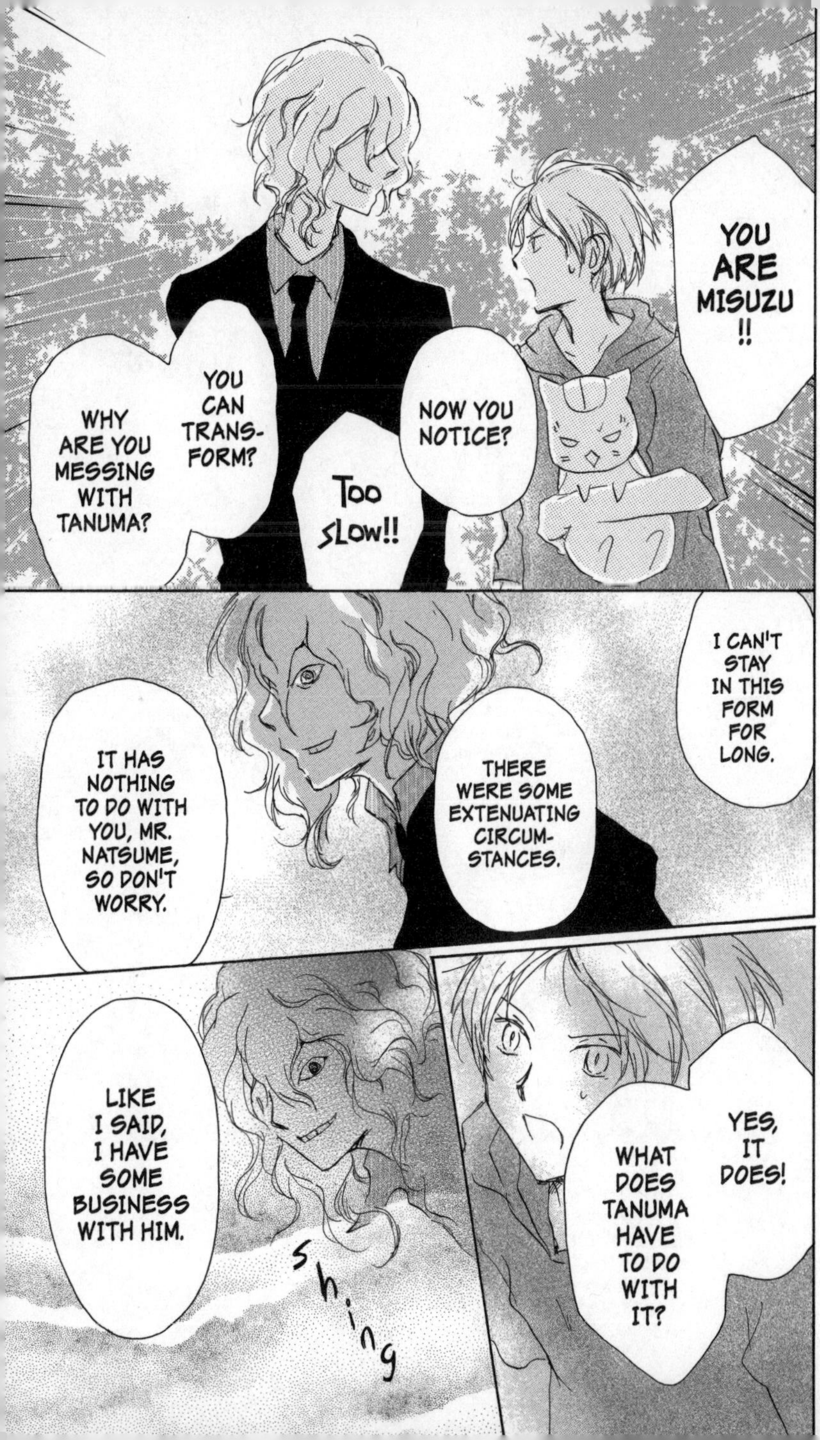
YOU ARE MISUZU!!
NOW YOU NOTICE?
TOO SLOW!!
YOU CAN TRANSFORM?
WHY ARE YOU MESSING WITH TANUMA?
I CAN'T STAY IN THIS FORM FOR LONG.
THERE WERE SOME EXTENUATING CIRCUMSTANCES.
IT HAS NOTHING TO DO WITH YOU, MR. NATSUME, SO DON'T WORRY.
YES, IT DOES!
WHAT DOES TANUMA HAVE TO DO WITH IT?
LIKE I SAID, I HAVE SOME BUSINESS WITH HIM.
shing

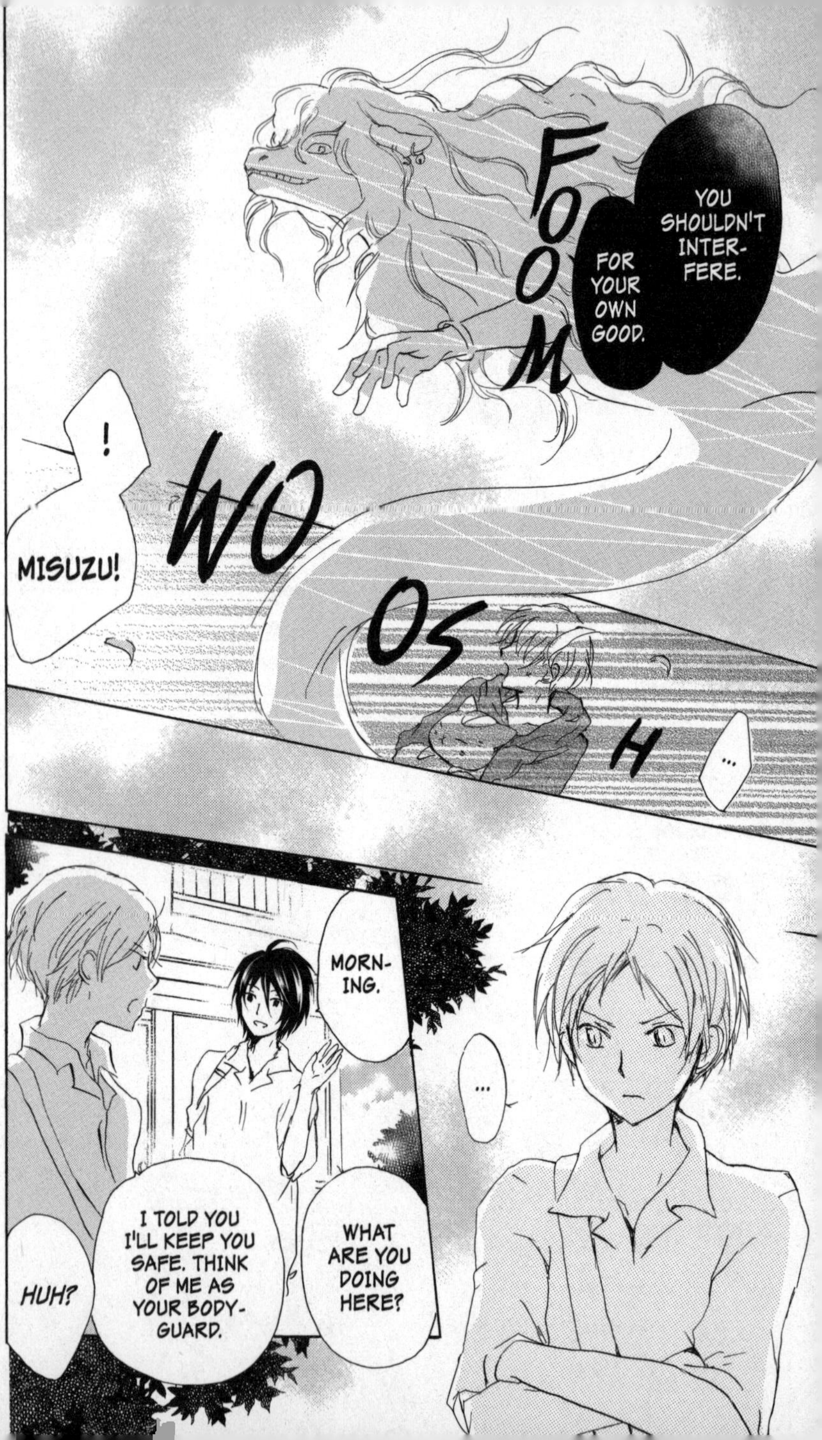
FOOM
YOU SHOULDN'T INTER-FERE.
FOR YOUR OWN GOOD.
!
MISUZU!
WOOSH
...
...
MORN-ING.
WHAT ARE YOU DOING HERE?
I TOLD YOU I'LL KEEP YOU SAFE. THINK OF ME AS YOUR BODY-GUARD.
HUH?

03

✻ Anime movie, part 1

During its theatrical run, my sister looked up the showtimes and took me to theaters in Kumamoto and Fukuoka prefectures whenever I had a chance to go. I was thrilled that some places put up pop-up exhibits or sold merchandise, because of the local connection. The audience was truly diverse in age and gender.
I couldn't wait to report on all this to everyone who worked on the anime. I wanted to thank all the theater staff for their preparations, and for handing out flyers and pamphlets. And thank you to everyone who turned out. It would make me happy if one day you remember a theater as the one you watched the Natsume movie in.

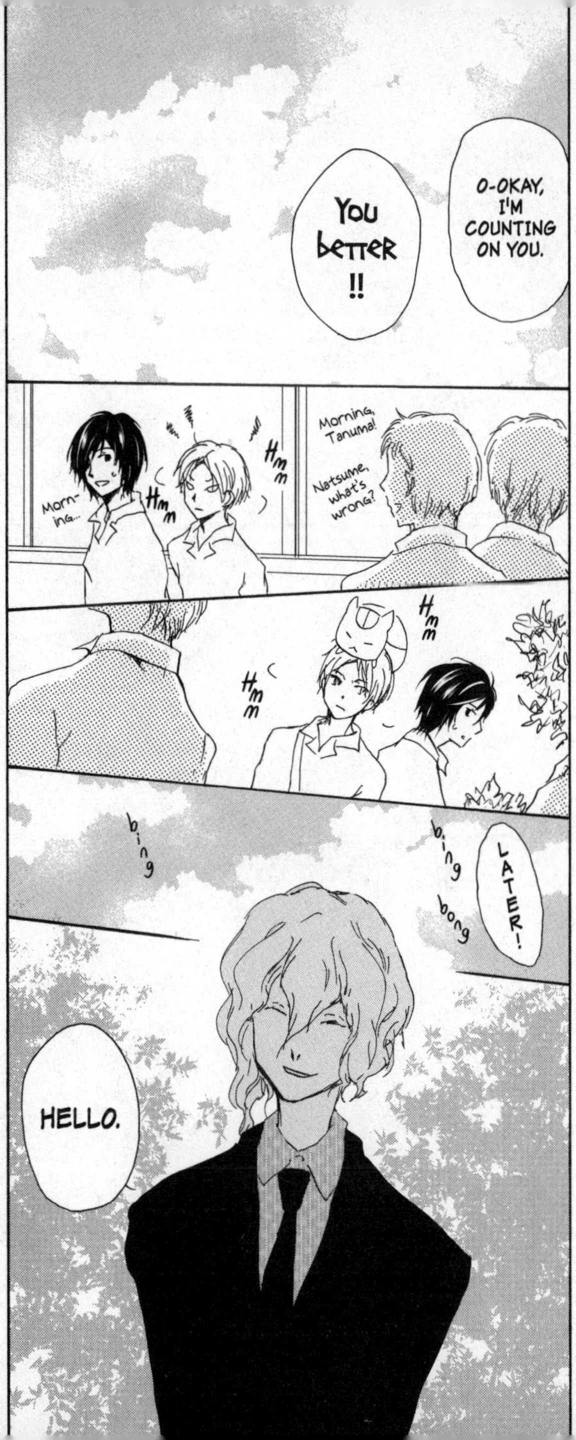
O-OKAY, I'M COUNTING ON YOU.
You better!!
Morning, Tanuma!
Natsume, what's wrong?
Hmm
Hmm
Morning...
Hmm
Hmm
LATER!
bing bong
bing
HELLO.

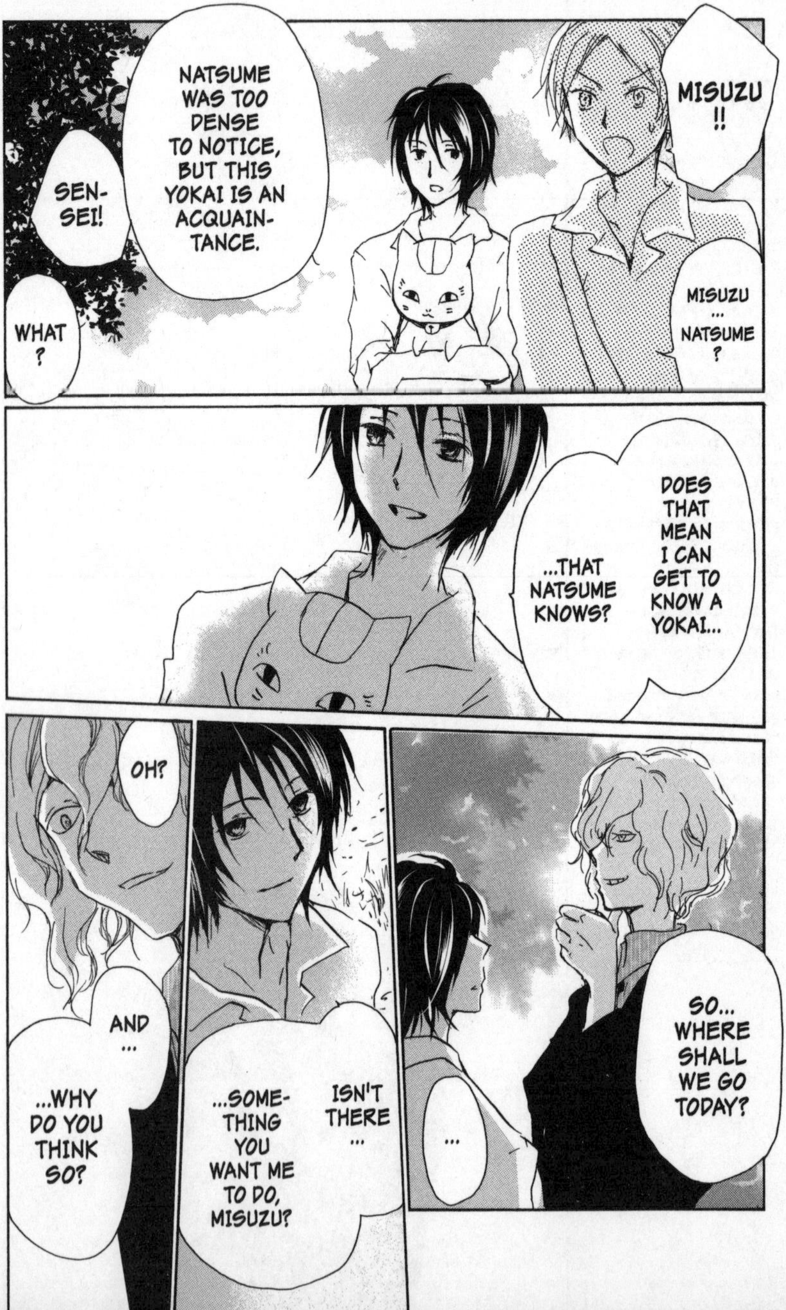
MISUZU !!
MISUZU ... NATSUME ?
NATSUME WAS TOO DENSE TO NOTICE, BUT THIS YOKAI IS AN ACQUAIN-TANCE.
SEN-SEI!
WHAT ?
DOES THAT MEAN I CAN GET TO KNOW A YOKAI...
...THAT NATSUME KNOWS?
SO... WHERE SHALL WE GO TODAY?
...
ISN'T THERE ...
...SOME-THING YOU WANT ME TO DO, MISUZU?
OH?
AND ...
...WHY DO YOU THINK SO?

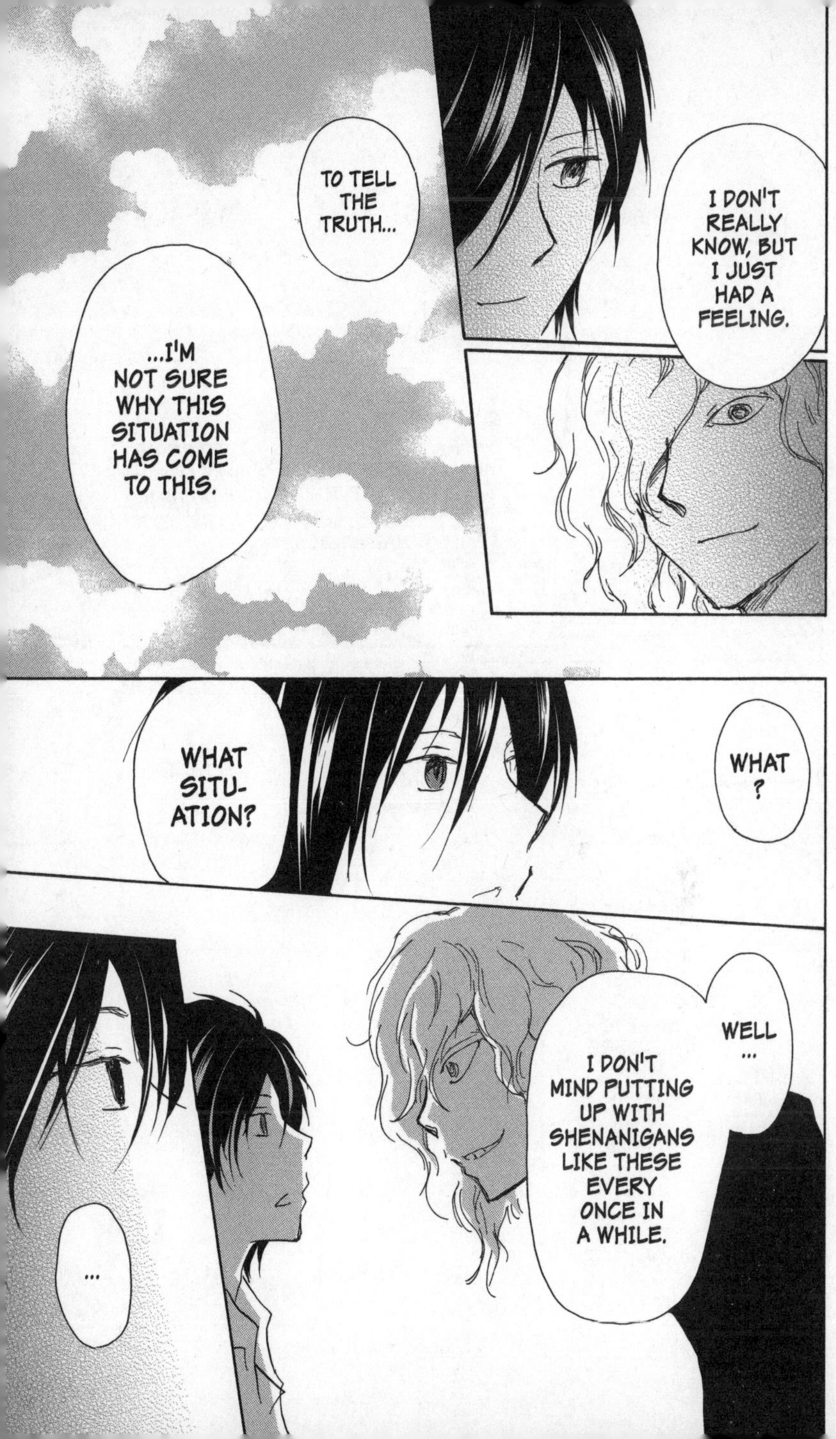
TO TELL THE TRUTH...
I DON'T REALLY KNOW, BUT I JUST HAD A FEELING.
...I'M NOT SURE WHY THIS SITUATION HAS COME TO THIS.
WHAT?
WHAT SITU-ATION?
WELL...
I DON'T MIND PUTTING UP WITH SHENANIGANS LIKE THESE EVERY ONCE IN A WHILE.
...

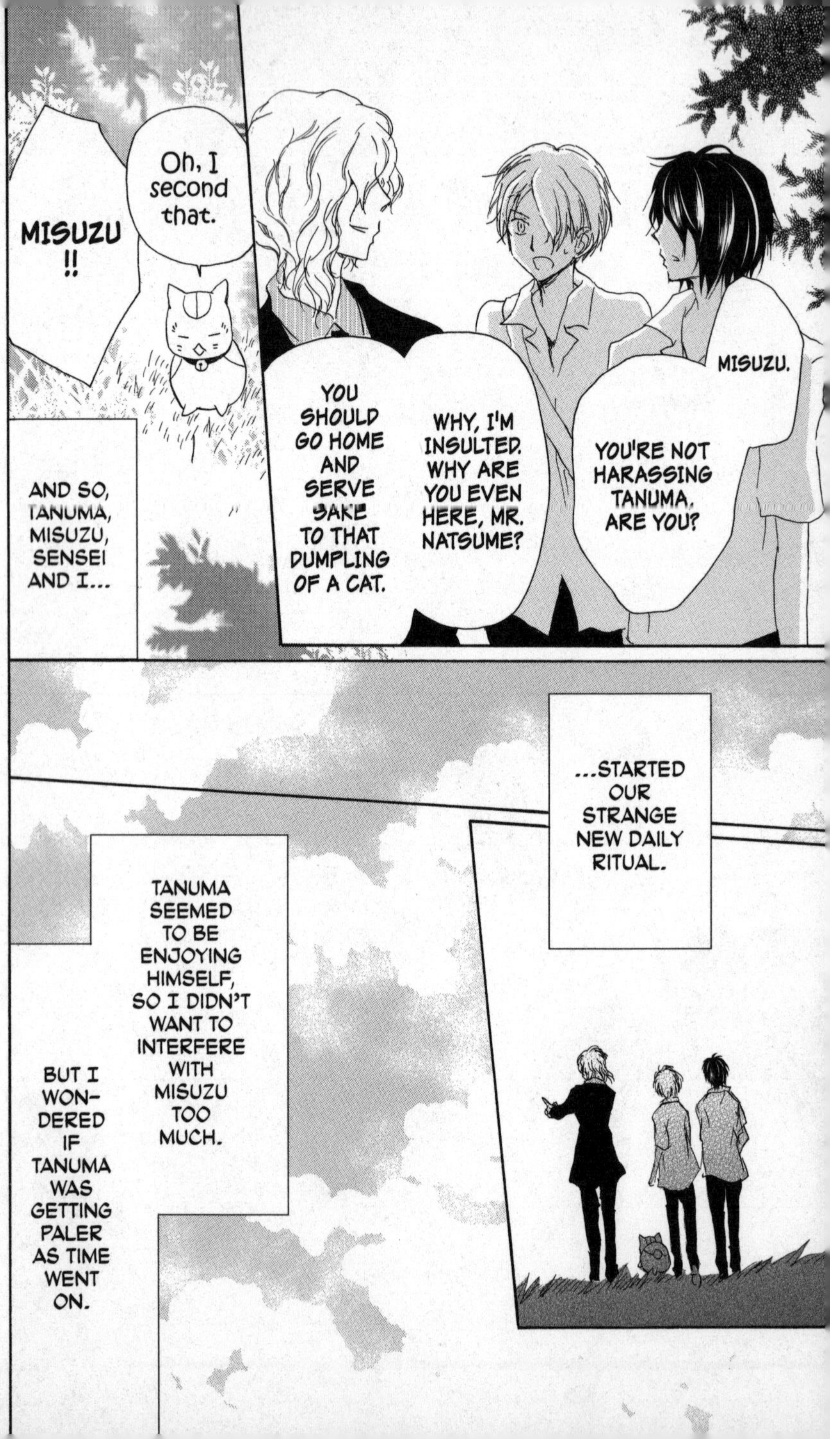
MISUZU.
YOU'RE NOT HARASSING TANUMA, ARE YOU?
WHY, I'M INSULTED. WHY ARE YOU EVEN HERE, MR. NATSUME?
YOU SHOULD GO HOME AND SERVE SAKE TO THAT DUMPLING OF A CAT.
Oh, I second that.
MISUZU!!
AND SO, TANUMA, MISUZU, SENSEI AND I...
...STARTED OUR STRANGE NEW DAILY RITUAL.
TANUMA SEEMED TO BE ENJOYING HIMSELF, SO I DIDN'T WANT TO INTERFERE WITH MISUZU TOO MUCH.
BUT I WONDERED IF TANUMA WAS GETTING PALER AS TIME WENT ON.

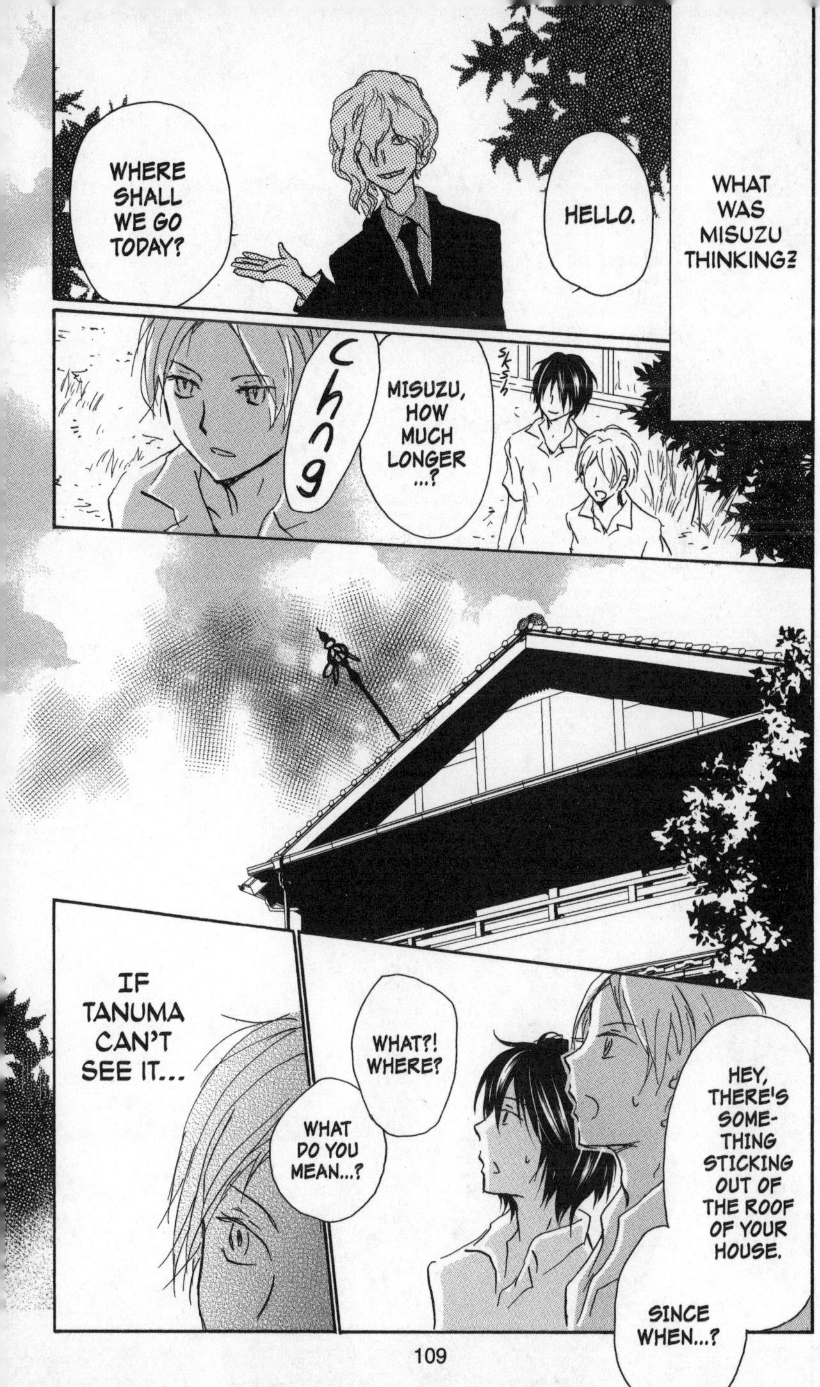
WHAT WAS MISUZU THINKING?
HELLO.
WHERE SHALL WE GO TODAY?
MISUZU, HOW MUCH LONGER ...?
chng
sksh
HEY, THERE'S SOME-THING STICKING OUT OF THE ROOF OF YOUR HOUSE.
WHAT?! WHERE?
SINCE WHEN...?
WHAT DO YOU MEAN...?
IF TANUMA CAN'T SEE IT...

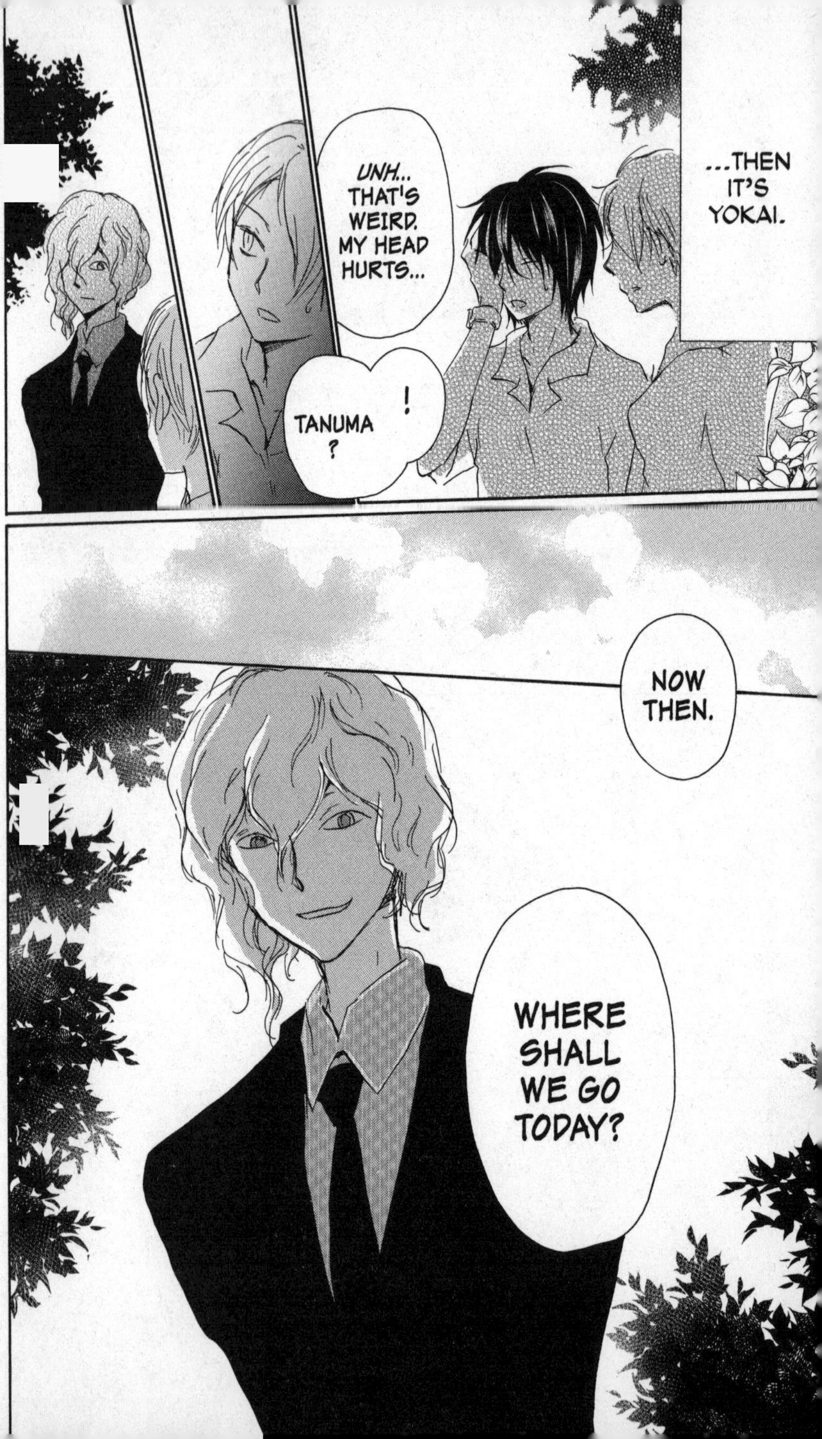
...THEN IT'S YOKAI.
UNH... THAT'S WEIRD. MY HEAD HURTS...
TANUMA?!
NOW THEN.
WHERE SHALL WE GO TODAY?

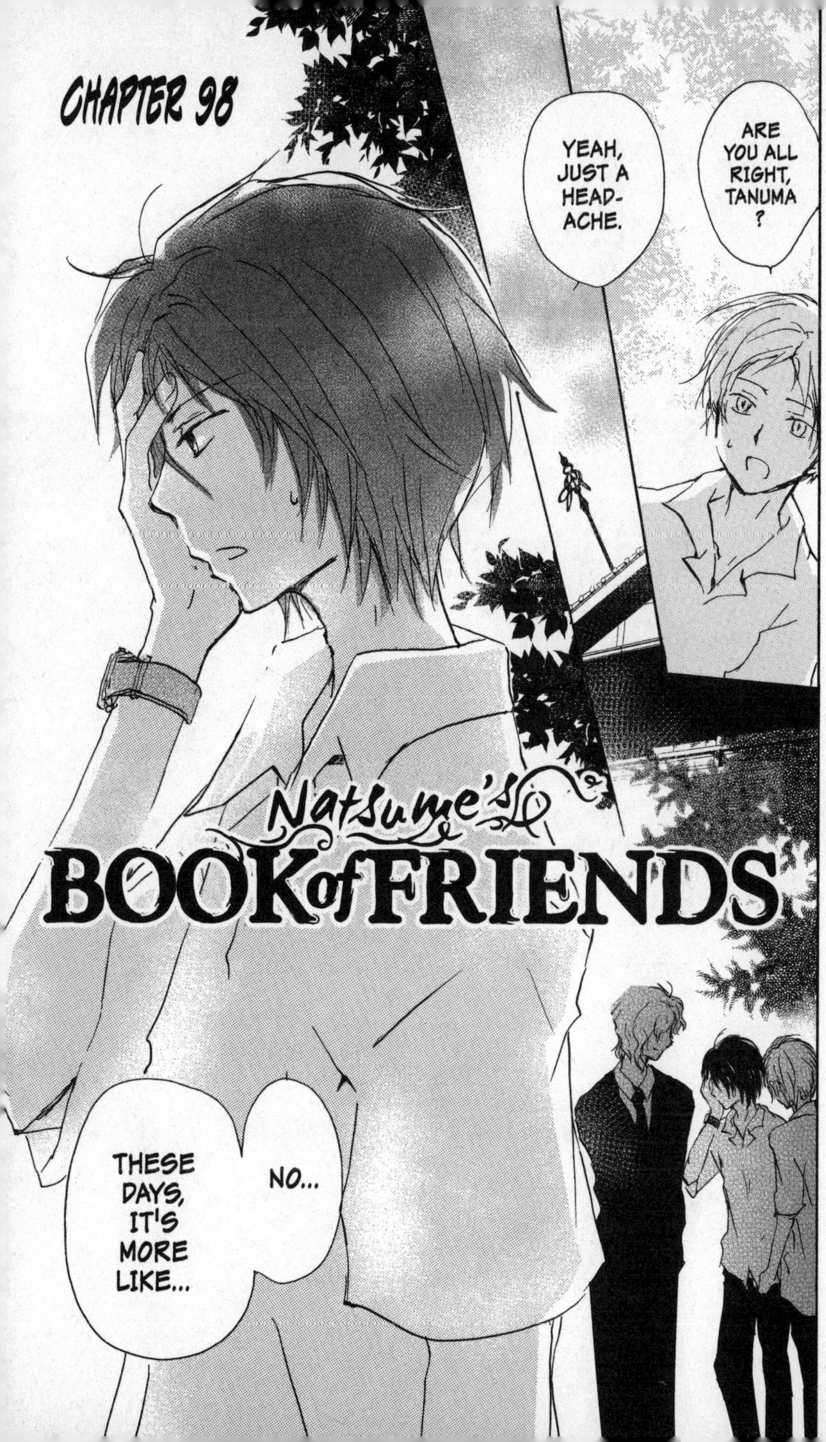
CHAPTER 98
ARE YOU ALL RIGHT, TANUMA?
YEAH, JUST A HEAD-ACHE.
Natsume's BOOK of FRIENDS
NO...
THESE DAYS, IT'S MORE LIKE...

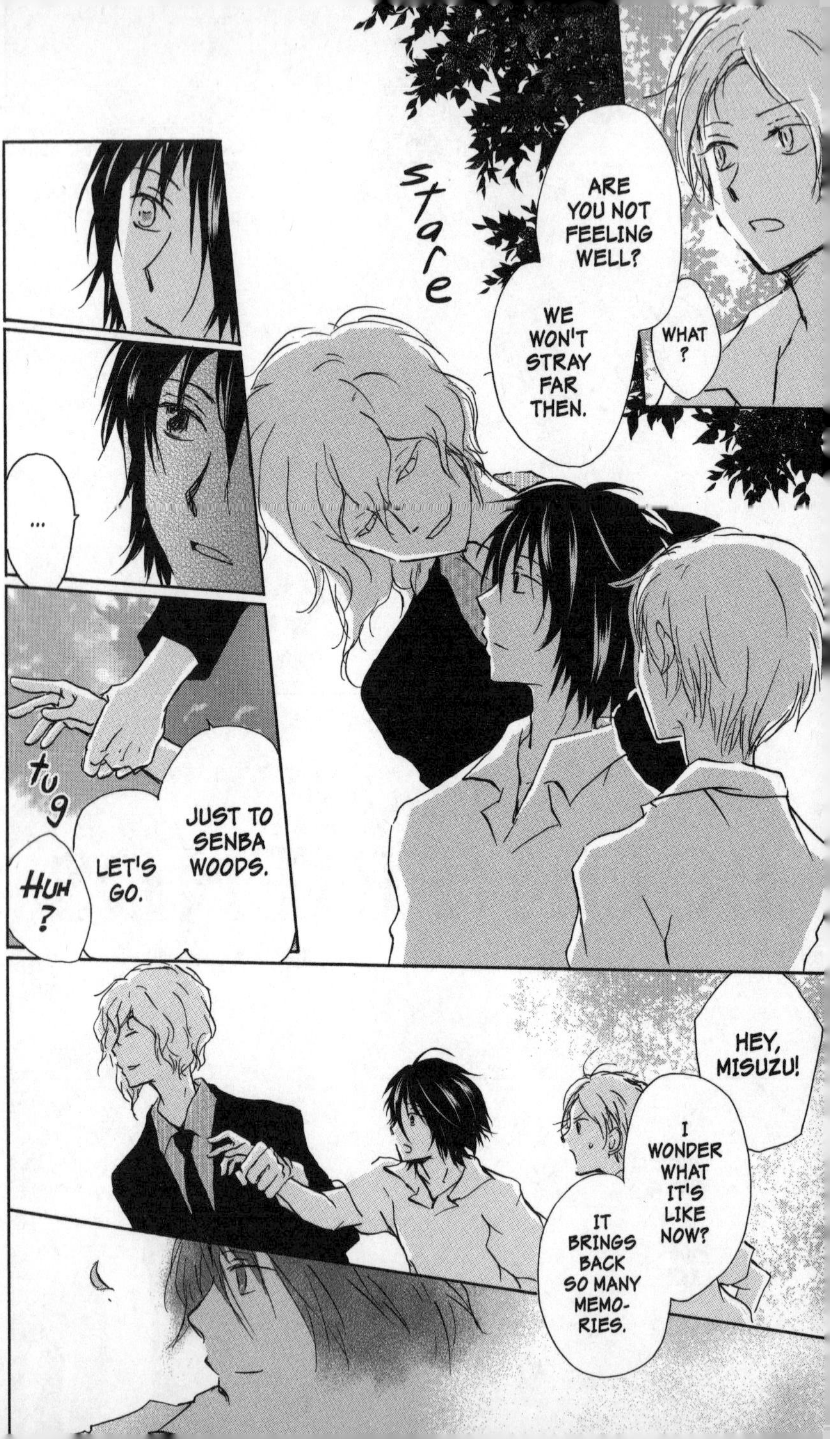
ARE YOU NOT FEELING WELL?
WHAT?
Stare
WE WON'T STRAY FAR THEN.
...
JUST TO SENBA WOODS.
LET'S GO.
tug
HUH?
HEY, MISUZU!
I WONDER WHAT IT'S LIKE NOW?
IT BRINGS BACK SO MANY MEMORIES.

...

WHAT ARE YOU DOING, MISUZU?

TAKING WALKS TO PLACES I USED TO GO.

WHY ARE YOU MAKING TANUMA COME ALONG?

WHY, INDEED?

...

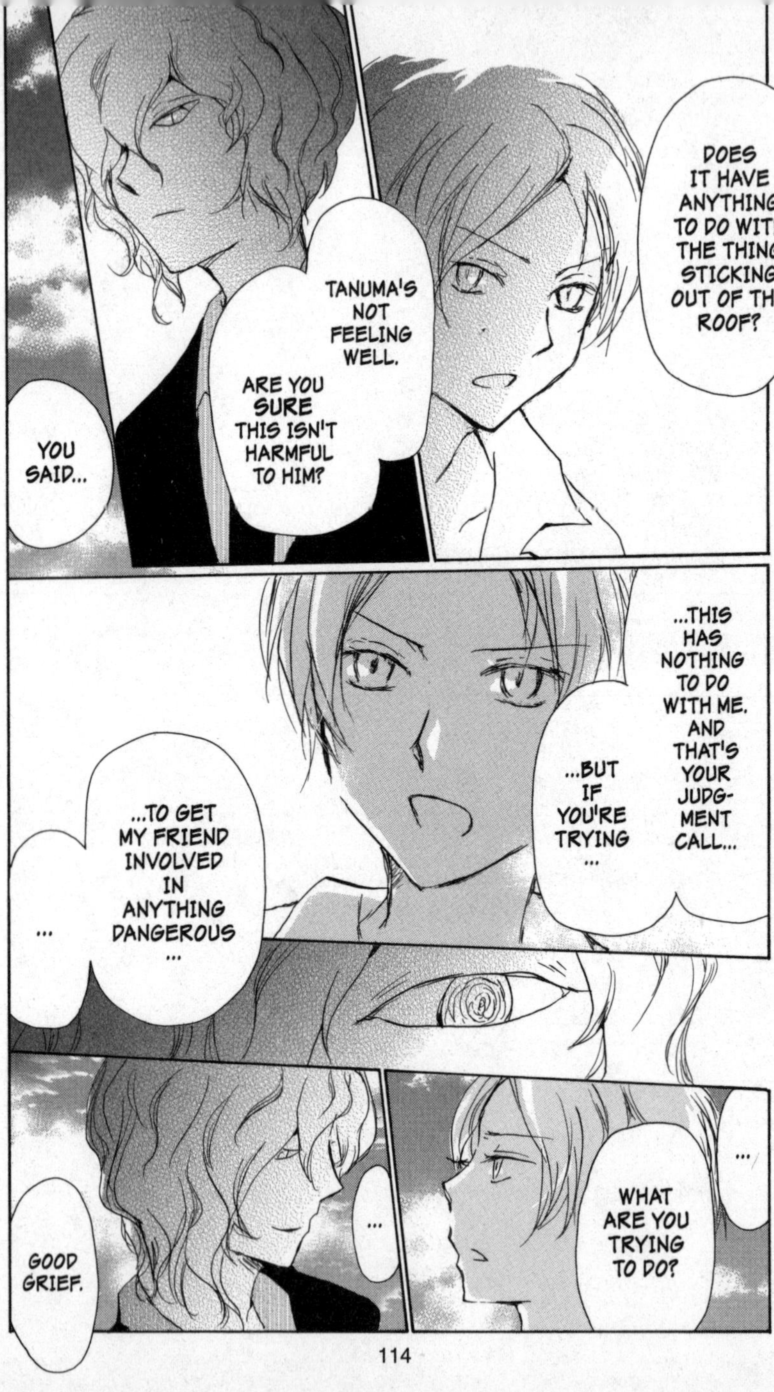
DOES IT HAVE ANYTHING TO DO WITH THE THING STICKING OUT OF THE ROOF?
TANUMA'S NOT FEELING WELL.
ARE YOU SURE THIS ISN'T HARMFUL TO HIM?
YOU SAID...
...THIS HAS NOTHING TO DO WITH ME. AND THAT'S YOUR JUDGMENT CALL...
...BUT IF YOU'RE TRYING ...
...TO GET MY FRIEND INVOLVED IN ANYTHING DANGEROUS ...
...
...
WHAT ARE YOU TRYING TO DO?
...
GOOD GRIEF.

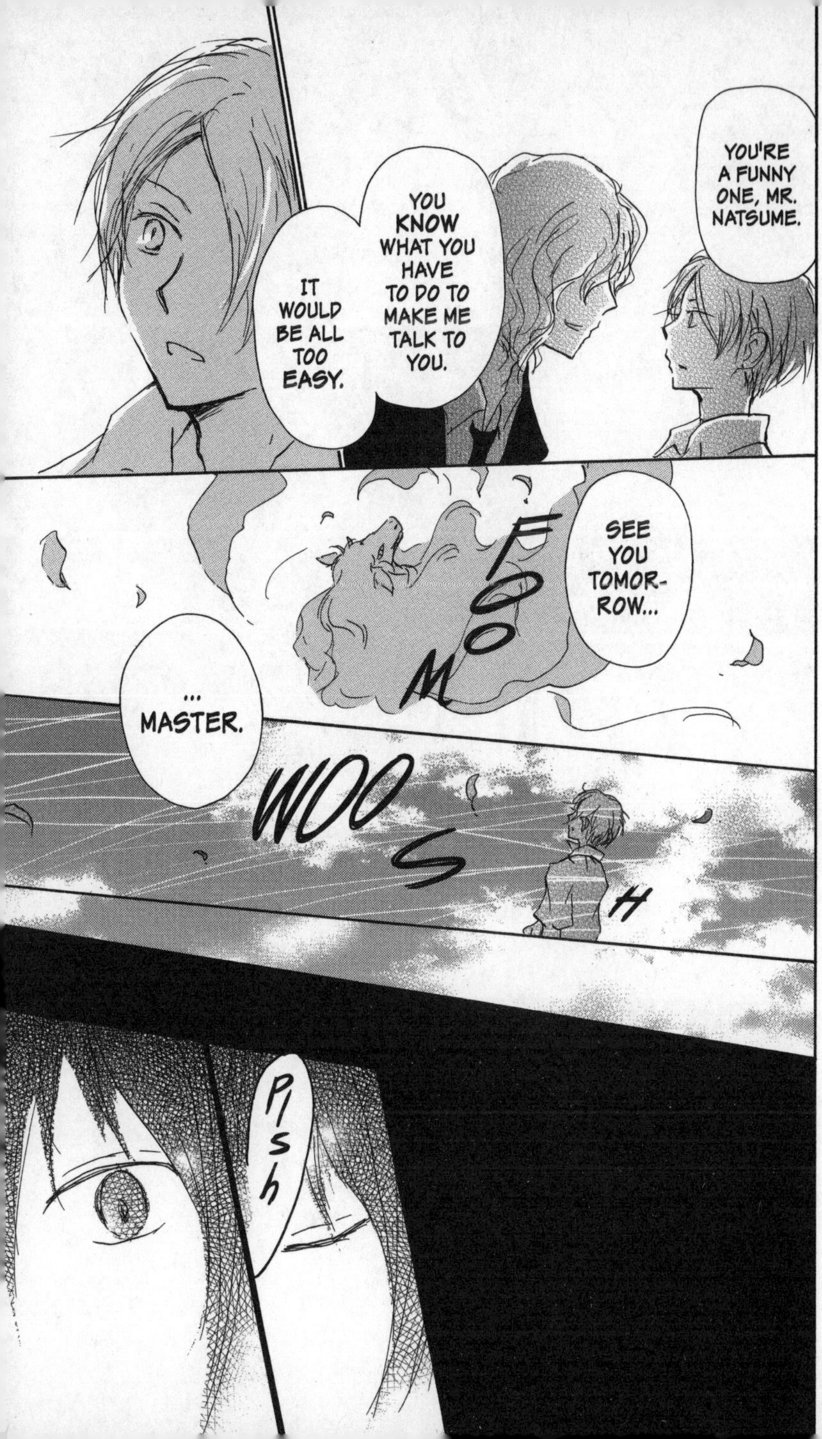
YOU'RE A FUNNY ONE, MR. NATSUME.
YOU KNOW WHAT YOU HAVE TO DO TO MAKE ME TALK TO YOU.
IT WOULD BE ALL TOO EASY.
SEE YOU TOMOR-ROW...
FOOOM
... MASTER.
WOOSH
Pish

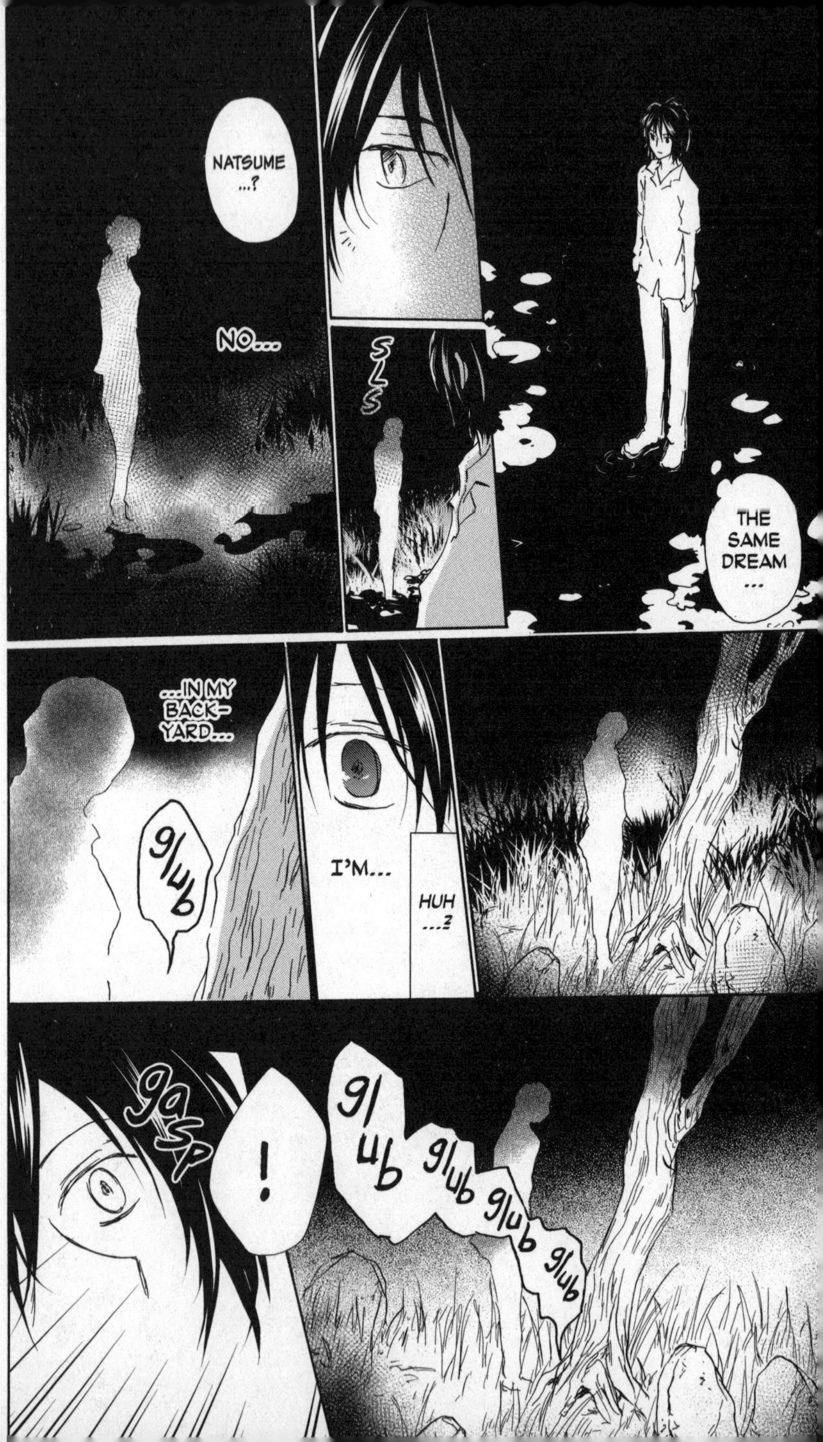
THE SAME DREAM ...
SLS
NATSUME ...?
NO...
HUH ...?
I'M...
...IN MY BACK-YARD...
glub
glub glub glub glub
!
gasp

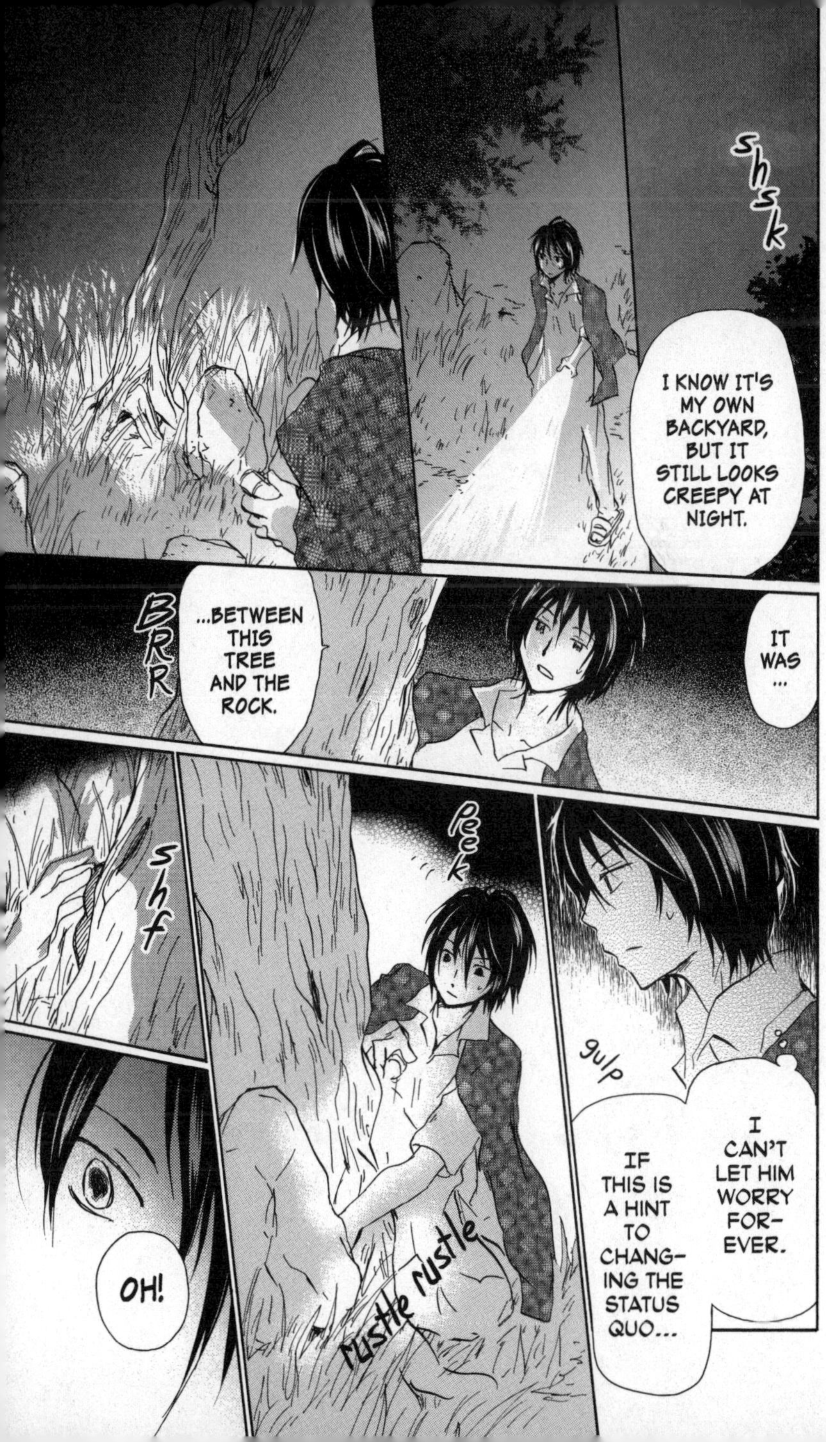
shsk
I KNOW IT'S MY OWN BACKYARD, BUT IT STILL LOOKS CREEPY AT NIGHT.
IT WAS...
...BETWEEN THIS TREE AND THE ROCK.
BRRR
I CAN'T LET HIM WORRY FOR-EVER.
IF THIS IS A HINT TO CHANG-ING THE STATUS QUO...
gulp
Peek
rustle rustle
shf
OH!

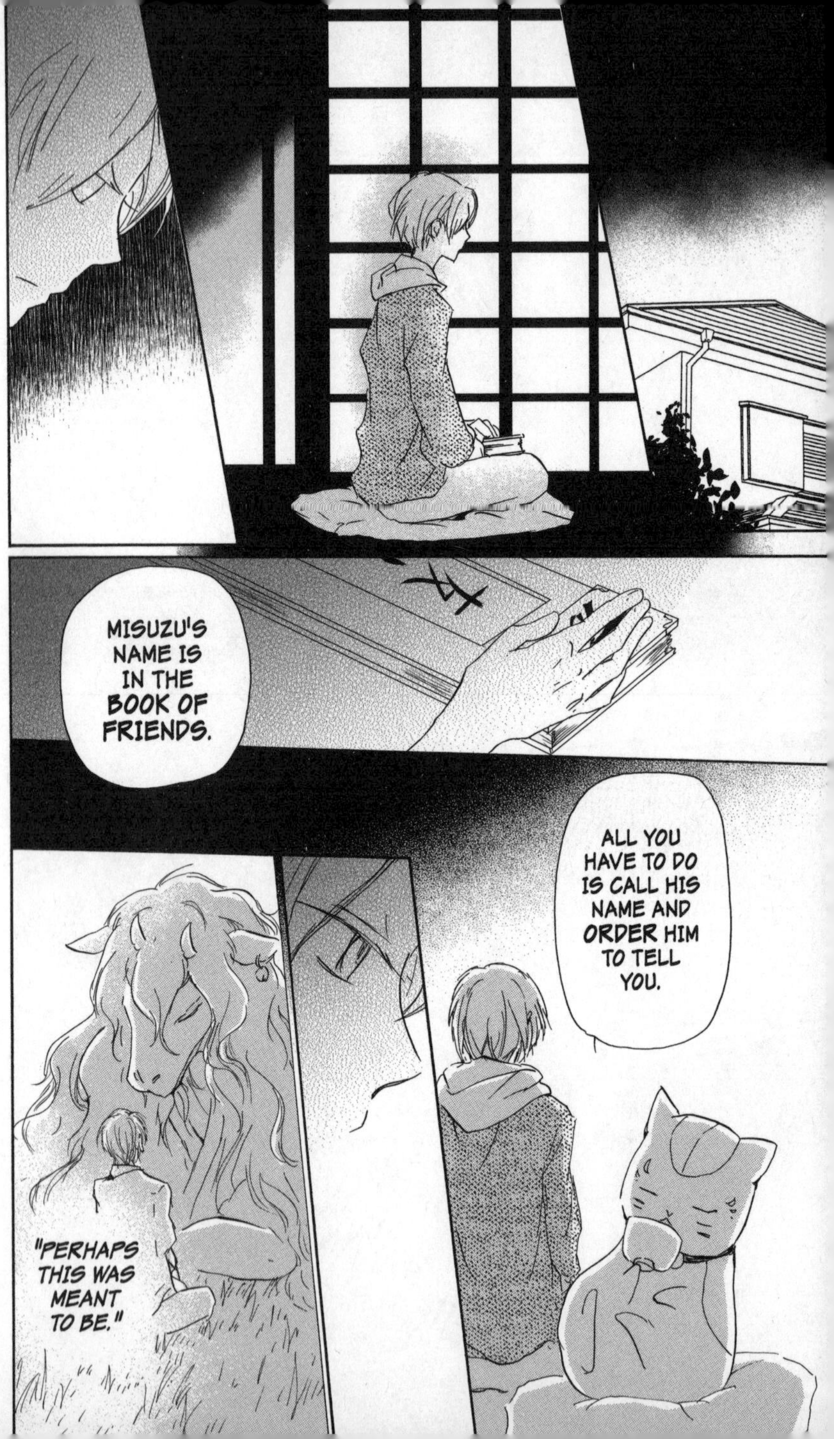
MISUZU'S NAME IS IN THE BOOK OF FRIENDS.
ALL YOU HAVE TO DO IS CALL HIS NAME AND ORDER HIM TO TELL YOU.
"PERHAPS THIS WAS MEANT TO BE."

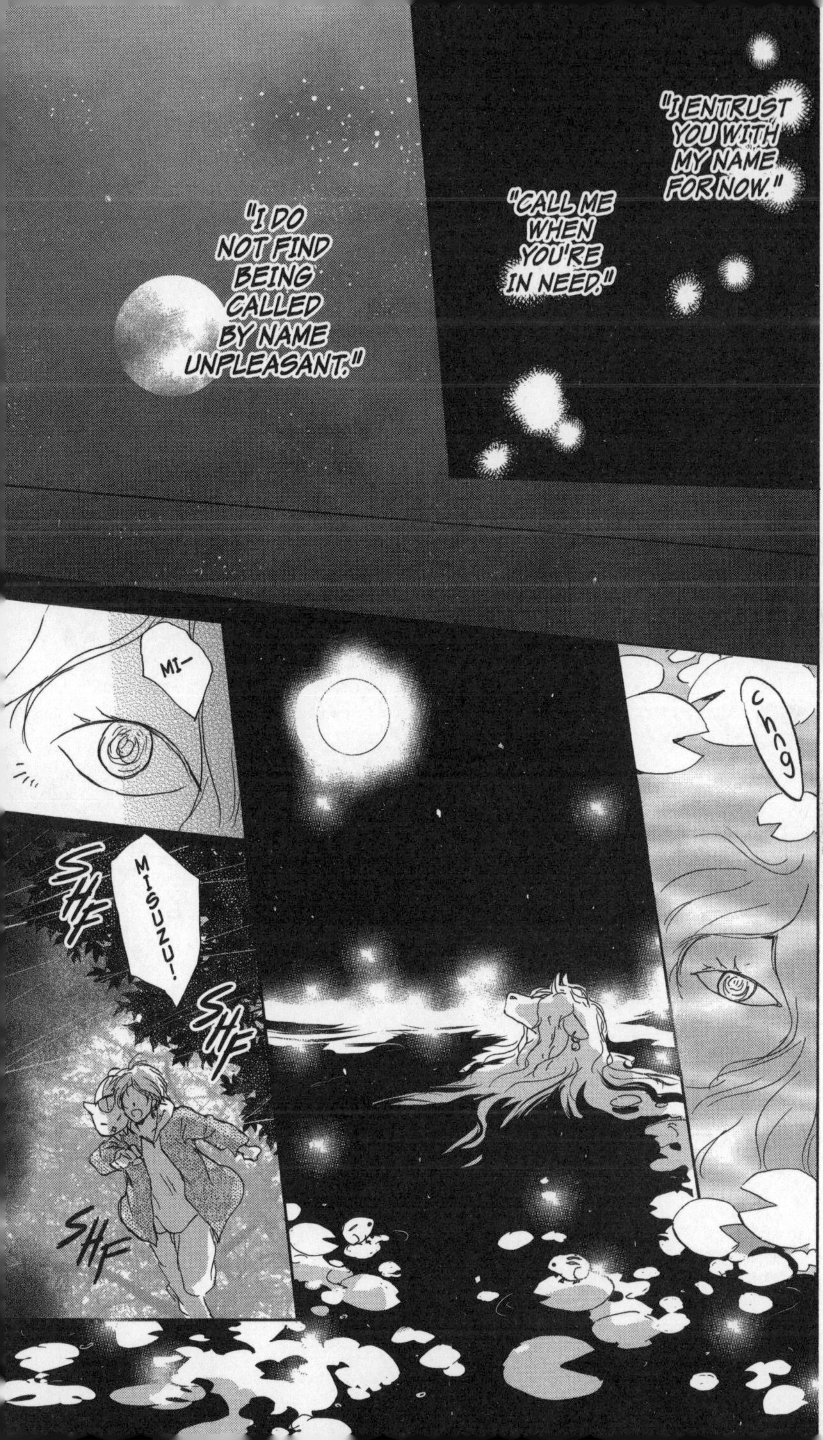
"I ENTRUST YOU WITH MY NAME FOR NOW."
"CALL ME WHEN YOU'RE IN NEED."
"I DO NOT FIND BEING CALLED BY NAME UNPLEASANT."
chng
MI-
MISUZU!
SHF
SHF
SHF

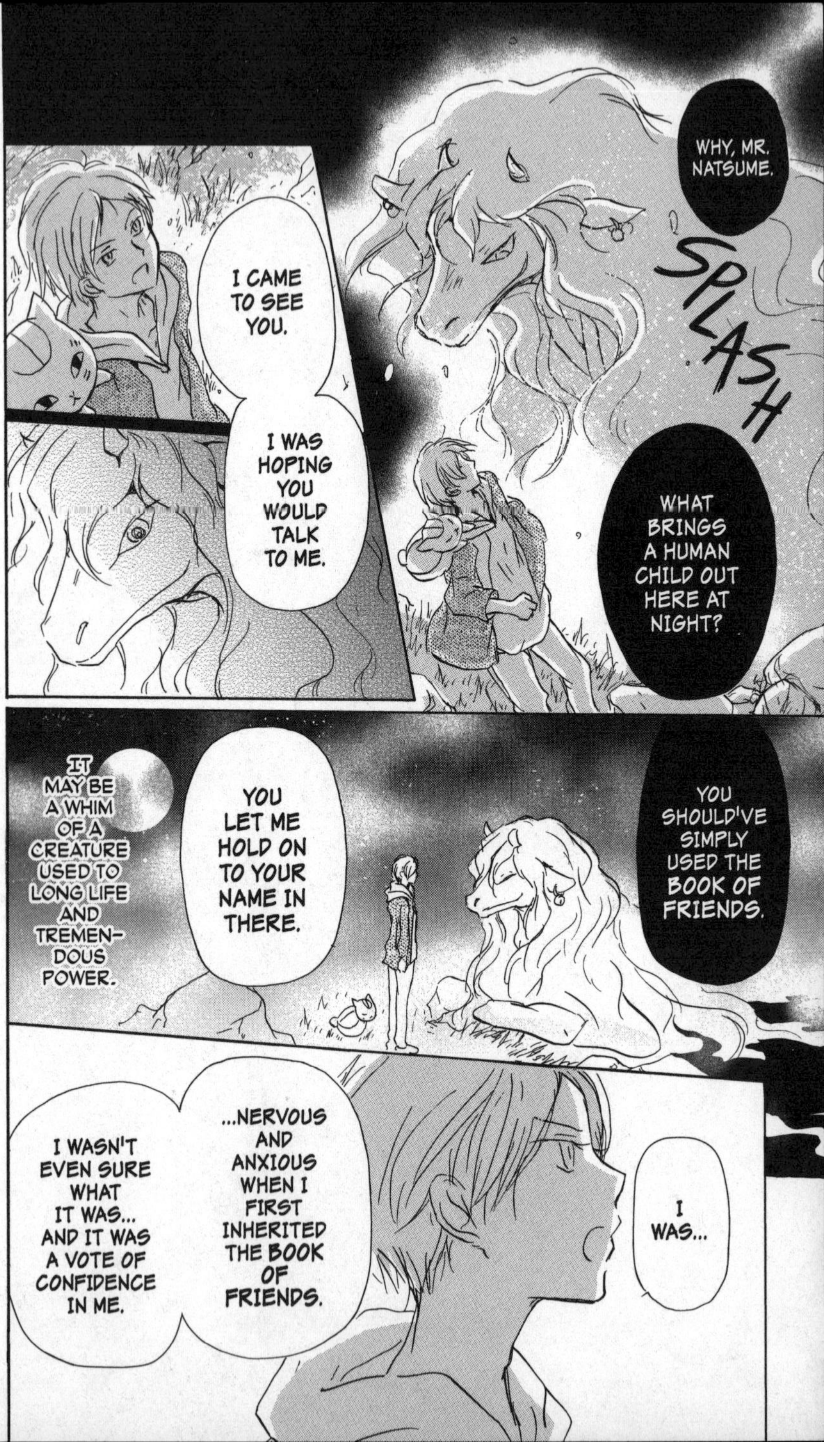
WHY, MR. NATSUME.
SPLASH
WHAT BRINGS A HUMAN CHILD OUT HERE AT NIGHT?
I CAME TO SEE YOU.
I WAS HOPING YOU WOULD TALK TO ME.
YOU SHOULD'VE SIMPLY USED THE BOOK OF FRIENDS.
YOU LET ME HOLD ON TO YOUR NAME IN THERE.
IT MAY BE A WHIM OF A CREATURE USED TO LONG LIFE AND TREMENDOUS POWER.
I WAS...
...NERVOUS AND ANXIOUS WHEN I FIRST INHERITED THE BOOK OF FRIENDS.
I WASN'T EVEN SURE WHAT IT WAS... AND IT WAS A VOTE OF CONFIDENCE IN ME.

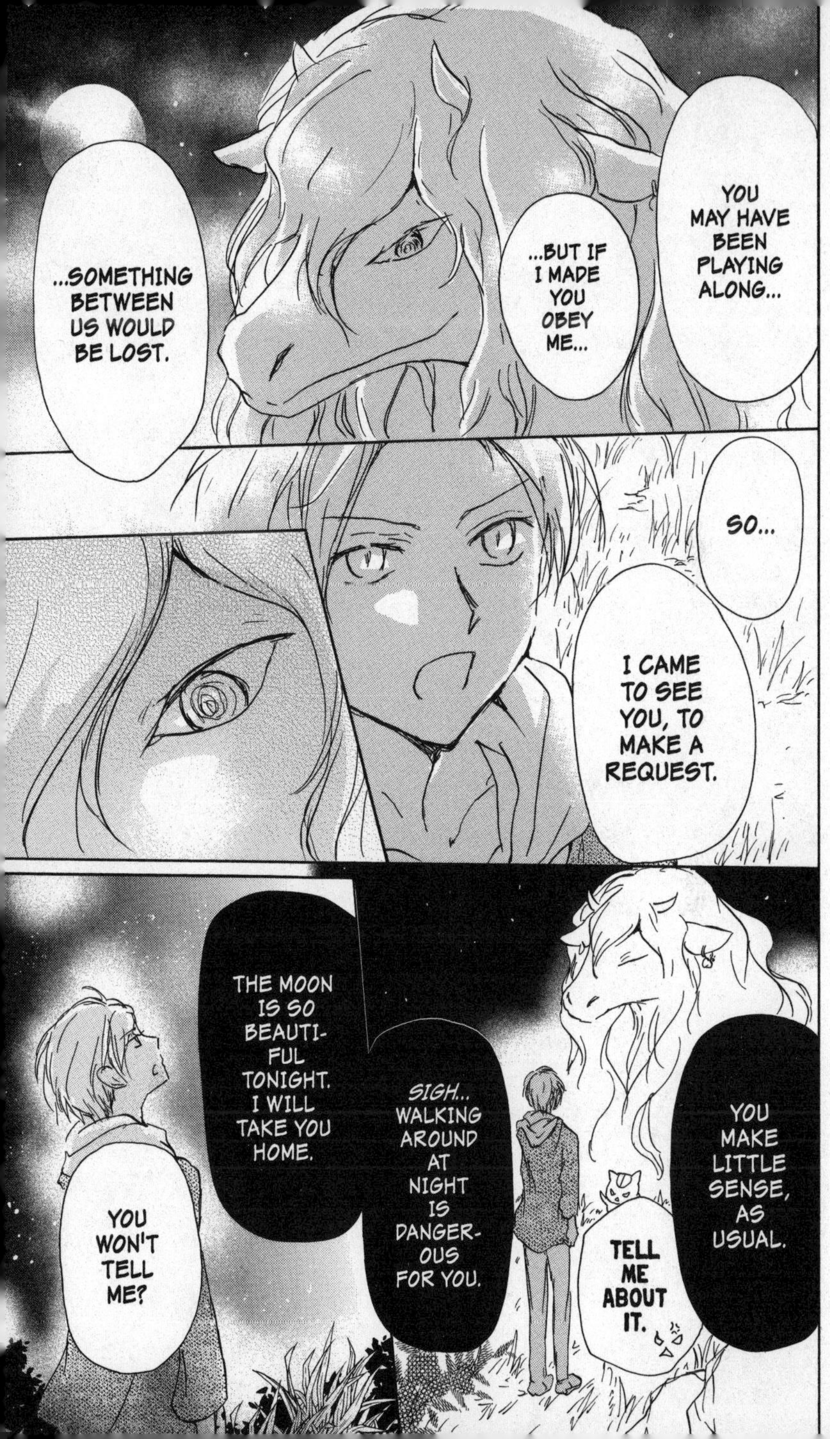
YOU MAY HAVE BEEN PLAYING ALONG...
...BUT IF I MADE YOU OBEY ME...
...SOMETHING BETWEEN US WOULD BE LOST.
SO...
I CAME TO SEE YOU, TO MAKE A REQUEST.
YOU MAKE LITTLE SENSE, AS USUAL.
TELL ME ABOUT IT.
SIGH... WALKING AROUND AT NIGHT IS DANGER-OUS FOR YOU.
THE MOON IS SO BEAUTI-FUL TONIGHT. I WILL TAKE YOU HOME.
YOU WON'T TELL ME?

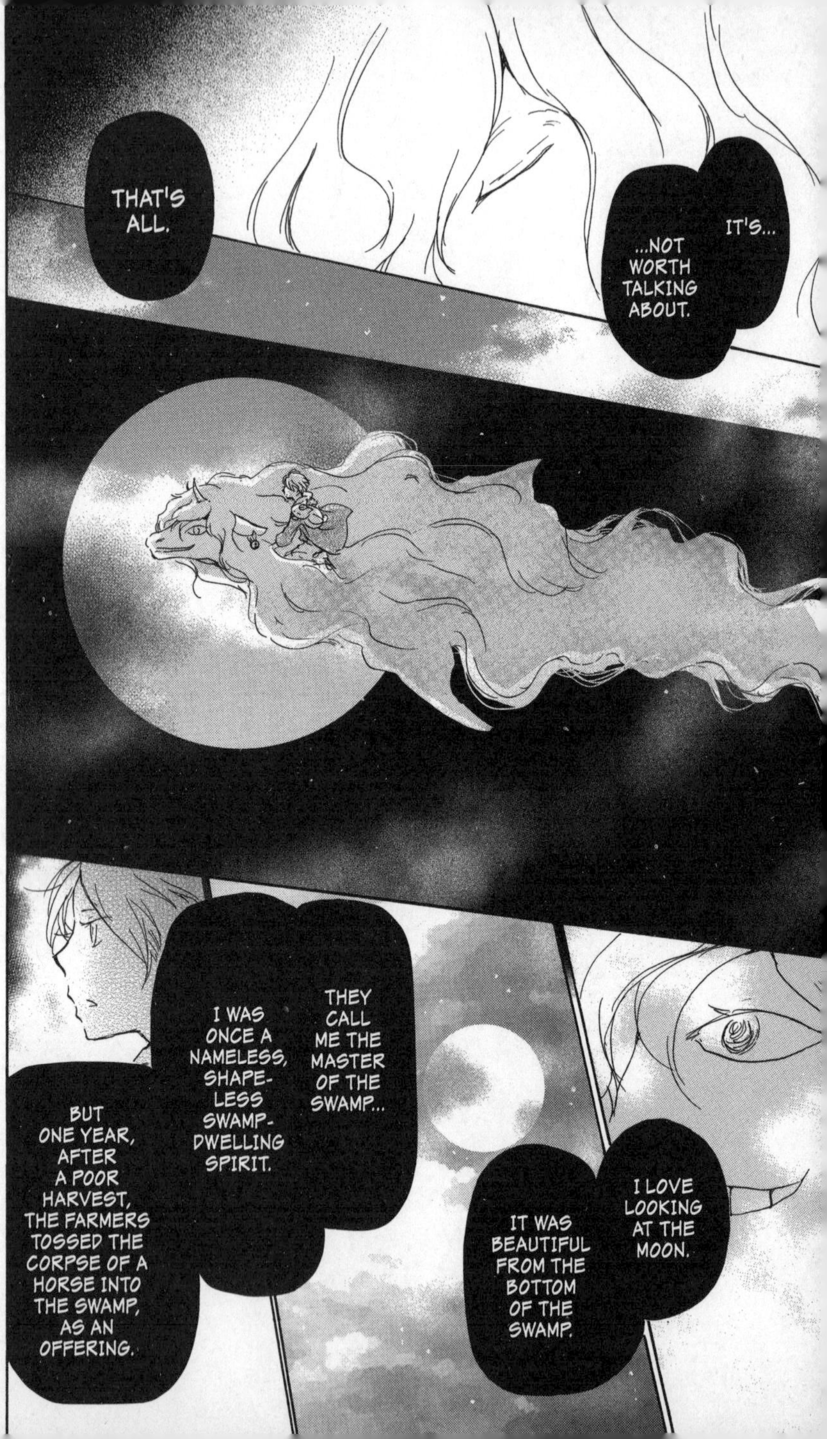
IT'S...
...NOT WORTH TALKING ABOUT.
THAT'S ALL.
I LOVE LOOKING AT THE MOON.
IT WAS BEAUTIFUL FROM THE BOTTOM OF THE SWAMP.
THEY CALL ME THE MASTER OF THE SWAMP...
I WAS ONCE A NAMELESS, SHAPE-LESS SWAMP-DWELLING SPIRIT.
BUT ONE YEAR, AFTER A POOR HARVEST, THE FARMERS TOSSED THE CORPSE OF A HORSE INTO THE SWAMP, AS AN OFFERING.

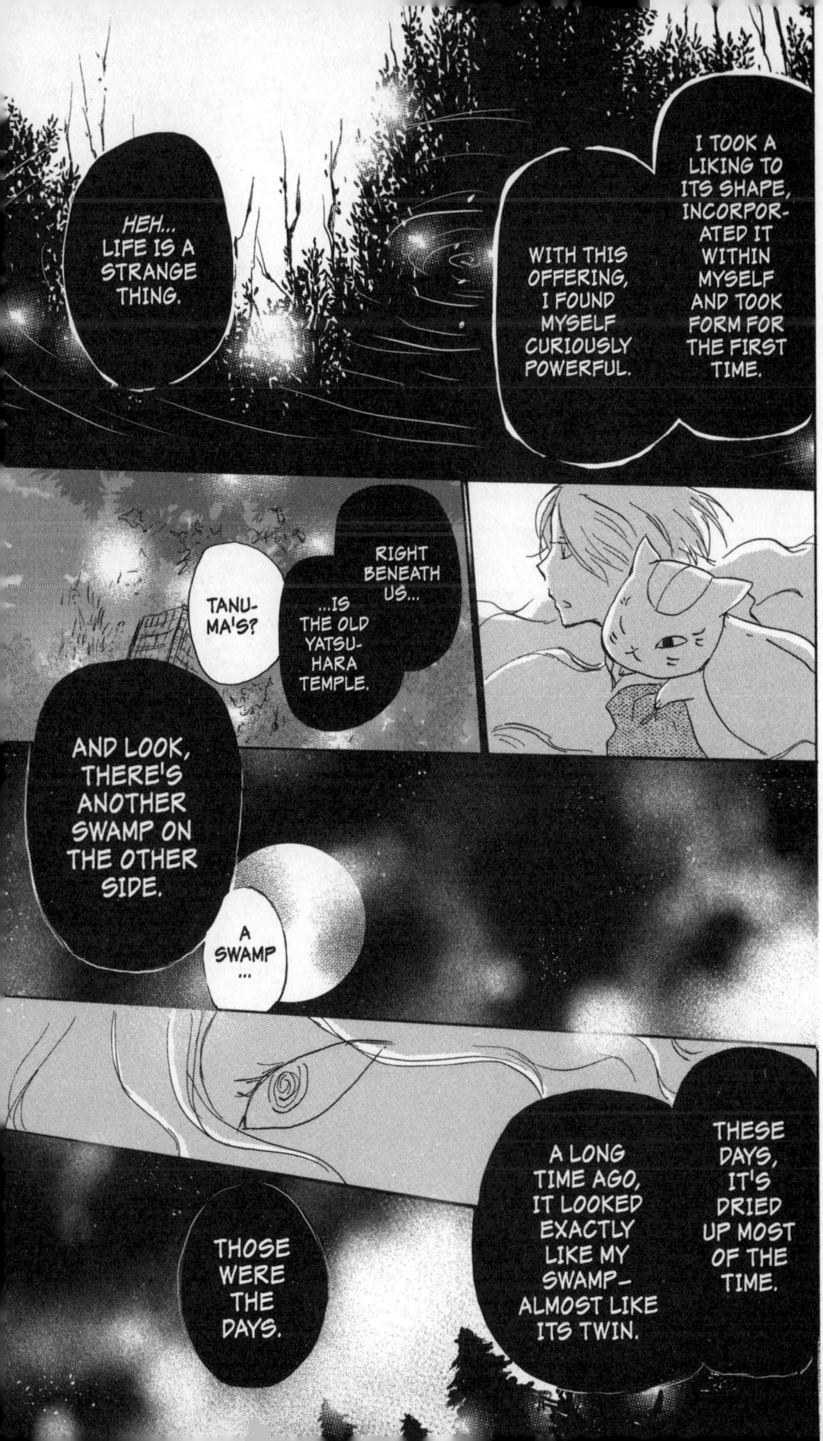
I TOOK A LIKING TO ITS SHAPE, INCORPORATED IT WITHIN MYSELF AND TOOK FORM FOR THE FIRST TIME.
WITH THIS OFFERING, I FOUND MYSELF CURIOUSLY POWERFUL.
HEH... LIFE IS A STRANGE THING.
RIGHT BENEATH US...
...IS THE OLD YATSUHARA TEMPLE.
TANUMA'S?
AND LOOK, THERE'S ANOTHER SWAMP ON THE OTHER SIDE.
A SWAMP...
THESE DAYS, IT'S DRIED UP MOST OF THE TIME.
A LONG TIME AGO, IT LOOKED EXACTLY LIKE MY SWAMP—ALMOST LIKE ITS TWIN.
THOSE WERE THE DAYS.

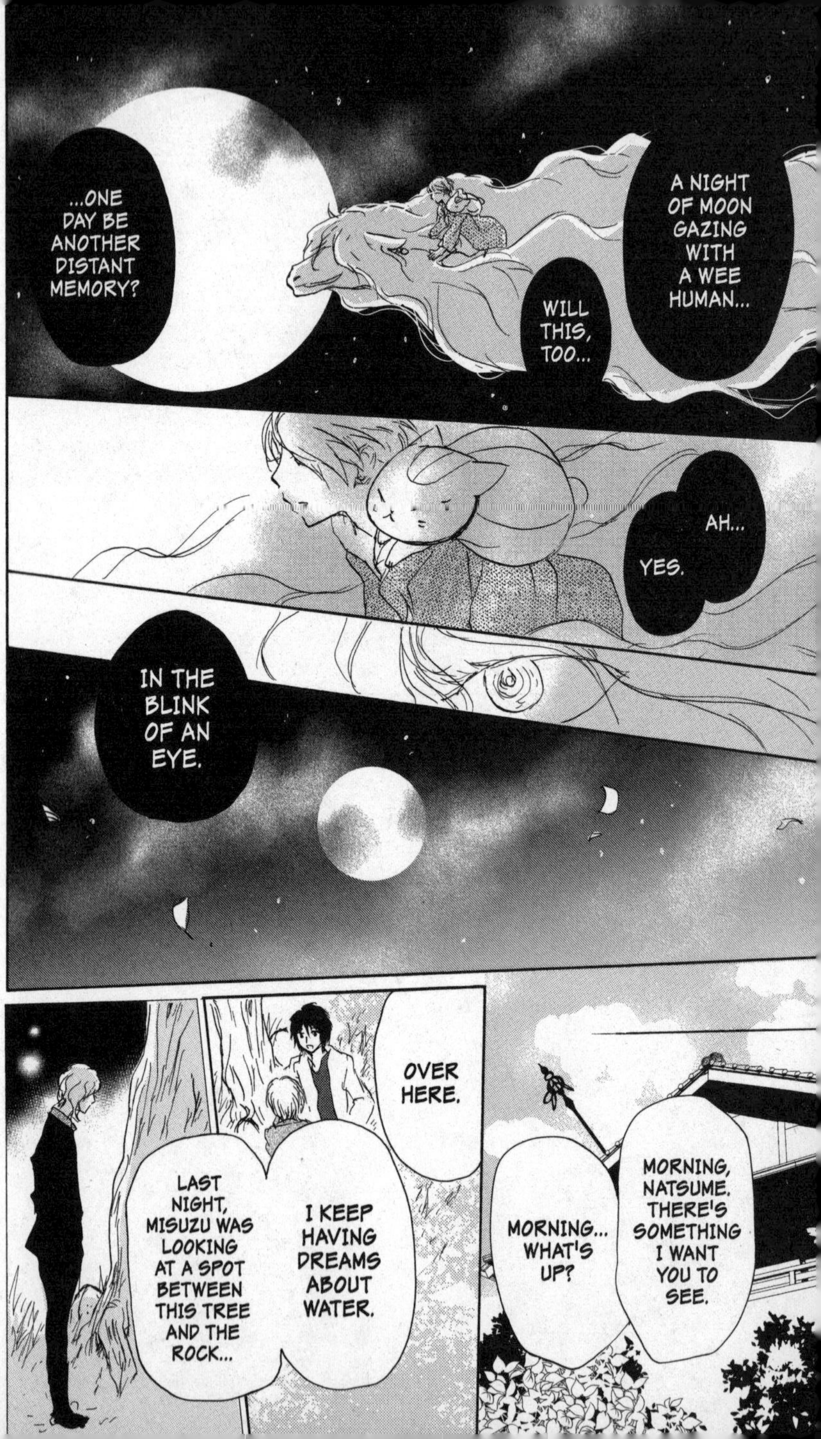
A NIGHT OF MOON GAZING WITH A WEE HUMAN...
WILL THIS, TOO...
...ONE DAY BE ANOTHER DISTANT MEMORY?
AH...
YES.
IN THE BLINK OF AN EYE.
MORNING, NATSUME. THERE'S SOMETHING I WANT YOU TO SEE.
MORNING... WHAT'S UP?
OVER HERE.
I KEEP HAVING DREAMS ABOUT WATER.
LAST NIGHT, MISUZU WAS LOOKING AT A SPOT BETWEEN THIS TREE AND THE ROCK...

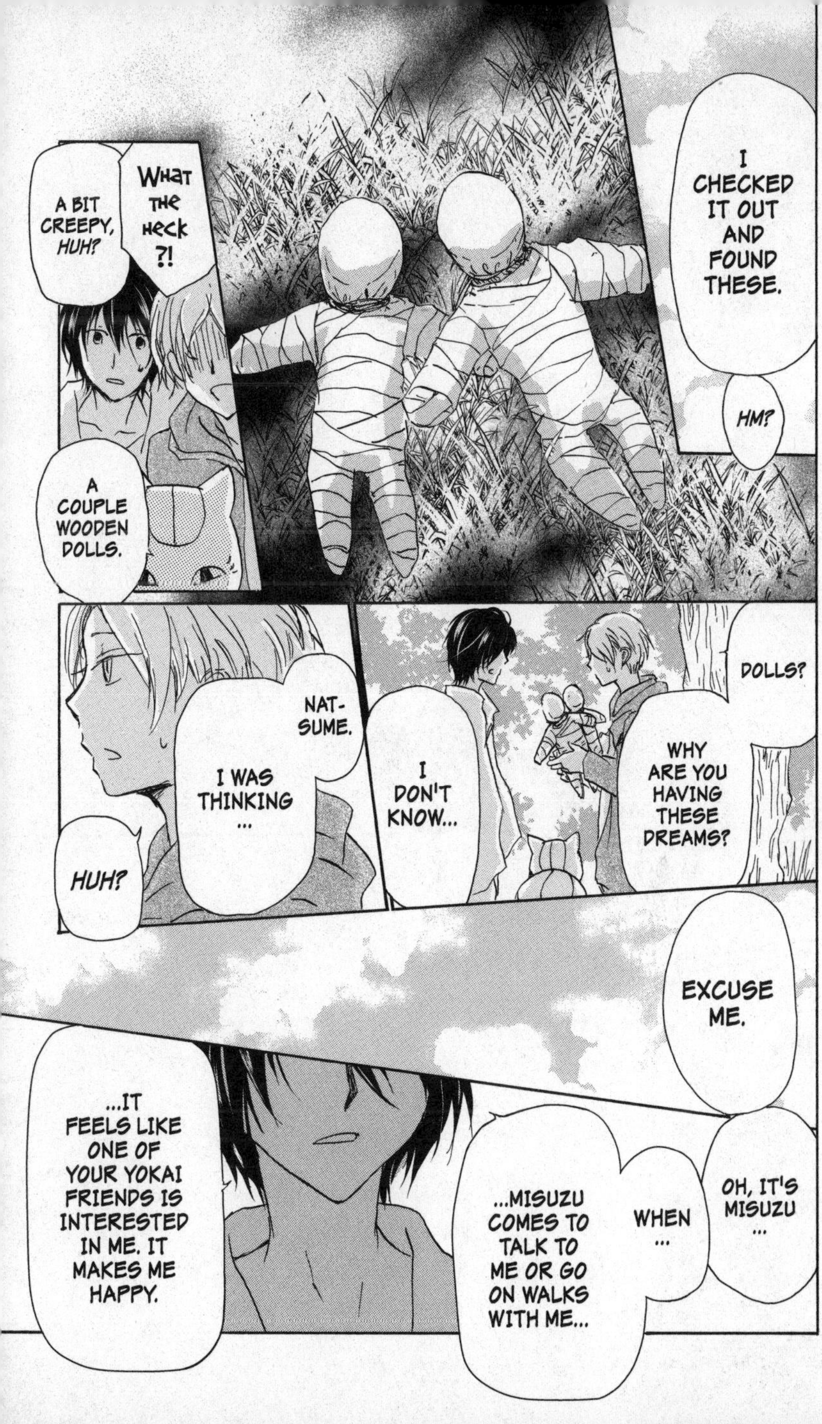
I CHECKED IT OUT AND FOUND THESE.
HM?
WHAT THE HECK?!
A BIT CREEPY, HUH?
A COUPLE WOODEN DOLLS.
DOLLS?
WHY ARE YOU HAVING THESE DREAMS?
I DON'T KNOW...
NAT-SUME.
I WAS THINKING...
HUH?
EXCUSE ME.
OH, IT'S MISUZU...
WHEN...
...MISUZU COMES TO TALK TO ME OR GO ON WALKS WITH ME...
...IT FEELS LIKE ONE OF YOUR YOKAI FRIENDS IS INTERESTED IN ME. IT MAKES ME HAPPY.

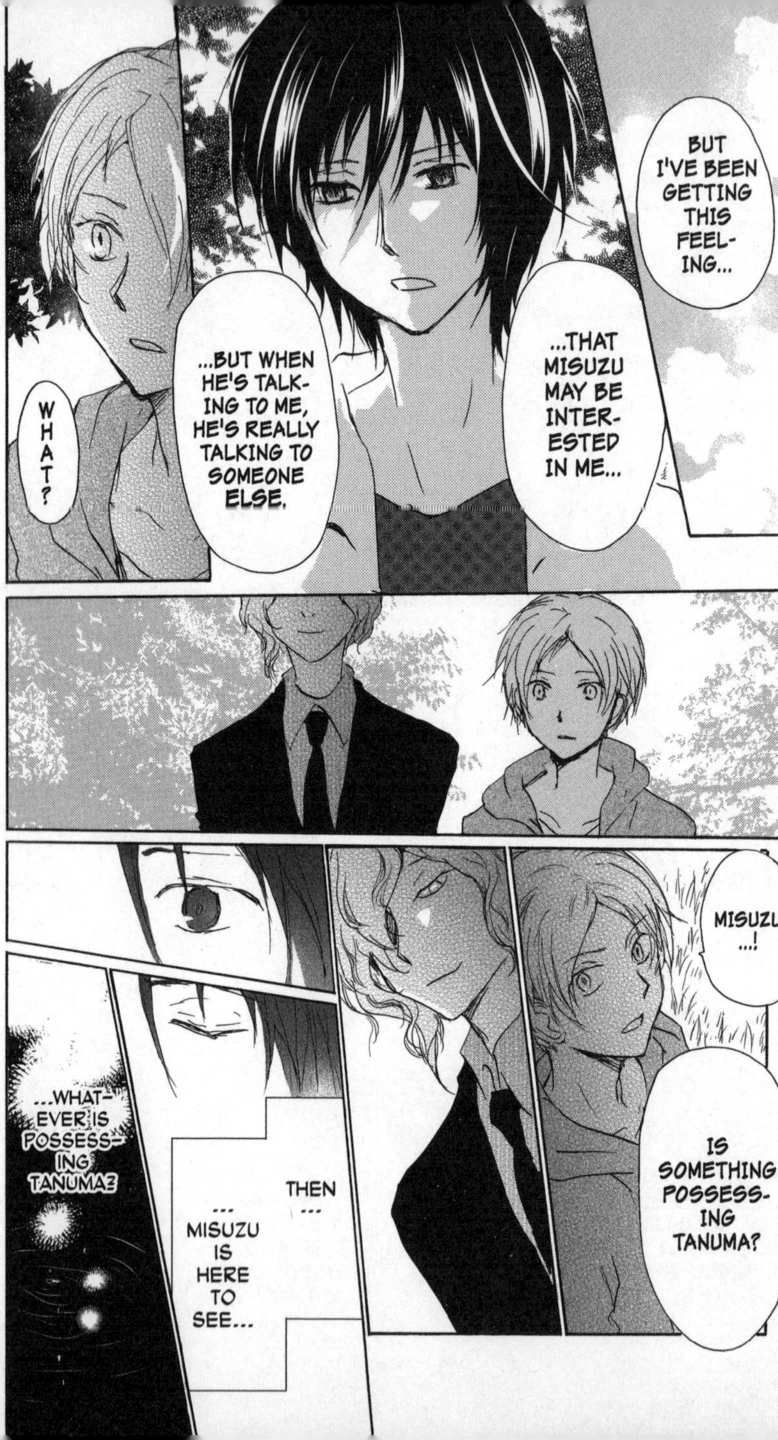
BUT I'VE BEEN GETTING THIS FEEL-ING...
...THAT MISUZU MAY BE INTER-ESTED IN ME...
...BUT WHEN HE'S TALK-ING TO ME, HE'S REALLY TALKING TO SOMEONE ELSE.
WHAT?
MISUZU ...!
IS SOMETHING POSSESS-ING TANUMA?
THEN ...
... MISUZU IS HERE TO SEE...
...WHAT-EVER IS POSSESS-ING TANUMA?

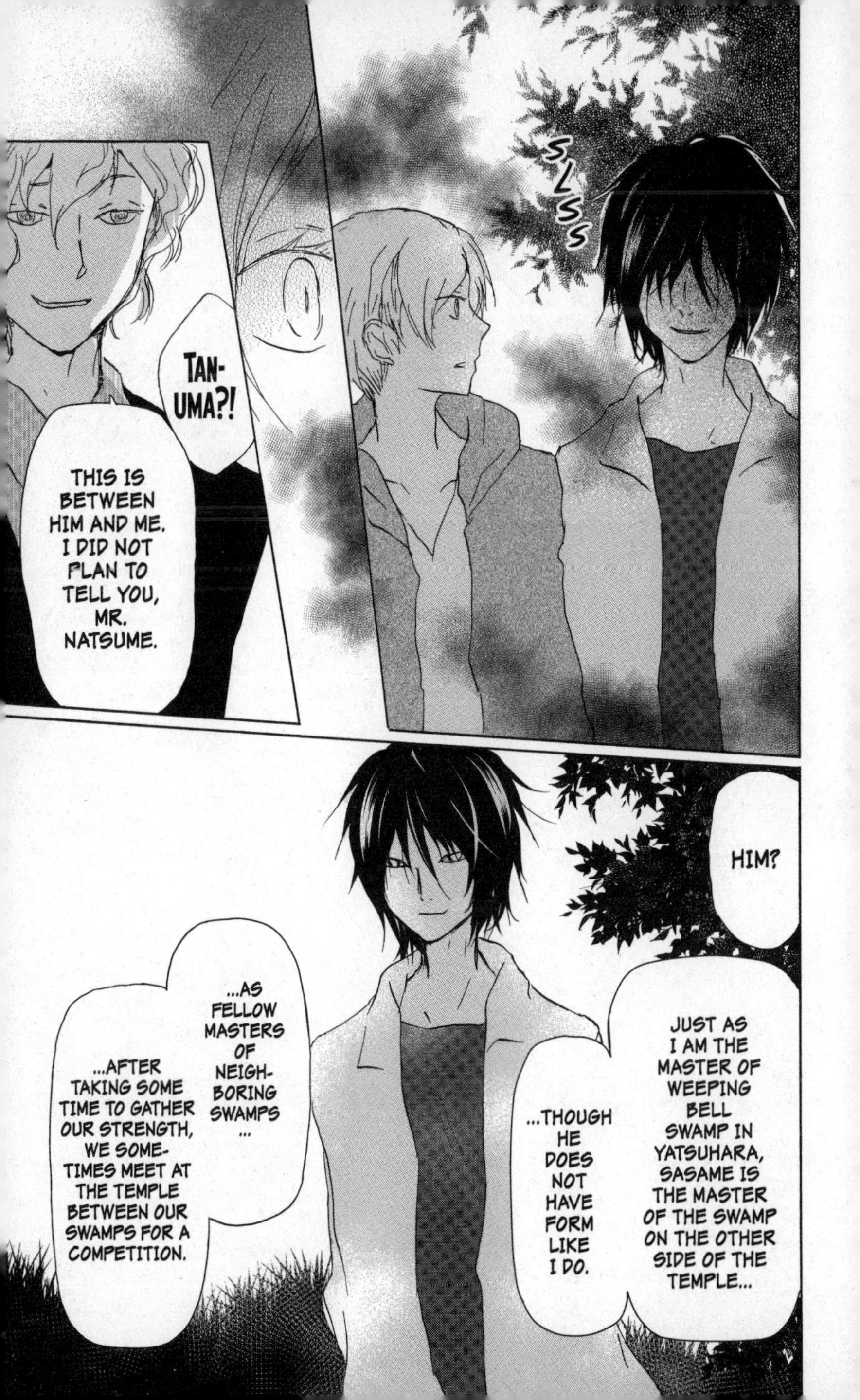
SLSS
TAN-UMA?!
THIS IS BETWEEN HIM AND ME. I DID NOT PLAN TO TELL YOU, MR. NATSUME.
HIM?
JUST AS I AM THE MASTER OF WEEPING BELL SWAMP IN YATSUHARA, SASAME IS THE MASTER OF THE SWAMP ON THE OTHER SIDE OF THE TEMPLE...
...THOUGH HE DOES NOT HAVE FORM LIKE I DO.
...AS FELLOW MASTERS OF NEIGH-BORING SWAMPS...
...AFTER TAKING SOME TIME TO GATHER OUR STRENGTH, WE SOME-TIMES MEET AT THE TEMPLE BETWEEN OUR SWAMPS FOR A COMPETITION.

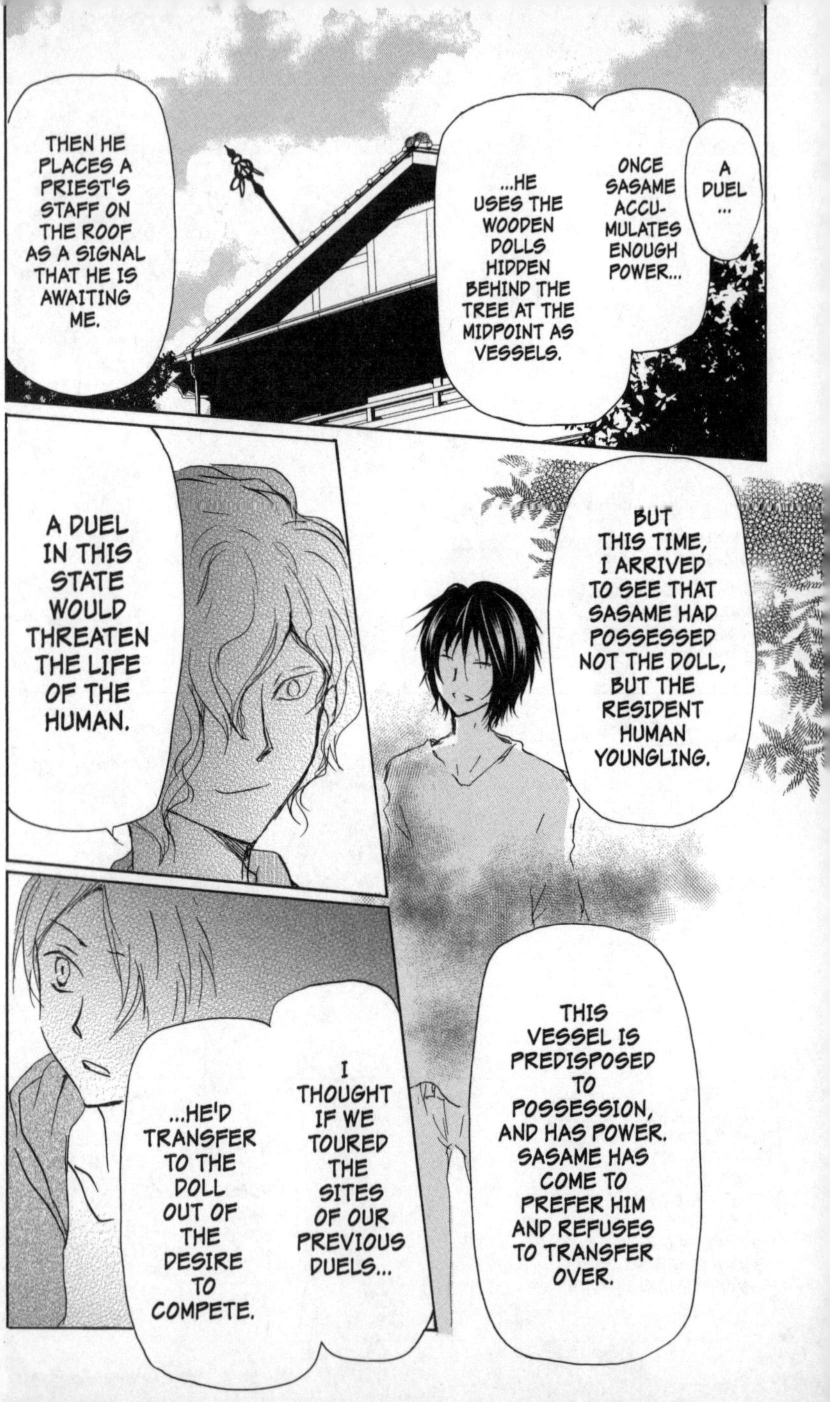
A DUEL...
ONCE SASAME ACCUMULATES ENOUGH POWER...
...HE USES THE WOODEN DOLLS HIDDEN BEHIND THE TREE AT THE MIDPOINT AS VESSELS.
THEN HE PLACES A PRIEST'S STAFF ON THE ROOF AS A SIGNAL THAT HE IS AWAITING ME.
BUT THIS TIME, I ARRIVED TO SEE THAT SASAME HAD POSSESSED NOT THE DOLL, BUT THE RESIDENT HUMAN YOUNGLING.
THIS VESSEL IS PREDISPOSED TO POSSESSION, AND HAS POWER. SASAME HAS COME TO PREFER HIM AND REFUSES TO TRANSFER OVER.
A DUEL IN THIS STATE WOULD THREATEN THE LIFE OF THE HUMAN.
I THOUGHT IF WE TOURED THE SITES OF OUR PREVIOUS DUELS...
...HE'D TRANSFER TO THE DOLL OUT OF THE DESIRE TO COMPETE.

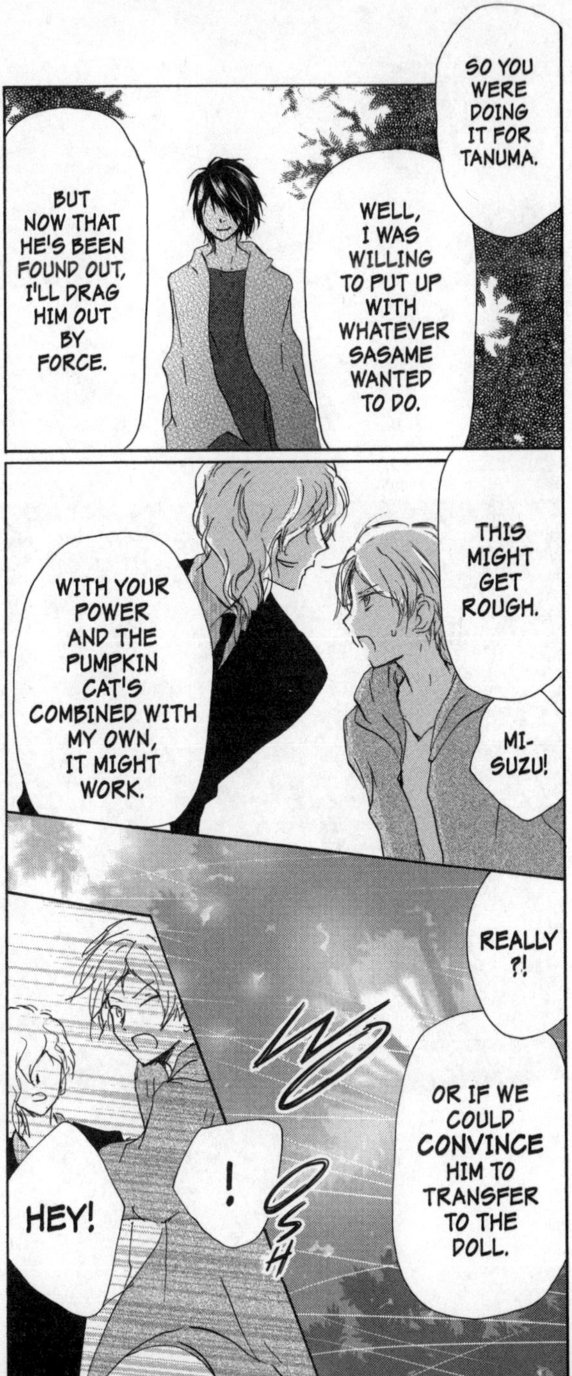
SO YOU WERE DOING IT FOR TANUMA.
WELL, I WAS WILLING TO PUT UP WITH WHATEVER SASAME WANTED TO DO.
BUT NOW THAT HE'S BEEN FOUND OUT, I'LL DRAG HIM OUT BY FORCE.
THIS MIGHT GET ROUGH.
WITH YOUR POWER AND THE PUMPKIN CAT'S COMBINED WITH MY OWN, IT MIGHT WORK.
MI-SUZU!
REALLY?!
OR IF WE COULD CONVINCE HIM TO TRANSFER TO THE DOLL.
WOOSH
!
HEY!

04

✻Anime movie, part 2

The *Natsume's Book of Friends* movie has finished its theatrical run. The movie thoughtfully crafted a warm, lonesome but kind world that really draws you in. As I watched the credits roll in the theater, I recognized each name from seasons 1-6 and the OVA. I was sad to miss the names that didn't take part in this project, happy over the new names added for the movie, and was overcome with so many emotions. It's fun to draw manga, but it's sometimes lonely doggedly working by myself, with only the desire to entertain my readers to keep me company. Now that I'm included on a team like this as the original creator, maintaining connections with all these different people...well, it was very encouraging. I'll keep working hard so I can continue to make manga people will enjoy, so please continue with your support.

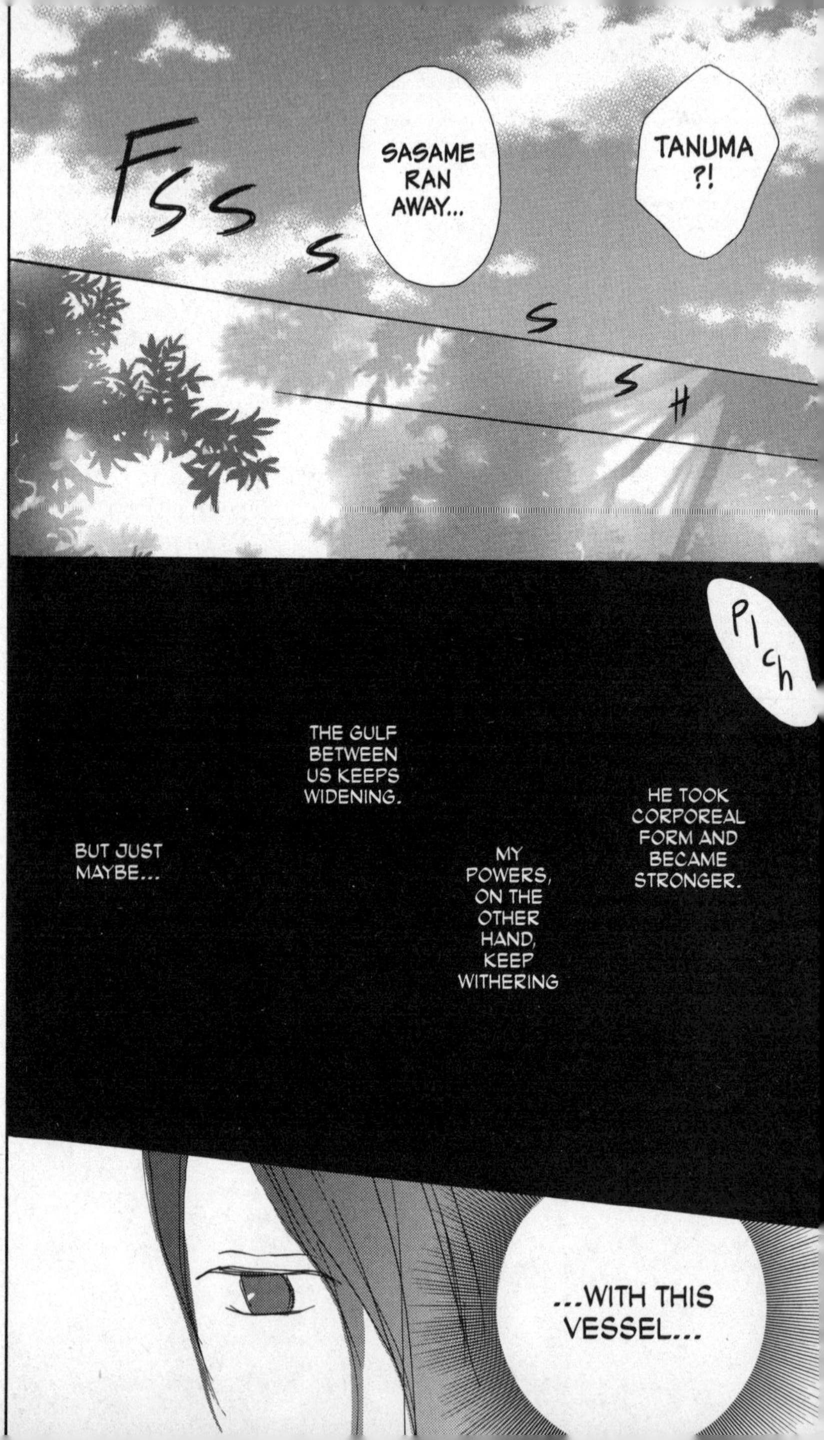
TANUMA ?!
SASAME RAN AWAY...
FSSSSSH
Plch
HE TOOK CORPOREAL FORM AND BECAME STRONGER.
MY POWERS, ON THE OTHER HAND, KEEP WITHERING
THE GULF BETWEEN US KEEPS WIDENING.
BUT JUST MAYBE...
...WITH THIS VESSEL...

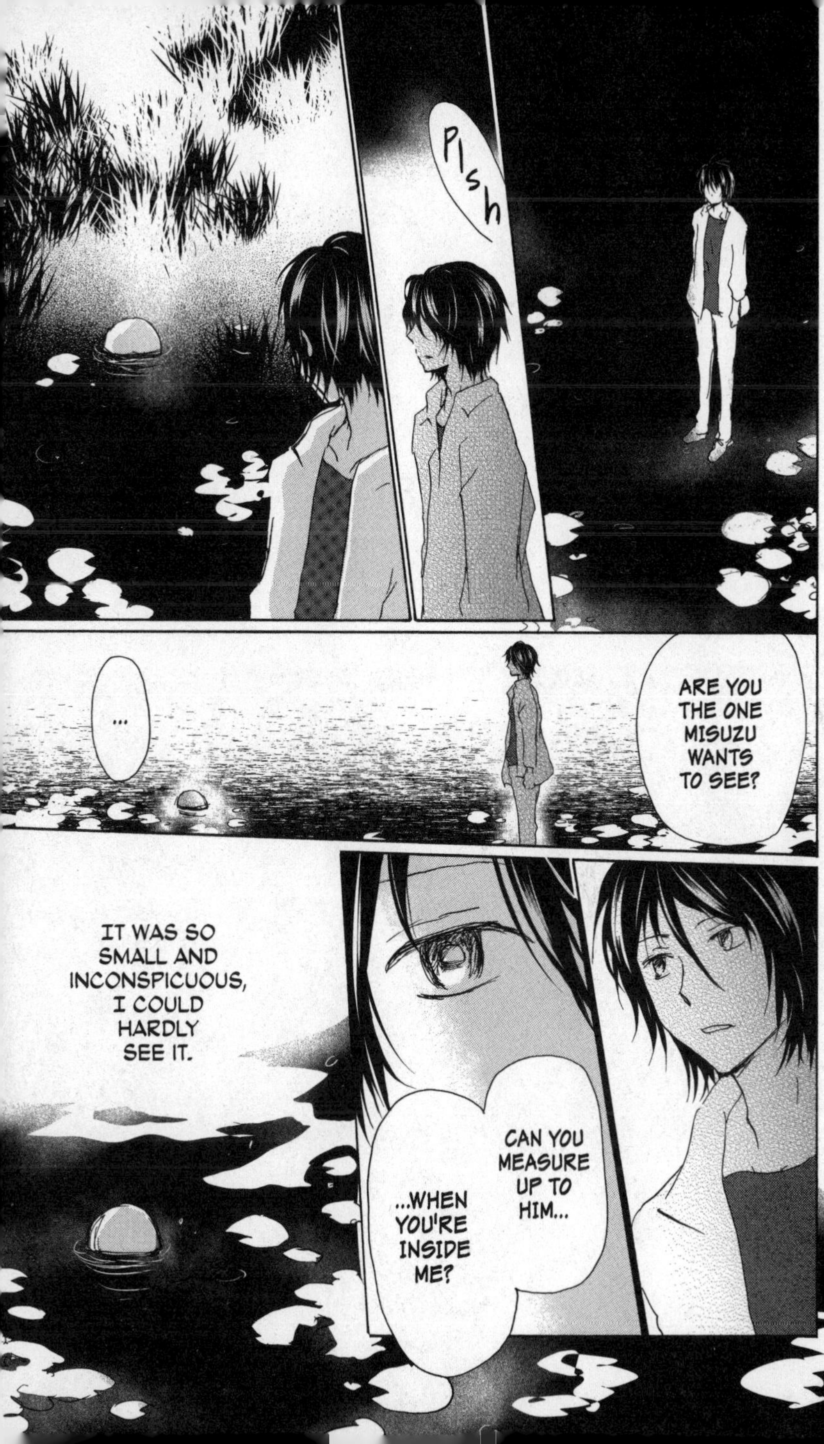
Plish
ARE YOU THE ONE MISUZU WANTS TO SEE?
...
CAN YOU MEASURE UP TO HIM...
...WHEN YOU'RE INSIDE ME?
IT WAS SO SMALL AND INCONSPICUOUS, I COULD HARDLY SEE IT.

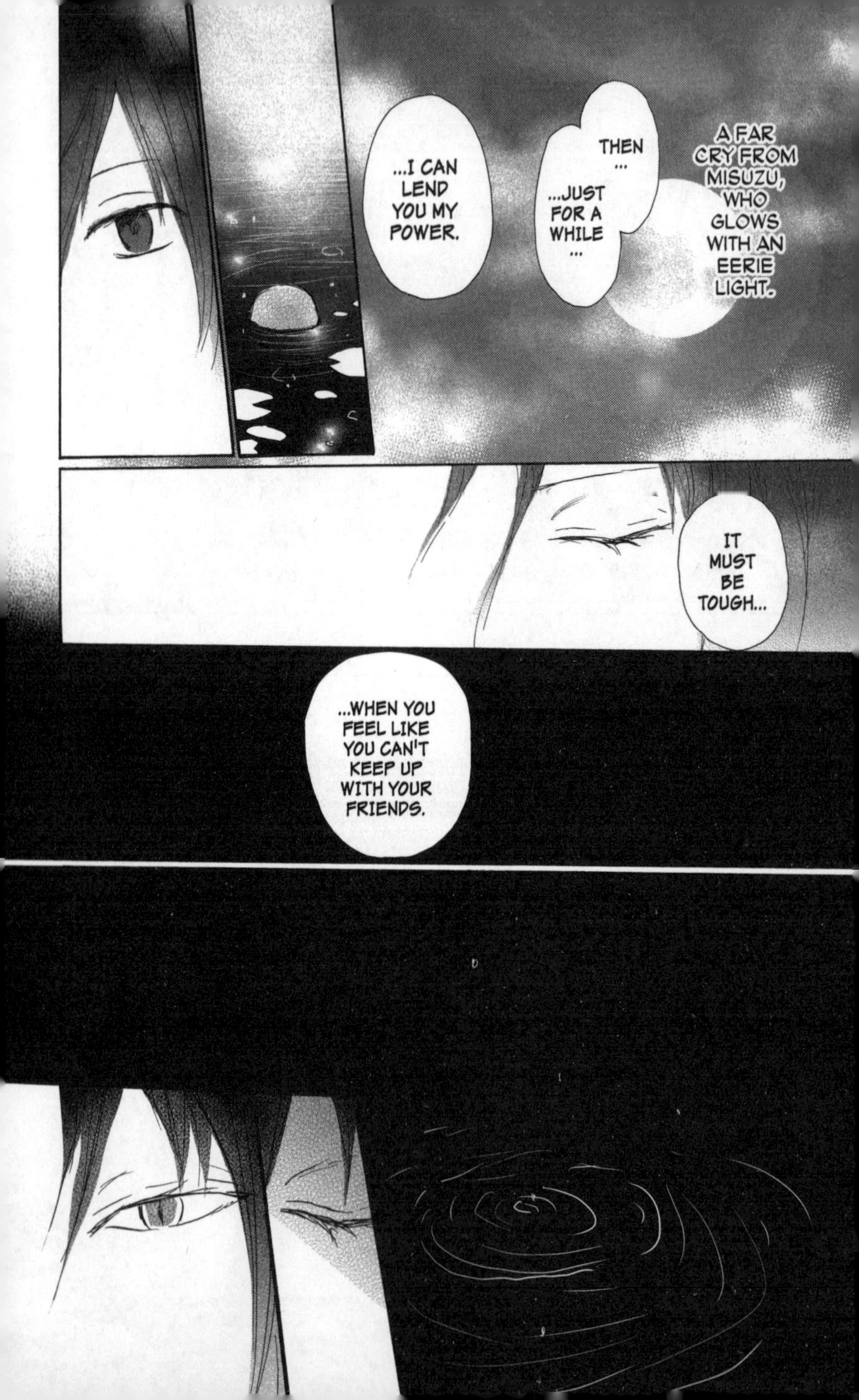
A FAR CRY FROM MISUZU, WHO GLOWS WITH AN EERIE LIGHT.
THEN...
...JUST FOR A WHILE...
...I CAN LEND YOU MY POWER.
IT MUST BE TOUGH...
...WHEN YOU FEEL LIKE YOU CAN'T KEEP UP WITH YOUR FRIENDS.

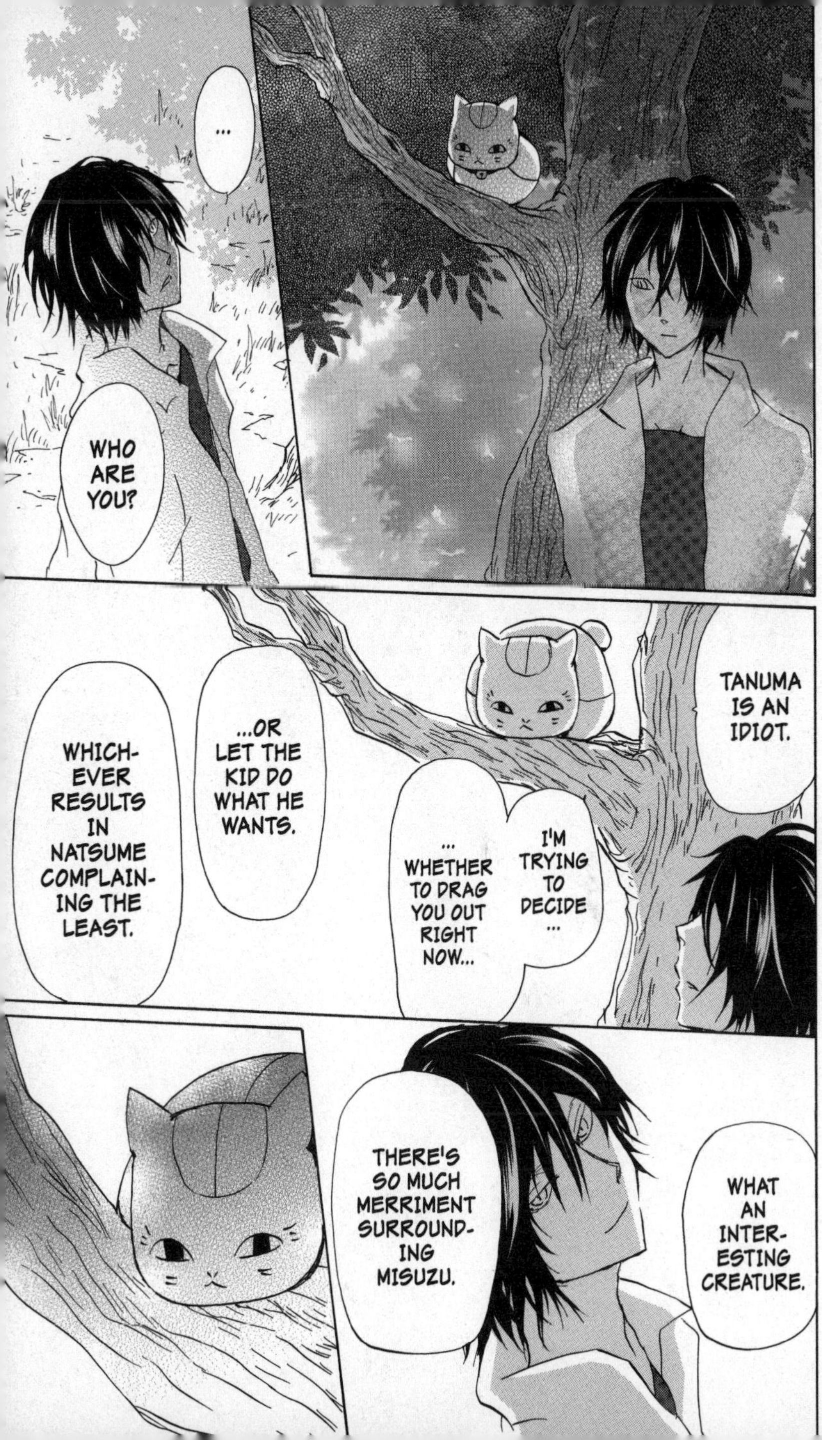
...
WHO ARE YOU?
TANUMA IS AN IDIOT.
I'M TRYING TO DECIDE...
...WHETHER TO DRAG YOU OUT RIGHT NOW...
...OR LET THE KID DO WHAT HE WANTS.
WHICH-EVER RESULTS IN NATSUME COMPLAIN-ING THE LEAST.
WHAT AN INTER-ESTING CREATURE.
THERE'S SO MUCH MERRIMENT SURROUND-ING MISUZU.

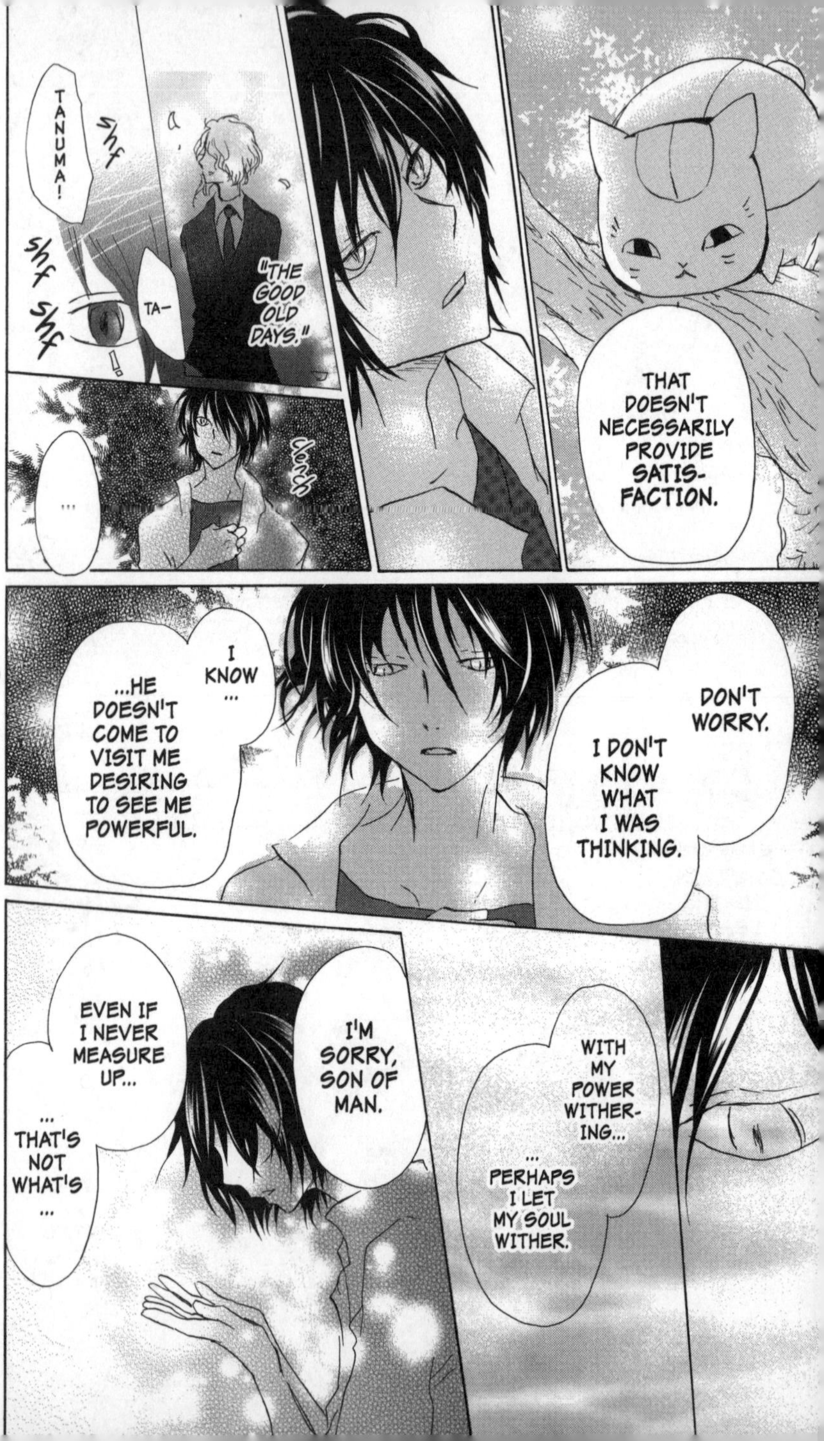
THAT DOESN'T NECESSARILY PROVIDE SATIS-FACTION.
TANUMA!
shf
TA-
"THE GOOD OLD DAYS."
shf shf
!
...
clench
DON'T WORRY.
I DON'T KNOW WHAT I WAS THINKING.
I KNOW...
...HE DOESN'T COME TO VISIT ME DESIRING TO SEE ME POWERFUL.
WITH MY POWER WITHER-ING...
...PERHAPS I LET MY SOUL WITHER.
I'M SORRY, SON OF MAN.
EVEN IF I NEVER MEASURE UP...
...THAT'S NOT WHAT'S...

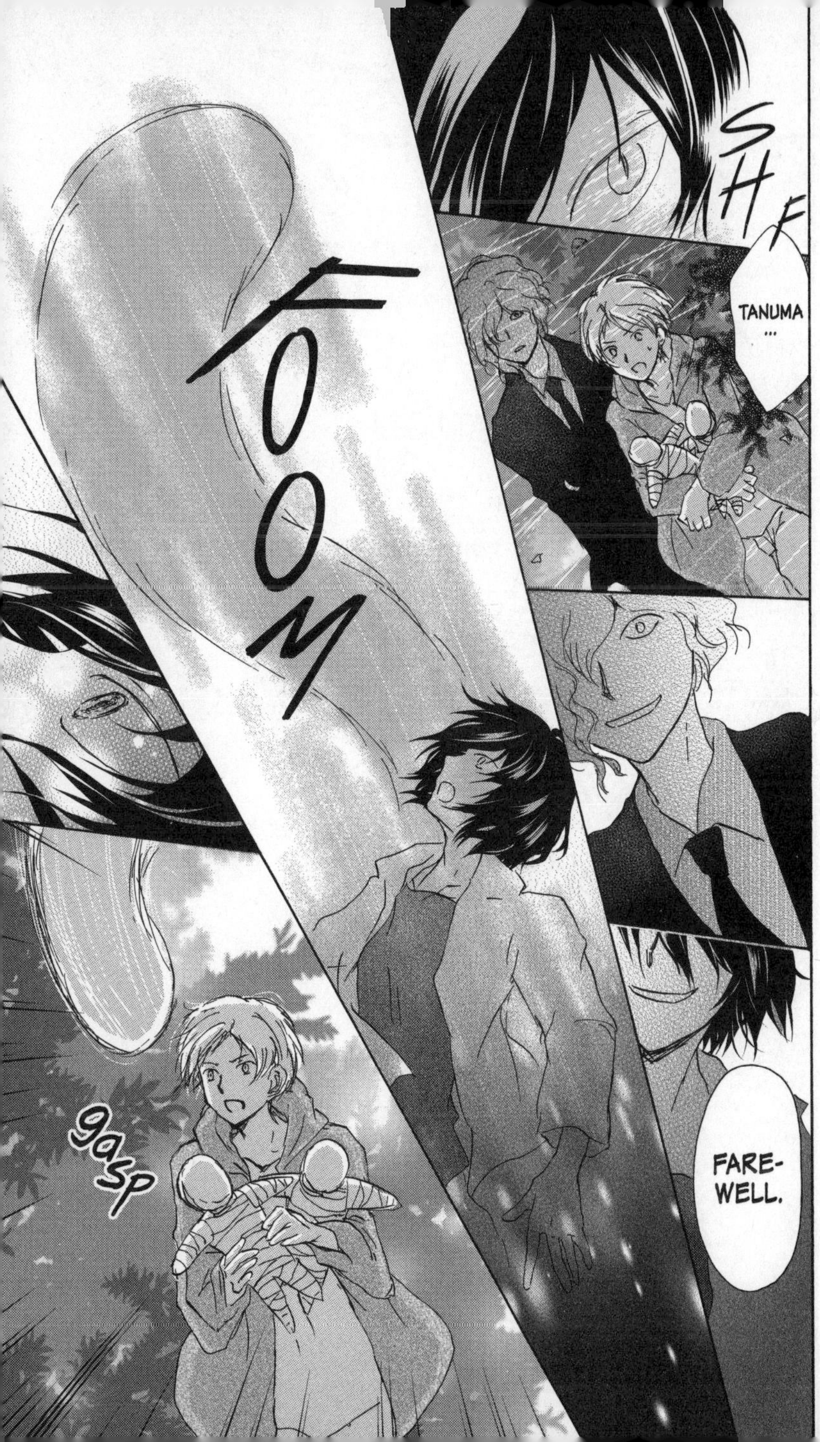
SHF
TANUMA ...
FARE-WELL.
FOOM
gasp

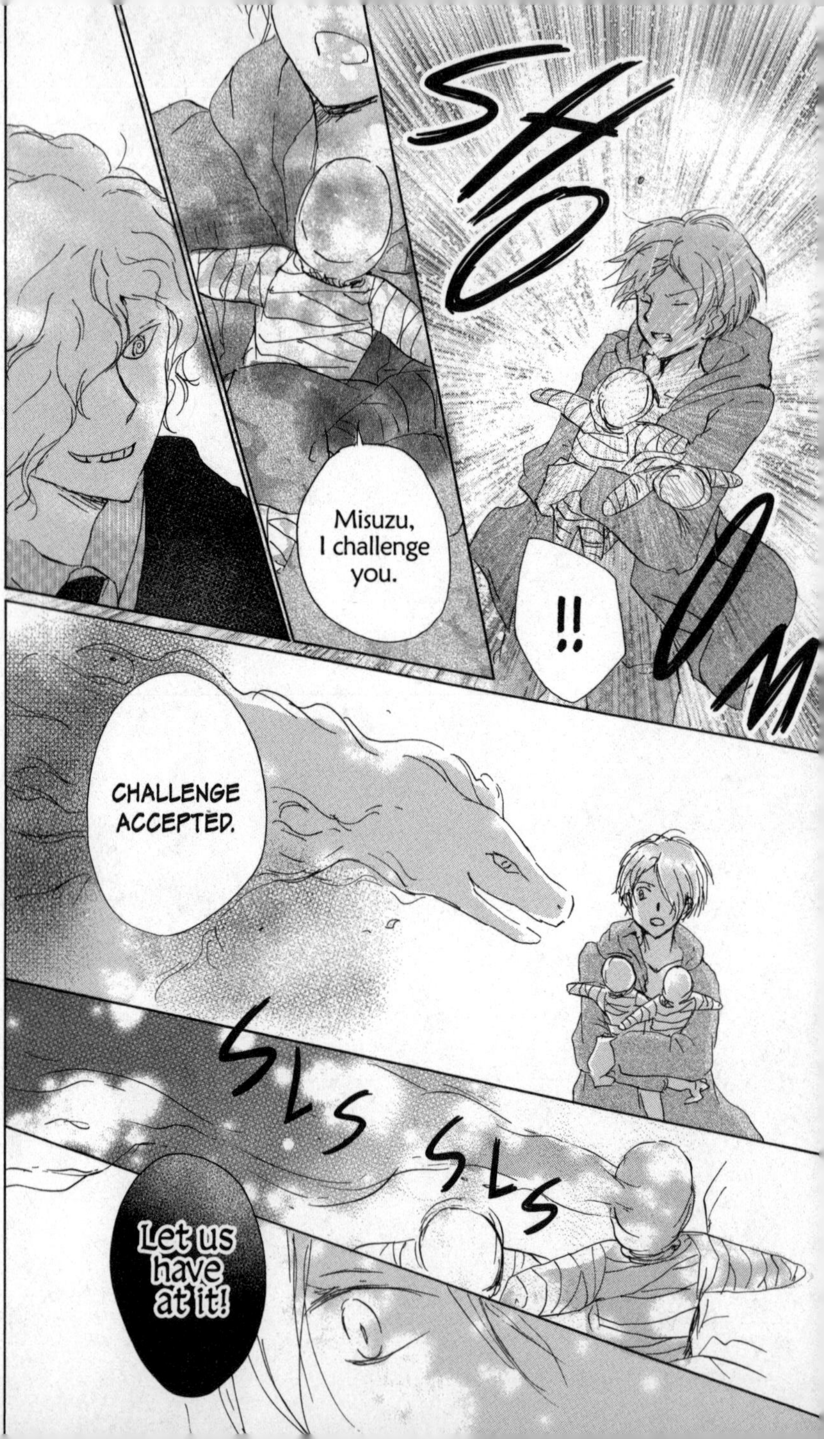
SHOOM
!!
Misuzu, I challenge you.
CHALLENGE ACCEPTED.
SLSS
SLSS
Let us have at it!

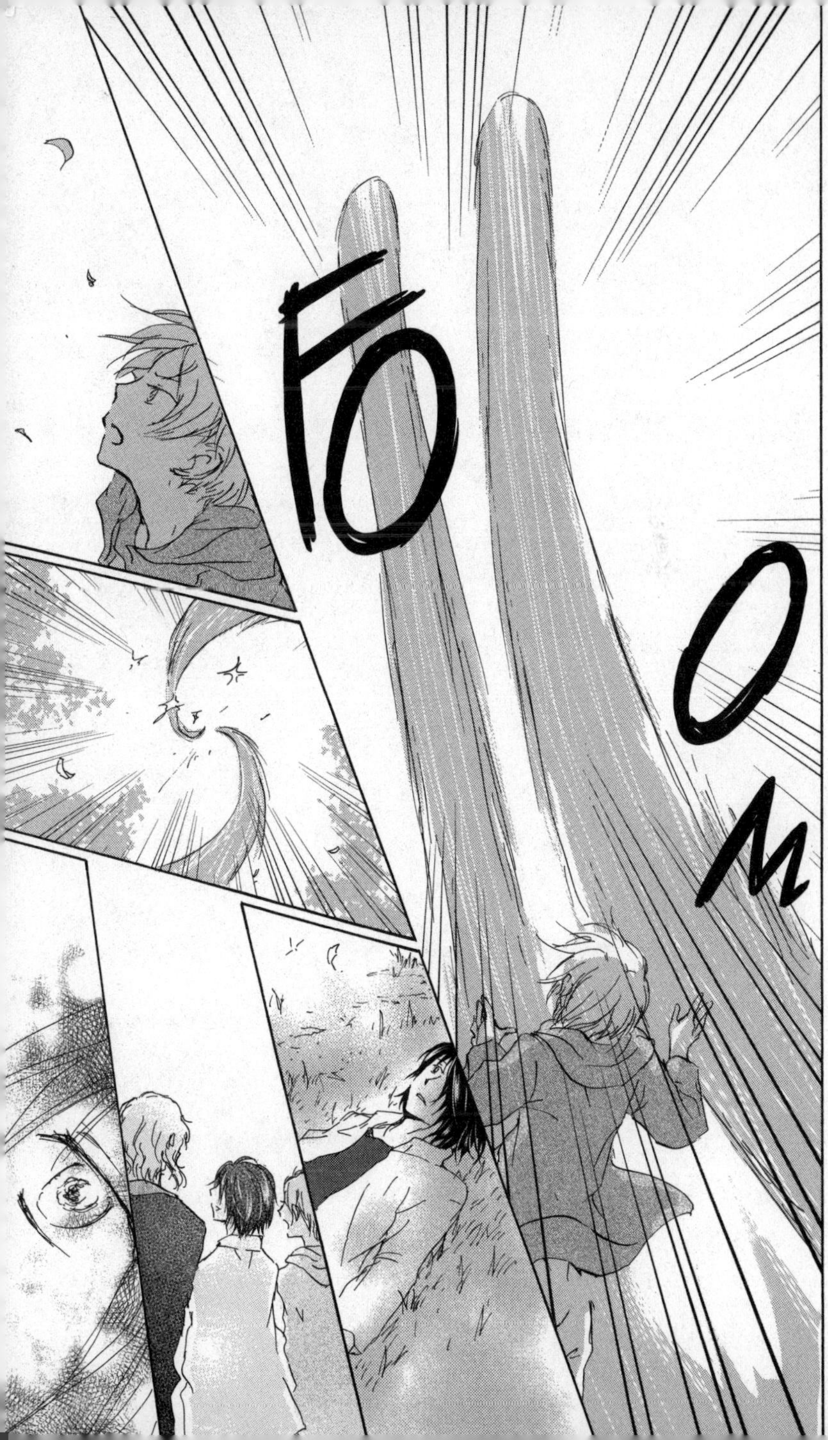
FOOOM

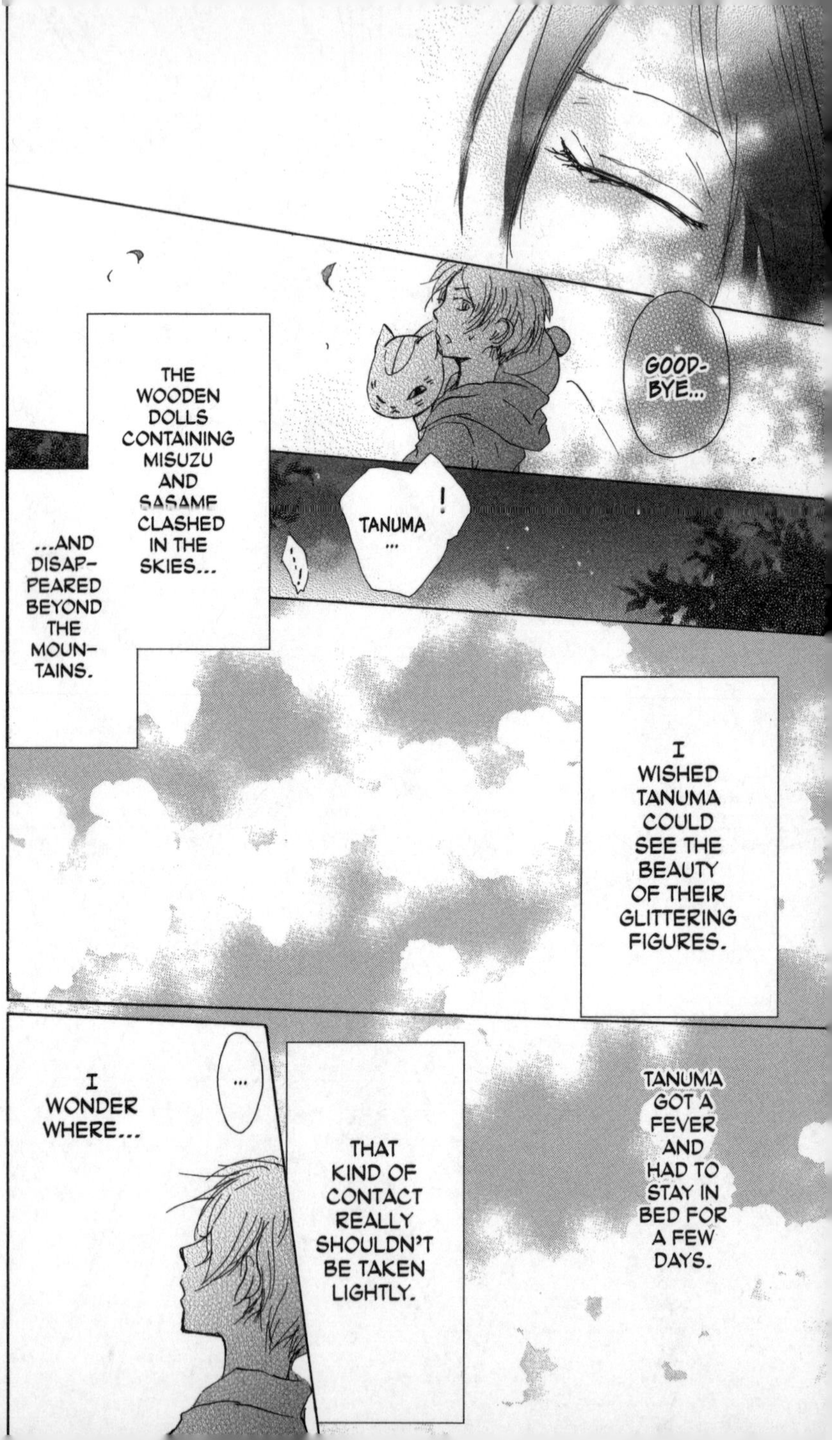
GOOD-BYE...
!
TANUMA ...
...!
THE WOODEN DOLLS CONTAINING MISUZU AND SASAME CLASHED IN THE SKIES...
...AND DISAPPEARED BEYOND THE MOUNTAINS.
I WISHED TANUMA COULD SEE THE BEAUTY OF THEIR GLITTERING FIGURES.
TANUMA GOT A FEVER AND HAD TO STAY IN BED FOR A FEW DAYS.
THAT KIND OF CONTACT REALLY SHOULDN'T BE TAKEN LIGHTLY.
...
I WONDER WHERE...

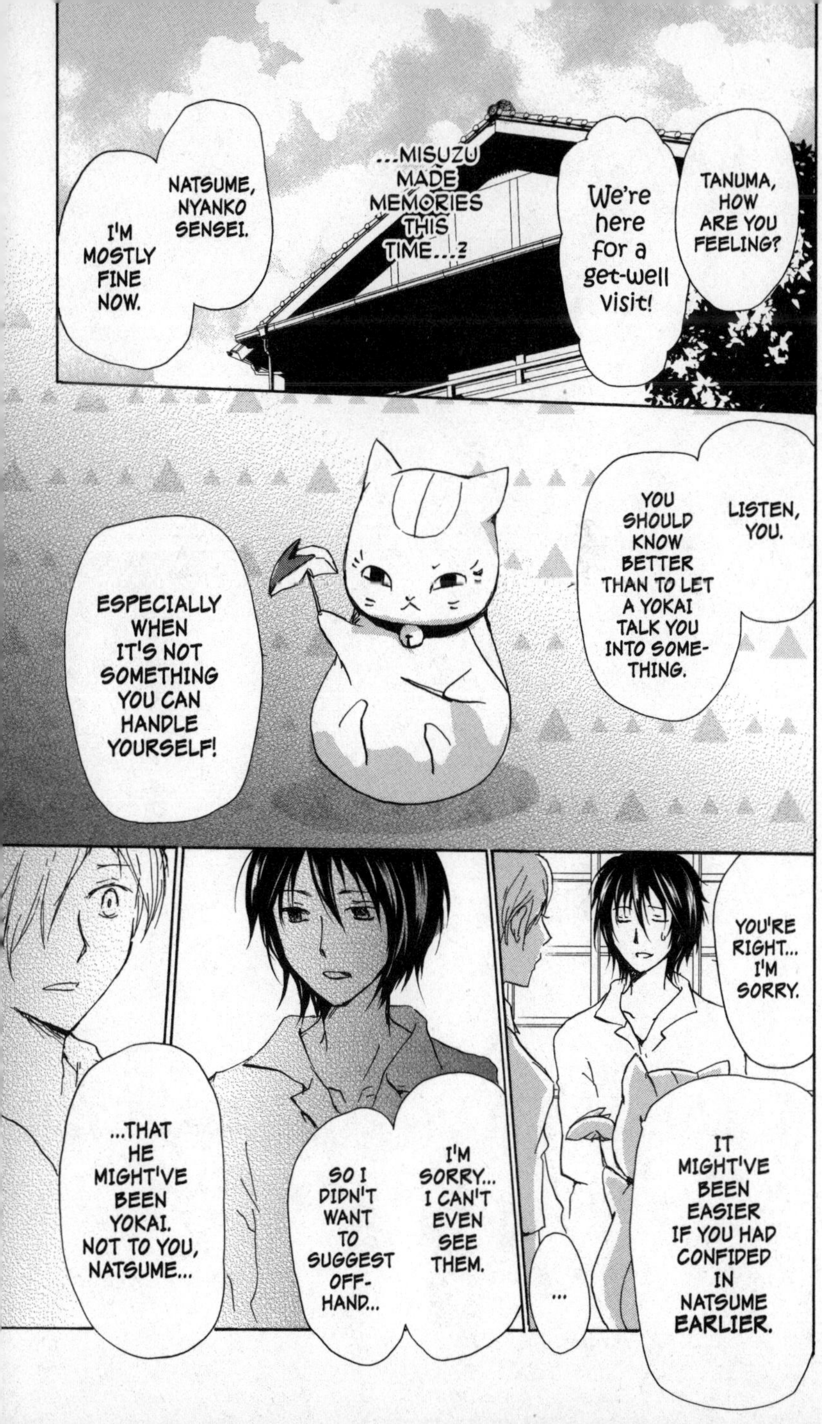

TANUMA, HOW ARE YOU FEELING?
We're here for a get-well visit!
...MISUZU MADE MEMORIES THIS TIME...?
NATSUME, NYANKO SENSEI.
I'M MOSTLY FINE NOW.
LISTEN, YOU.
YOU SHOULD KNOW BETTER THAN TO LET A YOKAI TALK YOU INTO SOME-THING.
ESPECIALLY WHEN IT'S NOT SOMETHING YOU CAN HANDLE YOURSELF!
YOU'RE RIGHT... I'M SORRY.
IT MIGHT'VE BEEN EASIER IF YOU HAD CONFIDED IN NATSUME EARLIER.
...
I'M SORRY... I CAN'T EVEN SEE THEM.
SO I DIDN'T WANT TO SUGGEST OFF-HAND...
...THAT HE MIGHT'VE BEEN YOKAI. NOT TO YOU, NATSUME...

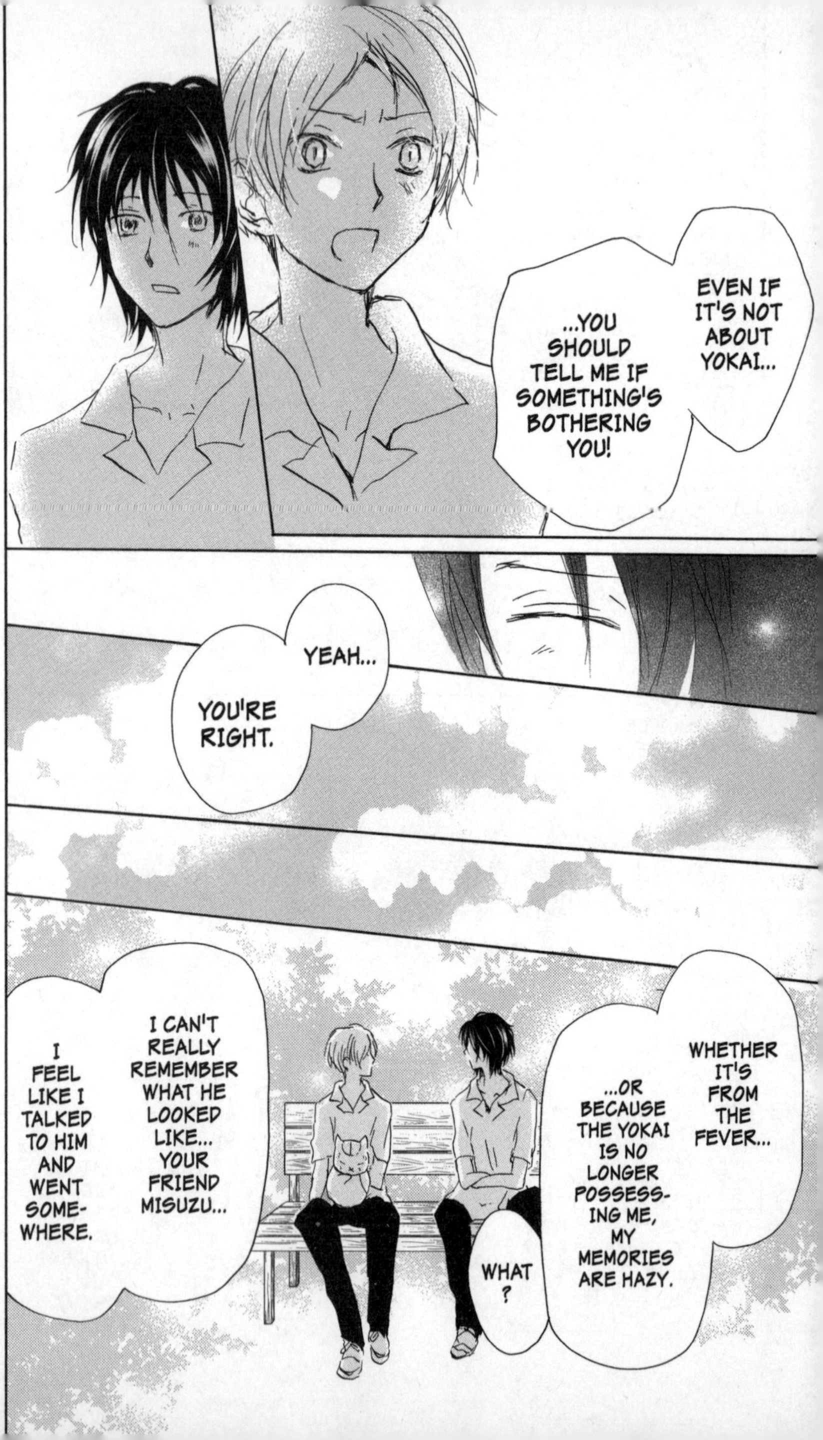
EVEN IF IT'S NOT ABOUT YOKAI...
...YOU SHOULD TELL ME IF SOMETHING'S BOTHERING YOU!
YEAH...
YOU'RE RIGHT.
WHETHER IT'S FROM THE FEVER...
...OR BECAUSE THE YOKAI IS NO LONGER POSSESS-ING ME, MY MEMORIES ARE HAZY.
WHAT?
I CAN'T REALLY REMEMBER WHAT HE LOOKED LIKE... YOUR FRIEND MISUZU...
I FEEL LIKE I TALKED TO HIM AND WENT SOME-WHERE.

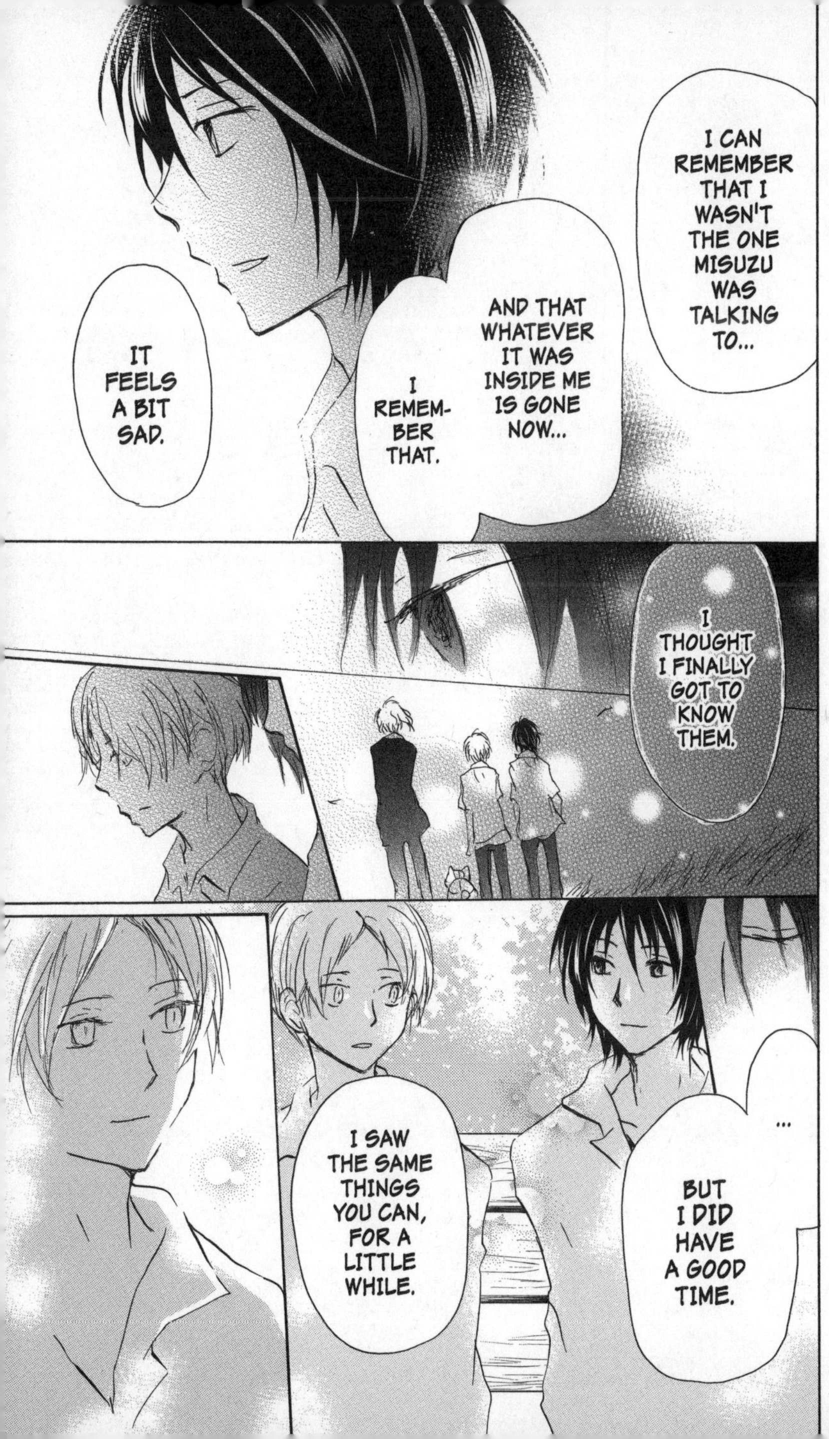
I CAN REMEMBER THAT I WASN'T THE ONE MISUZU WAS TALKING TO...
AND THAT WHATEVER IT WAS INSIDE ME IS GONE NOW...
I REMEMBER THAT.
IT FEELS A BIT SAD.
I THOUGHT I FINALLY GOT TO KNOW THEM.
...
BUT I DID HAVE A GOOD TIME.
I SAW THE SAME THINGS YOU CAN, FOR A LITTLE WHILE.

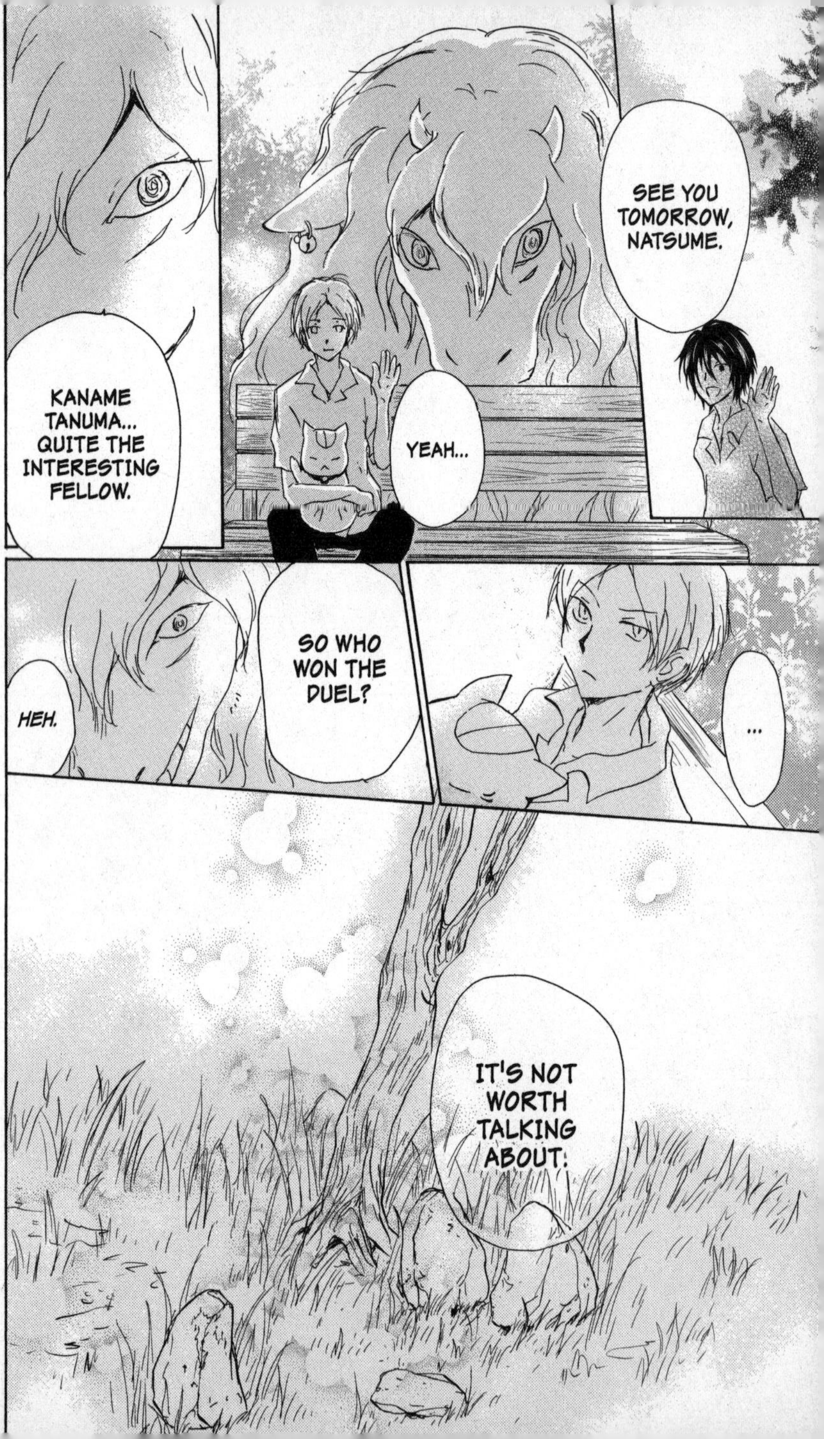
SEE YOU TOMORROW, NATSUME.
YEAH...
KANAME TANUMA... QUITE THE INTERESTING FELLOW.
...
SO WHO WON THE DUEL?
HEH.
IT'S NOT WORTH TALKING ABOUT.

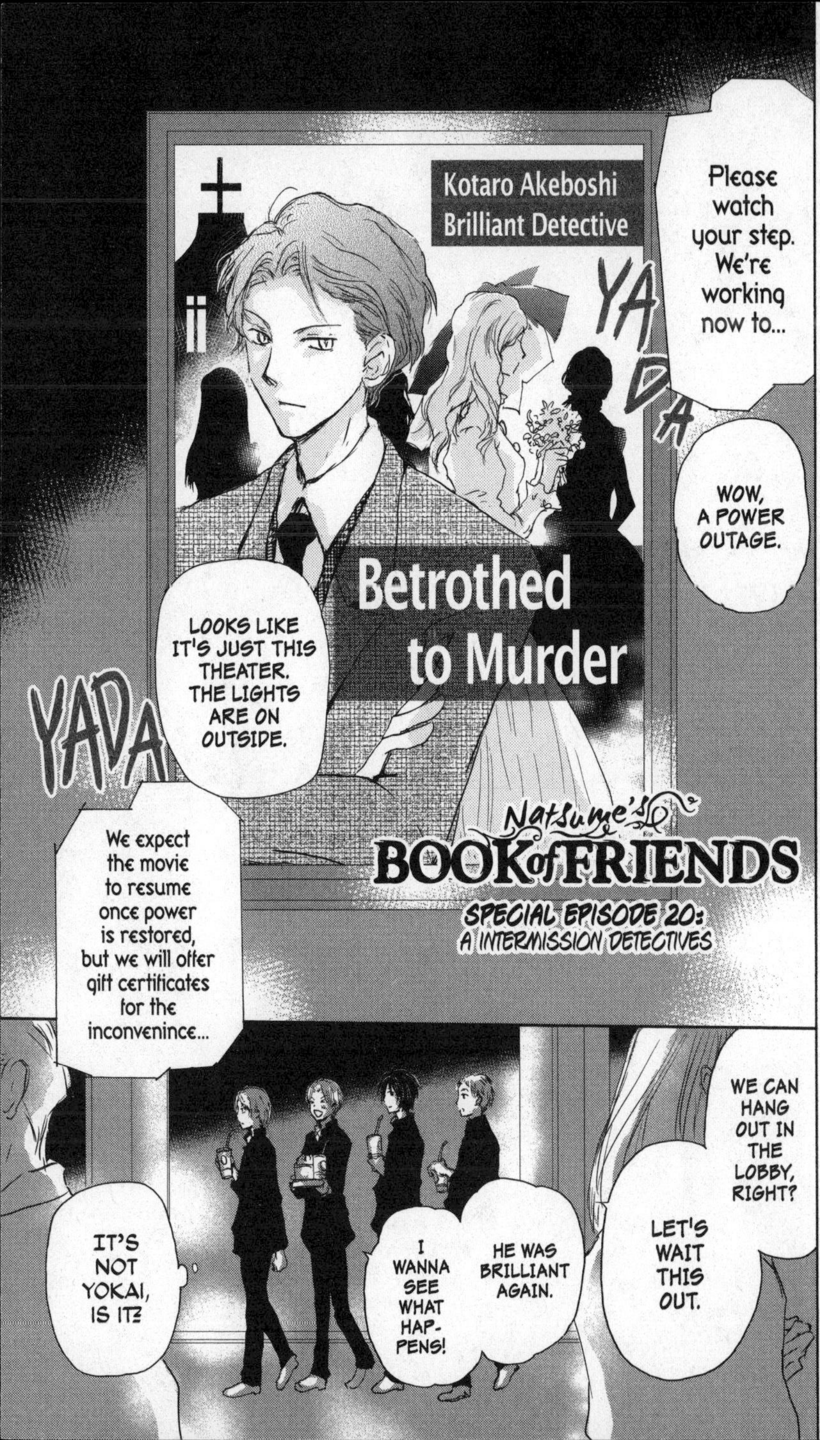
Please watch your step. We're working now to...
YADA YADA
Kotaro Akeboshi Brilliant Detective
WOW, A POWER OUTAGE.
Betrothed to Murder
LOOKS LIKE IT'S JUST THIS THEATER. THE LIGHTS ARE ON OUTSIDE.
YADA
Natsume's BOOK of FRIENDS
SPECIAL EPISODE 20: A INTERMISSION DETECTIVES
We expect the movie to resume once power is restored, but we will offer gift certificates for the inconvenince...
WE CAN HANG OUT IN THE LOBBY, RIGHT?
LET'S WAIT THIS OUT.
HE WAS BRILLIANT AGAIN.
I WANNA SEE WHAT HAP-PENS!
IT'S NOT YOKAI, IS IT?

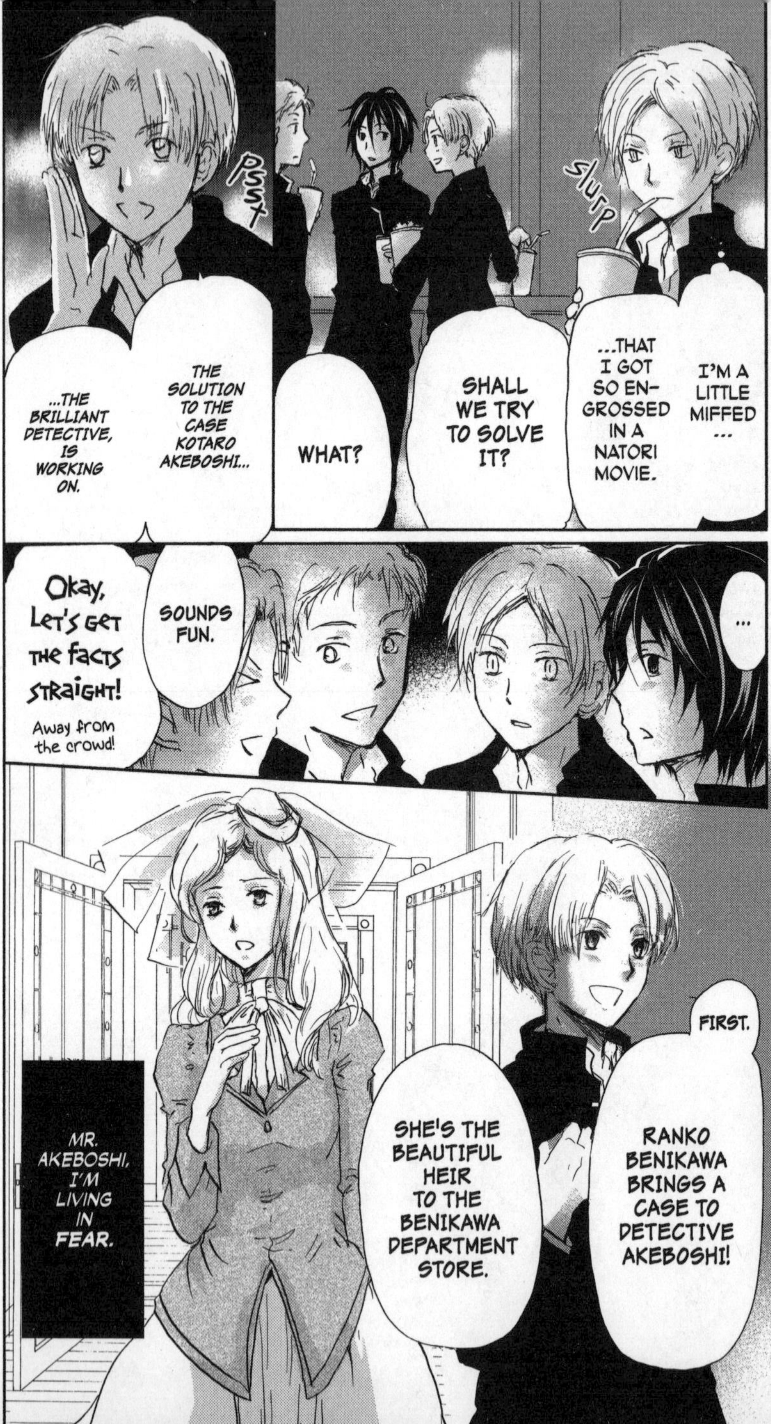
SLURP
I'M A LITTLE MIFFED...
...THAT I GOT SO EN-GROSSED IN A NATORI MOVIE.
SHALL WE TRY TO SOLVE IT?
WHAT?
PSST
THE SOLUTION TO THE CASE KOTARO AKEBOSHI...
...THE BRILLIANT DETECTIVE, IS WORKING ON.
...
SOUNDS FUN.
Okay, Let's get the facts straight!
Away from the crowd!
FIRST.
RANKO BENIKAWA BRINGS A CASE TO DETECTIVE AKEBOSHI!
SHE'S THE BEAUTIFUL HEIR TO THE BENIKAWA DEPARTMENT STORE.
MR. AKEBOSHI, I'M LIVING IN FEAR.

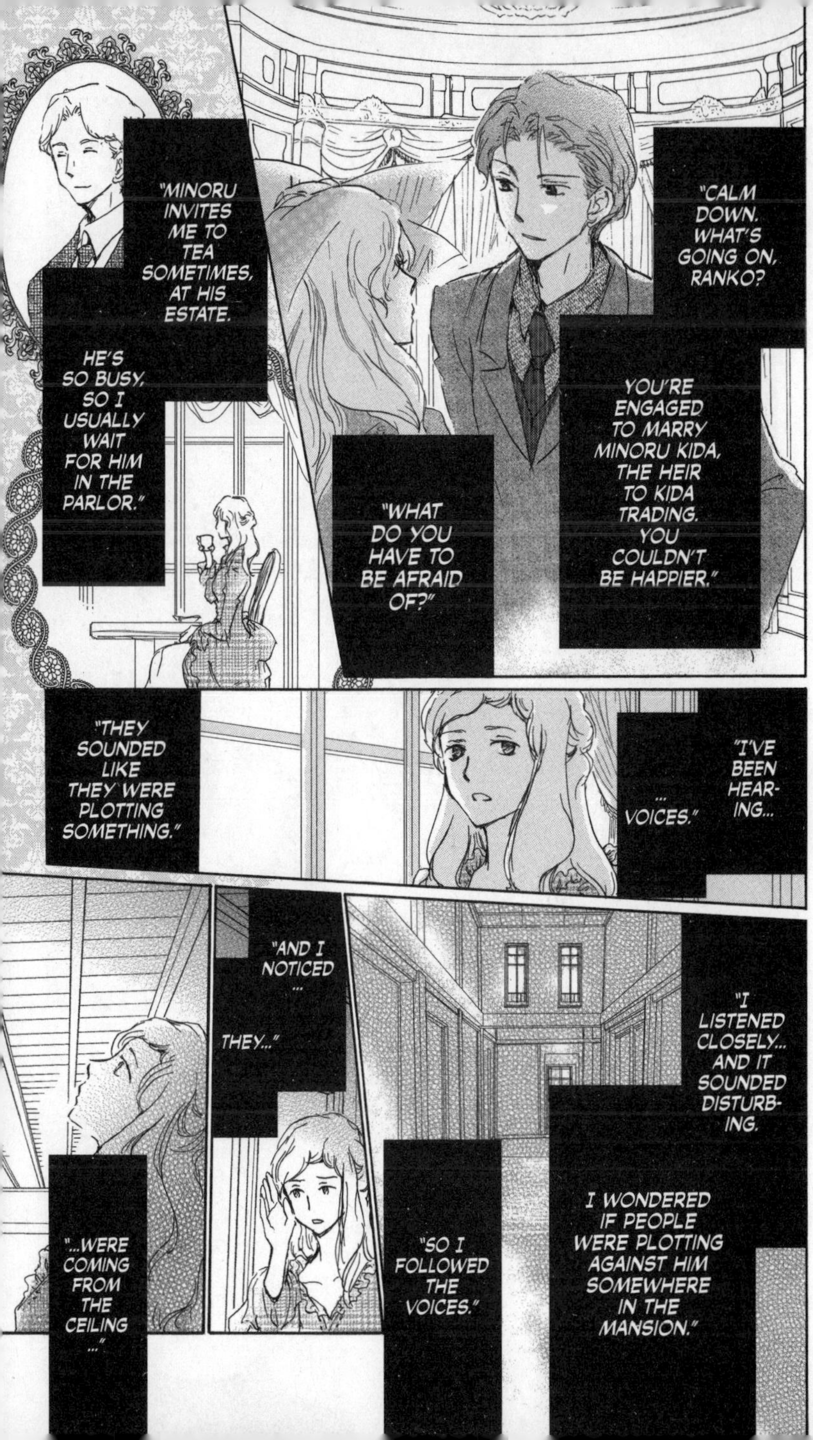
"CALM DOWN. WHAT'S GOING ON, RANKO?
YOU'RE ENGAGED TO MARRY MINORU KIDA, THE HEIR TO KIDA TRADING. YOU COULDN'T BE HAPPIER."
"WHAT DO YOU HAVE TO BE AFRAID OF?"
"MINORU INVITES ME TO TEA SOMETIMES, AT HIS ESTATE.
HE'S SO BUSY, SO I USUALLY WAIT FOR HIM IN THE PARLOR."
"I'VE BEEN HEARING...
...VOICES."
"THEY SOUNDED LIKE THEY WERE PLOTTING SOMETHING."
"I LISTENED CLOSELY... AND IT SOUNDED DISTURBING.
I WONDERED IF PEOPLE WERE PLOTTING AGAINST HIM SOMEWHERE IN THE MANSION."
"SO I FOLLOWED THE VOICES."
"AND I NOTICED ...
THEY..."
"...WERE COMING FROM THE CEILING ..."

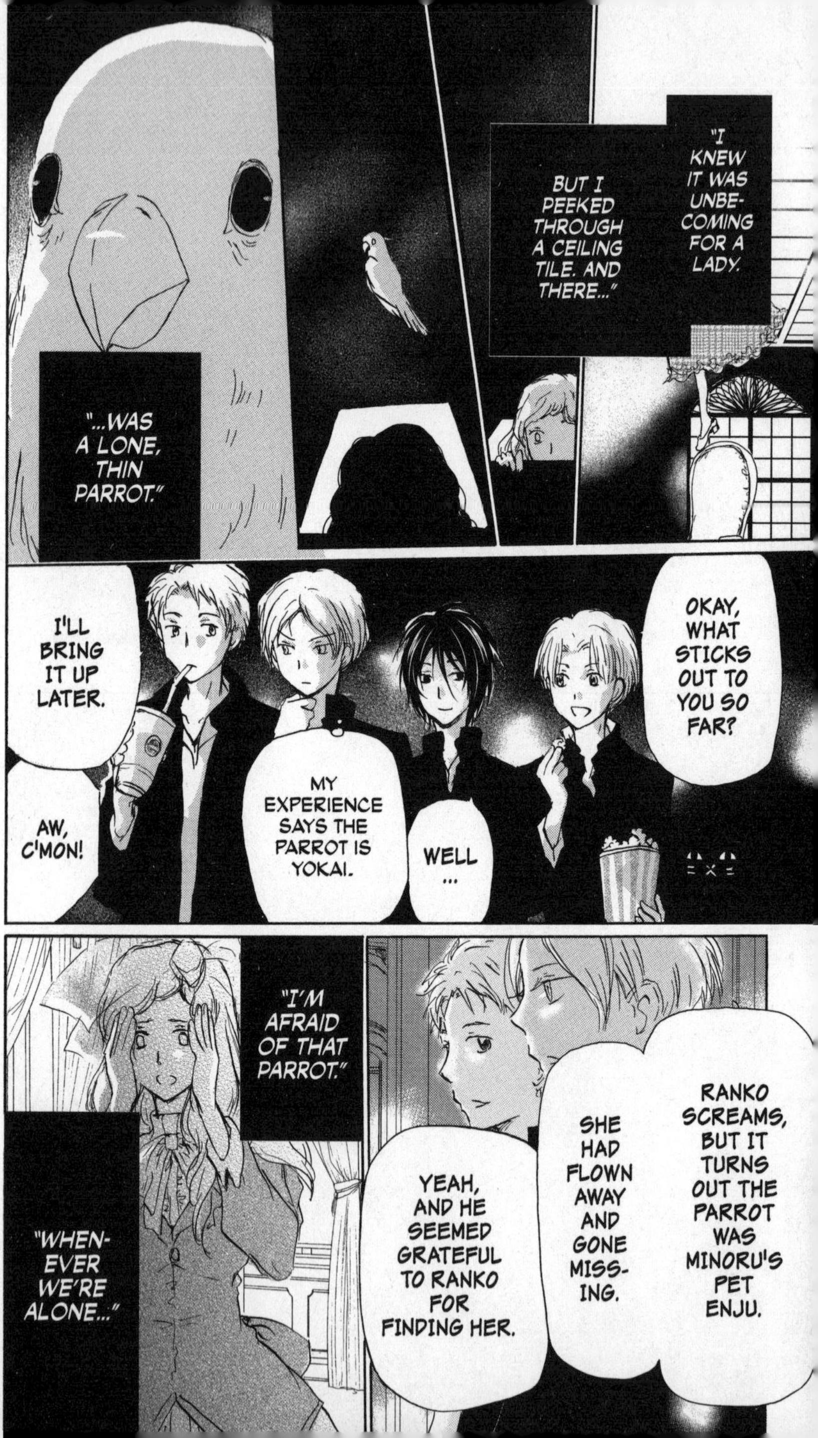
"I KNEW IT WAS UNBE-COMING FOR A LADY.
BUT I PEEKED THROUGH A CEILING TILE. AND THERE..."
"...WAS A LONE, THIN PARROT."
OKAY, WHAT STICKS OUT TO YOU SO FAR?
WELL ...
MY EXPERIENCE SAYS THE PARROT IS YOKAI.
I'LL BRING IT UP LATER.
AW, C'MON!
RANKO SCREAMS, BUT IT TURNS OUT THE PARROT WAS MINORU'S PET ENJU.
SHE HAD FLOWN AWAY AND GONE MISS-ING.
YEAH, AND HE SEEMED GRATEFUL TO RANKO FOR FINDING HER.
"I'M AFRAID OF THAT PARROT."
"WHEN-EVER WE'RE ALONE..."

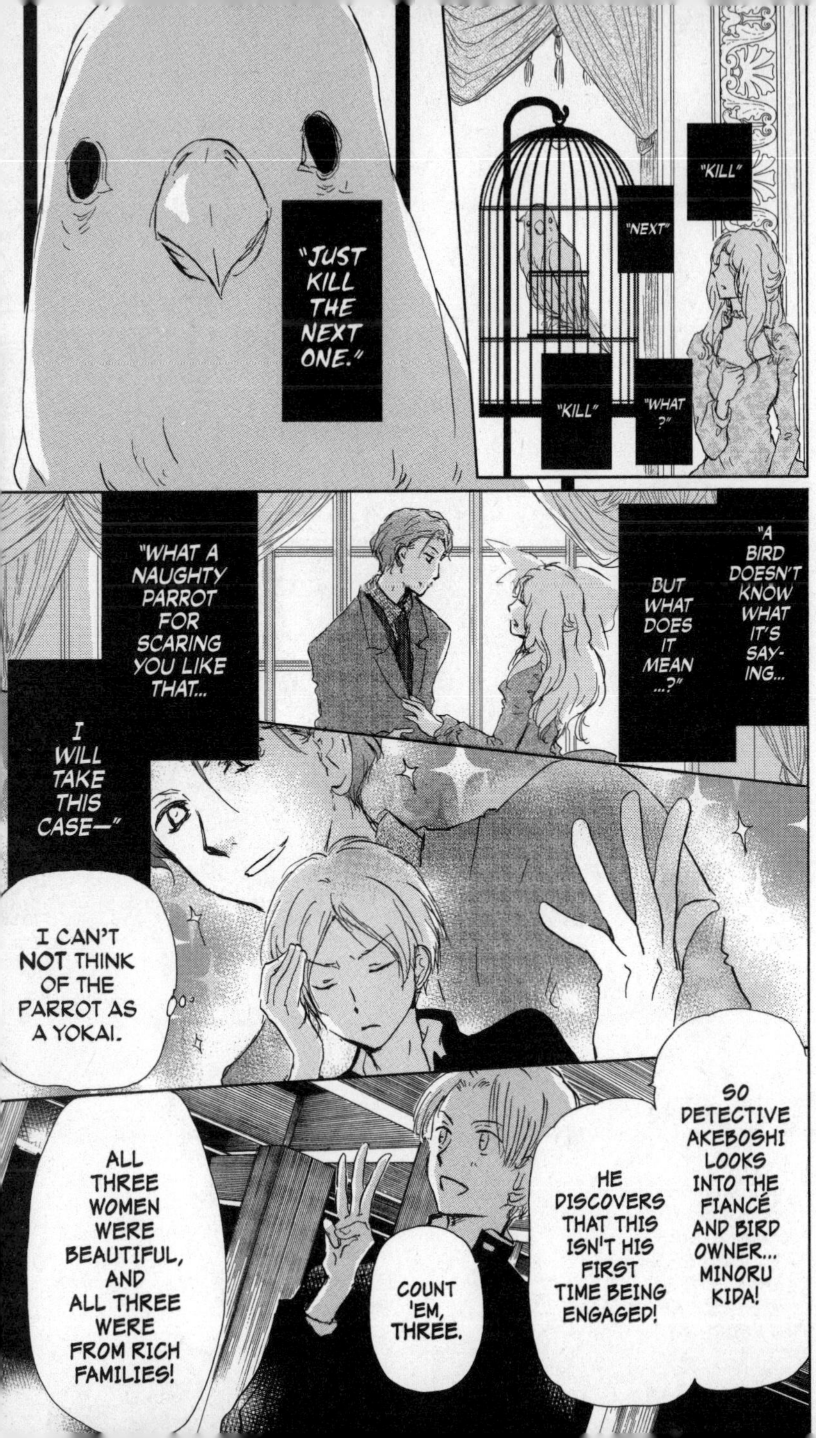
"KILL"
"NEXT"
"WHAT?"
"KILL"
"JUST KILL THE NEXT ONE."
"A BIRD DOESN'T KNOW WHAT IT'S SAYING...
BUT WHAT DOES IT MEAN...?"
"WHAT A NAUGHTY PARROT FOR SCARING YOU LIKE THAT...
I WILL TAKE THIS CASE—"
I CAN'T NOT THINK OF THE PARROT AS A YOKAI.
SO DETECTIVE AKEBOSHI LOOKS INTO THE FIANCÉ AND BIRD OWNER... MINORU KIDA!
HE DISCOVERS THAT THIS ISN'T HIS FIRST TIME BEING ENGAGED!
COUNT 'EM, THREE.
ALL THREE WOMEN WERE BEAUTIFUL, AND ALL THREE WERE FROM RICH FAMILIES!

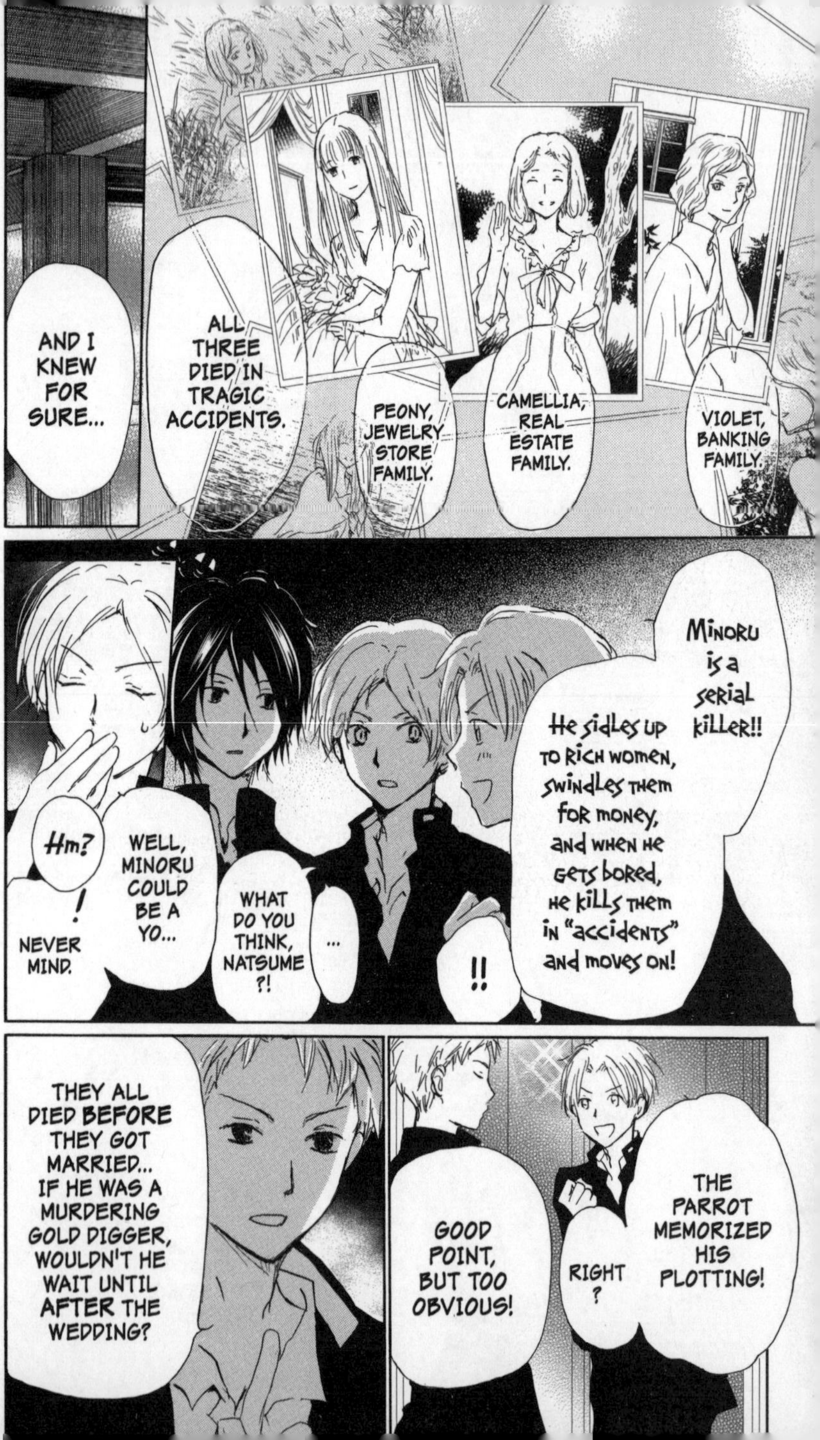
VIOLET, BANKING FAMILY.
CAMELLIA, REAL ESTATE FAMILY.
PEONY, JEWELRY STORE FAMILY.
ALL THREE DIED IN TRAGIC ACCIDENTS.
AND I KNEW FOR SURE...
Minoru is a serial killer!!
He sidles up to rich women, swindles them for money, and when he gets bored, he kills them in "accidents" and moves on!
!!
...
WHAT DO YOU THINK, NATSUME?!
WELL, MINORU COULD BE A YO...
Hm?
!
NEVER MIND.
THE PARROT MEMORIZED HIS PLOTTING!
RIGHT?
GOOD POINT, BUT TOO OBVIOUS!
THEY ALL DIED BEFORE THEY GOT MARRIED... IF HE WAS A MURDERING GOLD DIGGER, WOULDN'T HE WAIT UNTIL AFTER THE WEDDING?

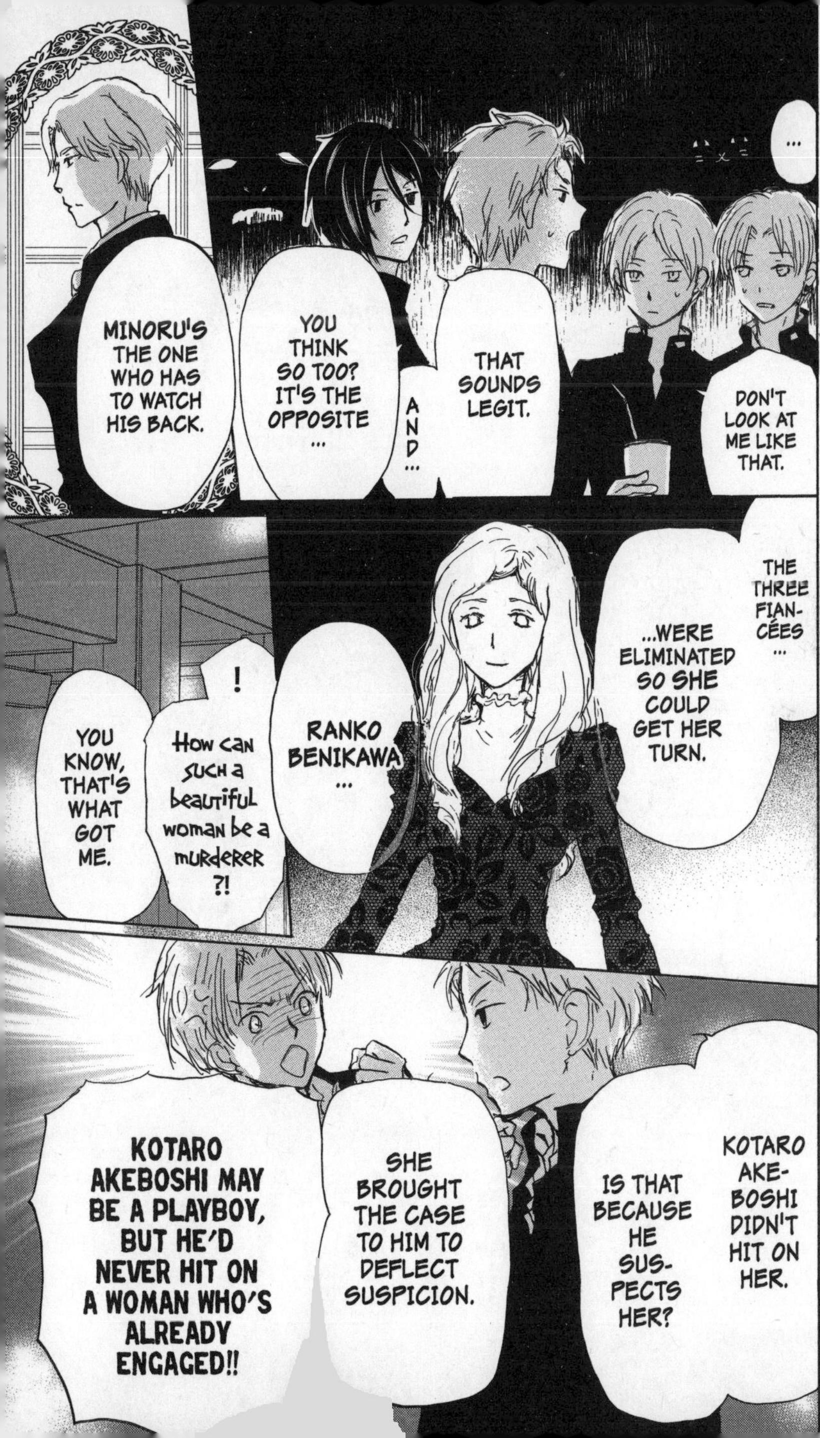
...
DON'T LOOK AT ME LIKE THAT.
THAT SOUNDS LEGIT.
AND...
YOU THINK SO TOO? IT'S THE OPPOSITE...
MINORU'S THE ONE WHO HAS TO WATCH HIS BACK.
THE THREE FIANCÉES...
...WERE ELIMINATED SO SHE COULD GET HER TURN.
RANKO BENIKAWA...
!
How can such a beautiful woman be a murderer?!
YOU KNOW, THAT'S WHAT GOT ME.
KOTARO AKEBOSHI DIDN'T HIT ON HER.
IS THAT BECAUSE HE SUSPECTS HER?
SHE BROUGHT THE CASE TO HIM TO DEFLECT SUSPICION.
KOTARO AKEBOSHI MAY BE A PLAYBOY, BUT HE'D NEVER HIT ON A WOMAN WHO'S ALREADY ENGAGED!!

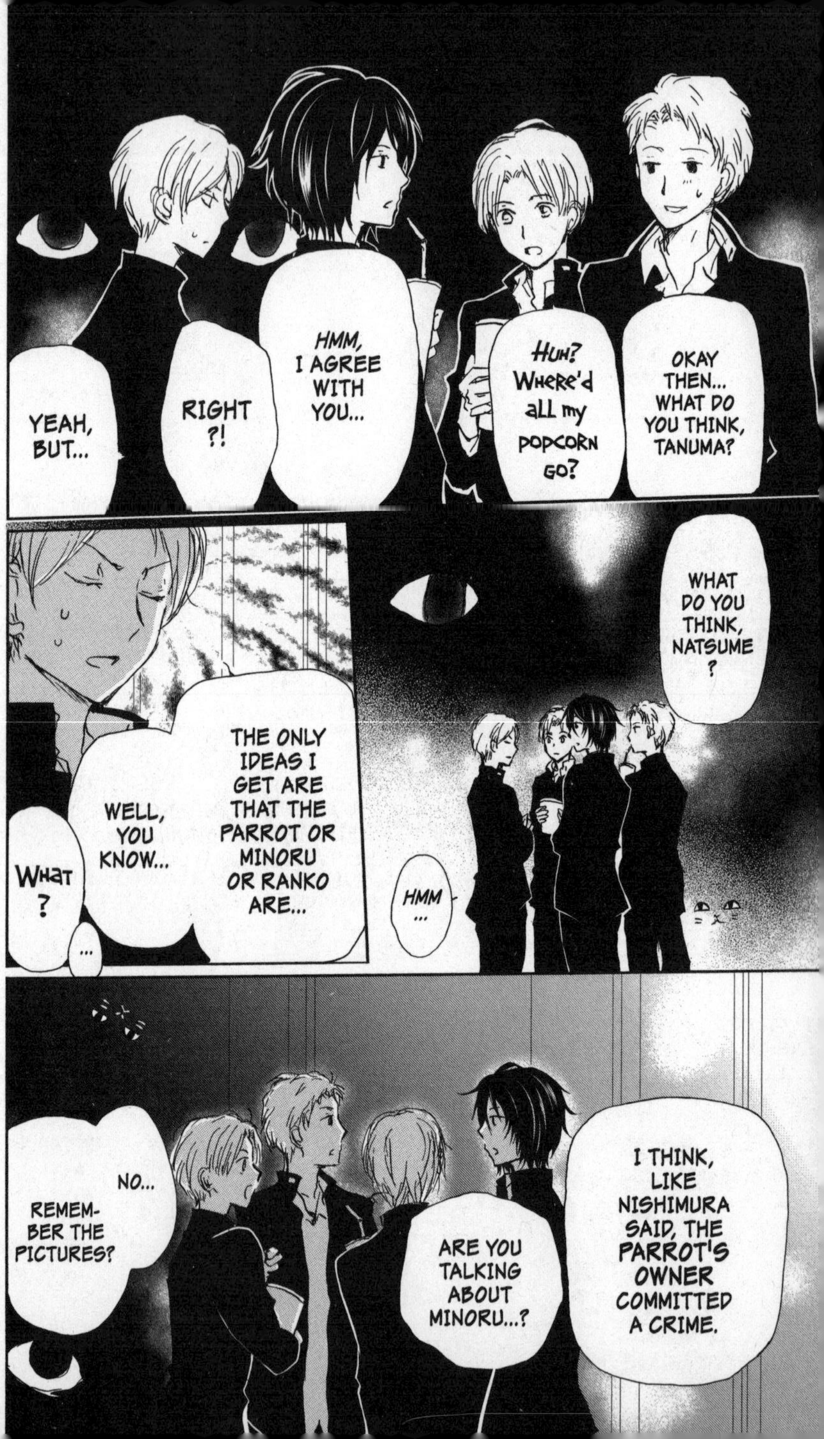
OKAY THEN... WHAT DO YOU THINK, TANUMA?
Huh? Where'd all my popcorn go?
HMM, I AGREE WITH YOU...
RIGHT?!
YEAH, BUT...
WHAT DO YOU THINK, NATSUME?
HMM...
THE ONLY IDEAS I GET ARE THAT THE PARROT OR MINORU OR RANKO ARE...
WELL, YOU KNOW...
What?
...
I THINK, LIKE NISHIMURA SAID, THE PARROT'S OWNER COMMITTED A CRIME.
ARE YOU TALKING ABOUT MINORU...?
NO...
REMEMBER THE PICTURES?

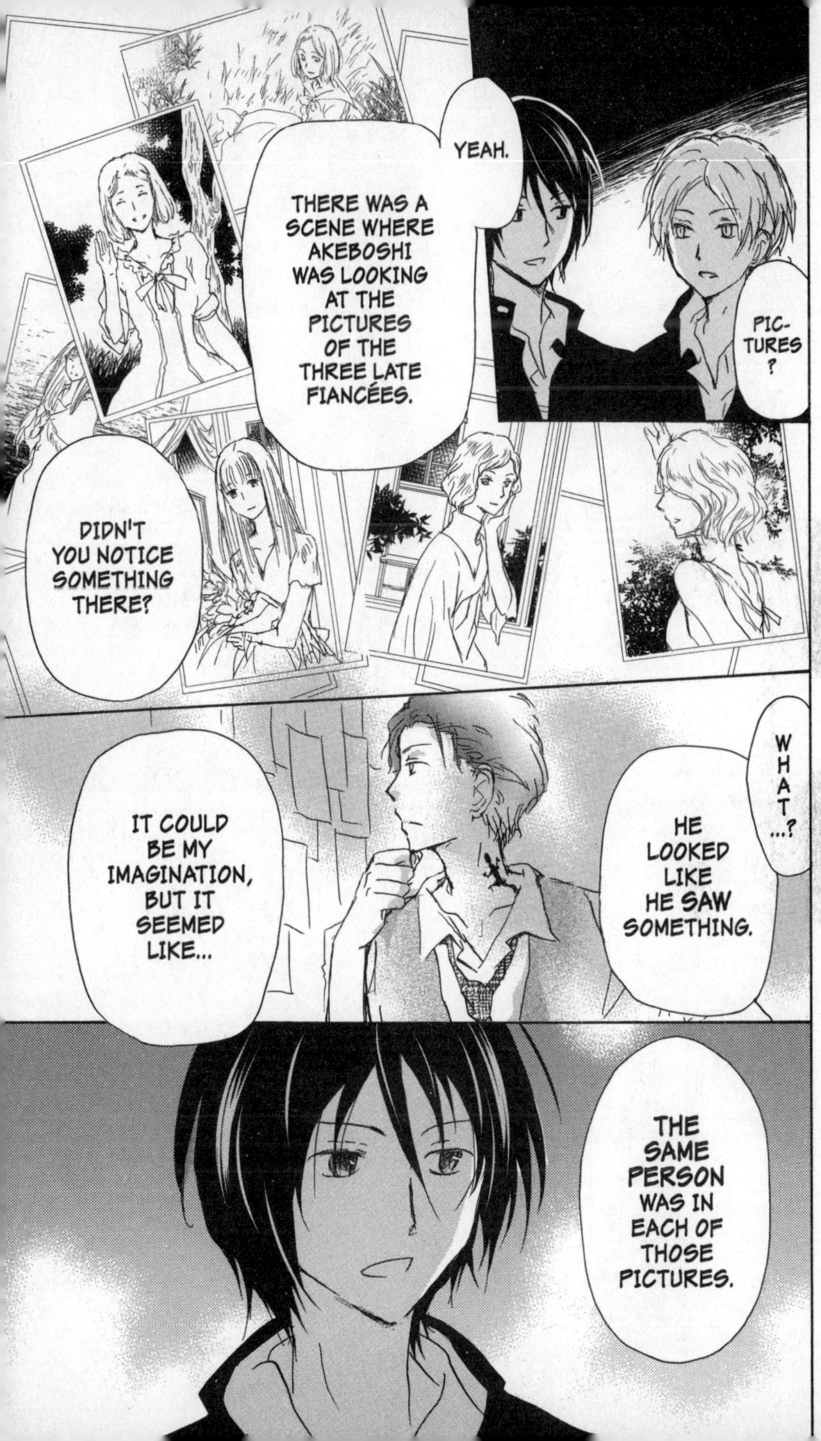
YEAH.
PICTURES?
THERE WAS A SCENE WHERE AKEBOSHI WAS LOOKING AT THE PICTURES OF THE THREE LATE FIANCÉES.
DIDN'T YOU NOTICE SOMETHING THERE?
WHAT...?
HE LOOKED LIKE HE SAW SOMETHING.
IT COULD BE MY IMAGINATION, BUT IT SEEMED LIKE...
THE SAME PERSON WAS IN EACH OF THOSE PICTURES.

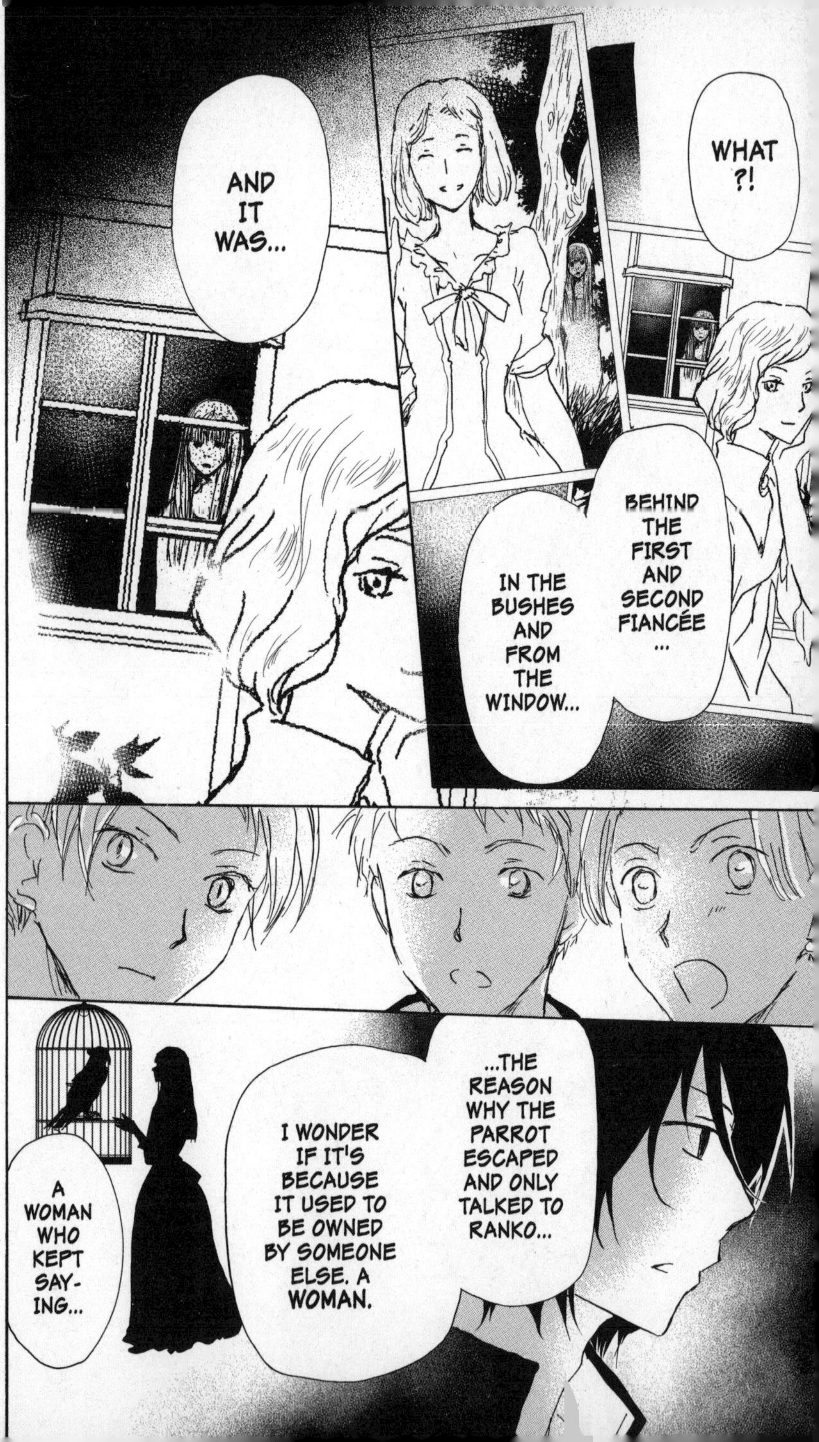
WHAT?!
AND IT WAS...
BEHIND THE FIRST AND SECOND FIANCÉE...
IN THE BUSHES AND FROM THE WINDOW...
...THE REASON WHY THE PARROT ESCAPED AND ONLY TALKED TO RANKO...
I WONDER IF IT'S BECAUSE IT USED TO BE OWNED BY SOMEONE ELSE. A WOMAN.
A WOMAN WHO KEPT SAY-ING...

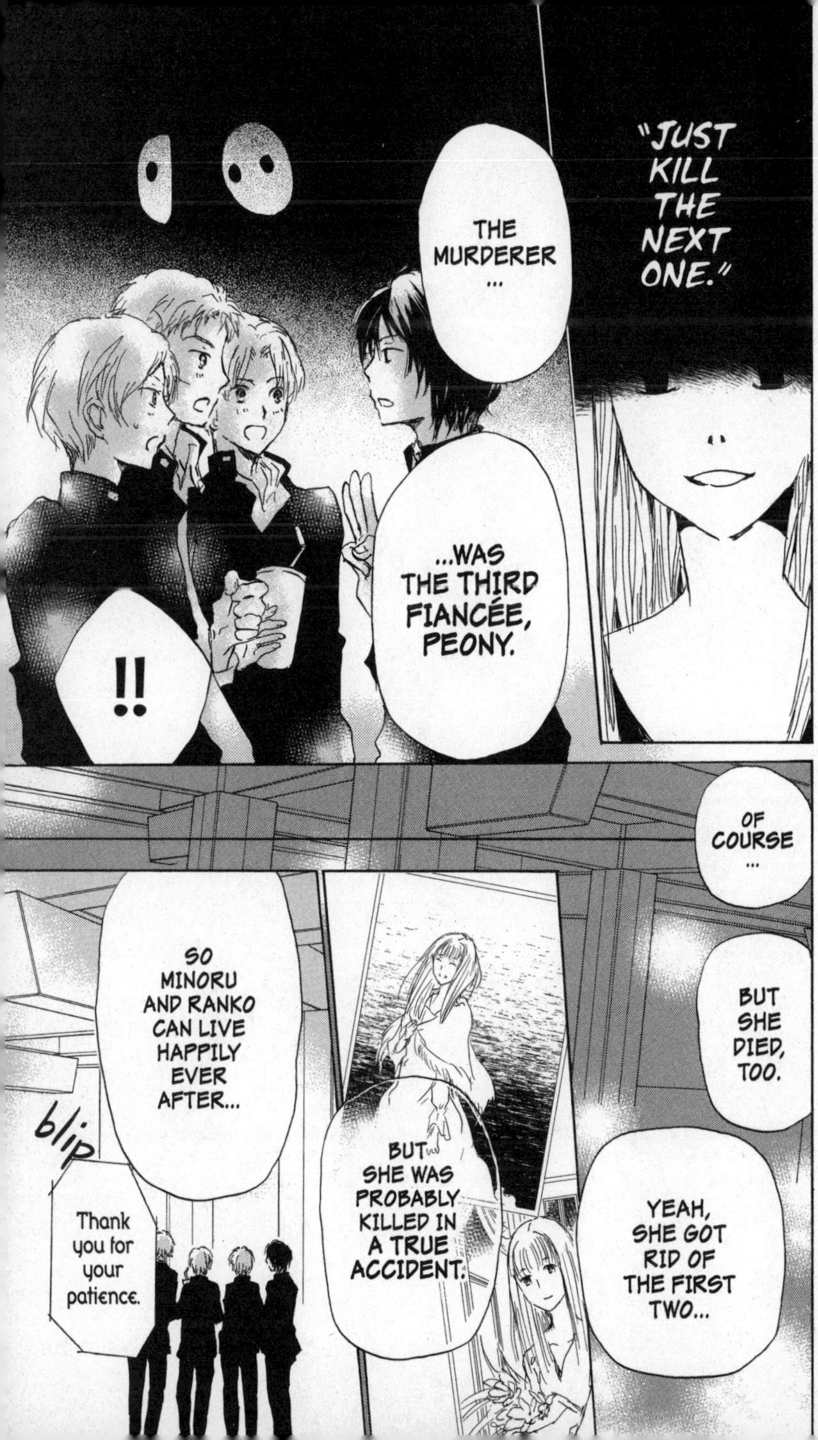

"JUST KILL THE NEXT ONE."
THE MURDERER ...
...WAS THE THIRD FIANCÉE, PEONY.
!!
OF COURSE ...
BUT SHE DIED, TOO.
YEAH, SHE GOT RID OF THE FIRST TWO...
SO MINORU AND RANKO CAN LIVE HAPPILY EVER AFTER...
BUT SHE WAS PROBABLY KILLED IN A TRUE ACCIDENT.
blip
Thank you for your patience.

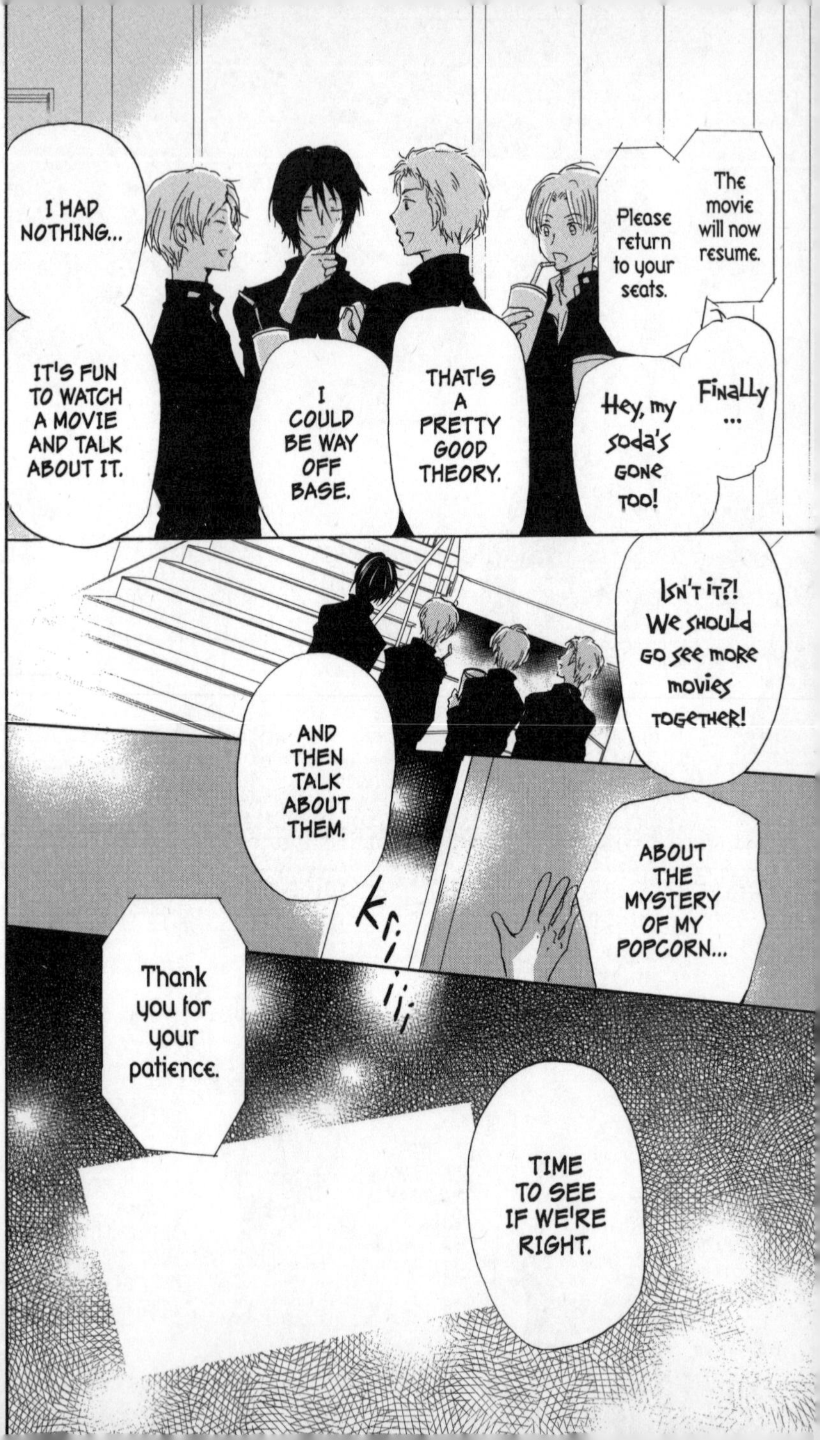
The movie will now resume.
Please return to your seats.
Finally...
Hey, my soda's gone too!
THAT'S A PRETTY GOOD THEORY.
I COULD BE WAY OFF BASE.
I HAD NOTHING...
IT'S FUN TO WATCH A MOVIE AND TALK ABOUT IT.
Isn't it?! We should go see more movies together!
AND THEN TALK ABOUT THEM.
ABOUT THE MYSTERY OF MY POPCORN...
kriiii
Thank you for your patience.
TIME TO SEE IF WE'RE RIGHT.

Natsume's BOOK of FRIENDS

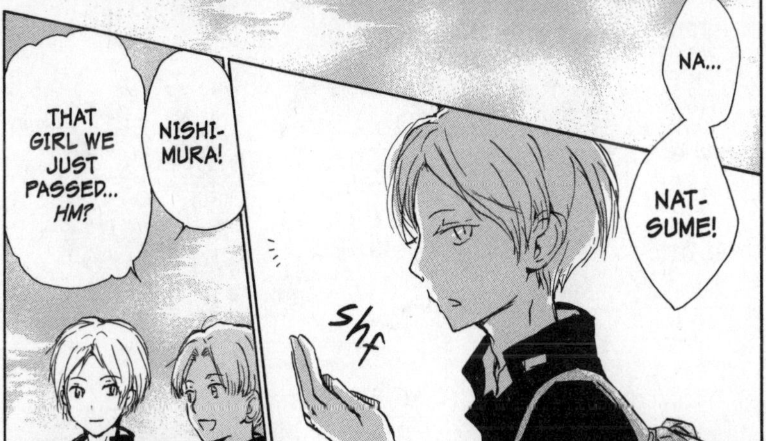
NA...
NAT-SUME!
shf
NISHI-MURA!
THAT GIRL WE JUST PASSED... HM?
WHAT'S THAT YOU'RE HOLDING? ORIGAMI?

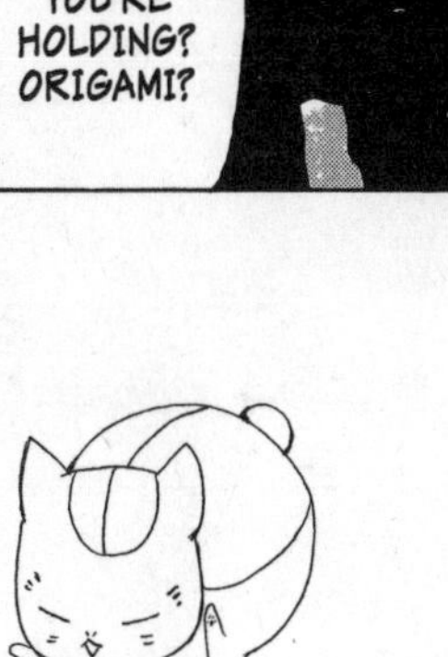

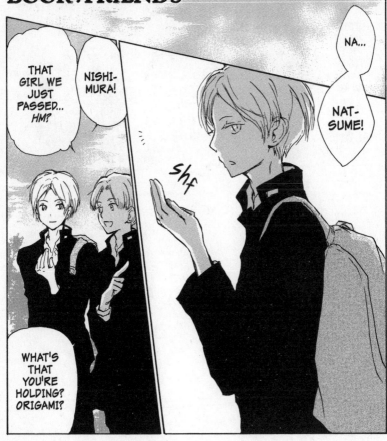

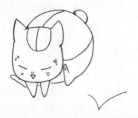

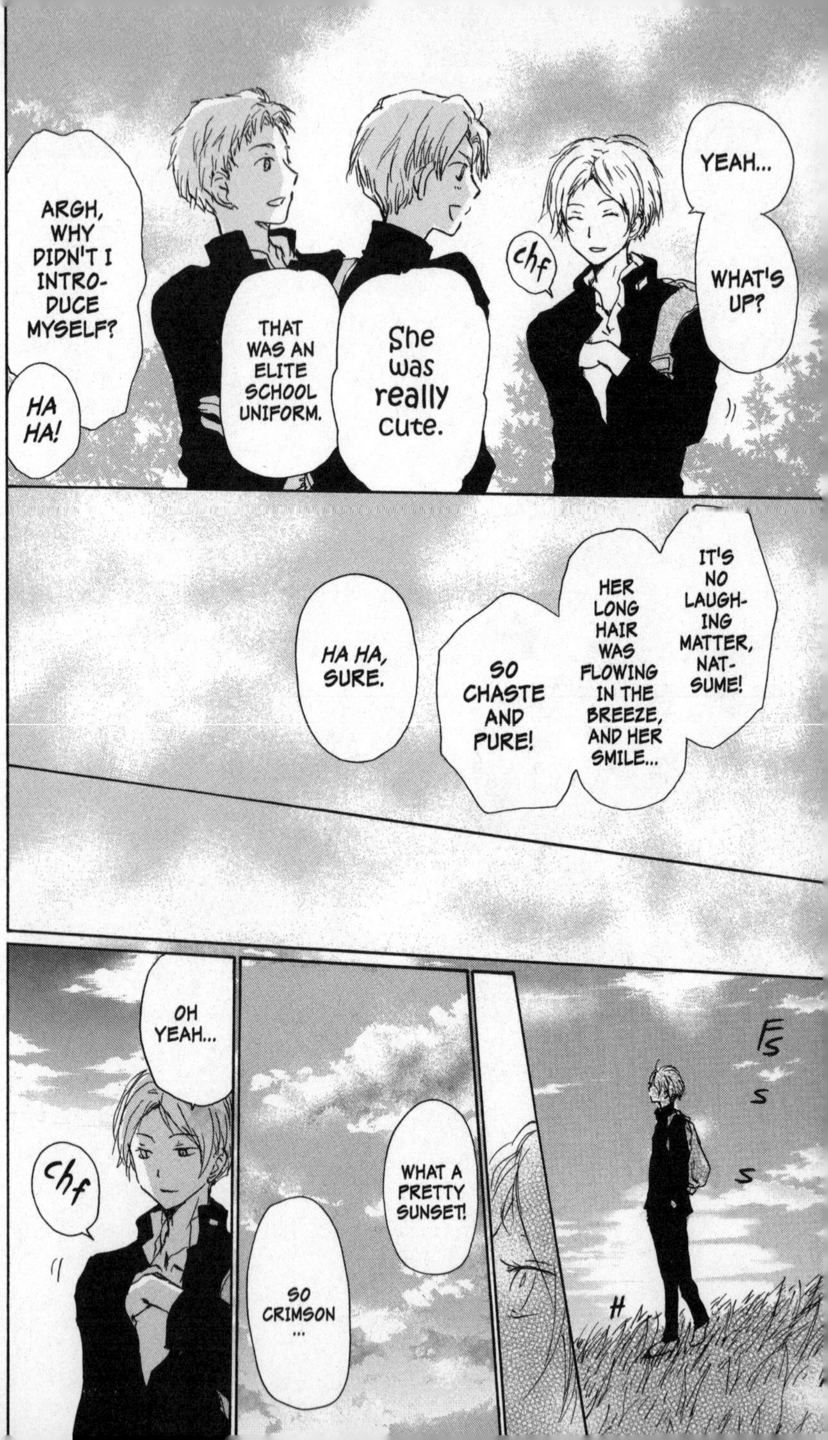
YEAH...
WHAT'S UP?
chf
She was really cute.
THAT WAS AN ELITE SCHOOL UNIFORM.
ARGH, WHY DIDN'T I INTRO-DUCE MYSELF?
HA HA!
IT'S NO LAUGH-ING MATTER, NAT-SUME!
HER LONG HAIR WAS FLOWING IN THE BREEZE, AND HER SMILE...
SO CHASTE AND PURE!
HA HA, SURE.
FSSS
WHAT A PRETTY SUNSET!
SO CRIMSON...
OH YEAH...
chf

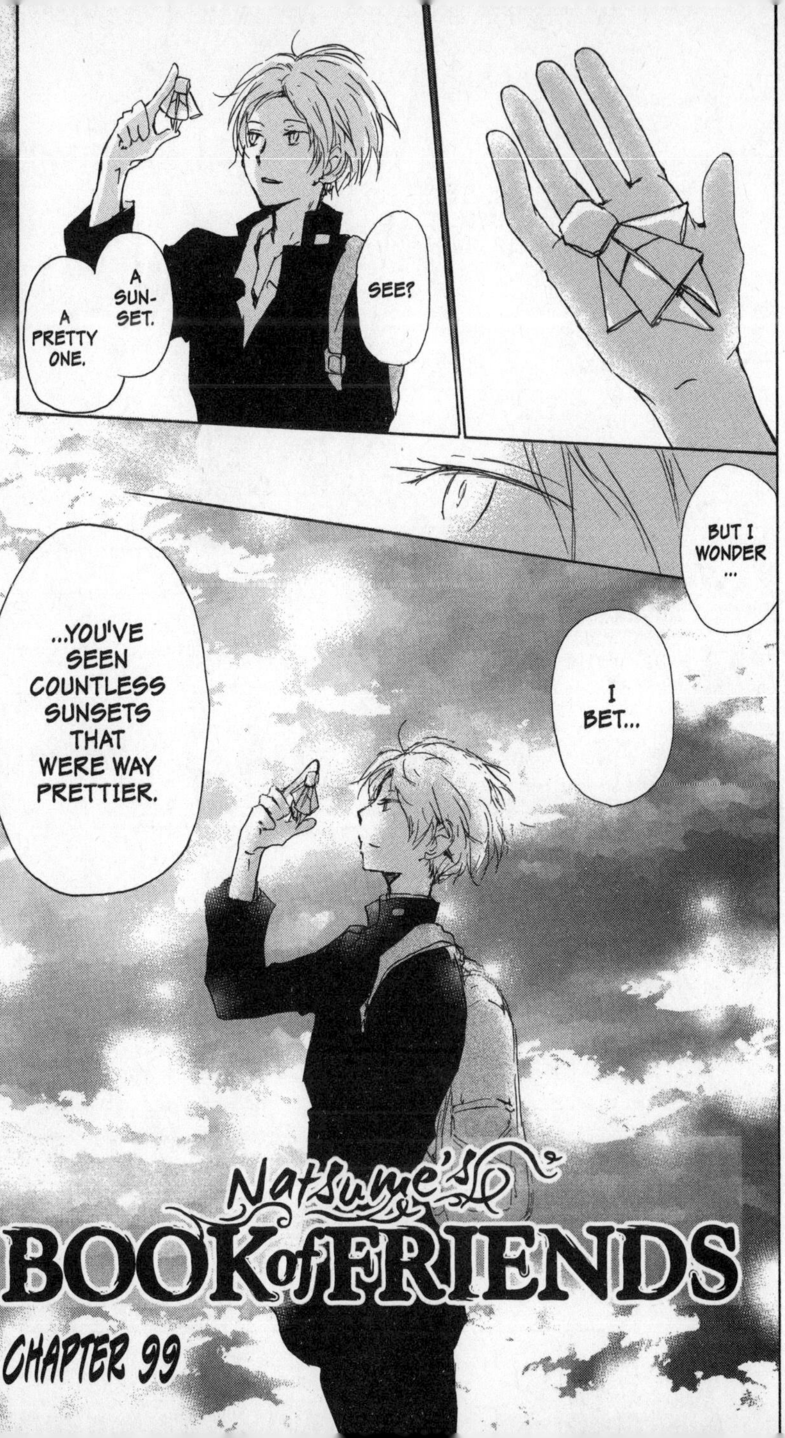
SEE?
A SUN-SET.
A PRETTY ONE.
BUT I WONDER ...
I BET...
...YOU'VE SEEN COUNTLESS SUNSETS THAT WERE WAY PRETTIER.
Natsume's BOOK of FRIENDS
CHAPTER 99

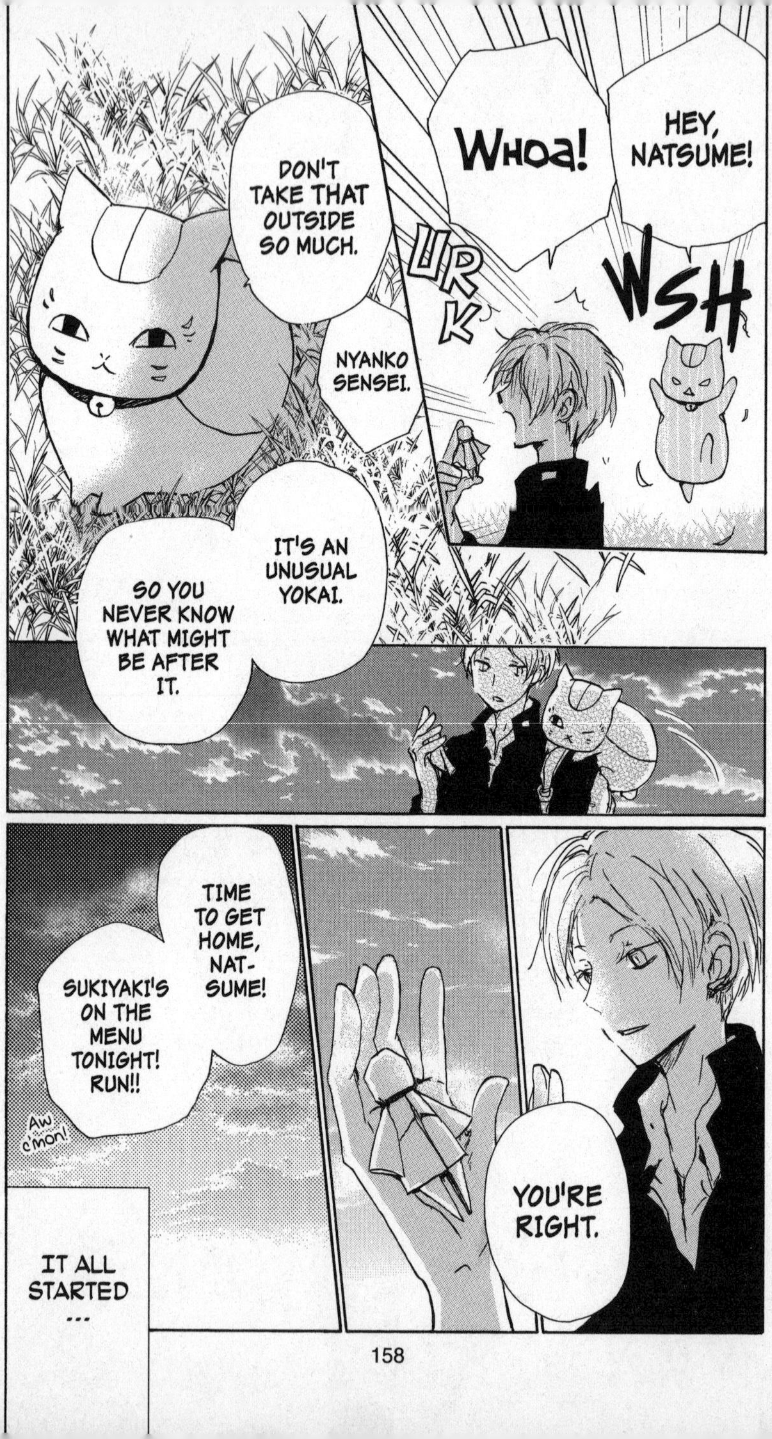
HEY, NATSUME!
WHOA!
WSH
URK
DON'T TAKE THAT OUTSIDE SO MUCH.
NYANKO SENSEI.
IT'S AN UNUSUAL YOKAI.
SO YOU NEVER KNOW WHAT MIGHT BE AFTER IT.
YOU'RE RIGHT.
TIME TO GET HOME, NAT-SUME!
SUKIYAKI'S ON THE MENU TONIGHT! RUN!!
Aw c'mon!
IT ALL STARTED ...

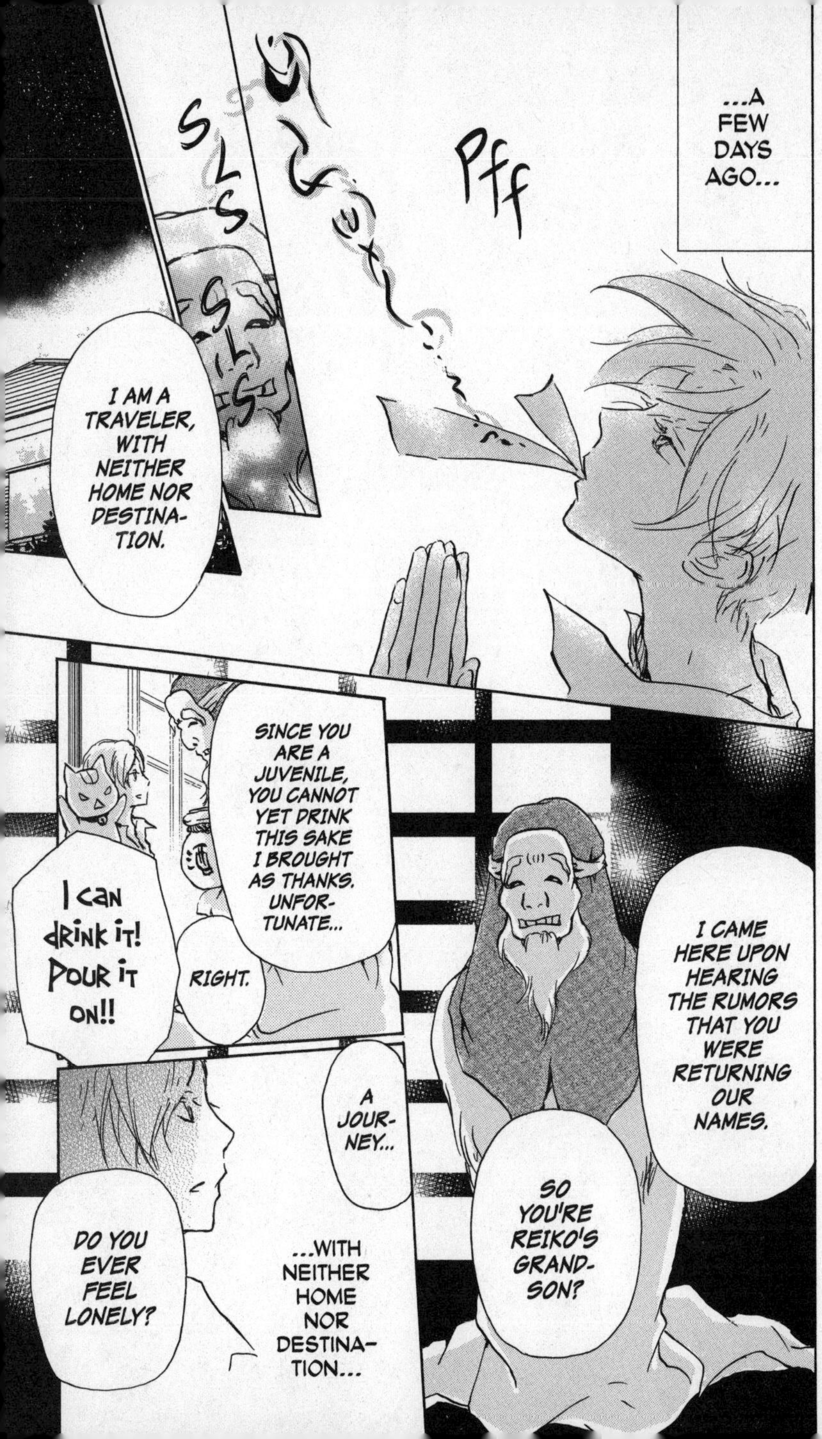
...A FEW DAYS AGO...
Pff
I AM A TRAVELER, WITH NEITHER HOME NOR DESTINATION.
I CAME HERE UPON HEARING THE RUMORS THAT YOU WERE RETURNING OUR NAMES.
SO YOU'RE REIKO'S GRANDSON?
SINCE YOU ARE A JUVENILE, YOU CANNOT YET DRINK THIS SAKE I BROUGHT AS THANKS. UNFORTUNATE...
RIGHT.
I can drink it! Pour it on!!
A JOURNEY...
...WITH NEITHER HOME NOR DESTINATION...
DO YOU EVER FEEL LONELY?

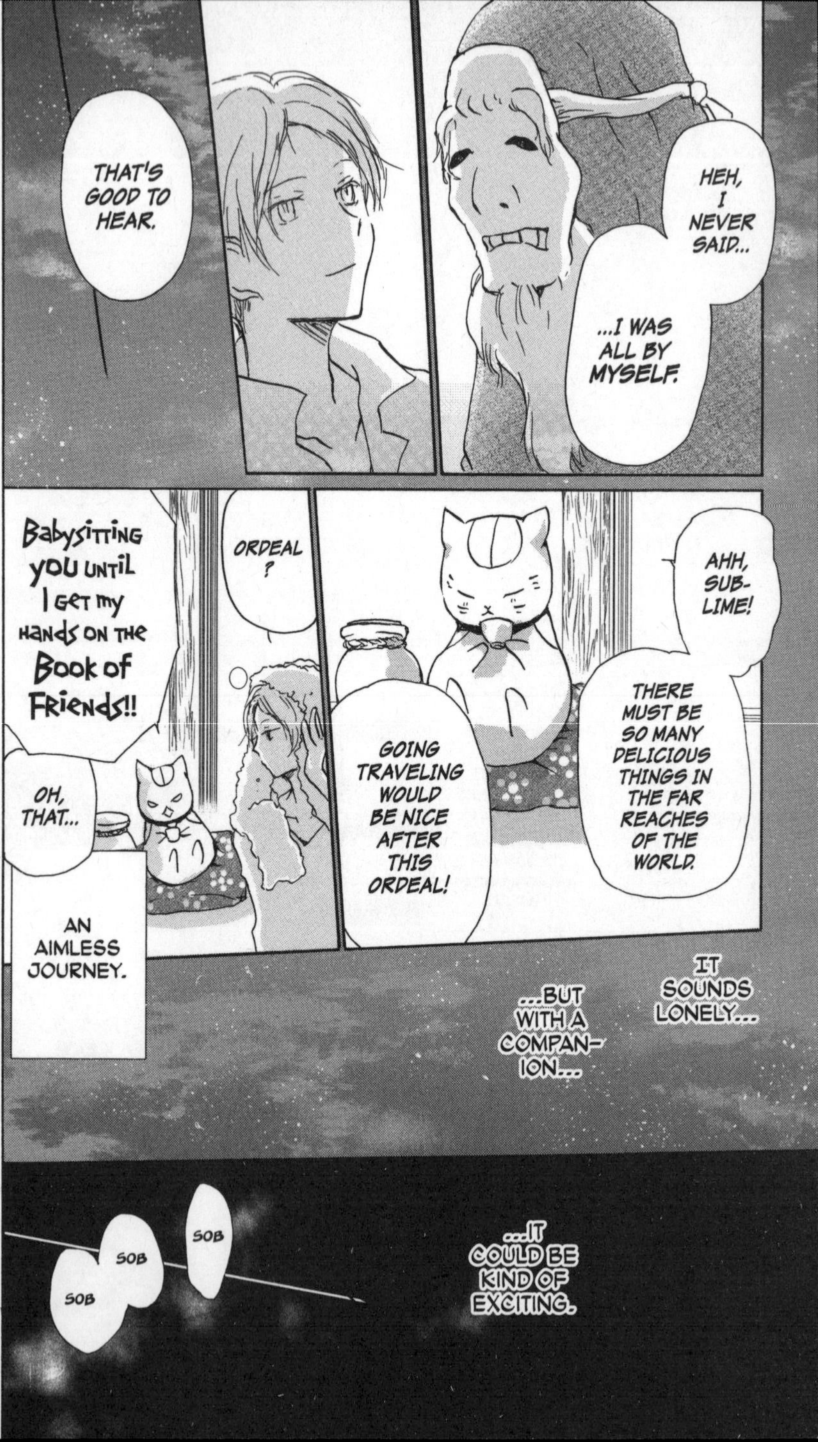
HEH, I NEVER SAID...
...I WAS ALL BY MYSELF.
THAT'S GOOD TO HEAR.
AHH, SUB-LIME!
THERE MUST BE SO MANY DELICIOUS THINGS IN THE FAR REACHES OF THE WORLD.
GOING TRAVELING WOULD BE NICE AFTER THIS ORDEAL!
ORDEAL?
Babysitting you until I get my hands on the Book of Friends!!
OH, THAT...
AN AIMLESS JOURNEY.
IT SOUNDS LONELY...
...BUT WITH A COMPANION...
...IT COULD BE KIND OF EXCITING.
SOB
SOB
SOB

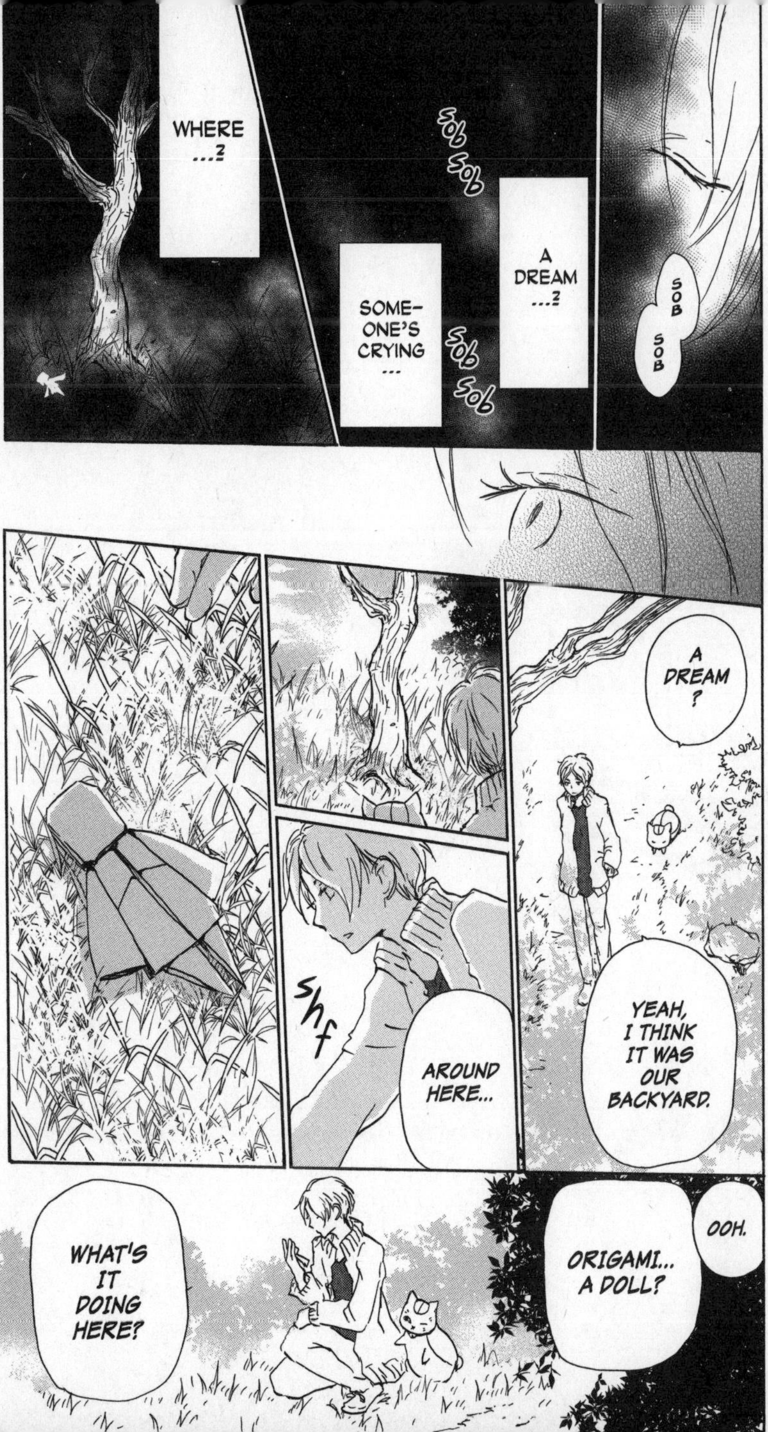
SOB SOB
sob sob
A DREAM...?
SOME-ONE'S CRYING...
sob sob
WHERE...?
A DREAM?
YEAH, I THINK IT WAS OUR BACKYARD.
shf
AROUND HERE...
OOH.
ORIGAMI... A DOLL?
WHAT'S IT DOING HERE?

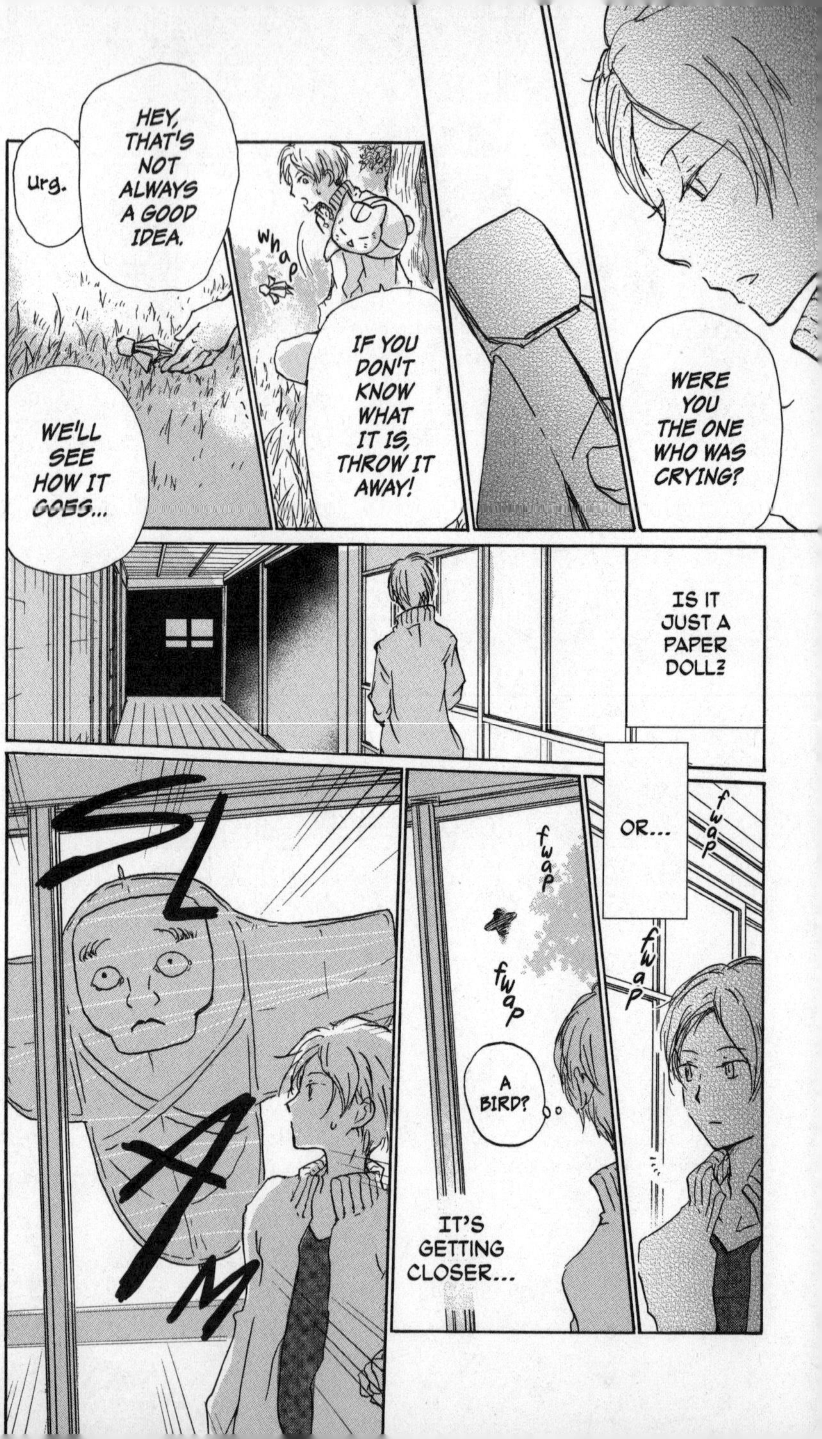
WERE YOU THE ONE WHO WAS CRYING?
IF YOU DON'T KNOW WHAT IT IS, THROW IT AWAY!
whap
HEY, THAT'S NOT ALWAYS A GOOD IDEA.
urg.
WE'LL SEE HOW IT GOES...
IS IT JUST A PAPER DOLL?
OR...
fwap
fwap
fwap
fwap
A BIRD?
IT'S GETTING CLOSER...
SLAM

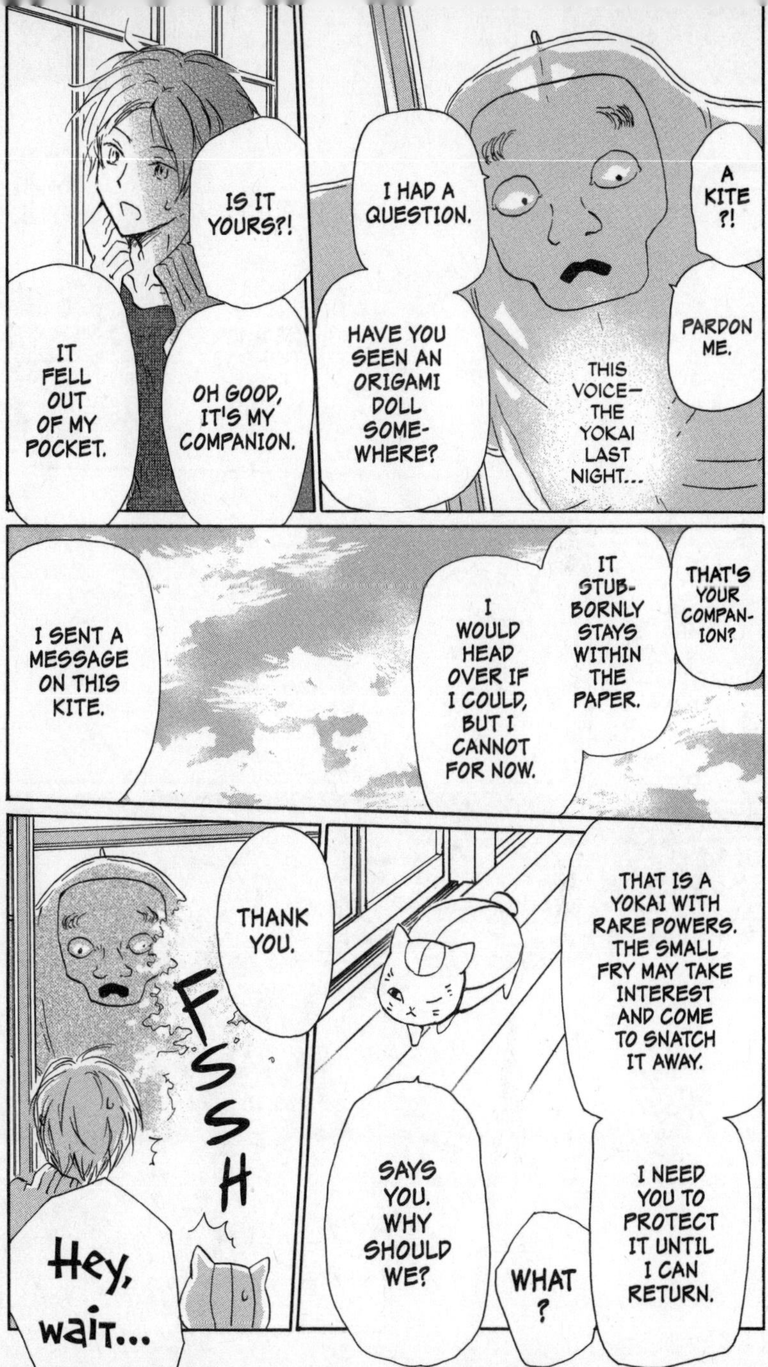
A KITE?!
I HAD A QUESTION.
PARDON ME.
THIS VOICE—THE YOKAI LAST NIGHT...
HAVE YOU SEEN AN ORIGAMI DOLL SOMEWHERE?
IS IT YOURS?!
OH GOOD, IT'S MY COMPANION.
IT FELL OUT OF MY POCKET.
THAT'S YOUR COMPANION?
IT STUBBORNLY STAYS WITHIN THE PAPER.
I WOULD HEAD OVER IF I COULD, BUT I CANNOT FOR NOW.
I SENT A MESSAGE ON THIS KITE.
THAT IS A YOKAI WITH RARE POWERS. THE SMALL FRY MAY TAKE INTEREST AND COME TO SNATCH IT AWAY.
I NEED YOU TO PROTECT IT UNTIL I CAN RETURN.
WHAT?
SAYS YOU. WHY SHOULD WE?
THANK YOU.
FSSH
Hey, wait...

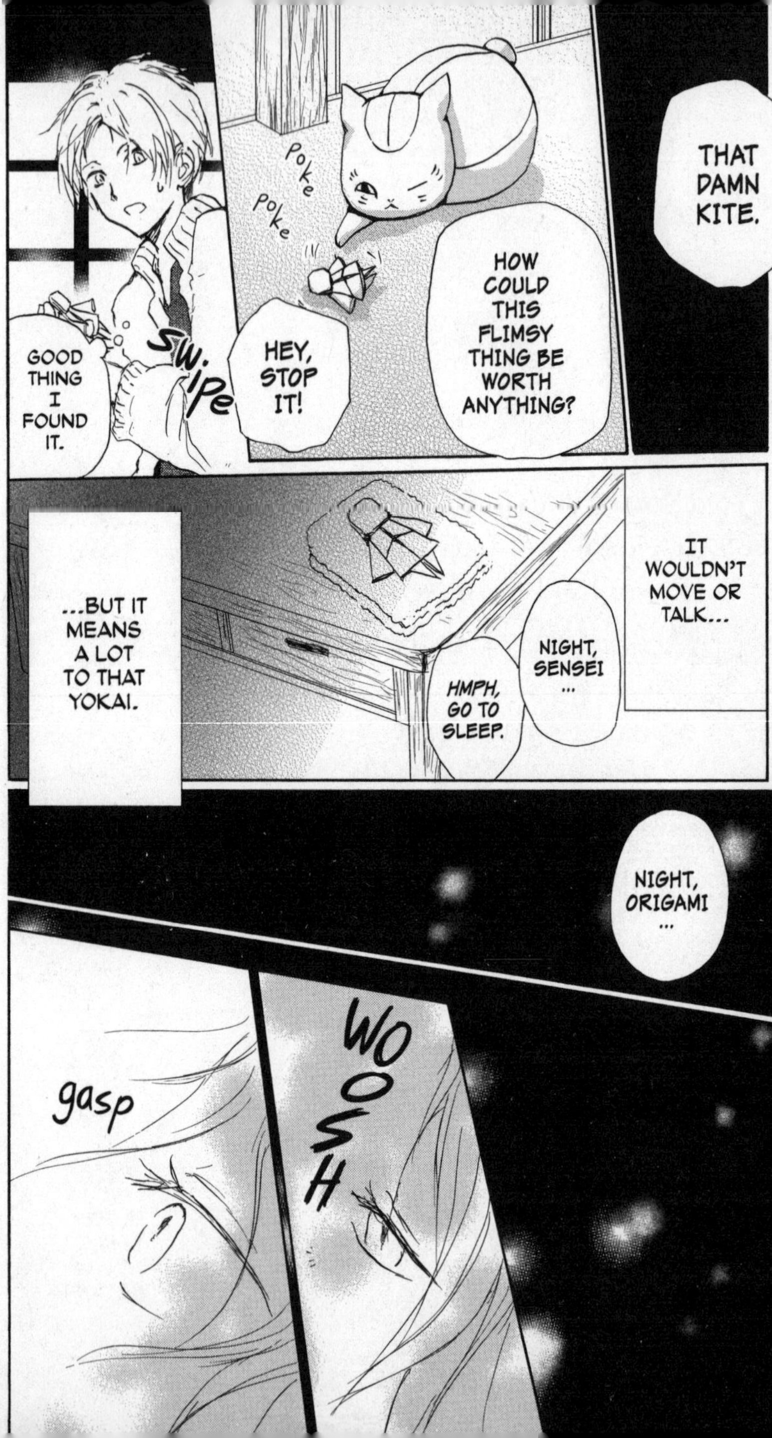
THAT DAMN KITE.
HOW COULD THIS FLIMSY THING BE WORTH ANYTHING?
Poke
Poke
HEY, STOP IT!
swipe
GOOD THING I FOUND IT.
IT WOULDN'T MOVE OR TALK...
NIGHT, SENSEI ...
HMPH, GO TO SLEEP.
...BUT IT MEANS A LOT TO THAT YOKAI.
NIGHT, ORIGAMI ...
WOOSH
gasp

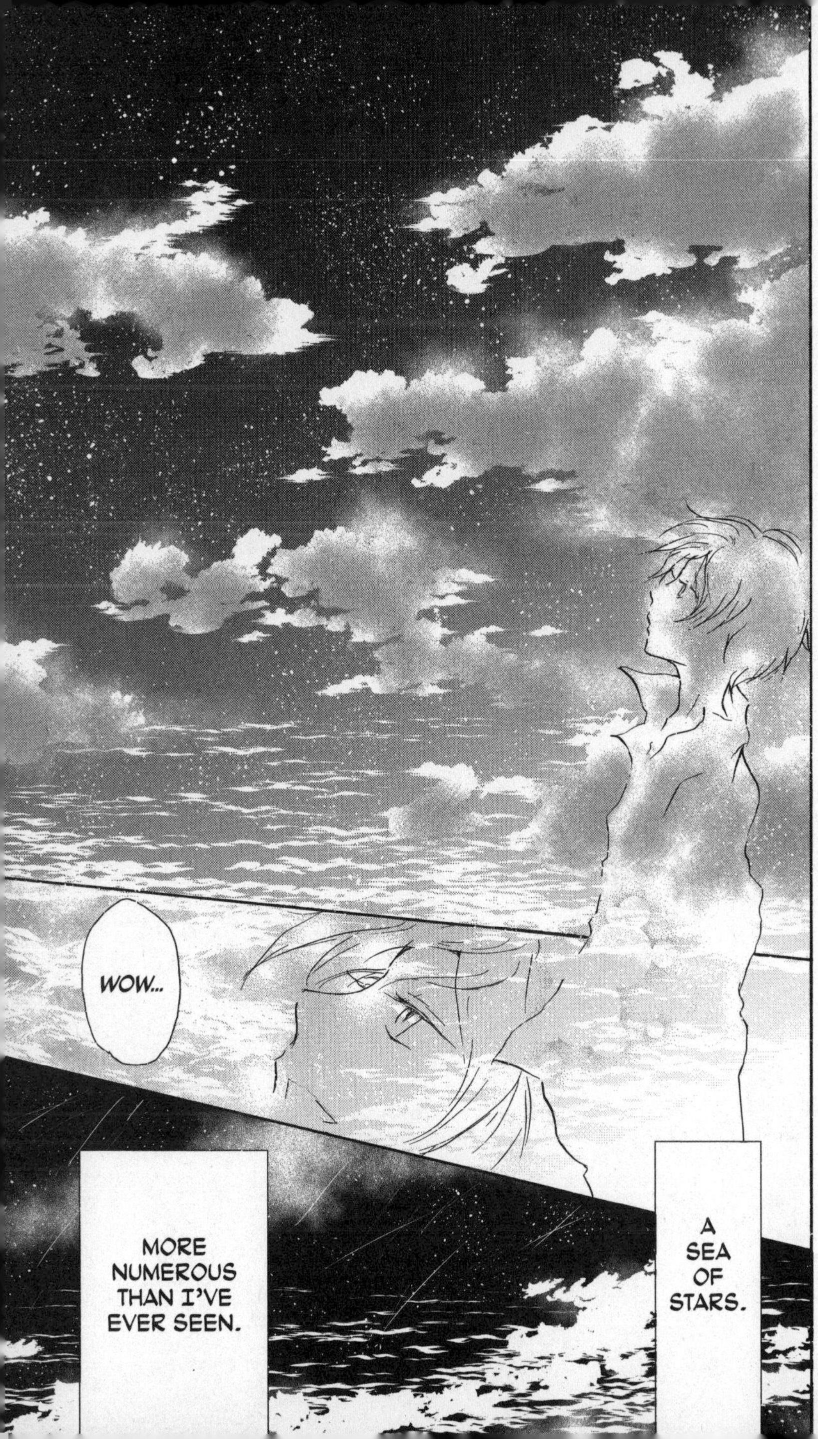
WOW...
A SEA OF STARS.
MORE NUMEROUS THAN I'VE EVER SEEN.

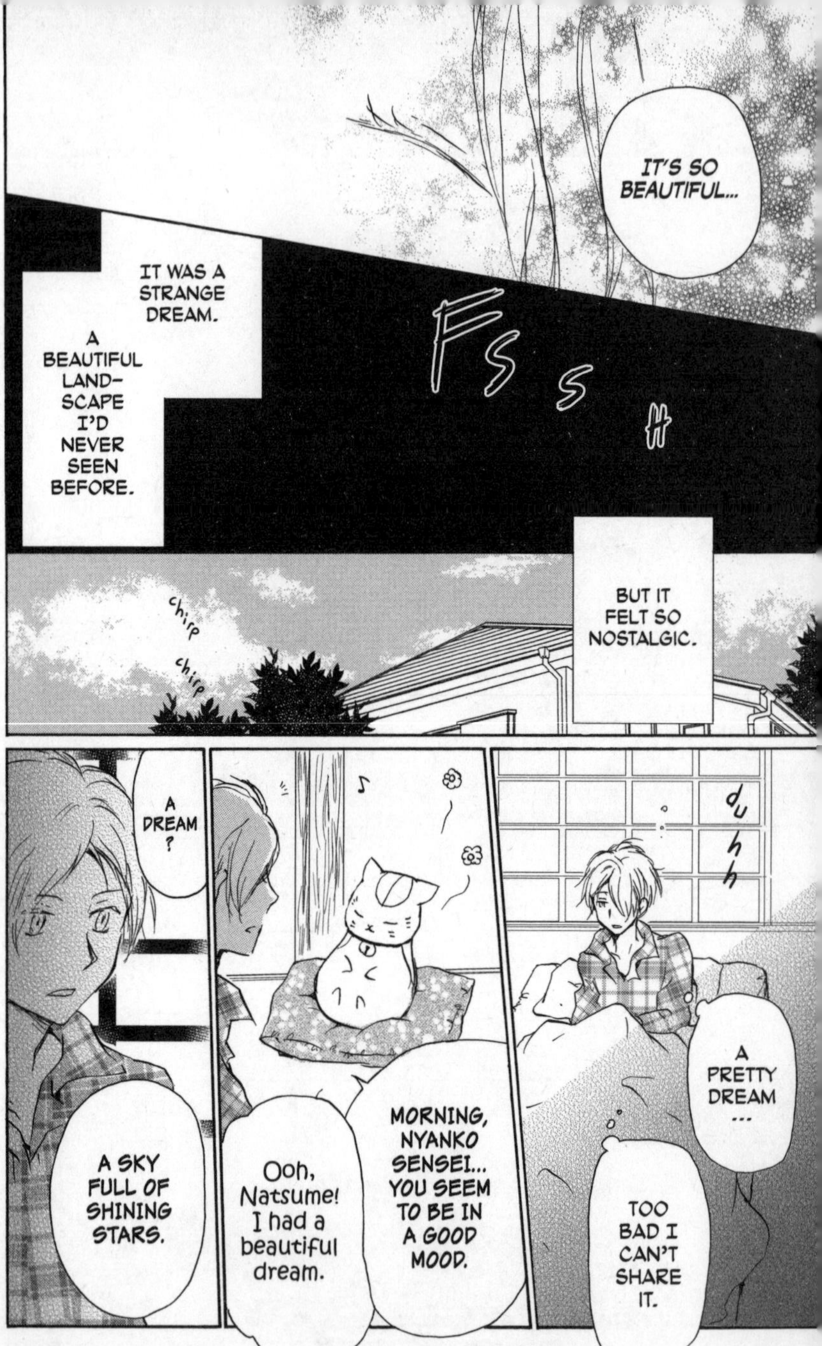
IT'S SO BEAUTIFUL...
FSSH
IT WAS A STRANGE DREAM.
A BEAUTIFUL LAND-SCAPE I'D NEVER SEEN BEFORE.
BUT IT FELT SO NOSTALGIC.
chirp
chirp
duhh
A PRETTY DREAM...
TOO BAD I CAN'T SHARE IT.
MORNING, NYANKO SENSEI... YOU SEEM TO BE IN A GOOD MOOD.
Ooh, Natsume! I had a beautiful dream.
A DREAM?
A SKY FULL OF SHINING STARS.

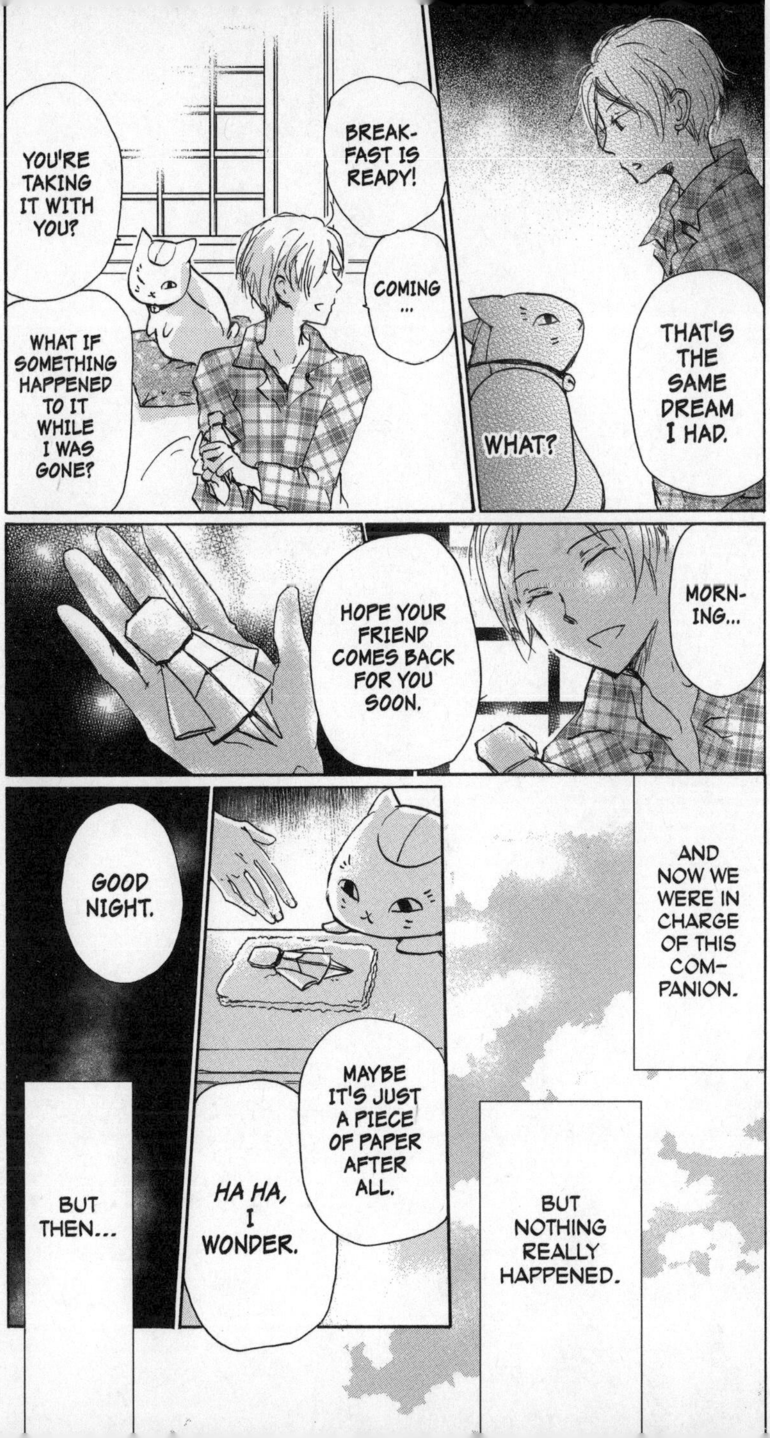
THAT'S THE SAME DREAM I HAD.
WHAT?
BREAKFAST IS READY!
COMING...
YOU'RE TAKING IT WITH YOU?
WHAT IF SOMETHING HAPPENED TO IT WHILE I WAS GONE?
MORNING...
HOPE YOUR FRIEND COMES BACK FOR YOU SOON.
AND NOW WE WERE IN CHARGE OF THIS COMPANION.
BUT NOTHING REALLY HAPPENED.
MAYBE IT'S JUST A PIECE OF PAPER AFTER ALL.
HA HA, I WONDER.
GOOD NIGHT.
BUT THEN...

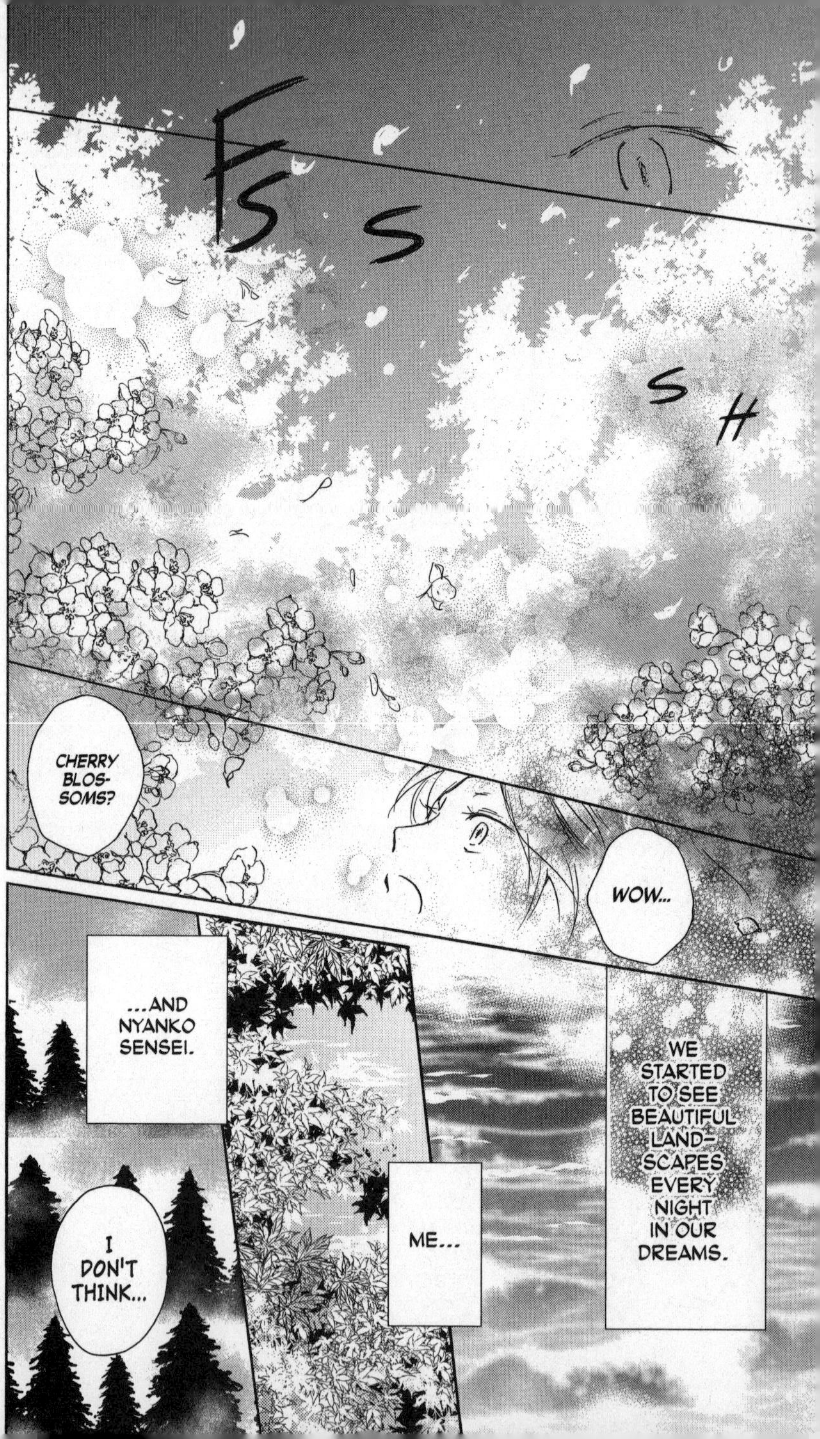
FSS
SH
WOW...
CHERRY BLOSSOMS?
WE STARTED TO SEE BEAUTIFUL LANDSCAPES EVERY NIGHT IN OUR DREAMS.
ME...
...AND NYANKO SENSEI.
I DON'T THINK...

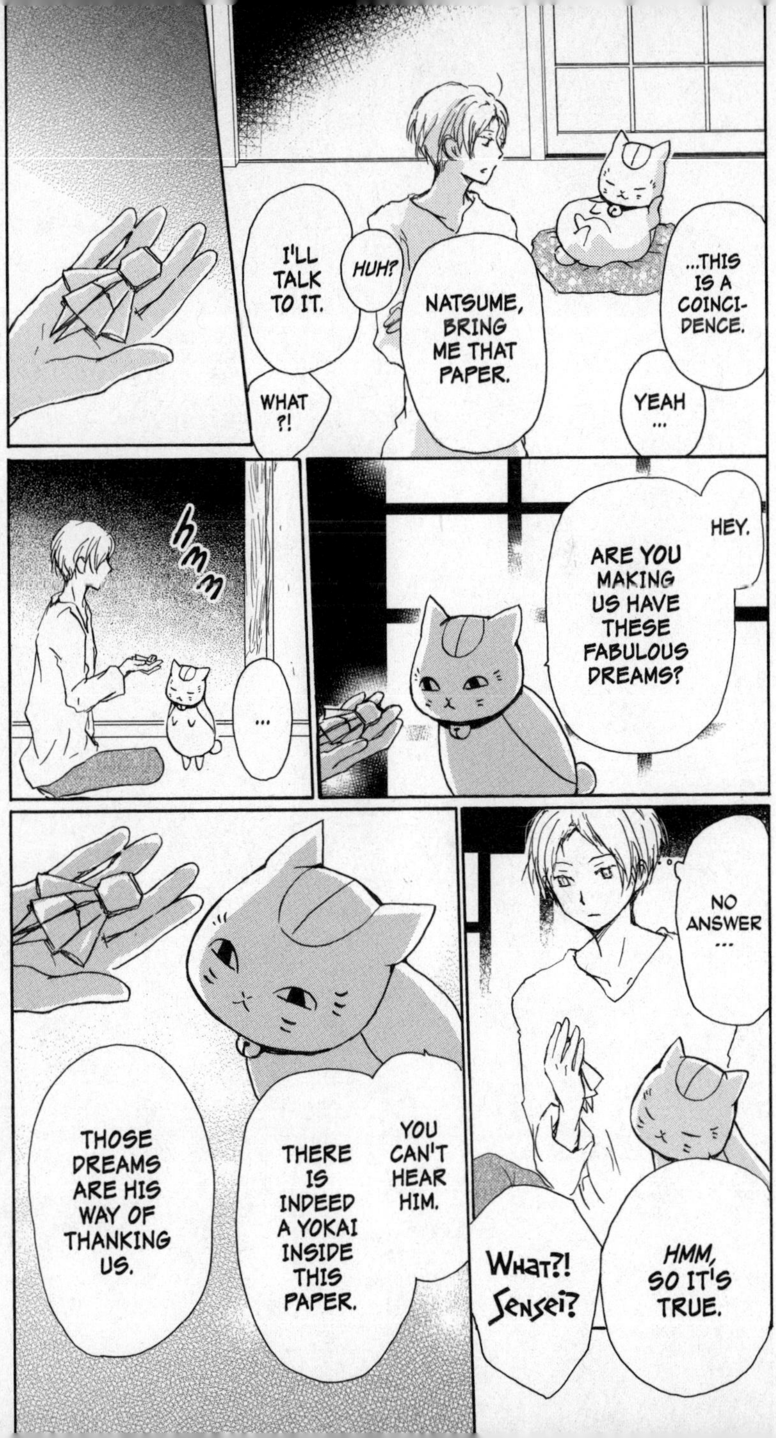
...THIS IS A COINCIDENCE.
YEAH...
NATSUME, BRING ME THAT PAPER.
HUH?
I'LL TALK TO IT.
WHAT?!
HEY.
ARE YOU MAKING US HAVE THESE FABULOUS DREAMS?
hmm
...
NO ANSWER...
HMM, SO IT'S TRUE.
What?! Sensei?
YOU CAN'T HEAR HIM.
THERE IS INDEED A YOKAI INSIDE THIS PAPER.
THOSE DREAMS ARE HIS WAY OF THANKING US.

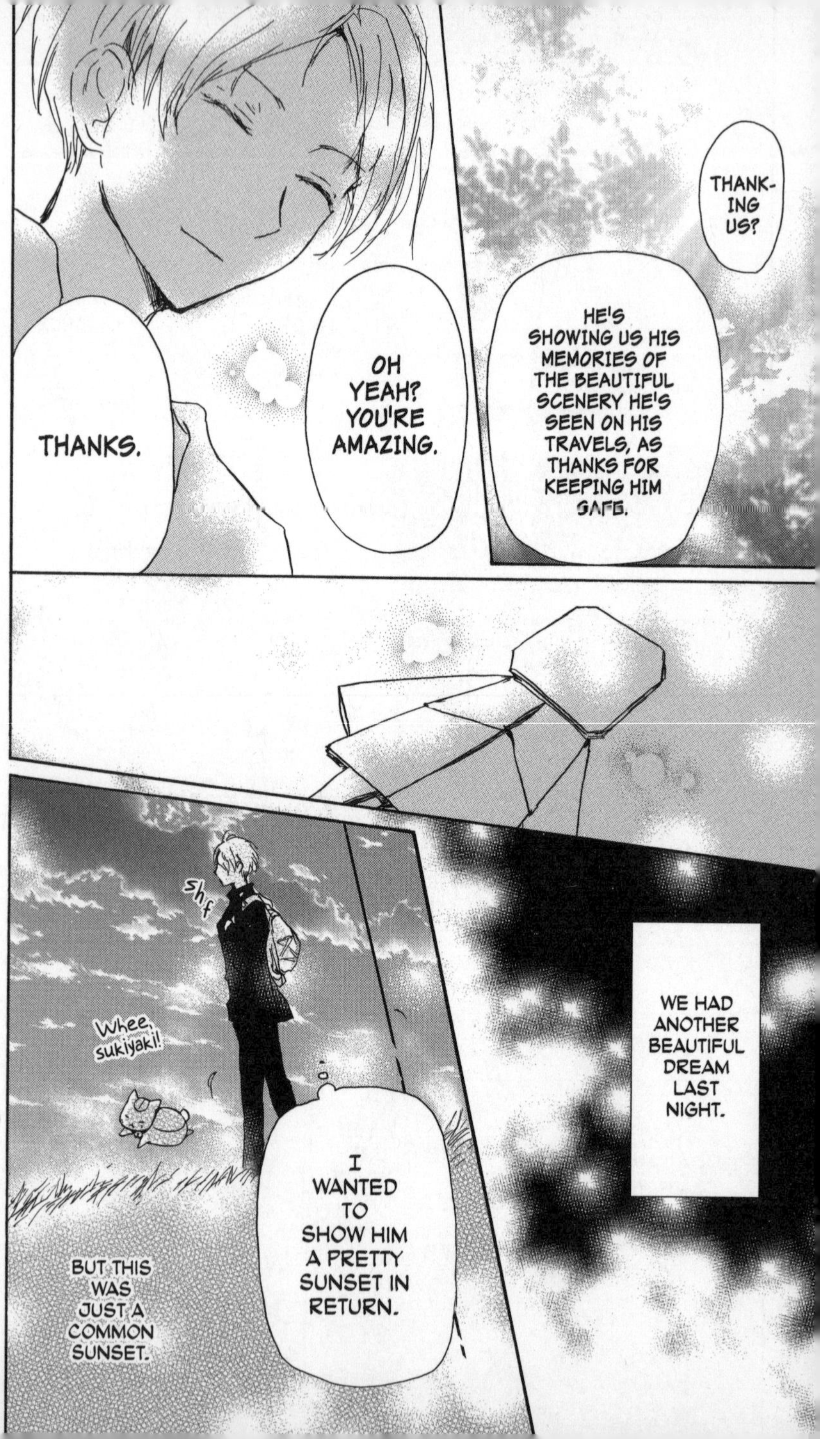
THANK-ING US?
HE'S SHOWING US HIS MEMORIES OF THE BEAUTIFUL SCENERY HE'S SEEN ON HIS TRAVELS, AS THANKS FOR KEEPING HIM SAFE.
OH YEAH? YOU'RE AMAZING.
THANKS.
WE HAD ANOTHER BEAUTIFUL DREAM LAST NIGHT.
shf
Whee, sukiyaki!
I WANTED TO SHOW HIM A PRETTY SUNSET IN RETURN.
BUT THIS WAS JUST A COMMON SUNSET.

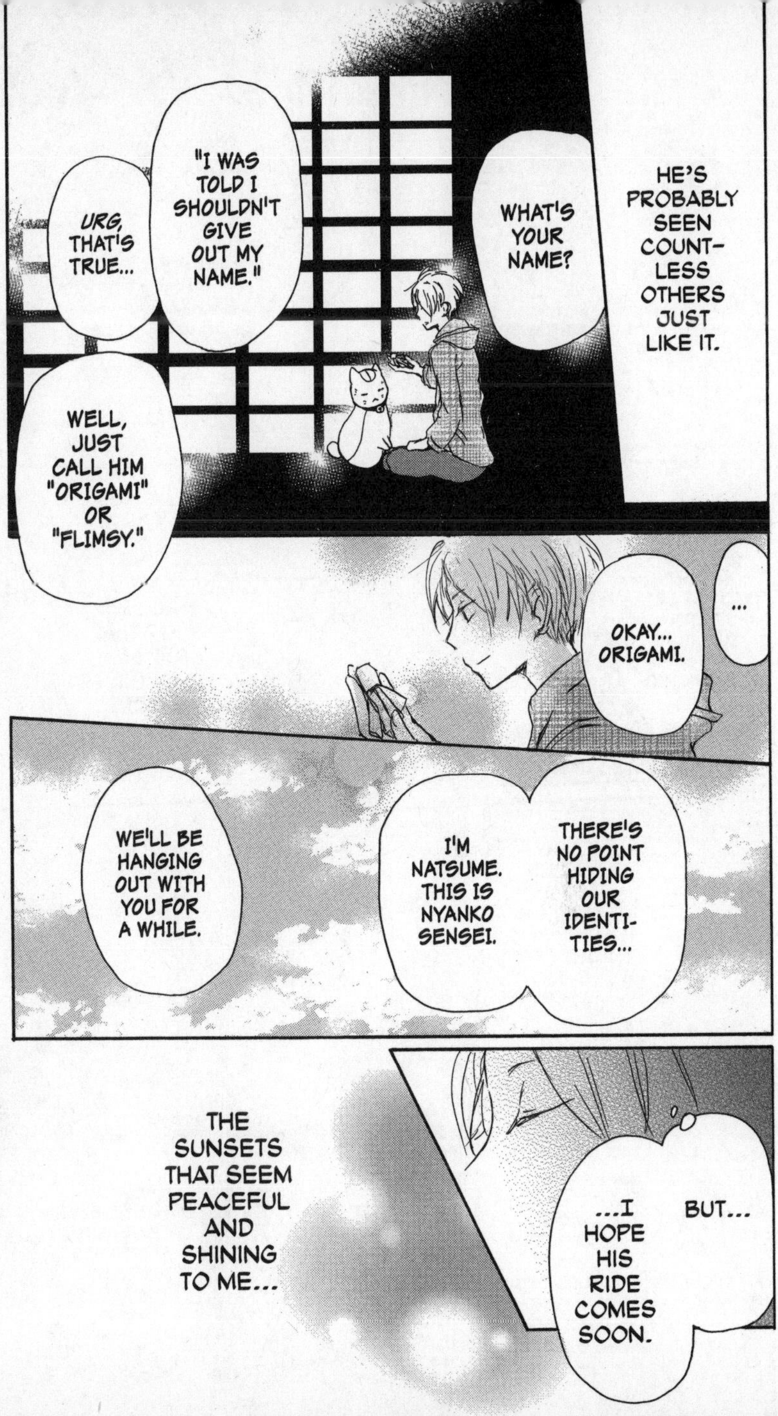
HE'S PROBABLY SEEN COUNT-LESS OTHERS JUST LIKE IT.
WHAT'S YOUR NAME?
"I WAS TOLD I SHOULDN'T GIVE OUT MY NAME."
URG, THAT'S TRUE...
WELL, JUST CALL HIM "ORIGAMI" OR "FLIMSY."
...
OKAY... ORIGAMI.
THERE'S NO POINT HIDING OUR IDENTI-TIES...
I'M NATSUME. THIS IS NYANKO SENSEI.
WE'LL BE HANGING OUT WITH YOU FOR A WHILE.
BUT...
...I HOPE HIS RIDE COMES SOON.
THE SUNSETS THAT SEEM PEACEFUL AND SHINING TO ME...

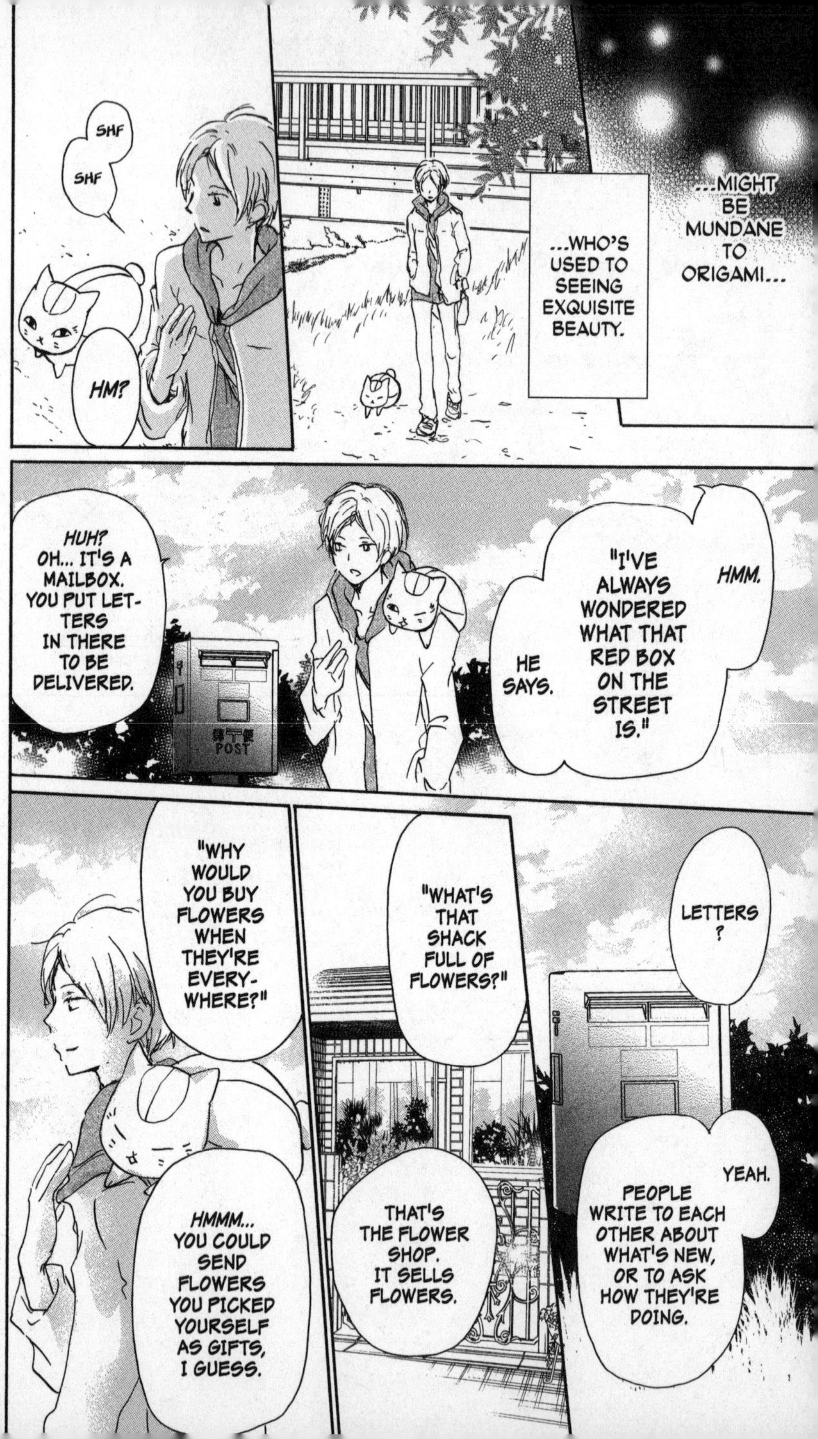
...MIGHT BE MUNDANE TO ORIGAMI...
...WHO'S USED TO SEEING EXQUISITE BEAUTY.
SHF SHF
HM?
HMM.
"I'VE ALWAYS WONDERED WHAT THAT RED BOX ON THE STREET IS."
HE SAYS.
HUH? OH... IT'S A MAILBOX. YOU PUT LET-TERS IN THERE TO BE DELIVERED.
POST
LETTERS?
YEAH.
PEOPLE WRITE TO EACH OTHER ABOUT WHAT'S NEW, OR TO ASK HOW THEY'RE DOING.
"WHAT'S THAT SHACK FULL OF FLOWERS?"
THAT'S THE FLOWER SHOP. IT SELLS FLOWERS.
"WHY WOULD YOU BUY FLOWERS WHEN THEY'RE EVERY-WHERE?"
HMMM... YOU COULD SEND FLOWERS YOU PICKED YOURSELF AS GIFTS, I GUESS.

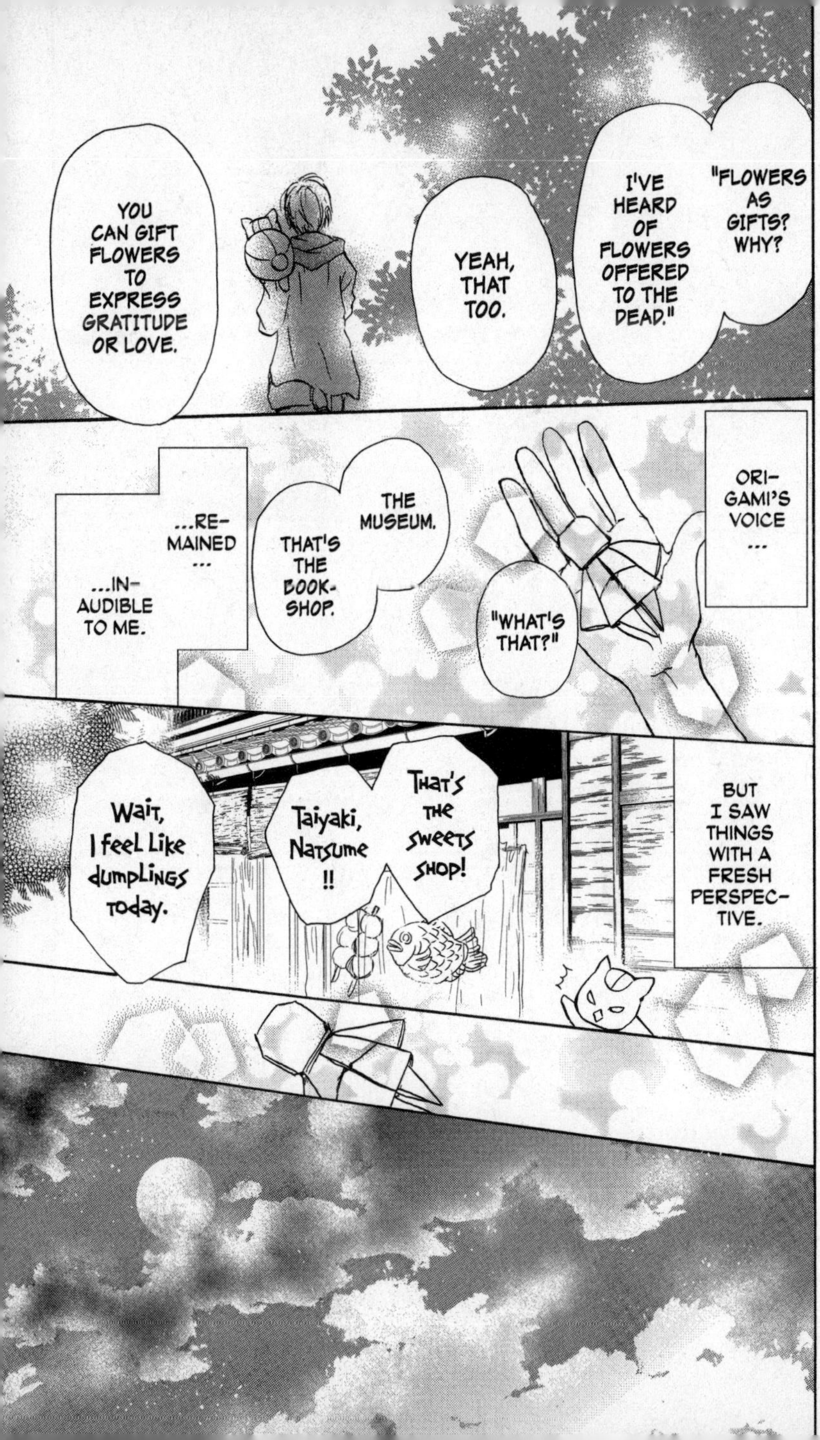
"FLOWERS AS GIFTS? WHY?
I'VE HEARD OF FLOWERS OFFERED TO THE DEAD."
YEAH, THAT TOO.
YOU CAN GIFT FLOWERS TO EXPRESS GRATITUDE OR LOVE.
ORI-GAMI'S VOICE...
"WHAT'S THAT?"
THE MUSEUM.
THAT'S THE BOOK-SHOP.
...RE-MAINED...
...IN-AUDIBLE TO ME.
BUT I SAW THINGS WITH A FRESH PERSPEC-TIVE.
That's the sweets shop!
Taiyaki, Natsume!!
Wait, I feel like dumplings today.

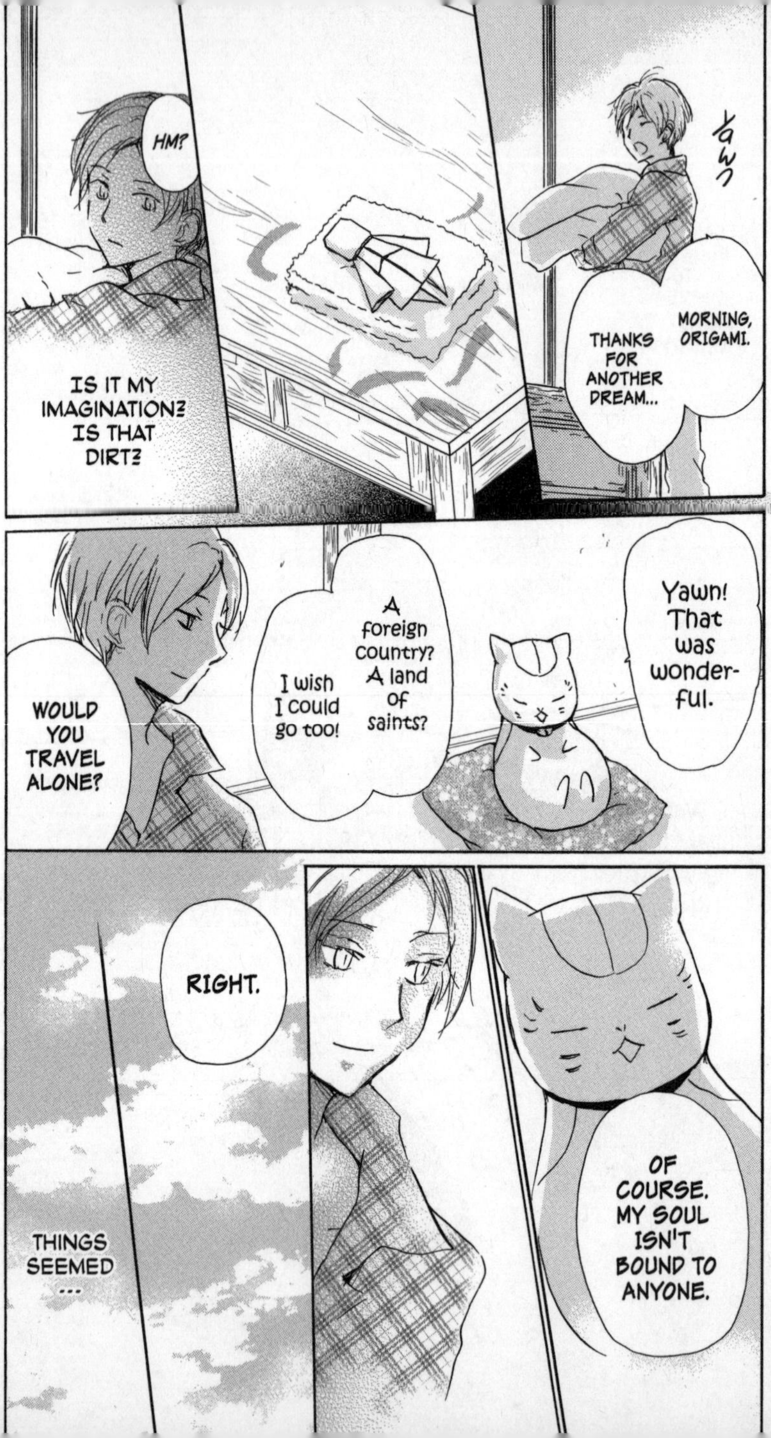
YAWN
MORNING, ORIGAMI.
THANKS FOR ANOTHER DREAM...
HM?
IS IT MY IMAGINATION? IS THAT DIRT?
Yawn! That was wonderful.
A foreign country? A land of saints?
I wish I could go too!
WOULD YOU TRAVEL ALONE?
OF COURSE. MY SOUL ISN'T BOUND TO ANYONE.
RIGHT.
THINGS SEEMED...

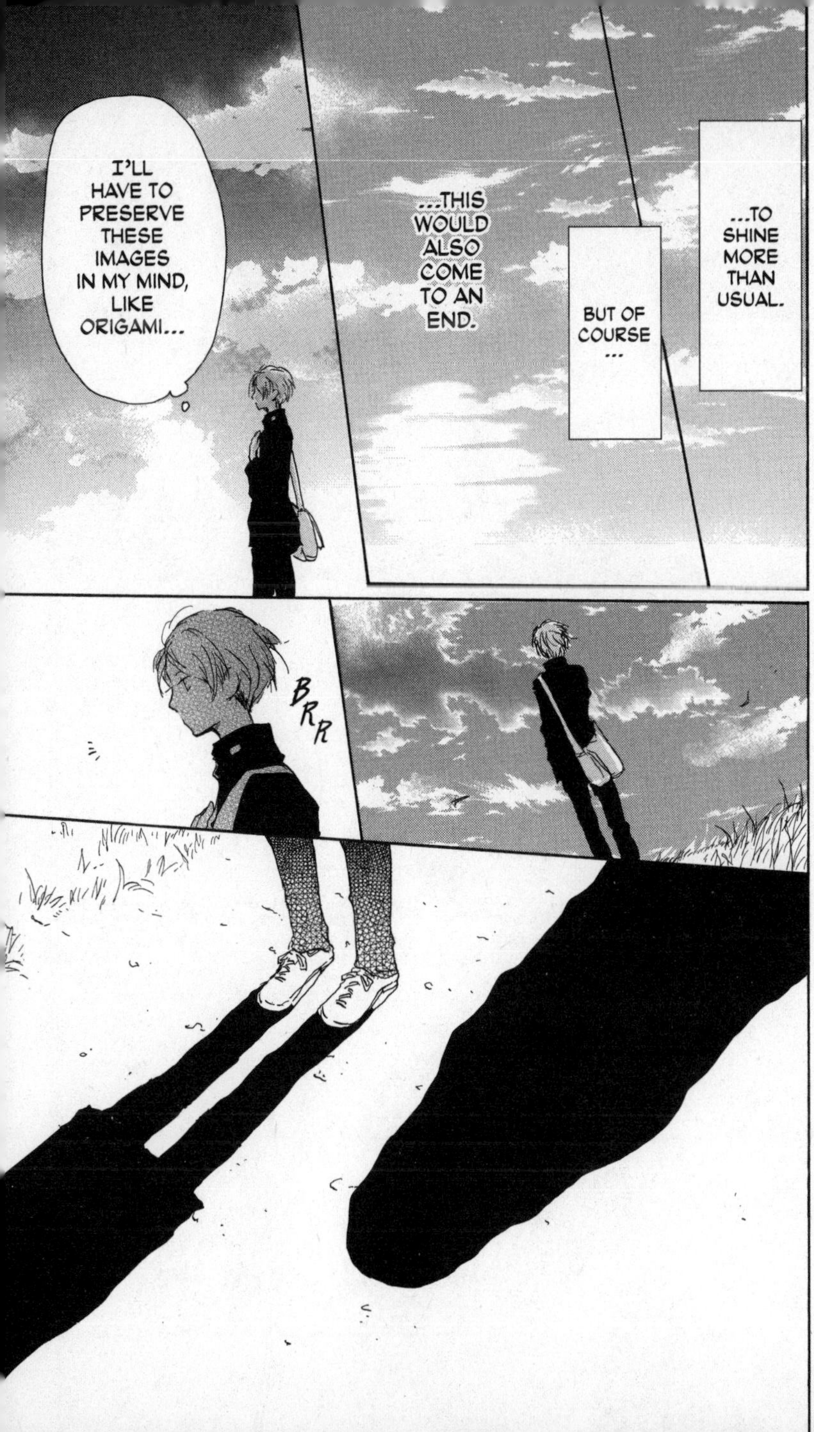
...TO SHINE MORE THAN USUAL.
BUT OF COURSE ...
...THIS WOULD ALSO COME TO AN END.
I'LL HAVE TO PRESERVE THESE IMAGES IN MY MIND, LIKE ORIGAMI...
BRR

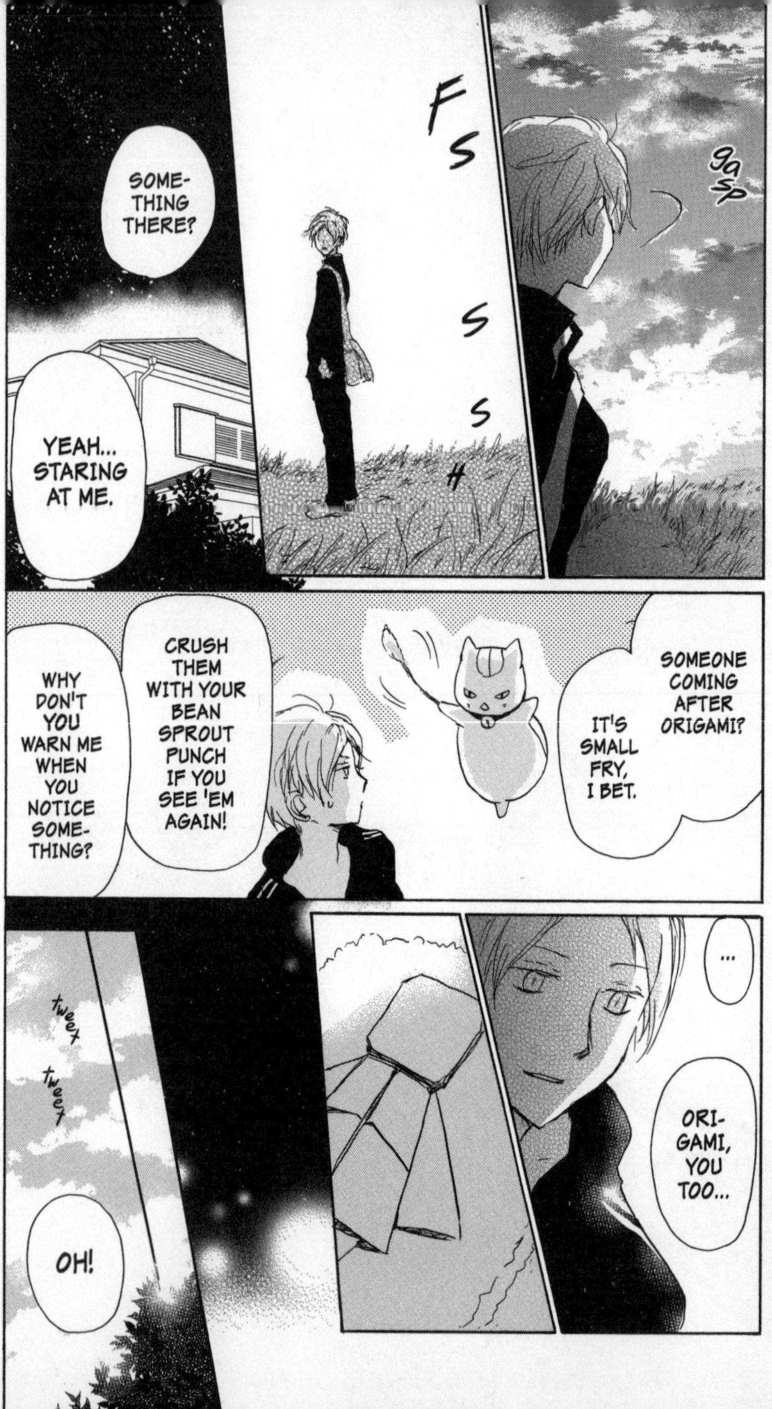
gasp
FSSSH
SOME-THING THERE?
YEAH... STARING AT ME.
SOMEONE COMING AFTER ORIGAMI?
IT'S SMALL FRY, I BET.
CRUSH THEM WITH YOUR BEAN SPROUT PUNCH IF YOU SEE 'EM AGAIN!
WHY DON'T YOU WARN ME WHEN YOU NOTICE SOME-THING?
...
ORI-GAMI, YOU TOO...
tweet tweet
OH!

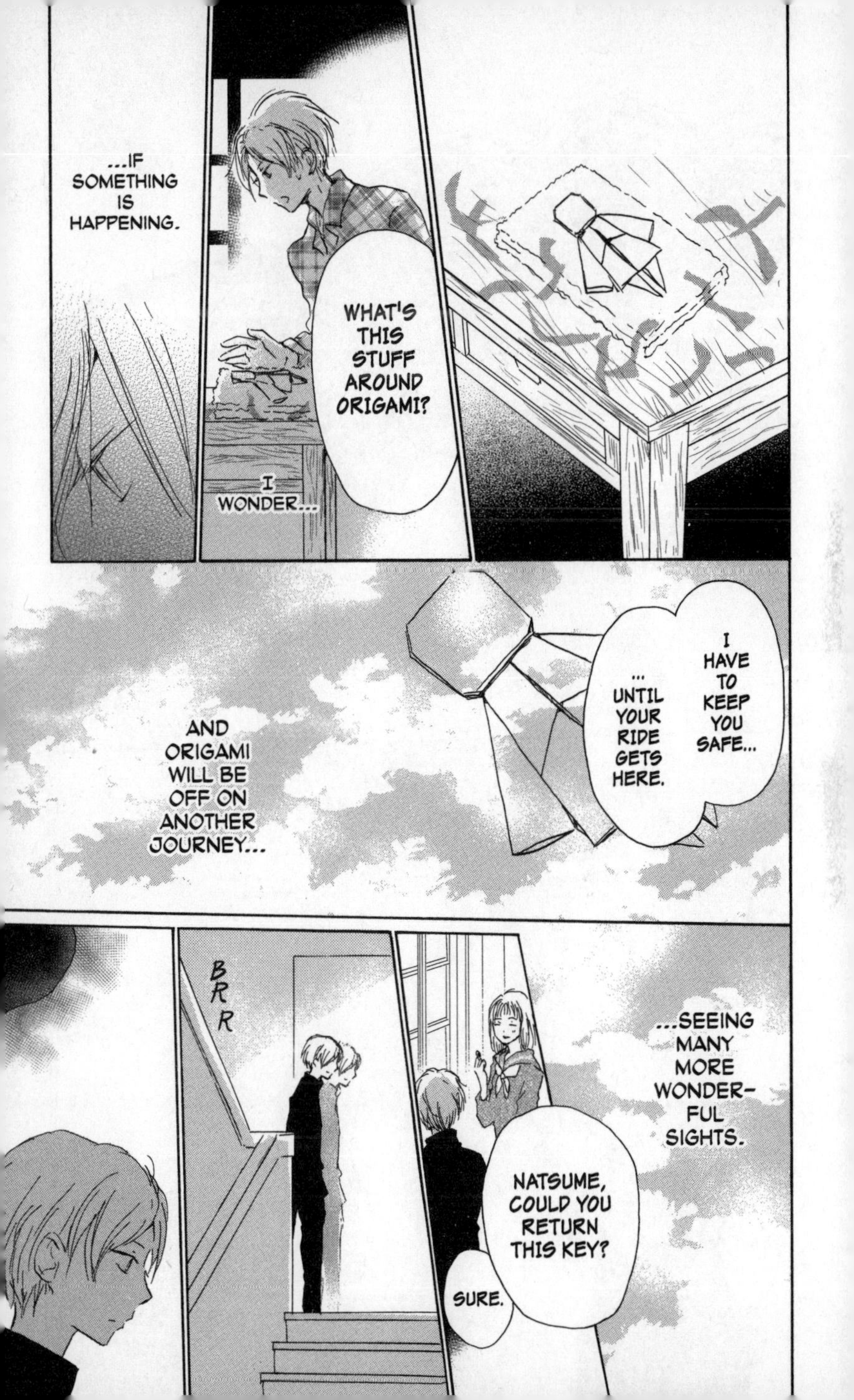
WHAT'S THIS STUFF AROUND ORIGAMI?
I WONDER...
...IF SOMETHING IS HAPPENING.
I HAVE TO KEEP YOU SAFE...
...UNTIL YOUR RIDE GETS HERE.
AND ORIGAMI WILL BE OFF ON ANOTHER JOURNEY...
...SEEING MANY MORE WONDER-FUL SIGHTS.
NATSUME, COULD YOU RETURN THIS KEY?
SURE.
BRR

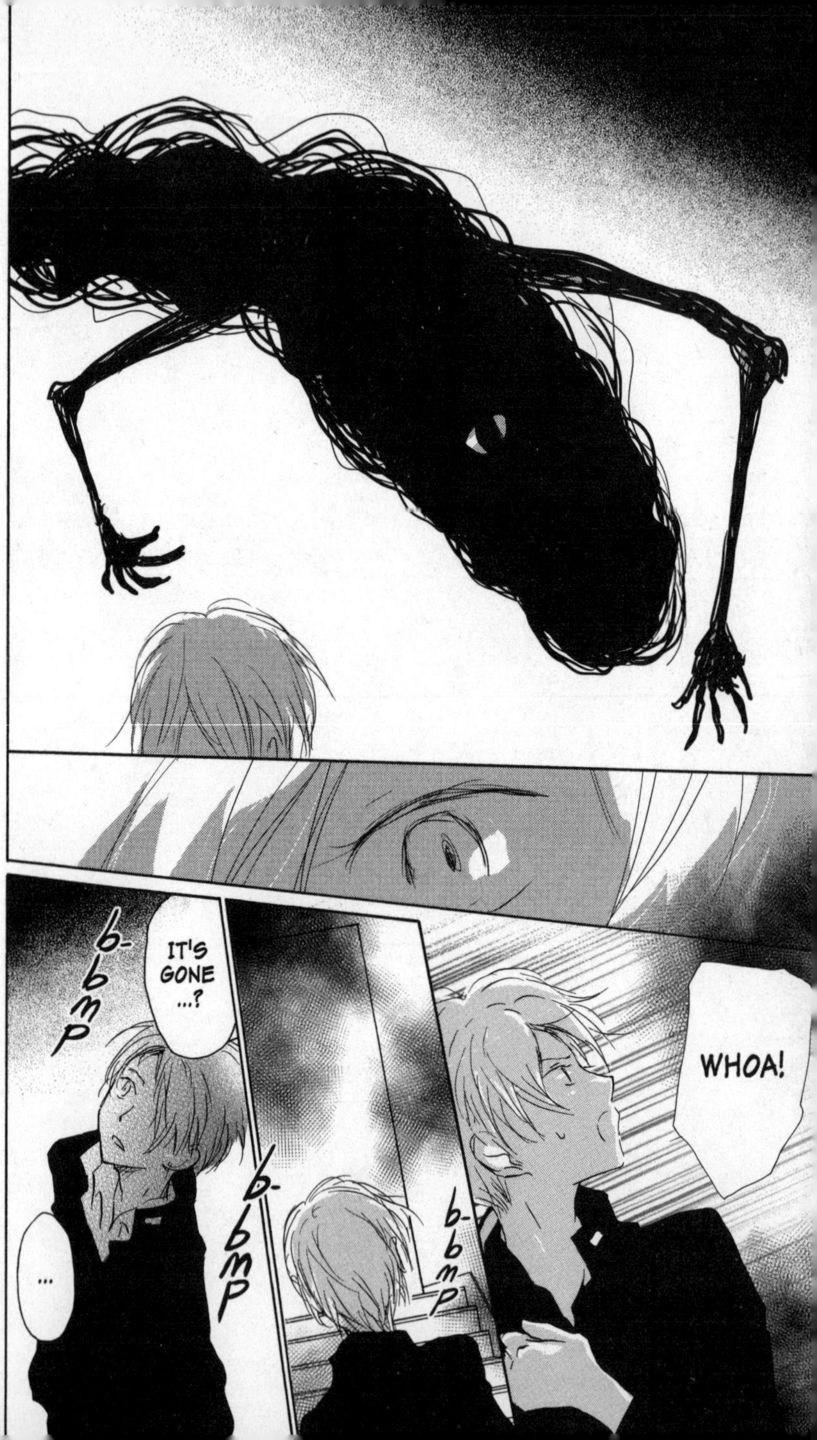
WHOA!
b-bmp
b-bmp
IT'S GONE ...?
b-bmp
...

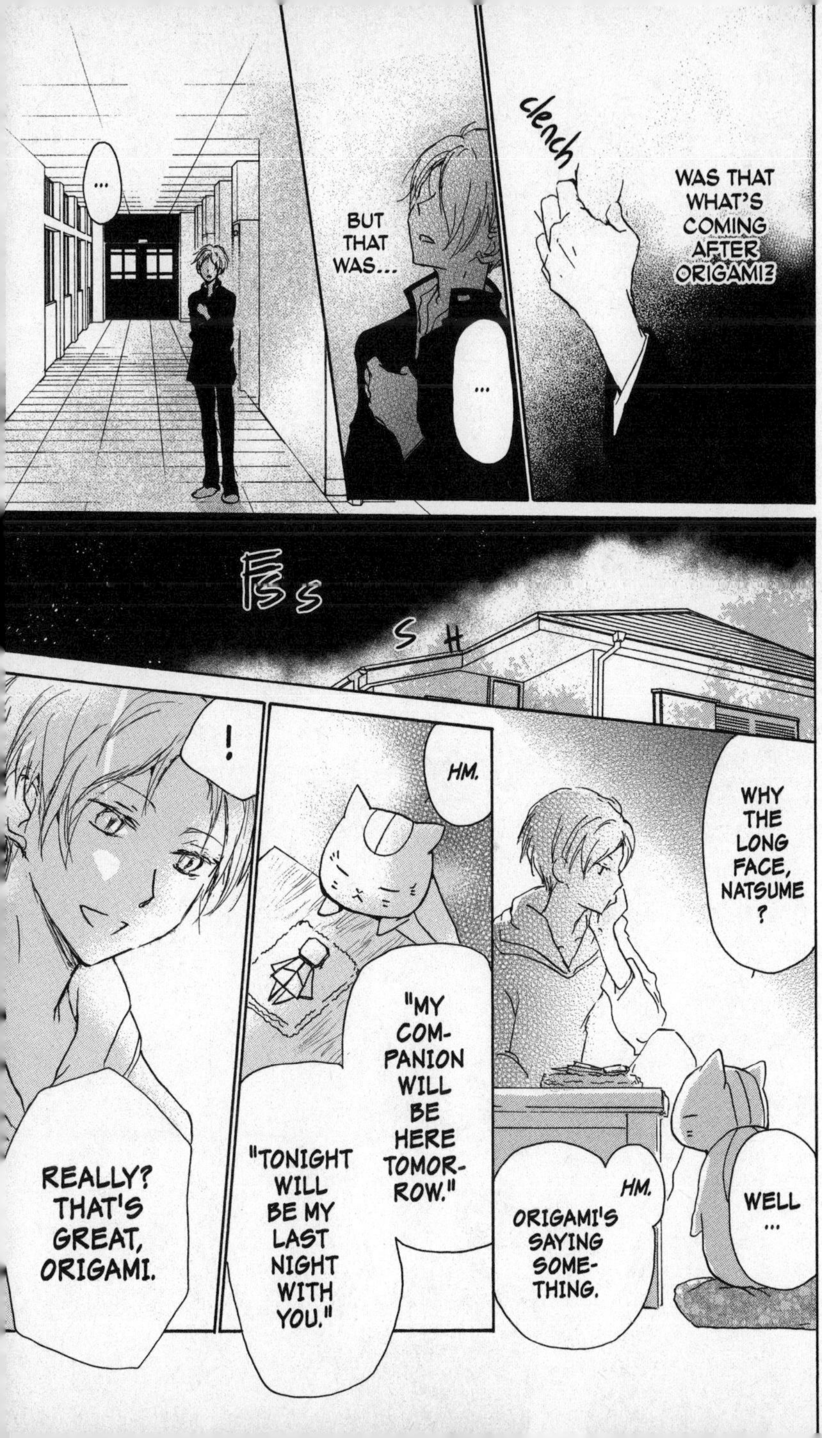
clench
WAS THAT WHAT'S COMING AFTER ORIGAMI?
BUT THAT WAS...
...
...
FSSSH
WHY THE LONG FACE, NATSUME?
WELL...
HM.
ORIGAMI'S SAYING SOME-THING.
HM.
"MY COM-PANION WILL BE HERE TOMOR-ROW."
"TONIGHT WILL BE MY LAST NIGHT WITH YOU."
!
REALLY? THAT'S GREAT, ORIGAMI.

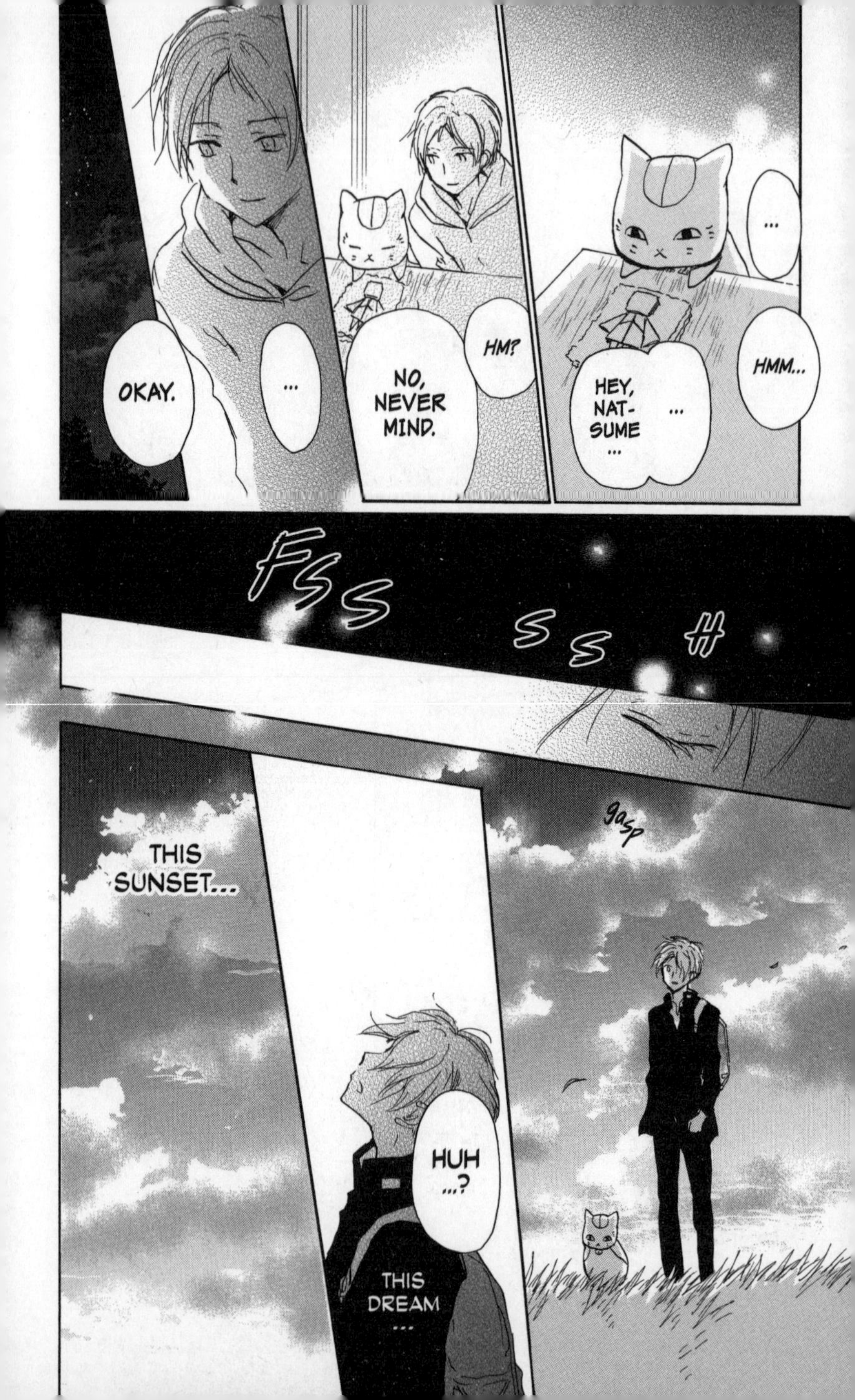
...
HMM...
HEY, NAT-SUME ...
...
HM?
NO, NEVER MIND.
...
OKAY.
FSSSSSH
gasp
HUH ...?
THIS DREAM ...
THIS SUNSET...

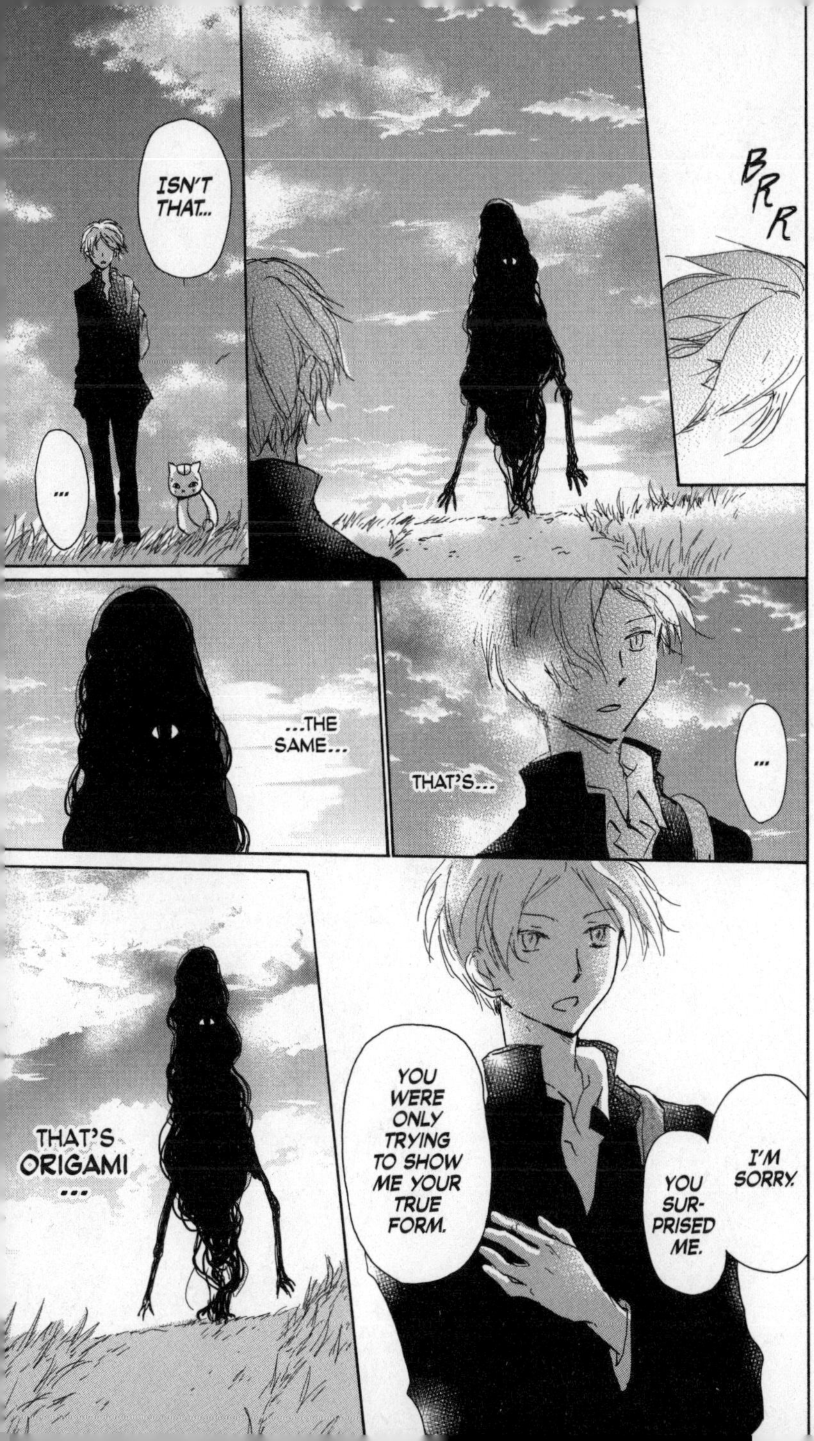
BRRR
ISN'T THAT...
...
...
THAT'S...
...THE SAME...
I'M SORRY.
YOU SURPRISED ME.
YOU WERE ONLY TRYING TO SHOW ME YOUR TRUE FORM.
THAT'S ORIGAMI...

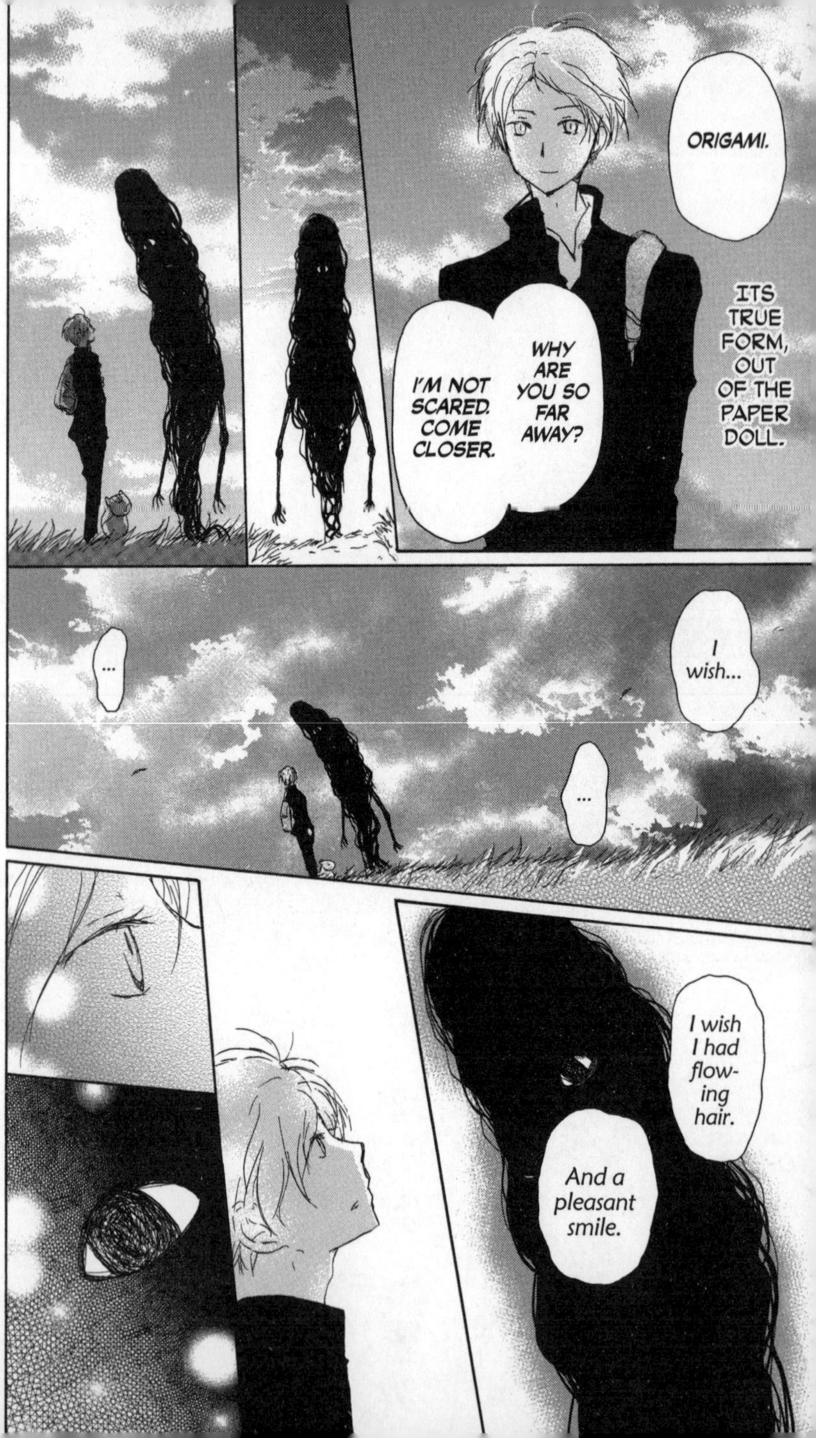
ORIGAMI.
ITS TRUE FORM, OUT OF THE PAPER DOLL.
WHY ARE YOU SO FAR AWAY?
I'M NOT SCARED. COME CLOSER.
I wish...
...
...
I wish I had flow-ing hair.
And a pleasant smile.

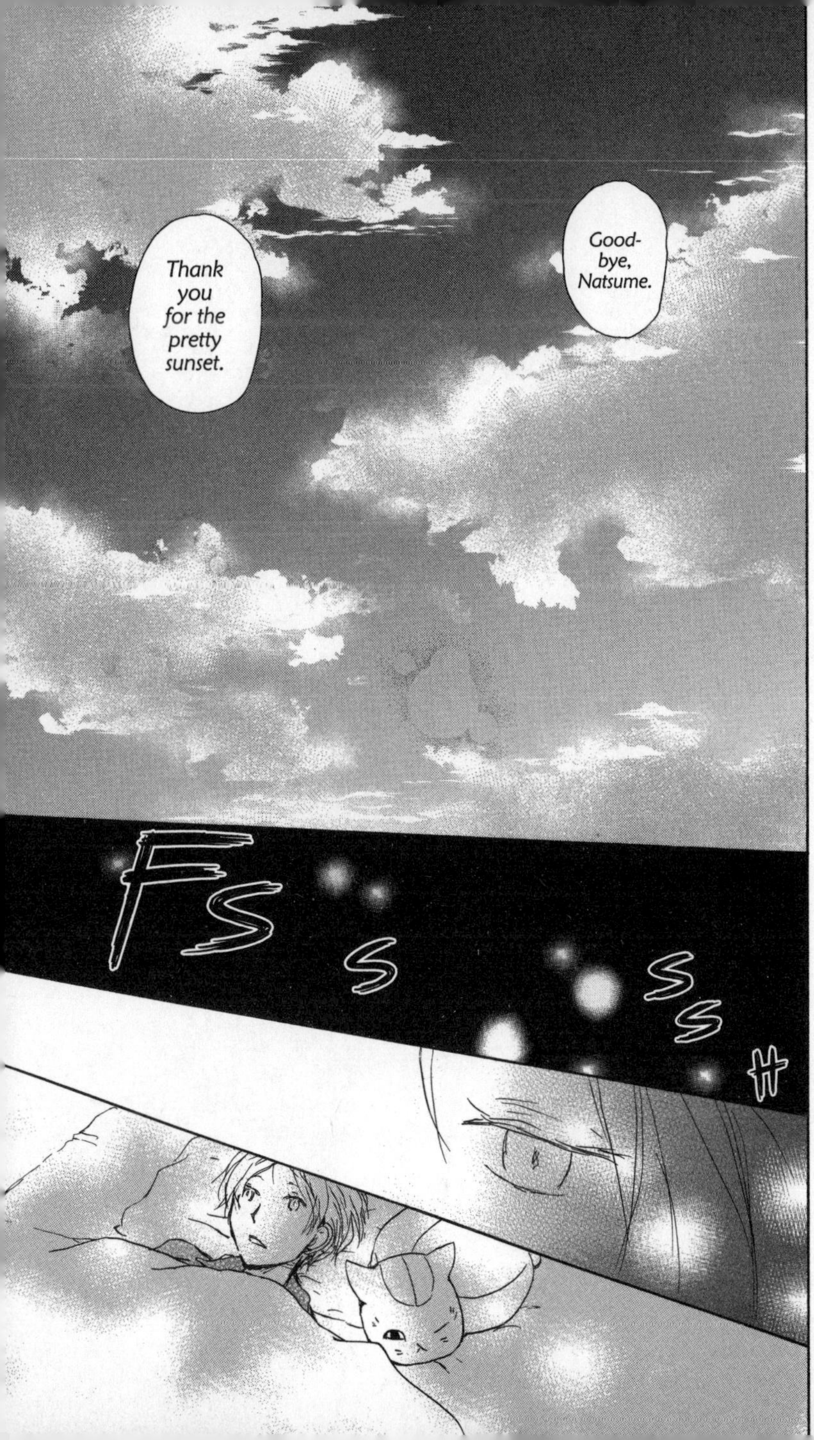
Good-bye, Natsume.
Thank you for the pretty sunset.
FSSSSH

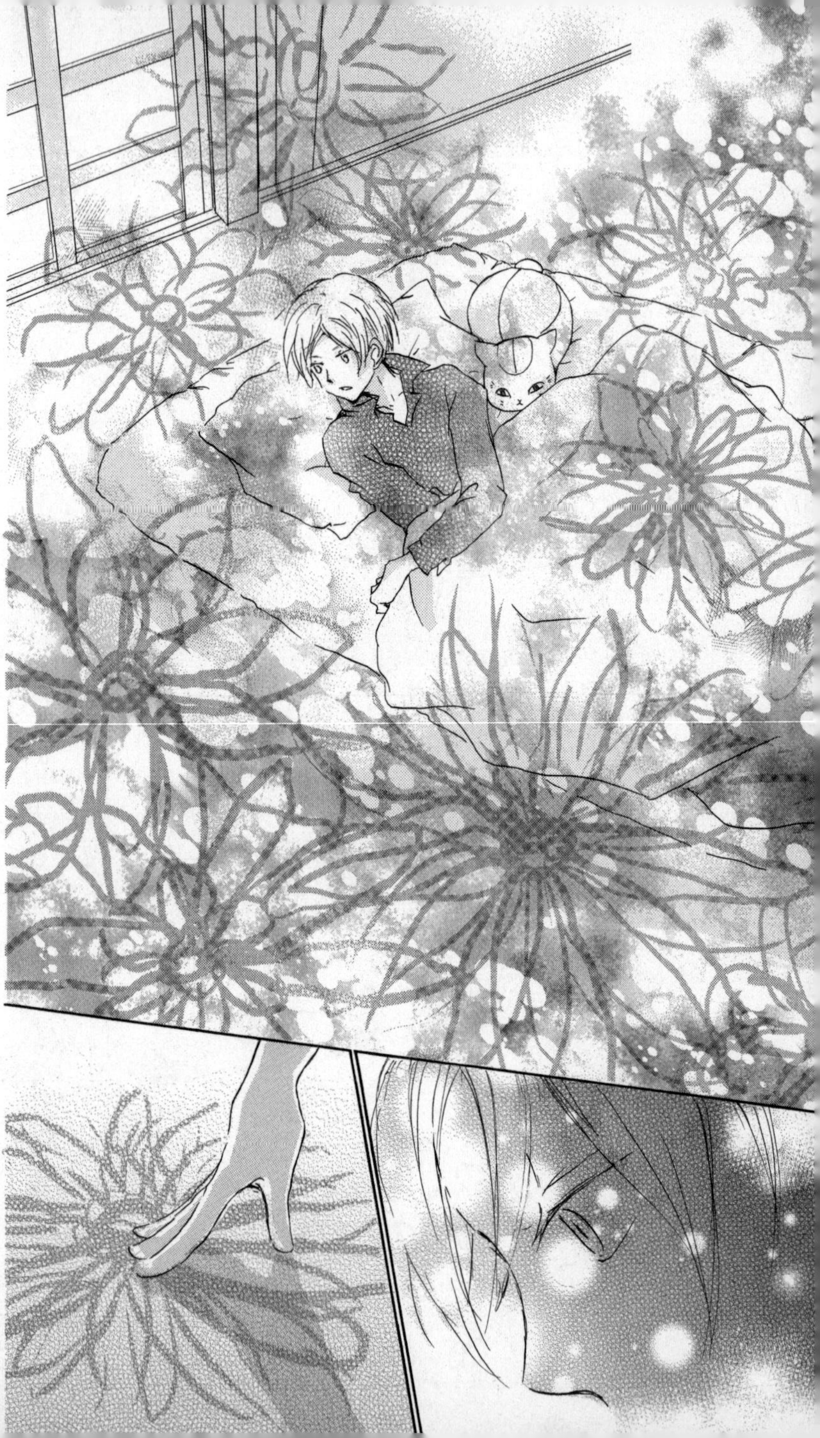

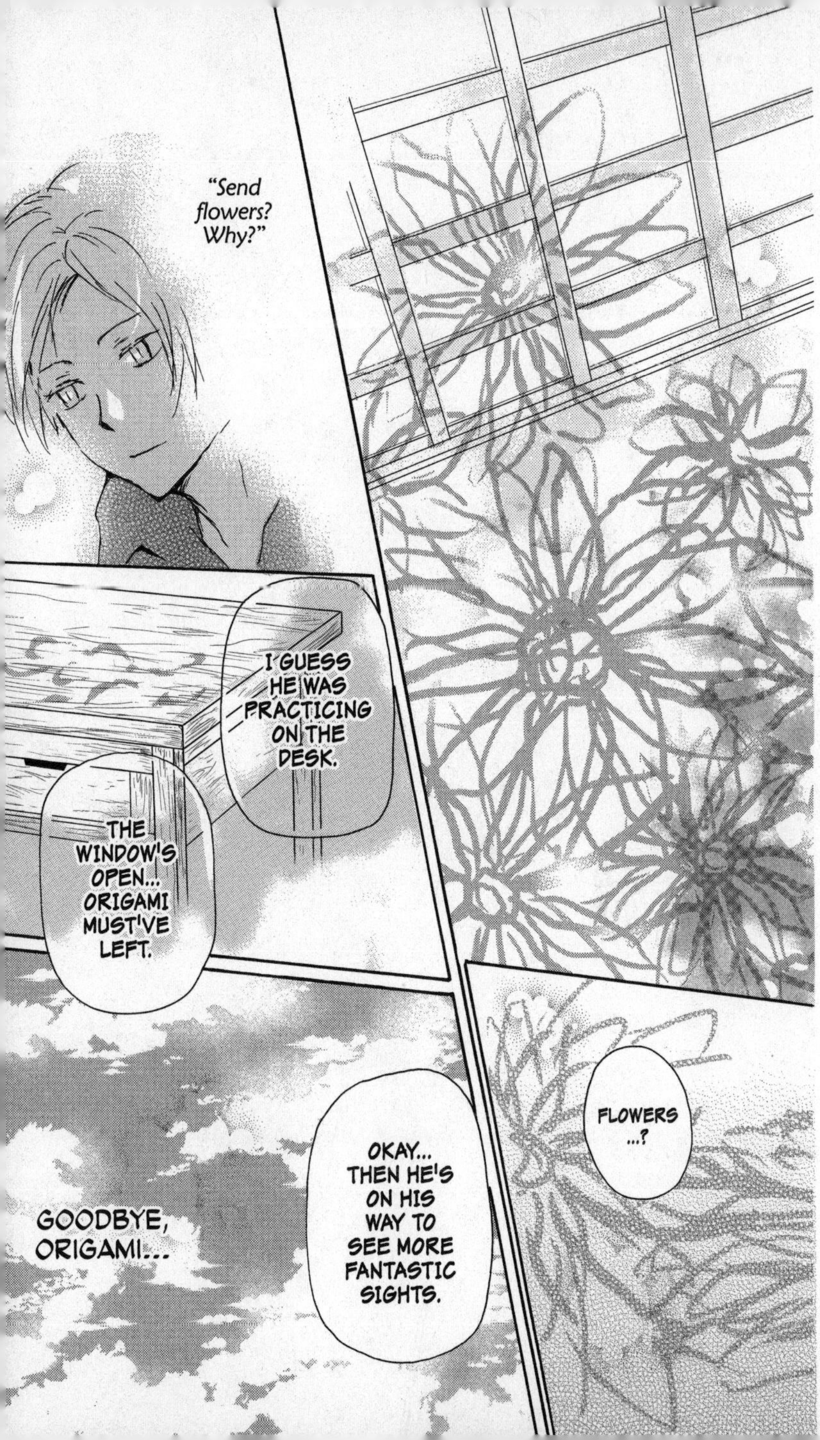
"Send flowers? Why?"
I GUESS HE WAS PRACTICING ON THE DESK.
THE WINDOW'S OPEN... ORIGAMI MUST'VE LEFT.
FLOWERS ...?
OKAY... THEN HE'S ON HIS WAY TO SEE MORE FANTASTIC SIGHTS.
GOODBYE, ORIGAMI...

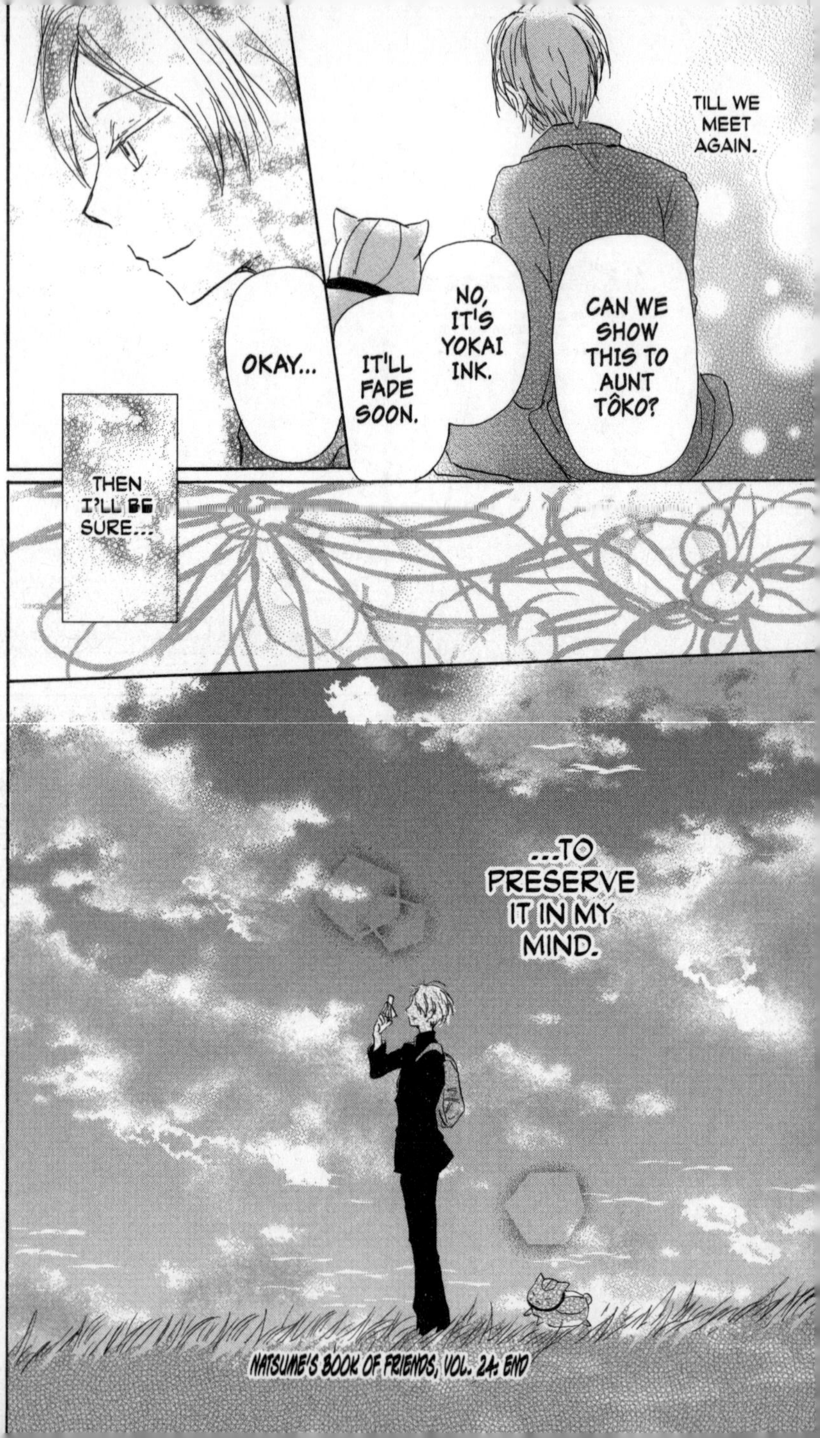
TILL WE MEET AGAIN.
CAN WE SHOW THIS TO AUNT TÔKO?
NO, IT'S YOKAI INK.
IT'LL FADE SOON.
OKAY...
THEN I'LL BE SURE...
...TO PRESERVE IT IN MY MIND.
NATSUME'S BOOK OF FRIENDS, VOL. 24: END

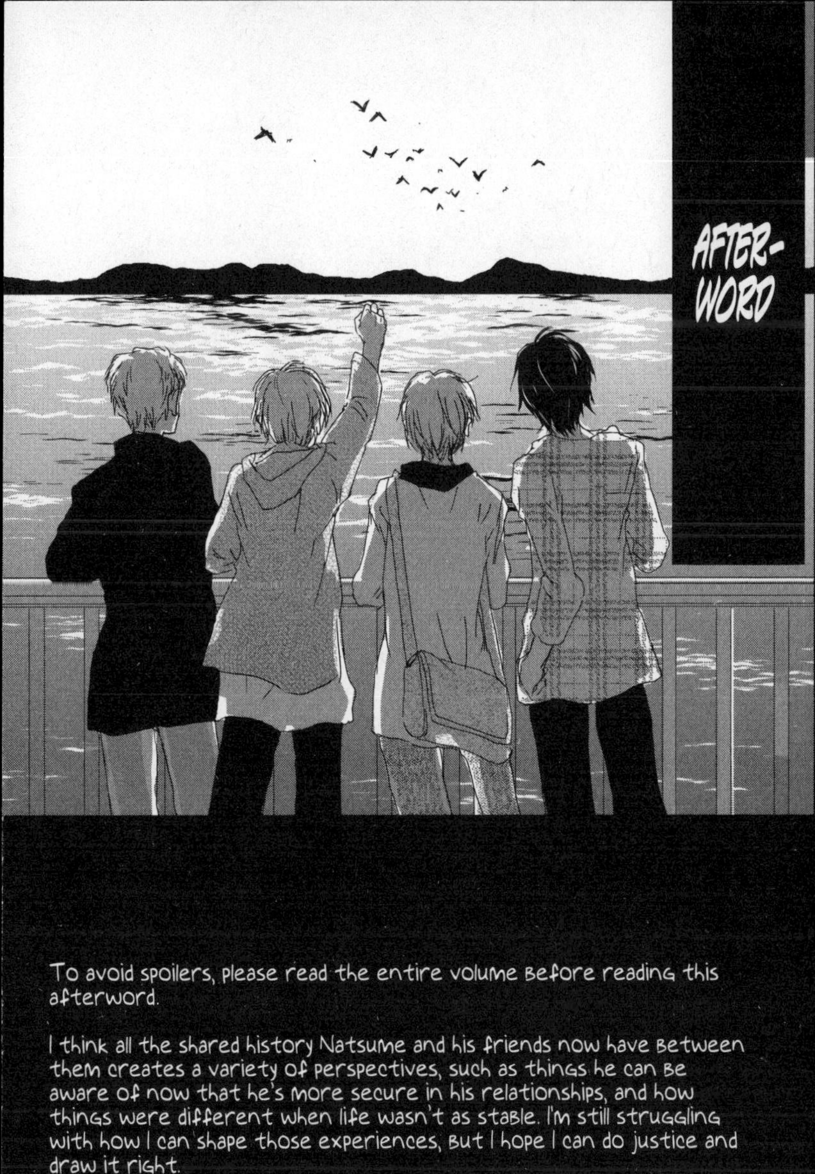

AFTER-WORD

To avoid spoilers, please read the entire volume before reading this afterword.

I think all the shared history Natsume and his friends now have between them creates a variety of perspectives, such as things he can be aware of now that he's more secure in his relationships, and how things were different when life wasn't as stable. I'm still struggling with how I can shape those experiences, but I hope I can do justice and draw it right.

CHAPTER 95-96 The Odd Couple

I still get nervous when I'm drawing Taki. Yokai don't really have boundaries, but Taki tries to clearly maintain hers. It's surprisingly difficult to show that difference without calling attention to it when Natsume is hanging out with them. It's tricky how it only takes one misstep, then Taki is no longer Taki and Natsume is no longer Natsume. But it's fun once I get working on it, and I'm glad I got to draw her family.

CHAPTER 97-98 A Suspicious Visitor

Tanuma, who stands by Natsume, may not be able to see yokai like his friend, but he has his own special abilities that other people do not possess. At the same time, there are things that can never be the same. When I draw Tanuma, I feel like Natsume is trying to close the distance between them for a change. You'd think they'd be great buddies by now, but there's still a bit of awkwardness. It's strange to blame it on Tanuma, but there it is. I'm just happy I got to work on this story, since I've had the idea ever since I drew the illustration for the afterword of the volume where he made his first appearance.

SPECIAL EPISODE 20 Intermission Detectives

The anime came up with "The Brilliant Detective" as a title for a movie starring Natori, so I've been happily wondering where I could sneak in a mention of it. I only had twelve pages to work with, but it ran in the magazine during the theatrical release of the anime movie, so I took the plunge. I hope Natsume and his friends can make some good memories at the movies.

CHAPTER 99 Beautiful Dreamer

I wanted to go back to the usual Natsume. It's my opinion that a brief encounter that seems mundane to one person can be unforgettable for someone else.

Yuki Midorikawa
is the creator of *Natsume's Book of Friends*, which was nominated for the Manga Taisho (Cartoon Grand Prize). Her other titles published in Japan include *Hotarubi no Mori e* (Into the Forest of Fireflies), *Hiiro no Isu* (The Scarlet Chair) and *Akaku Saku Koe* (The Voice That Blooms Red).

NATSUME'S BOOK OF FRIENDS
Vol. 24
Shojo Beat Edition

STORY AND ART BY Yuki Midorikawa

Translation & Adaptation Lillian Olsen
Touch-up Art & Lettering Sabrina Heep
Design Jimmy Presler
Editor Pancha Diaz

Natsume Yujincho by Yuki Midorikawa

First published in Japan in 2019 by HAKUSENSHA, Inc., Tokyo.
English language translation rights arranged with HAKUSENSHA, Inc., Tokyo.

Printed in the USA

Published by VIZ Media, LLC
P.O. Box 77010
San Francisco, CA 94107

10 9 8 7 6 5 4 3 2 1
First printing, June 2020

VIZ MEDIA
viz.com

ratings.viz.com
RATED T TEEN

PARENTAL ADVISORY
NATSUME'S BOOK OF FRIENDS is rated T for Teen and is recommended for ages 13 and up. This volume contains fantasy violence.

Shojo Beat
shojobeat.com

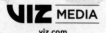

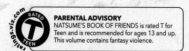

SURPRISE!

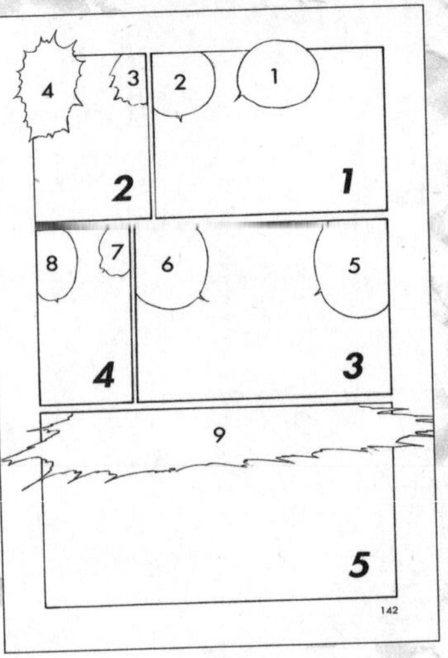
1
2
3
4
5
6
7
8
9
142

You may be reading the wrong way!

It's true: In keeping with the original Japanese comic format, this book reads from right to left—so action, sound effects, and word balloons are completely reversed. This preserves the orientation of the original artwork—plus, it's fun! Check out the diagram shown here to get the hang of things, and then turn to the other side of the book to get started!

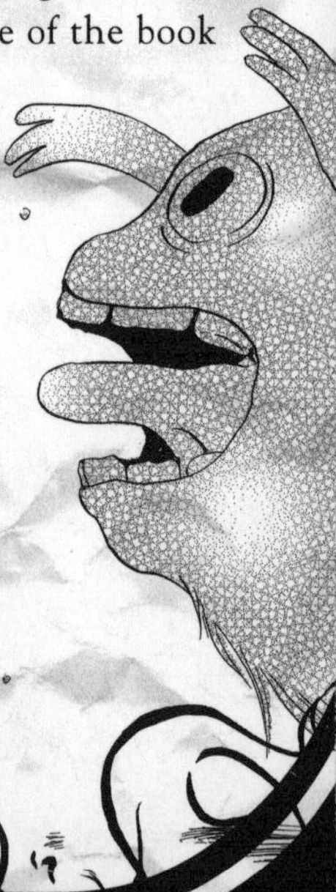

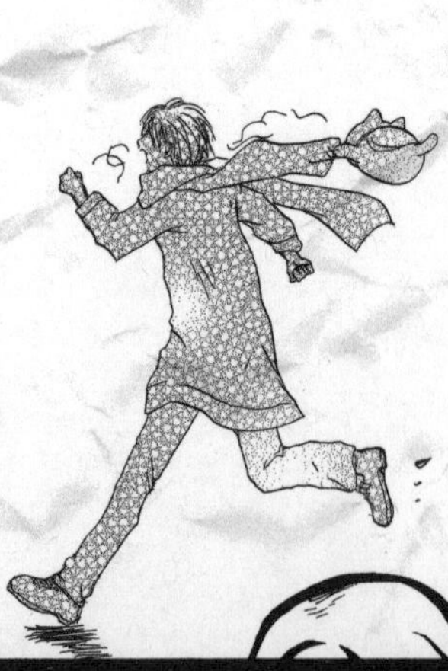

Natsume's
BOOK of FRIENDS

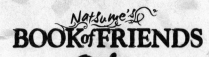

VOLUME 24 CONTENTS

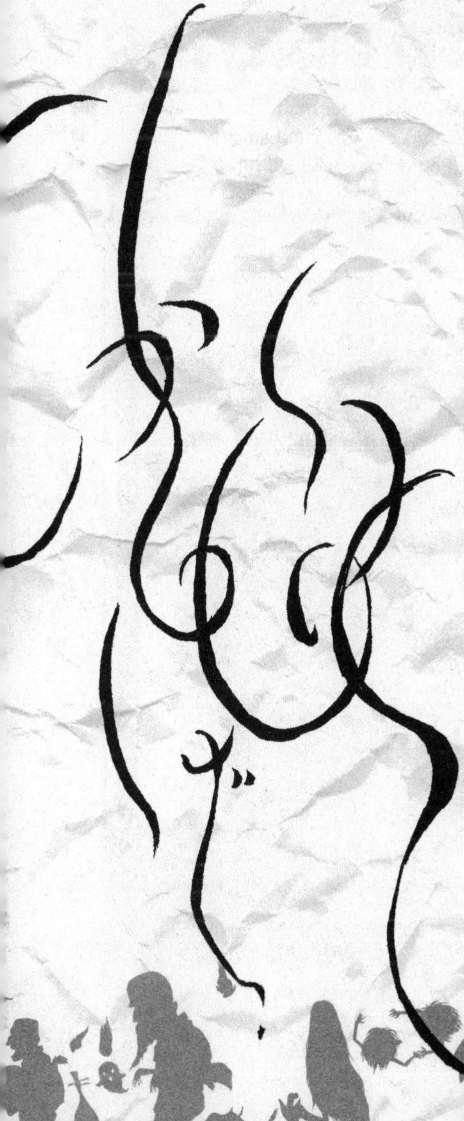

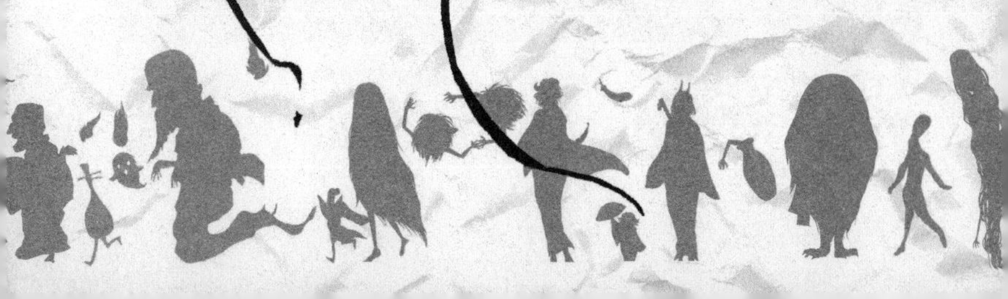

Shojo Beat

Natsume's BOOK of FRIENDS

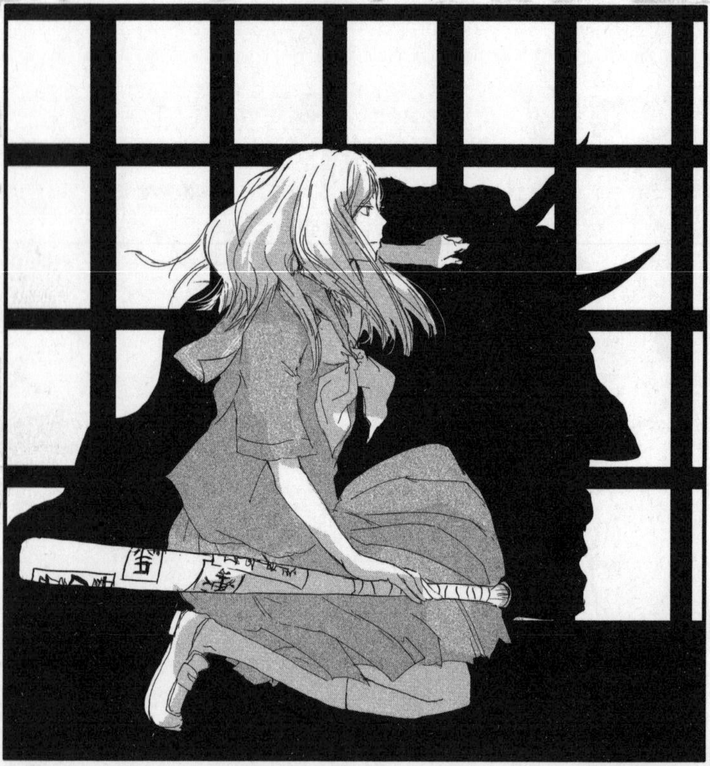

STORY and ART by
Yuki Midorikawa

VOLUME 24